AN HISTORICAL AND HISTORIOGRAPHICAL
COMMENTARY ON SUETONIUS'
LIFE OF C. CALIGULA

AMERICAN PHILOLOGICAL ASSOCIATION
American Classical Studies

Series Editor

Matthew S. Santirocco

Number 32

An Historical and Historiographical
Commentary on Suetonius'
Life of C. Caligula

by
Donna W. Hurley

Donna W. Hurley

AN HISTORICAL
AND HISTORIOGRAPHICAL
COMMENTARY ON SUETONIUS'
LIFE OF C. CALIGULA

Scholars Press
Atlanta, Georgia

AN HISTORICAL AND HISTORIOGRAPHICAL COMMENTARY ON SUETONIUS'
LIFE OF C. CALIGULA

by
Donna W. Hurley

© 1993
The American Philological Association

Library of Congress Cataloging in Publication Data
Hurley, Donna W.
   An historical and historiographical commentary on Suetonius' Life
of C. Caligula/ by Donna W. Hurley
      p. cm. — (American classical studies; no. 32)
   Includes bibliographical references.
   ISBN 1–55540–880–X (cloth). — ISBN 1–55540–881–8 (pbk.)
   1. Suetonius, ca. 69–ca. 122. Caligula. 2. Caligula, Emperor of
Rome, 12–41. 3. Rome—History—Caligula, 37–41. 4. Roman emperors-
-Biography.   I. Title.   II. Series.
DG283.S83H87   1993
937'.07'092—dc20   93–13723
                                                        CIP

Printed in the United States of America
on acid-free paper

Introduction

When Suetonius' *Life of Caligula* has not been accepted uncritically as a mine for historical fact, it has been dismissed as gossip. The *monstrum* especially has not been taken seriously. A commentary by J. A. Maurer stopped after chapter 21, the point at which Suetonius leaves his *princeps* behind. It is, to be sure, the most outrageous of Suetonius' biographies but not because its author approached his task differently. As Tacitus said, nothing had been written *sine ira et studio*, and toward the emperor Gaius it was all anger. Unlike the assessments of Germanicus or Nero, for instance, about whom threads of differing opinions can be traced, the tradition about Gaius is amazingly uniform. It had been in the interest of no one, especially Claudius, to rescue the reputation of the unsuccessful princeps who was best treated as an aberration, and so a vulgate developed quickly and soon took written form. For all Suetonius' rearranging, he did not make things up and is our most important witness of what the first century had to say about Gaius.

I

The *Lives of the Caesars* were influential throughout antiquity, and the large number of manuscripts that have survived indicate that they were read heavily in the later Middle Ages and Renaissance.[1] Suetonius' portraits were apparently accepted as psychologically plausible until modern scholarship judged their author merely a diligent and mechanical collector. All are constructed in the same way; rubrics of related characteristics, good and bad, are gathered within a quasi-chronological outline (birth, accession, death). At the turn of the century Friedrich Leo advanced the idea that Suetonius, influenced perhaps by his own *De viris illustribus,* had transferred to political figures categories properly belonging to literary men, what he called "Alexandrian biography," ostensibly the creation of Alexandrian scholarship. He saw Suetonius making no effort to individualize

---

[1] For the large number of manuscripts, Reynolds 399. On his reputation and influence, Macé 401–9; Steidle 9–12; Townend 1967, 96–108; Lounsbury 27–61.

his emperors or to create unified portraits, an assessment that persists despite
Wolf Steidle's radical correction in *Sueton und die antike Biographie* (1951).
Steidle proposed that Suetonius did create organically consistent and dramatically
satisfying portraits, each held together by an overarching theme, cruelty in the
case of Gaius. His work has stimulated numerous structural analyses of the *Lives*,
and the result is an appreciation of the ancient biographer's organizational skills
and control of his data.[2]

There can be no question that Suetonius accomplished what he set out to do.
His organization is careful and sometimes even clever, his transitions neat, his
parallels stylish; rhetorical flourishes abound, especially in the "middle lives" of
which the *Life of Caligula* is one.[3] Gaius' disrespect for his associates marches
neatly from close relatives to more distant ones, then on to friends and finally to
the Roman people as a whole; his favors to citizens descend systematically
through the orders as does his cruel treatment of these same groups. A rubric of
licentiousness is followed by extravagance (or parsimony) which is followed in
turn by extraordinary money-raising measures, not only in the *Life* of Gaius but
also in the *Lives* of Julius, Augustus, Tiberius and Nero. Whether or not an appreciation of these structures convinces that the whole of Suetonius' effort is
more than the sum of its parts depends on the reader's satisfaction with the portraits themselves. The checkerboard emperors still float disembodied without
benefit of context.

The *Life of Caligula* is different from Suetonius' other *Lives* only because the
number of "bad" rubrics so far outweighs the "good" and because the demarca-
tion between them is so very clearly marked in the text: *hactenus quasi de
principe, reliqua ut de monstro narranda sunt*. The number of "bad" rubrics is
increased when those that enhance the images of other emperors (appearance,
pastimes, military activities) turn pejorative when referred to him. Milestones on
his journey from birth to death form a sketchy framework. Suetonius always begins with ancestry, but for Gaius this becomes a "mini-biography" of his father
Germanicus with its own rubrics and framing narration. Gaius' birth, childhood
and youth follow and then his accession and the propitious opening of his reign,

---

[2] Leo 11–27. Alcide Macé's comprehensive *Essai sur Suétone* (1900) was the first full treatment
of Suetonius. Caligula was one of the emperors whom Steidle chose to analyze in detail (68–87).
On organization and style, Mouchova ("Rubrik und Erzählung") 17–64; Gugel; Cizek. For a good
summation of Suetonius' weaknesses, Flach; for his virtues, Lounsbury; for a balanced assessment, Wallace-Hadrill 1983, 19–22. The history of Suetonian scholarship has been summarized
well by Mouchova (9–15) and Gugel (11–22).

[3] The "middle lives" (Tiberius–Nero) are distinct from the first two (Julius and Augustus) that
show evidence of wide research and the last ones (Galba–Domitian) that are very brief. The differ-
ences have prompted speculation that the last were written first (Bowersock; *contra*, Townend
1959; Bradley 1973).

all included in the "good" division of the *Life*. Chronology returns (after a fashion) when the expedition to the German frontier in chapters 39–40 is described in a "bad" rubric of trivial military exploits. Then come the events at the end of his life, his return home, the assassination and its aftermath, all appropriately in the *monstrum* portion. An interruption in the account of events of his youth anticipates the tyrant to come, and the suspense of the assassination is increased when a chapter on portents intervenes.

Suetonius had a long list of books to his credit, many of them compilations of all manner of things from boys' games to insults. His literary career was combined with service to both Trajan and Hadrian in the prestigious posts of *a studiis, a bibliothecis,* and *ab epistulis* to which he rose as a protegee of the Younger Pliny, also a successful equestrian careerist. The *Lives* were written while Suetonius was in Hadrian's court and perhaps after he had been dismissed (A.D. 122?). Although it has been suggested that his negative experience with Hadrian colored his judgments, most attempts to uncover the moral assumptions that lie behind his work have found him representative of his class and age and a reliable servant of the imperial establishment. From the vantage point of the second century and a firmly established principate, he was certain how a good emperor should behave and what made a bad one. It is not surprising that his catalog of virtues and vices finds a parallel in Pliny's *Panegyricus* for Trajan.[4] The heavy burden of opprobrium that Gaius the *monstrum* bears seems at first monolithic and obvious, but close examination of exactly what it is that Suetonius objects to provides insight into the rather finely balanced tension between tyrannical behavior and the acceptable expression of an emperor's role. It was often not what he did but how he did it that mattered.

The biographer makes his judgments known by selection and arrangement. Only occasionally does he use the first person, as when he takes credit for referring Gaius' swift swings between bravado and timorousness to an underlying *valitudo mentis* or points out the illogic of those who accepted the myth that Gaius was born in the camp when they should have known that it did not fit the facts. His reasoning in these instances cannot be faulted, and modern historians may wish that he had shared more of it and had spent a larger portion of his energies on original research like his occasional forays into the correspondence of Augustus, the *acta diurna* and inscriptions. With these his prose is direct, and he as much as footnotes such documents, just as he does the oral tradition that he taps now and again. What is most particular about Suetonius is this thoroughness and

---

[4] For Suetonius' relationship to the imperial establishment, Della Corte; Bradley 1976; Wallace-Hadrill 1981, 1983; Gascou ("L'Image du Prince chez Suétone") 717–73. For Suetonius making a veiled attack on Hadrian, Carney. For the connection with the *Panegyricus,* Wallace-Hadrill 1983, 145–47; Gascou 735–45.

attention to detail, qualities readily appreciated when they turn to something like research on the birthplace of Gaius, less so when they become pedantic in an irrelevant discussion of *puelli, puerae* and *puerperium*. But the great bulk of what is on his pages was not virgin data, and an occasional careful argument stands in contrast to the apparent lack of discrimination with which the catholic collector included whatever came his way. Now and again he retreats from full credence with a subjunctive verb or a "some even say," but he more often accepts his sources at face value and even insists vigorously on their authority. Remnants of incompletely digested material may surface as awkward and compressed sentences, and details leave their context behind, while traces of annalistic sources come through. It is this rather pedestrian recording of both fact and fiction that makes the Suetonius *Lives* such a rich treasure of the inherited tradition.

It has been well established that Suetonius, Tacitus and Cassius Dio frequently relied on the same annalistic history or histories for their basic information about first century events. One such history was begun by Aufidius Bassus and continued by the elder Pliny, but which of the two covered the short reign of Gaius is uncertain. Other candidates are Servilius Nonianus, Cluvius Rufus, and Fabius Rusticus, the latter two known to have written about the Neronian period.[5] In the *Life of Caligula* Suetonius refers to two authors by name: Pliny the Elder, almost certainly in his *Bella Germaniae*, claimed that Gaius was born in his father's legionary camp, and Cn. Cornelius Lentulus Gaetulicus, the commander of the Army of Upper Germany whom Gaius executed for treason, was responsible for the story that Gaius was born at Tibur; he had probably flattered the emperor in an encomiastic poem. Beyond this it becomes conjecture. The contemporary history of Seneca the Elder, who lived into the reign of Gaius, may have furnished some scarce positive information, if not to Suetonius, then perhaps to the first century historians. Suetonius records a great many sayings, collections of which have been postulated,[6] perhaps those of Passienus Crispus or even of Gaius himself. Tacitus knew the memoirs of the younger Agrippina, but if they covered life under Gaius, there is no indication that Suetonius used them. Pamphlet literature surely existed at one time and probably lies behind the pejorative anecdotes and jokes that found their way into the general accounts. It is possible that Suetonius relied directly on polemical texts of this sort since he preserves more of this material than is found in the parallel texts.

Although *The Life of Caligula* is the richest source of detail about Gaius, it is not much help in establishing the sequence of events for his reign. Gaius makes a

---

[5] For the shared sources, Syme 1958, 287–303, 688–92; Questa 1963; Momigliano 1932a; Townend, 1960, 1964; for the possibility of Cluvius, Mommsen 1870; for a summary of first century writers, Wilkes.

[6] Townend 1960.

few cameo appearances in the late Tiberian years of Tacitus' *Annales* and is mentioned in passing in other works, but the loss of Books 7 and 8 is great indeed. One would love to know what Suetonius' older and more skeptical contemporary wrote about Gaius, certainly nothing very complimentary and surely much that was ironic. Book 59 of Cassius Dio's *Roman History* has survived about three-quarters intact and in epitome for the last year of Gaius' reign. Dio, writing near the beginning of the third century, must have relied heavily on the first century annalistic history or histories, and this is where parallels with the Suetonius *Life* can be seen. The long period of Roman history that he covered precluded his doing broad research, and the more esoteric texts and much of the oral tradition that Suetonius and Tacitus used were less available to him in any case. Unfortunately, Dio's practice of strategy notes for a ten-year period before he began to write was responsible for many errors of fact, and an apparent conflation of sources for this period makes his work still more unreliable, but without it there would be little chronological basis at all for events of 37–41.[7]

The writings of contemporaries who had met or knew Gaius are of special interest. The younger Seneca was present in his court and later in the courts of Claudius and Nero, where he would have been privy to the anecdotes and jokes that circulated. His random and uniformly hostile comments about Gaius furnish the best unobstructed view of what Gaius' own generation among Rome's upper classes thought of him and show the vulgate assessment taking shape. One anecdote is particularly instructive: Gaius challenged Jupiter with a line from Homer, "Lift me or I will lift you." Seneca provides context for the quotation in a banquet and pantomimes that Gaius did not want disturbed by thunderstorms. But when Dio reports the same quotation, Gaius is on the Palatine hurling a personal thunderbolt at Jupiter on the Capitoline. Seneca tells the story one way, Dio's source another, but each had its origin in the same quotation and makes the same point about hubris.

Philo of Alexandria had also met Gaius in person and produced two texts that bear on his reign, *Legatio ad Gaium* and *In Flaccum*. Both were written no more than ten years after Gaius' death, probably a good deal sooner, and both describe a reprehensible Gaius from a non-Roman point of view. Philo had led a delegation to Rome to seek a ruling on the Jews' status after the pogrom in August of 38 in Alexandria; he found the emperor not very interested in their parochial concerns. The *Legatio* is highly rhetorical (everything happens in threes) and so is factually suspect, but it already contains elements of the canonical view of the volatile and erratic Gaius. Another Hellenized Jew who deals with Gaius' reign

---

[7] For Dio's sources, Millar 1964, 32–38; for the apparent conflation, Questa 1957a, 45–48, and see notes 42 and 94 in the commentary. The later Eutropius, Orosius, Aurelius Victor and the *Epitome de Caesaribus* are ultimately derivitive and provide little new.

was Flavius Josephus. Both Philo's tracts and Josephus' *Jewish War* and *Jewish Antiquities* are concerned with Gaius' insult to Jewish monotheism when he tried to place a colossal statue of himself in the temple in Jerusalem and with the role of "Herod" Agrippa, the Jewish prince who was Gaius' friend. But Josephus also records a disproportionately lengthy account of Gaius' assassination that betrays great interest in Roman *libertas* and senatorial prerogative. Its hostility to the entire Julian line indicates that Josephus was transmitting a post-Neronian reassessment of the Caligula story.[8]

II

The process of sorting an historical Gaius out from the anecdotal accretion began around the turn of the century. Until then the mad emperor was accepted very much as presented by Suetonius, since his was not only the most popular and accessible text (the other narratives are in Greek) but the most titillating as well. Hugo Willrich began the process of establishing context for the isolated anecdotes with a three-part series in *Klio* in 1903. Extremely partisan in defense of his subject and guilty of overcorrection, he thought that Gaius alone had the vision to see that the future of Rome demanded a divine monarchy based on an Eastern model instead of ersatz Republican institutions. J. P. V. D. Balsdon's 1934 *The Emperor Gaius (Caligula),* which remained the standard scholarly study until recently, continued Willrich's rationalizations but avoided his excessive enthusiasm. Balsdon's Gaius is inexperienced, conceited and tactless and responded harshly to the threats posed by his insecure position. Since then the sorting process has been helped by the careful investigation of individual problems and by non-literary evidence, especially the *Acta Fratrum Arvalium,* available in part for his entire reign and now fairly complete for A.D. 38. The scholarship of the past fifty years has been brought together in a full-length study by Anthony A. Barrett, *Caligula, The Corruption of Power*, a long overdue update of Balsdon's *Gaius*. Barrett follows Balsdon but is less forgiving. His Gaius is culpable, although not mad, and he finds his reign fairly unremarkable.[9] Some details of chronology remain uncertain but his life has been arranged as follows:

---

[8] Jewish matters were incidental from the Roman point of view, and neither the *Life of Caligula* nor other extant Roman sources are interested. Tacitus perhaps was to judge from his passing reference to Gaius' attempt to install his statue in the temple in Jerusalem in the *Historiae*. For discussion of Josephus and his sources, Mommsen 1870; Timpe 1960; Feldman 1962; Ritter; Wiseman 1991, xii–xiv.

[9] Ludwig Quidde's thinly disguised assimilation of Gaius to the Kaiser Wilhelm II (*Caligula; eine Studie über römischen Cäsarenwahnsinn* 1894) took the text at face value. Willrich's series in *Klio* was followed by Gelzer's collection of the available evidence for the "Iulius (Caligula)" entry in the *Real Encyclopeadia* (1918) that anticipated Balsdon. Gaius has been judged variously an

Born in A.D. 12, Gaius was given a role in the public expression of the impe-rial house when he was present as the little soldier Caligula with the Army of Lower Germany and probably in Syria as well. After Germanicus died in 19, Gaius lived in Rome with his mother, great-grandmother Livia, and then his grandmother Antonia until 30 or 31 when he was summoned to join Tiberius on Capreae to be groomed (more or less) for the principate. Tiberius died in March of 37, and Gaius inherited his wealth and position after suppressing the claims of his cousin and co-heir, the young Tiberius Gemellus. He played his role well during the first summer when he distributed Tiberius' legacies and money of his own and dedicated the temple of Augustus. Childless (a first wife had died earlier that year), he married for the second time and joined his sister Drusilla to M. Aemilius Lepidus, who provided much-needed security when he was placed in the line of succession. Drusilla was the link that legitimized the arrangement. If she bore a child, so much the better. In the autumn Gaius fell ill to a malady which was perceived as life-threatening, and after he recovered, perhaps around the end of the year (the time is uncertain), there were indications of trouble. His potential rival Tiberius Gemellus was killed (probably), and his former father-in-law M. Junius Silanus was tried and sentenced. A number of new persons were installed among the Arval Brethern in May of 38 in what seems to indicate a reorganiza-tion of his inner circle. Gaius' arrangements were shaken, however, when Drusilla died in June. After a trip to Syracuse he returned to Rome to preside over her deification, probably on September 23. Shortly thereafter he married again; the legitimate child still eluded him.

The year 39 was difficult for Gaius. He had genuine reason for distrusting those around him and became overtly confrontational with the senate. The se-quence of events is unclear, but he celebrated the deified Drusilla's birthday with a massive display, married a fourth wife (this time the already pregnant Caesonia), restored the *crimen maiestatis,* put on an elaborate show with a bridge of boats across the Bay of Naples and then, at the beginning of September, left Rome for Lugdunum. He had at some point discovered that his former brother-in-law Aemilius Lepidus was conspiring for the principate and that Gaetulicus was planning a coup from his base with the Army of Upper Germany. Both men were executed for treason; the news about Gaetulicus reached Rome in October.

Gaius spent the winter in Gaul and was at Lugdunum on January 1 of A.D. 40. Although he had arranged for a massive muster of forces on the German fron-tier, campaigns against Germany or Britain or both did not take place. He visited the Rhine armies, participated in some minor military exercises planned to give

---

alcoholic (Jerome 1923) and an inept victim of senatorial hostility (Momigliano 1932b). Arther Ferrill's recent *Caligula, Emperor of Rome* (1991) returns to the view that Gaius was a madman.

legitimacy to his title of *imperator,* received a British chieftain into custody, staged a show of some sort on the Channel coast and turned home. If the trip was intended to strengthen his position, it was not a success. Back on the outskirts of Rome by May, he did not enter the city until his birthday on the last day of August and then with only an ovation, although he had at one point surely intended to come home in triumph. The atmosphere was very tense in the final months of the year as more than one group sought to eliminate him and he retaliated with prosecutions. Time ran out on January 24, A.D. 41, when he was ambushed by his own praetorian tribunes at the *ludi Palatini.*

Gaius did Rome no harm. In the first place, there was no time. Ironically, the very brevity of his reign makes a contribution to history since his quick coming and going provide two points at which the transfer of power can be observed, an important marker for how the office of princeps was understood.[10] His public measures (or since it is unclear how decisions were made, things done on his watch) fit more often than not into the continuum of the early Empire. Gaius revived a number of Augustan practices that had lapsed during the reign of Tiberius; the equestrian census was restored, the public account books were opened, and he tried to return elections to the voting assemblies. His new taxes were unpopular, but taxes themselves were scarcely a novelty. He encouraged the practice of remembering the emperor in wills, but tried at least to do without the pernicious *crimen maiestatis.* Rome's border territories were disposed according to established norms.

There had long been a choice between annexing principalities as provinces or more informal control of them as client states or tribes ruled by "friendly kings" loyal to the emperor as their patron. Tiberius preferred annexation and Gaius returned to the policy of Augustus.[11] Claudius preserved all of his border arrangements and any number of other initiatives as well. With the marginal exception of Jewish affairs, historical events cross his reign quite unremarkably. Gaius was passive in the face of disruptive anti-Semitism in Alexandria, and it took Claudius to restrain both Jews and Greeks. In the Jewish homeland the conflict over his statue almost triggered armed uprising; only his sudden death saved the situation. The fault lay not in the original idea, for a statue of a Roman emperor in an existing temple had become standard, but in Gaius' unwise refusal to back off when it became clear that the program was causing difficulty.[12] It is interesting that both of these crises were interpreted in terms of his character. Neither issue reached critical proportions until the time of Nero.

---

[10] Timpe 1962, 71–75; Veyne 1990, 332–33, 340; Jakobson and Cotton.
[11] Balsdon 1934a 202–3; Magie 514–15; Luttwak 20–40.
[12] Smallwood, 1961; Smallwood 1981, 174–80, 235–50; Barrett 1989, 184–91.

Tiberius was the one out of step, especially with the ceremonial aspects of the principate that defined the emperor's job for the populace. Gaius understood his public role and played it according to the precedent that Augustus had set. He quite properly gave and presided over *munera,* and even if he sometimes failed to respond graciously to the wishes of the crowd and stormed out in a rage, he no doubt behaved as prescribed most of the time. But would inappropriate behavior of this sort have seemed so very serious if he had been a successful emperor? Even at the end, he still had his following. His entertainments were lavish and he threw money from the roof; there were always volunteers to kiss his feet. But support did not run deep and died along with him, and it was not centered where it mattered in any case. Gaius' abysmal relationship with the senate, the social stratum to which he himself belonged, was the source of his rapid failure and of the horrific reputation that he left behind. What the senate expected was reasonable scope for ambition and the license to maintain its status as Rome's elite. In dealing with it, an emperor had to operate at closer quarters than with the populace, and his personal qualities, his behavior (his manners) made a difference. Gaius' two elderly predecessors had managed a workable relationship but did not prove useful models for the inexperienced and apparently uneducable young man. It was madness for him to drop the pretense of civility as he seems to have done in 39 or to favor the equestrians openly in an edict the next year. If respect, not power, was what an emperor had to give, his talent for insult was a disaster. The senate paid him back since it was the judgment of the literate upper class that found its way into the surviving texts.[13]

Is the mad emperor then to be explained away as the product of a hostile press with inexperience and a lack of tact his besetting sins? Gaius' apparently random murders were no doubt responses to genuine threats prosecuted under the *crimen maiestatis;* he had a right to protect himself. He married multiple wives in an impatient but not irrational chase after the legitimate child who would leave him less vulnerable to as assassin's dagger. Other anecdotes are exaggerated or simply not true, and everything that he did was given the worst possible construction by his critics. The inescapable impression is that of an exposed young man flailing about, trying ever more desperately to shore up a deteriorating position without success. But how did his relationship with the senate become so disastrous so quickly and why did he break with such a large number of persons close to him, both family and retainers, within so short a time? Proximity obviously did not breed trust. Josephus wrote that Gaius was "unmindful of friendships," and it is fact that he could not or did not nurture the reciprocal loyalties that he needed to

---

[13] For emperor and senate, Talbert 163–64; Veyne 1990, 411–13; for its revenge, Momigliano 1932b, 214–16

maintain his position over a long period. When a group within the praetorian tribunes, the colonels in his private army, turned against him, the end was at hand.
The strong emphasis on the personality of the emperor that is implicit in the
Suetonius' *Lives* is appropriate because behavior was the key to what made a
"good" or "bad" emperor. With Gaius, the focus has remained there both by default and because it was an especially serious issue in his case.

Josephus, Dio, and Philo provide character sketches that are consistent with
one another and present an internally cohesive constellation of traits, and corrob-
orating anecdotes, including those that are not true, show what was thought of
him. Gaius was not a generic *monstrum* but above all erratic and moody,
occasionally generous, more often cruel, self-aggrandizing, untrusting and un-
trustworthy, impatient of advice, quick to take offense, insistent on his own way,
arrogant and possessed of a hot temper and a nasty tongue. His sadism is typical
of all tyrants, but the rest is quite particular and no doubt accurate in a general
way. He must have been extraordinarily difficult if not impossible to deal with, at
the very least the wrong person for a job that required a component of public
relations skills. The ancient judgment that he possessed *furiosa inconstantia* or a
turbida mens must be taken seriously for what it is, an impressionistic reaction to
his chaotic behavior. The temptation to go further and transform the lay description into a diagnosis according to the categories of modern psychiatric disease is
seemingly irresistible[14] but has its limits. The evidence is selective hearsay drawn
from what seemed especially noteworthy in ancient Rome. But if the picture were
complete and cultural specifics could be taken into consideration adequately, one
or more among the wide range of psychoses or personality disorders might be
found to fit. There is no need to choose between the schizophenic and the inexperienced innocent, a polarity that has often stalled discussion about Gaius. It is
possible to provide context and rationale for most of his erratic actions and still
leave room for a seriously flawed individual at their center.

                                    III

How Gaius' story was told is a part of the story itself. His contemporaries and
near contemporaries interpreted their experience with him in ways that reflected
their needs or fit their preconceptions. Several themes return. His reign was always viewed antithetically, fair beginnings turned into miserable savagery, and

---

[14] The assumption is that since psychiatry is a branch of scientific medicine, the trained clinician
should be able to examine the evidence and reach a conclusion that the ancients could not. Most
pursuasive are those that have stayed within the generalized character sketch, the best not surprisingly the joint work of a classicist and psychiatrist who suggest anxiety or mania (Massaro and
Montgomery 1978). Less credible suggestions from Jerome, Sachs, Esser (133–39), Lucus.

this led to the postulation that he "changed." Although vulnerable from the beginning, he does appear to have grown ever more isolated and suspicious as time passed; after 39 the absence of trust between him and the senate was no longer hidden, and it may well be true that he was increasingly seduced by his powerful position. But the important change lay in the perception of those whom he disappointed. The senate always hoped for better treatment than it got with each new emperor. As Tacitus wrote, "The best day is the first day after a bad princeps." Gaius' honeymoon was over quickly, the disappointment greater because his association with the legendary Germanicus had exaggerated initial expectations. Philo, writing not long after Gaius was killed, already draws a firm line between the enthusiastic reception that the new emperor received and the utter depravity that followed. Dio followed sources that pointedly contrasted Gaius' dutiful behavior toward those close to him with his betrayal of those same persons. Suetonius' *princeps–monstrum* divide reflects the schematic pattern without benefit of chronology.

A comparison between Gaius and his ancestor of the same name, the dictator Gaius Julius Caesar, was unavoidable, but he was no *divus* and always came off second best. Suetonius chose the comparison as the climax of the *Life of Caligula* and ends with the statement that every Julius Caesar with the *praenomen* Gaius after the time of Cinna had suffered a violent death, but it was the ancient tradition, not Suetonius, that first made this obvious connection between the two. The name alone was more than enough to prompt it, and their stabbing deaths at the hands of men named Cassius was a strong second. Josephus wrote that the assassination of this "last" Caesar brought a century of despotism to a fitting close since it came exactly one hundred years after the first consulship of the Great Dictator. The connection led to broader observations about ambition, both kingly and divine, and about leaders who appealed directly to the populace over the heads of the senate. These were not misplaced notions, but modern readers should not be drawn too quickly into judging Gaius a second Caesar. The evidence is biased.

In similar fashion, it was Gaius' critics (not modern scholars) who were responsible for the image of him following in the footsteps of his great-grandfather Marc Antony. The story goes that his character was formed under the spell of Antony's daughter Antonia, in whose house he spent several allegedly formative years, and under the influence of his "tyrant teachers," Herod Agrippa and Antiochus of Commagene, who taught him the ways of Eastern potentates.[15] He was criticized for managing the client states on Rome's eastern borders to benefit his Oriental cronies, for his interest in the cult of Isis and things Egyptian and for

---

[15] Willrich 97–100, 297–304; Gelzer 382; Balsdon 1934a, 13–14; Garzetti 1975, 85. Ceausescu (1973) suggests that Gaius pursued a conscious policy of reincluding the East.

his threat to remove himself to Alexandria. Returning the revenues of eighteen years to Antiochus along with his kingdom was unusual; yet Gaius did not stray so far from the policy of other Julio-Claudian emperors as is assumed. Emperors who found themselves in conflict with the senate (potentially all) might wish to retreat from Rome. Augustus visited Egypt where he viewed the breastplate of Alexander (even if he did not put it on) and had a temple begun for Antony finished for himself. He perhaps built a private shrine on the Palatine for Isis, the Egyptian goddess who had arrived in Rome to stay.[16]

But client kings deprived the senators of employment as provincial governors, and Gaius also took away the last legion under senate control when he divided the province of Africa and gave its military responsibilities to an imperial legate. So long as the senate defined itself as the elite body of the Empire, its prestige lay in Rome, and it had a vested interest in maintaining the Augustan interpretation of the Civil War and its central image of victory over Antony, the Battle of Actium. When the consuls celebrated the anniversary of the battle in September of 39, Gaius (we are told) would have been angry no matter which of his two ancestors, Augustus or Antony, had been honored or left out. It is uncertain what sort of trial balloon or balloons Gaius sent up. Perhaps he wanted Antony remembered along with Augustus in connection with Actium or expressed displeasure with his treatment by Rome's writers of epic history or commissioned a biography of his father that assimilated him to Augustus' worthy opponent. When Claudius' turn came, he chose "by Augustus" as his personal oath on the one hand and honored Antony's birthday on the other. He got by with it; Gaius, as was often the case, did not.[17] But Gaius could not and did not turn his back on Augustus, for to have done so would have been to turn his back on the principate itself and to repudiate his own position. To see a reinstatement of Antony among the *imagines* of the dynasty as a rejection of Augustus is to follow the lead of senatorial prejudice. "Preference for the East" was in part at least a metaphor for an emperor's failure to deal graciously with the Rome-centered senate.

As Gaius' quasi-legitimate successor, Claudius was faced with a problem. Both uncle and nephew gained the principate by the same claim of family, but Gaius did not have useful coattails with the perverse exception of his erratic behavior that served his successor well. How better to dismiss this embarrassing failure than to encourage the idea that he was mad? Almost everything said about Gaius finds a reply in the tradition about Claudius. The unpopular measures that were reversed (new taxes, for instance) provided occasions for him to position himself

---

[16] Taylor 142–46; Barrett 1989, 221.

[17] The double loyalty of Gaius and Claudius is the same as that attached to Germanicus, who felt conflicting joy and sadness when he remembered Actium's winner and loser on his vist to the battle site in A.D. 18; his emotional response may have been retrojected from the reign of Gaius.

favorably in respect to his predecessor. Rather more difficult were the measures
that he chose to continue. When he reaffirmed what Gaius had initiated (necessary
because Gaius' *acta* were annulled), it was recorded as his own. The proposed expedition to Britain was especially troublesome since Claudius would himself
invade successfully three years later, and Gaius' aborted attempt was treated as an
absurdity. The honorific titles that Gaius bestowed on Antonia, Claudius' very
slender link with the *gens Iulia,* are confirmed by a sacrifice for "Antonia
Augusta" in January of the year following her death. But when Claudius granted
them again, he did more than merely take the credit since he needed his mother
for himself uncontaminated by association with Gaius. And so the story was put
forth that she had refused to take the titles from Gaius and that he did not follow
her ostensibly good advice, insulted her, drove her to her death, perhaps even
poisoned her. There was scarcely time for all this since she died within weeks of
Tiberius.[18] The considerable effort to put distance between her and her grandson
makes it certain that the Antony-Antonia-Gaius association was real in contemporary perception.

Not only Claudius but other members of Gaius' circle, those who had accepted
provinces, consulships, and adlections to the Arval Brotherhood and who
survived to pursue successful careers, had to appear to have served him with
something less than enthusiasm. Always available was the excuse that the
malicious emperor had intended to kill the survivors and indeed would have if
only he had lived a little longer. All Rome wanted to be thought among his
enemies once it was safe. Specific persons "rescued" by Gaius' timely death were
Memmius Regulus, Cassius Longinus, and Publius Petronius, all supposedly under
suspicion when he died. Others, like Valerius Asiaticus, who shouted "Would that
I had done it!" in the aftermath of the assassination, would claim that they had
long cherished hostile feelings. Even Gaius' praetorian prefects and freedman
climbed on board the conspiracy in the eleventh hour.

Lastly, Gaius' behavior provoked laughter as well as outrage. Why should everything that was said about him have been serious? As the *Apocolocyntosis*
demonstrates, there were certainly jokes about Claudius, and Gaius provided a
quantity of raw material. His failure to maintain a decent relationship with the
senate lay behind the charge that his only friends were actors, gladiators and
charioteers and spawned the joke that the priests of his cult were his wife, his
uncle and his horse, the last of whom might have to take on the consulship as
well. It was his litter bearers, the servants of his luxury, not his bodyguard, who
came to his aid when he was attacked. They were the only ones left in his camp.
His vanity prompted jokes about baldness, and his extravagance extended the list

---

18 Noted by Charlesworth, 1933b, 107–8.

of birds that he sacrificed to his *numen* to satisfy a gourmand's palate. Stories about "Little Boots" gathered around his divine pretensions, his obsession with the races, his Isiac dabbling and not surprisingly, his shoes.

* * *

The aim in this commentary is twofold, to furnish historical context and explanation (when possible) for the isolated anecdotes in the Suetonius *Life* and to try to understand why the stories about Gaius were told as they were; the fabric of anecdote is historical fact in its own right. Along the way I point out Suetonius' organization and parallels with the broader tradition. Because of its fuller apparatus, I have used Maximilian Ihm's *editio maior* of the Suetonius *Lives* (Teubner 1911) but nonetheless deal with textual problems only when cruces have found their way into the text proper or when an alternate reading prompts a change that is both persuasive and meaningful.

The help of my mentors at Columbia University and Barnard College is thankfully acknowledged. I am grateful to Professors Alan Cameron, Roger Bagnall, Lydia Lenaghan, James Rives and William V. Harris for their many specific suggestions. I also need to thank the referees of this text for pointing out from the objectivity of their greater distance the questions that I had begged. In his capacity as Chair of the Editorial Board for APA Monographs, Professor Matthew S. Santirocco's interest has been continuously encouraging. Dr. Richard L. Munich, Professor of Clinical Psychiatry, Cornell University Medical College, and Deborah Carson, Nurse Clinician, Comprehensive Epilepsy Center, The New York Hospital, have helped me interpret the medical information.

I am most indebted, of course, to the detailed and patient historical investigation that has tackled both Gaius and the early Empire over the years. The very recent (1992) Italian commentary on the *Life of Caligula* by Gianni Guastella appeared after my own work was substantially finished, but I have been able to include some insights that it has provided. I take full responsibility for my own (perhaps excessive) skepticism about what the ancients said about Gaius.

Finally, I must acknowledge my family's patience in living with me while I have lived with Caligula.

New York, New York, April 1993

Abbreviations

Classical authors and texts are cited according to the form suggested in the *Oxford Classical Dictionary*. Chapter and paragraph numbers in the commentary without attribution are to the Suetonius *Life of Caligula: C. Suetoni Tranquilli de vita Caesarum libri VIII. Liber IIII C. Caligula*. Edited by M. Ihm. Leipzig, 1907. References to the text of Cassius Dio's *Roman History* are to E. Cary's Loeb Classical Library edition unless the greater detail of the Boissevain edition is pertinent. The following abbreviations are also used in this commentary.

Anth. Lat.: Buecheler, F., and A. Riese, eds. *Anthologia Latina.* 2 vols. Leipzig, 1906. Reprint: Amsterdam, 1964.

Chron. Min.: Mommsen, T., ed. *Chronica Minora Saec. IV, V, VI, VII.* In *Monumenta Germaniae Historiae.* Vols. 9–11. Berlin, 1892. Reprint. Munich, 1981.

CRF: Ribbeck, O., ed. *Comicorum Romanorum Fragmenta (Comicorum Romanorum praeter Plautum et Terentium Fragmenta).* Vol. 2 of *Scaenicae Romanorum Poesis Fragmenta.* 2 vols. Leipzig, 1897–1898. Reprint. Hildesheim, 1962.

Docs.: Smallwood, E. M., ed. *Documents Illustrating the Principates of Gaius, Claudius and Nero.* Cambridge, 1967.

DMS-III-R: American Psychiatiric Association. *Diagnostic and Statistical Manual of Mental Disorders.* 3rd ed. Revised. Washington, D. C., 1987.

EJ: Ehrenberg, V., and A. H. M. Jones, eds. *Documents Illustrating the Reigns of Augustus and Tiberius.* 2nd ed. Oxford, 1955.

PA: Platner, S. B. *A Topographical Dictionary of Ancient Rome.* Compiled and revised by T. Ashby. London, 1929.

PIR[1]: Dessau, H., E. Krebs, and P. von Rohden, eds. *Prosopographia Imperii Romani Saec. I, II, III.* Berlin, 1896–1898.

PIR[2]: Stein, A., and L. Petersen, eds. *Prosopographia Imperii Romani Saec. I, II, III.* 2nd ed. Berlin, 1933–.

RE: Pauly, A., G. Wissowa, and W. Kroll, eds. *Real-Encyclopädie der klassischen Altertumswissenschaft, Stuttgart,* 1893–.

RIC[2]: Sutherland, C. H. V., and R. A. G. Carson, eds. *The Roman Imperial Coinage.* 2nd ed. Vol. 1. London, 1984.

Rel. Reiff.: Reifferscheid, A., ed. *C. Suetoni Tranquilli praeter Caesarum libros reliquiae.* Leipzig, 1860. Reprint. Hildesheim, 1971.

Schol. Juv.: P. Wessner, P., ed. *Scholia in Iuvenalem Vetustiora.* Leipzig, 1931.

TGF: Snell, B., R. Kannicht, and S. Radt, eds. *Tragicorum Graecorum Fragmenta.* 4 vols. Göttingen, 1977–1986.

TLL: Thesaurus Linguae Latinae. Leipzig, 1900–.

TRF: Ribbeck, O., ed. *Tragicorum Romanorum Fragmenta.* Vol. 1 of *Scaenicae Romanorum Poesis Fragmenta.* 2 vols. Leipzig, 1897–1898. Reprint. Hildesheim, 1962.

Commentary: Suetonius' *Life of Caligula*

There could be no better way for a biographer to begin an estimate of the emperor Gaius (*PIR²* I. 217) than with his father Germanicus Julius Caesar (*PIR²* I. 221), beneath the aegis of whose reputation he assumed the principate. Suetonius' *Lives* normally begin with a survey of the subject's ancestry but with no other of this length. Germanicus merited special treatment because he was an important player in the Julio-Claudian saga in his own right. After he died, his *amici* who were counting on being near the center of power when he became princeps were left without a focus for their ambition and found it in their interest to cast him as a foil to the emperor Tiberius (Tiberius Julius Caesar Augustus, *PIR²* C. 941) and to keep alive the myth of the perfect general and amicable prince. The name of Germanicus was cash in hand for both his son Gaius and his brother Claudius (Tiberius Claudius Nero Germanicus, *PIR²* C. 942; Suet. *Cl.* 11.2). But his reputation was not quite so simple; Tacitus paints a less enthusiastic picture of him (Borzsák 1970, Ross, Rutland, Pelling), although he too knew the encomiastic source that Suetonius used. Suetonius makes some small acknowledgment that the very favorable tradition could be questioned (*ut opinio fuit*, 2; *quin et.. ferunt*, 5) but in general he accepts it whole.

This "mini-biography" (1–6) opens with an economical summary of Germanicus' career. The first two sentences correspond to the two major phases of his activity, his service on the Northern frontier (1.1) and the final period in the East (1.2). The three finite verbs in the first sentence divide phase one into three parts: the facts of his parentage, adoption and accelerated honors (*gessit*), his involvement in the mutiny of the Army of Lower Germany (*compescuit*), and his German campaigns and the triumph of A.D. 17 (*triumphavit*). In the second sentence his mission to the Orient is grammatically and logically subordinate to his death (*obiit non sine veneni suspicione*).

1.1 *Germanicus, C. Caesaris pater:* Germanicus was born on May 24 (*ILS* 108; *EJ* p. 49; *Docs.* no. 3, p.11) most probably in 15 B.C. (Levick 1966, 238–39; Summer, 421–23). Germanicus Julius Caesar was his name after his adoption by his uncle, the future emperor Tiberius. His original name is unattested but as an eldest son he probably carried his father's (Nero Claudius Drusus, below; Mommsen 1878, 262). Suetonius' subject, the emperor Gaius (Caligula) was Gaius <Iulius> Caesar (Germanicus) and after he became emperor, Gaius Caesar Augustus Germanicus. The Julius never occurs. The conspicuous juxtaposition of Germanicus and Gaius Caesar here at the beginning of the text introduces the comparison between them that is implicit throughout the *Life,* and anticipates a second comparison, that of Gaius with his famous ancestor, another Gaius Julius Caesar, with which the text ends (60).

Drusi et minoris Antoniae filius: Germanicus' father was Nero Claudius Drusus (Germanicus), called Drusus the Elder (*PIR²* C. 857), the younger brother of the emperor Tiberius, the son of Tiberius Claudius Nero and of Livia Drusilla (*PIR²* L. 210). Livia later married Augustus Caesar (Gaius Julius Caesar Augustus, *PIR²* I. 215), then still Octavianus Caesar, not long before Drusus' birth in 38 B.C. (Suet. *Aug.* 62.2; *Tib.* 4.3; *Cl.* 1.1; Tac. *Ann.* 1.10.5; Dio 58.44.1–5; Vell. 2.95.1). When Drusus died in 9 B.C., the senate gave him and his heirs the *cognomen* Germanicus in recognition of his military successes in Germany (Suet. *Cl.* 1.3; Dio 55.2.3; Ov. *Fast.* 1.597). Germanicus' mother (Gaius' grandmother) was Antonia Minor (*PIR²* A. 885), the younger daughter of Marcus Antonius and of Octavia (*PIR²* O. 45), the sister of Augustus. Germanicus possessed an impressive ancestry with Claudian nobility on his father's side and political prestige on his mother's. The descent from Antony was important both for him (Tac. *Ann.* 2.43.5, 53.2) and for Gaius (on 23.1).

a Tiberio adoptatus: After the unexpected deaths of his grandsons and heirs Gaius and Lucius Caesar (*PIR²* I. 216 and 222), Augustus tried yet again to assure that he would found a dynasty by adopting his stepson Tiberius and his last surviving grandson Agrippa Postumus (*PIR²* I. 214) and by having Tiberius adopt Germanicus. The date was June 26, A.D. 4 (*EJ* p. 49). Those who thought that a serious conflict existed between Tiberius and Germanicus interpreted the adoption of Germanicus as reluctant inasmuch as Tiberius had a son of his own, Drusus Julius Caesar, or Drusus the Younger (*PIR²* I. 144; Tac. *Ann.* 1.3.5; Suet. *Tib.* 15.2; Dio 55.13.2).

quaesturam quinquennio ante quam per leges liceret: Young princes were marked destined for great careers when they were allowed to hold positions in the *cursus honorum* before the legal age (e.g., Tiberius, Dio 53.28.3; Drusus the Elder, Dio 54.10.4; Gaius and Lucius Caesar, Tac. *Ann.* 1.3.2; Dio 55.9.2, 9–10). During the early Empire the normal minimum age for the quaestorship seems to have been twenty-five (Summer 422–23; Talbert 17–18). Germanicus became quaestor at the beginning of A.D. 7 when he was twenty (Dio 55.31.1).

post eam consulatum statim gessit: He skipped the praetorship and proceeded directly (*statim*) to the consulship in A.D. 12 (8.1; also Dio 56.26.1; *EJ* no. 141, p. 97).

missusque ad exercitum in Germaniam: Germanicus served under Tiberius both in Pannonia in A.D. 7–9 (Dio 55.31–56.17) and on the German frontier in 11. In 12 he was in Rome for his consulship, and in 13 Augustus sent him to take command of the eight legions of the Armies of Upper and Lower Germany (8.3; Tac. *Ann.* 1.3.5; Vell. 2.123.1; Dio 57.3.1).

excessu Augusti nuntiato: Augustus died on August 19, A.D. 14 (Suet. *Aug.* 100.1; *EJ* p. 50). The news found Germanicus taking the census in Gaul (Tac. *Ann.* 1.31.2, 33.10).

Here follows the briefest possible summary of the mutiny that took place at the death of Augustus among the four legions stationed near the site of present day Cologne (Tac. *Ann.* 1.31–49; Dio 57.5; Vell. 2.125.1–4). Both the three frontier legions stationed in Pannonia and these that comprised the Army of Lower Germany took advantage of the potential for instability at the time of Augustus' death to press for more benefits and better conditions. Tiberius sent Drusus to deal with the uprising in Pannonia (Tac. *Ann.* 1.24.1), and Germanicus was already in position to deal with the one on the Rhine. Through a combination of concessions and repressive measures he restored discipline but does not seem to have exercised much leadership. He bought the legionaries off, forged a letter from Tiberius promising what he had no authority to deliver and in the end turned them loose on one another to settle scores. In the midst of the crisis, the legionaries offered to swear to Germanicus rather than to Tiberius. As a biographer Suetonius is interested only in the political potential for Germanicus; elsewhere he gives the real causes of the mutiny: *flagitabant ambo exercitus multa extra ordinem, ante omnia ut aequarentur stipendio praetorianis* (Suet. *Tib.* 25.2). The uprising followed the model of a labor-management dispute, not a revolution; once grievances were redressed, it lost its momentum (Liechtenhan 52–67). For other references to the mutiny and Gaius' involvement with it, see 9 and 48.

legiones universas imperatorem Tiberium pertinacissime recusantis... compescuit: Suetonius commonly exaggerates (*universas*). The legions in Lower Germany were the only ones that opted for Germanicus as an alternative to Tiberius.

et sibi summam rei p. deferentis: Cf. Dio 57.6.2. The army, gathered in a nasty mood, offered *imperium* to Germanicus as the man on the spot.[1] The offer was made amidst threats and demands, and Germanicus extricated himself from the situation with difficulty (Tac. *Ann.* 1. 34–5; Dio 57.5).

incertum pietate an constantia maiore: Attractive motives are assigned to Germanicus' refusal to accept the legions' backing. His *pietas* was loyalty to Tiberius (*flexit ad victorias triumphosque Tiberii, praecipuis laudibus celebrans quae apud Germanias illis cum legionibus pulcherrima fecisset*, Tac. *Ann.* 1.34.4). *Constantia maior*, his unwillingness to betray a more abstract trust, seems to be what Tacitus describes when he writes, *quasi scelere contaminaretur*,

---

[1] Availability was crucial. The emperor Vitellius (A. Vitellius, *PIR¹* V. 499) had been with the legions of Lower Germany for only a matter of weeks before he was saluted *imperator* in A.D. 69 (Tac. *Hist.* 1.52.1, 1.57).

praeceps tribunali desiluit...moriturum potius quam fidem exueret clamitans (Tac. *Ann.* 1.35.4). Germanicus did not need to insert himself into so precarious a situation and march on Rome. Augustus' plan was still in effect (scarcely begun), and patience was an option. His own position depended on the legitimacy of his adoptive father Tiberius.

atque hoste mox devicto triumphavit: After restoring discipline Germanicus campaigned indecisively in Germany in the autumn of A.D. 14 and again during the summers of 15 and 16. He was recalled to Rome by Tiberius where he celebrated a triumph on May 26, A.D. 17 (Tac. *Ann.* 2.41.2). The enemy had in no sense been "thoroughly conquered" (*devicto*). A dupondius that recalls his triumph (*RIC*[2] Gaius no. 57, p. 112) shows him in his triumphal quadriga on the obverse and as *imperator* on the reverse. Its legend, *signis recept devictis Germ S C,* suggests that *devincere* was the word officially chosen to describe the outcome of his war, regardless of its less than conclusive results.[2] Note also *cum signis devictarum gentium ina[uratis* describing the same campaigns on the *Tabula Siarensis* (frag. 1 line 11, González).

Chapter two of Germanicus' career, his Eastern command. Opinion hostile to Tiberius saw Germanicus' recall from Germany, his triumph and even his appointment as overseer of affairs in the Orient as a ruse to detach him from the Rhine legions with whom he was popular and as a way of getting him out of Rome. *Maius imperium* (below) was, however, a very powerful command to bestow on someone who was not trusted.

1.2 consul deinde iterum creatus: Germanicus' second consulship was in A.D. 18. His partner was Tiberius, who was holding his third (Tac. *Ann.* 2.53.1; *EJ* p. 41; *CIL* 4.1885). January 1 found Germanicus at Actium, the site of Augustus' victory over Antony in 31 B.C., on his way to his command in the East.

ac prius quam honorem iniret ad componendum Orientis statum expulsus: Tiberius sent Germanicus to the provinces *quae mari dividuntur,* i.e., east of the Adriatic, and gave him *maius imperium,* a command that was not geographically limited but took precedence over those of all other Roman officials in the vicinity (Tac. *Ann.* 2.43.1). The special command was apparently necessary because of the unsettling effect of power struggles within the territories in the East that Rome controlled through client kings (Tac. *Ann.* 2.5.1, 42.5). The

---

[2] For a suggestion that *devictus* meant considerably less than subjugated when it occurred as a coin legend, Christ 504–33. For various assessments of Germanicus' activity east of the Rhine in these years, see Timpe (1968), Christ, Koestermann (1958), and Kessler.

strong participle *expulsus* is consistent with the notion that Tiberius was eager to remove Germanicus from the center of power (Tac. *Ann.* 2.5.1).

Armeniae regem devicisset: Germanicus' most important mission was to restore authority in Armenia, the buffer state between Rome and Parthia (Tac. *Ann.* 2.55.6). Attempts to control it as a client kingdom had been unsatisfactory and chaos there was nothing new (Tac. *Ann.* 2.1–4; Magie 483–85). When Germanicus arrived in A.D. 18, he confirmed the popular choice Zeno (afterwards Artaxias, *PIR²* A. 1168) as king (Tac. *Ann.* 2.56.1–3; Debevoise 151–52; Magie, 496–98). The solution held until 35 (Tac. *Ann.* 6.31–38; see on 14.3). Suetonius probably wrote *dedisset* (Lipsius, *apparatus*) here. *Devicisset* does not fit the facts because there was no king to subdue in Armenia (*incerti solutique et magis sine domino quam in libertate,* Tac. *Ann.* 2.4.2), and "giving" the crown appears to have been a motif for the event (*insigne regium capiti eius imposuit,* Tac. *Ann.* 2.56.3; *regem Artaxian Armeniis a Germanico datum,* Tac. *Ann.* 2.64.1). A didrachm shows Germanicus placing the crown on the head of a standing Artaxias (*RIC²* Gaius no. 59, p. 113; see Marrone, 218).[3]

Cappadociam in provinciae formam redigisset: *In provinciae formam redigere* = "reduce to the form of a province," the standard expression (Suet. *Jul.* 25.1; Tac. *Ann.* 2.42.4; Caes. *BGall.* 2.45.2; Vell. 2.97.4). Cappadocia had been a client state, but after its aged and long-time ruler King Archelaus (*PIR²* A. 1023) was summoned to Rome in A.D. 17 where he was put on trial and then died, Tiberius made it into a province (Tac. *Ann.* 2.42.2–4; cf. Suet. *Tib.* 37.4; Dio 57.17.3–7). Germanicus' specific responsibility seems to have been the installation of the *legatus: at Cappadoces in formam provinciae redacti Q. Veranium legatum accepere* (Tac. *Ann.* 2.56.4). Commagene became a province at the same time (Tac. *Ann.* 2.42.4; Jos. *AJ* 18.53; see 16.3).

annum agens aetatis quartum et tricensimum: Germanicus had passed his thirty-third birthday when he died on October 10, A.D. 19 (*EJ* p. 53; Tac. *Ann.* 2.72.2).

Cn. Calpurnius Piso (*PIR²* C. 287) was appointed *legatus* in the imperial province of Syria (2) at the same time that Germanicus was given *maius imperium.* Opinion hostile to Tiberius claimed that

---

[3] *Devicisset* is probably derived from the fact that kings are more often "conquered" than "given." The attraction of *hoste devicto* in reference to the Germans (1.1) may also have influenced the transmission. An alternate solution has been to assume that the king referred to here was not Zeno-Artaxias but Venones I who was deposed by his own people and escaped to Syria where he was killed (Tac. *Ann.* 2.1–4, 56.2, 58, 68; Jos. *AJ* 18.46–52; Baumgarten-Crusius and Maurer). But this is more *deiecisset* (Lipsius, *apparatus*) than *devicisset,* and Zeno-Artaxias is clearly the king central to the record of Germanicus' achievements in the East and is meant here.

Piso had been appointed to be a check on him (*ad spes Germanici coercendas,* Tac. *Ann.* 2.43.3). The relationship between the two proved disastrous, whether Tiberius had intended it or not. Each thought the other was exceeding his jurisdiction, and there was undoubtedly an underlying conflict of generations and personalities. Piso, "a man of intractable temper with a family history of hostility to the Caesars" (Syme 1958, 492) had already challenged Tiberius (Tac. *Ann.* 2.43.2, 1.74.5, 1.79.4; Syme 1956b, 18). He seems to have accepted the necessity of a single strong man at the center of Roman power but not the manifestation of hereditary monarchy that he confronted in the person of a young prince: *vix Tiberio concedere, liberos eius ut multum infra despectare* (Tac. *Ann.* 2.43.3). Their conflict escalated to the point that Piso abandoned his responsibilities in Syria. He attempted a return after Germanicus was dead but in the end settled for a defense of his actions in Rome (Tac. *Ann.* 2.69, 78–81). His departure from his command was certainly irregular, but whether he poisoned Germanicus is another matter. It was never proved (Tac. *Ann.* 3.14.1–3, 19.2; Questa 1957b, 314; Koestermann 1957, 368–69; Goodyear 1972–1981, at *Ann.* 2.73.4; Kessler 77–78). But Germanicus' friends were either convinced that he was or at least felt that they could take to court and use for their own advantage the rumors which were bound to accompany the unexpected death of a young man. They brought the poisoning story back to Rome and used it in the trial against his alleged murderer (Tac. *Ann.* 3.13.2). Suetonius returns to the poisoning and the circumstances surrounding Germanicus' death at 3.3.

diuturno morbo: "Slow" poisons were suspected. Cf. Tac. *Ann.* 2.70.1.

Antiochiae obiit: Antioch ('Αντιόχεια ἡ ἐπὶ Δάφνῃ) was the leading city of Syria and central for Roman operations in the East. Tacitus writes that Germanicus died at "Epidaphne" (*tribunal Epidaphnae quo in loco vitam finierat, Ann.* 2.83.2), either not understanding that ἐπὶ Δάφνῃ was merely the tag that differentiated this Antioch from others or because it had become the colloquial name for the city. The surrounding area contained pleasant villas, and Germanicus in all likelihood did reside (and die) "near Daphne," i.e., near the shrine of Apollo outside the city proper (Downey 19–20, 187, n. 105, 188).

non sine veneni suspicione: Suetonius is both cautiously circumspect and succinct. There was a story that Alexander the Great was also poisoned.[4]

nam praeter livores, qui toto corpore erant, et spumas, quae per os fluebant: Germanicus' friends opened their case against Piso in Antioch by exposing his body nude so that it could bear witness to poison as the cause of death. The details of the black and blue marks and the foaming at the mouth occur only

---

[4] The parallels between Germanicus and Alexander have been explained variously as the insertion of Tacitus (Syme 1958, 492, 771; Treves 159–69, Borzsák 1969), as a conscious program of Germanicus himself and of his circle (Tac. *Ann.* 2.73.1–3; Questa 1957b, 303–20) or as a charge by his enemies (Marrone 217–21). Imitation of Antony and Hercules are also a part of the Germanicus story in Tacitus (Tac. *Ann.* 2.13.1; Borzsák 1970, 288). See on 3.2 for further connection with Alexander.

in this text. Tacitus was skeptical about all the symptoms (*Ann.* 2.73.3, 3.12.4; Dio 57.18.9).

cremati quoque cor inter ossa incorruptum repertum est: cuius ea natura existimatur, ut tinctum veneno igne confici nequeat: The elder Pliny cites the speech of P. Vitellius (*PIR¹* V. 502), a friend of Germanicus and prosecutor of Piso, for the notion that the heart of a poisoned man would not burn: *Negatur cremari posse in iis qui cardiaco morbo obierint, negatur et veneno interemptis; certe exstat oratio Vitelli qua Gnaeum Pisonem eius sceleris coarguit hoc usus argumento, palamque testatus non potuisse ob venenum cor Germanici Caesaris cremari. contra genere morbi defensus est Piso* (*HN* 11.71). Both Tacitus and Pliny write as though they had this speech in hand. For Vitellius as Piso's prosecutor, Tac. *Ann.* 3.13.2; Suet. *Vit.* 2.3.

2 ***obiit autem, ut opinio fuit, fraude Tiberi, ministerio et opera Cn. Pisonis, qui sub idem tempus Syriae praepositus:*** *Obiit* picks up *obiit non sine veneni suspicione* (1.2). *Ut opinio fuit* expresses Suetonius' reservations about Piso's role. The argument for complicity between Tiberius and Piso is that the latter could never have acted with such belligerence as he did if he had not had the emperor's blessing (Koestermann 1957, 341, 352–53).

nec dissimulans offendendum sibi aut patrem aut filium, quasi plane ita necesse esset: "Not concealing the fact that he had to give offense to either the father [Tiberius] or the son [Germanicus]—as though this were an obvious necessity." Suetonius' comparative conditional clause implies that Piso's choice between the camps of Tiberius and Germanicus was not absolutely necessary. Cf. *ut opinio fuit* (above).

etiam aegrum Germanicum gravissimis verborum ac rerum acerbitatibus nullo adhibito modo adfecit: Tacitus and Dio are both specific about the allegations that Suetonius generalizes in *verba* and *res*. Piso forcibly broke up demonstrations of thanksgiving for Germanicus' temporary recovery, he hastened his death by magic, and his partisans showed unseemly curiosity about the illness (Tac. *Ann.* 2.69.2–3; Dio 57.18.9).

propter quae, ut Romam rediit, paene discerptus a populo: According to Tacitus, although Piso returned home confidently (*Ann.* 3.9), there was a demonstration (riot?) outside the *curia* later during his trial, and the mob threatened to punish him themselves and to deface his statues if the senate acquitted him (Tac. *Ann.* 3.14.4).

a senatu capitis damnatus est: Tacitus tells a more complicated story. Tiberius gave the case a preliminary hearing and referred it to the senate, presumably so that Piso could be tried under the *lex Cornelia de sicariis et veneficiis* (on 3.3). The trial was in two parts with an intermission between the prosecution and the defense. After the first half, Piso committed suicide in anticipation of conviction (Tac. *Ann.* 3.10–15; also Suet. *Tib.* 52.3; *Vit.* 2.3). Dio's version has Tiberius bring Piso before the senate; the trial was postponed and before it resumed, the defendant killed himself (ἀναβολήν τέ τινα ἐποιήσατο καὶ ἑαυτὸν κατεχρήσατο, 57.18.10). Dio's postponement is plausibly Tacitus' two-part trial, but it is difficult to reconcile Suetonius' flat statement of conviction with the other two accounts. Wanting to be brief (Germanicus, after all, not Piso, was his subject), he seems simply to have summed it up with *damnatus est,* the anticipated outcome.

The brief survey of Germanicus' life finished, Suetonius turns to his virtues, first in summary (3.1), then with concrete examples (3.2–3) and finally with the popularity that resulted from them (4–6). His virtues are arranged in the rubrics that form the pattern of this and all of Suetonius' *Lives*. The list was surely intended to contrast with the overwhelming list of Gaius' vices that will follow. Suetonius provides something close to an outline in the topic sentence with which this description opens. The generalization, *omnes Germanico corporis animique virtutes* is amplified by *formam et fortitudinem egregiam [corporis virtutes]* and *ingenium praecellens…benivolentiam… conciliandaeque hominum gratiae ac promerendi amoris studium [animi virtutes]*. Dio has a similar organization: κάλλιστος μὲν γὰρ τὸ σῶμα ἄριστος δὲ καὶ τὴν ψυχὴν ἔφυ, παιδείᾳ τε ἅμα καὶ ῥώμῃ διέπρεπε (Dio 57.18.6; more fully, 57.18.6–8). Other texts also contain eulogies (Tac. *Ann.* 2.13.1, 73.1–3; Jos. *AJ* 18.207–10).

3.1 *Omnes Germanico corporis animique virtutes, et quantas nemini cuiquam, contigusse satis constat:* The superlatives implied by *quantas nemini cuiquam* are explicit in Dio: κάλλιστος…ἄριστος…ἀνδρειότατος… ἡμερώτατα τῷ οἰκείῳ προσεφέρατο…πλεῖστον ἰσχύων (57.18.6).

formam et fortitudinem egregiam, ingenium in utroque eloquentiae doctrinaeque genere praecellens: In utroque eloquentiae doctrinaeque genere, "in both sorts of oratory and learning," refers to rhetoric and literature both Latin and Greek, described in greater detail in 3.2. After his death Germanicus' likeness on a *clipeus* was placed among those of other *auctores eloquentiae* and *scriptores* in the library attached to the temple of Apollo on the Palatine (Tac. *Ann.* 2.83.3). Oratorical ability was the only accomplishment of his father's that Gaius shared (10.1, 53). For Gaius' *clipeus,* see 16.4.

benivolentiam singularem conciliandaeque hominum gratiae ac promerendi amoris mirum et efficax st studium: Germanicus' amiability and popularity were central to his reputation. Suetonius clearly finds successful public relations efforts commendable (e.g., Gaius' funerals for his family, 15.1; his bridge at Baiae, 19).

formae minus congruebat gracilitas crurum, sed ea quoque paulatim repleta assidua equi vectatione post cibum: Formae picks up *formam* from the outline (above). Skinny shanks were a deformity and betrayed bad character as well, notably immodesty and cowardice (Couissin 250; *et quid est illud quod contumelia dicitur? ...iocatus est et in oculorum valitudinem et crurum gracilitatem,* Sen. *Dial.* 2.16.4; also Suet. *Dom.* 18.1). Gaius inherited them (50.1). But the difference was that Germanicus tried to improve his legs by exercise and thus erase a blot on his character. See on 50.1 for the underlying assumptions of physiognomy.

3.2 *hostem comminus saepe percussit:* Hand to hand fighting illustrates *fortitudo* (3.1). The only other testimony of Germanicus' personal bravery is his engagement of the enemy at close quarters in Germany: *conlato illic gradu certatum* (Tac. *Ann.* 2.20.3).

oravit causas etiam triumphalis: He pleaded cases in A.D. 10 and again in 12, the year of his consulship (Dio 56.24.7, 26.1). Both of these instances came after he had received the *ornamenta triumphalia* in 9 (Dio 56.17.2). This was evidence not only of *eloquentia* (3.1) but also of *civilitas* (cf. *civilis,* below), because with his prestige he did not need to prove himself by pleading cases in court.

atque inter cetera studiorum monimenta reliquit: Studiorum monimenta = "written records of his learning." Germanicus was a man of letters (Ov. *Fast.* 1.19–26). Extant works attributed to him are a paraphrasing translation from the Greek of Aratus' *Phaenomena* and two Latin epigrams, each with its Greek version (*Anth. Lat.* nos. 708, 709, pp. 174–75). The *Phaenomena,* an influential Hellenistic work on astronomy, had already attracted Latin translators. The attribution of a version to Germanicus is uncertain (Gain 20).

et comedias Graecas: Shortly after he became emperor, Claudius produced a comedy in honor of Germanicus perhaps written by Germanicus himself (Rolfe 1913–1914 at Suet. *Cl.* 11.2).

domi forisque civilis: Applied to an emperor *civilis* meant unpretentious, behaving as an ordinary citizen or (more accurately) affecting to: καὶ πλεῖστον ἰσχύων ἅτε Καῖσαρ ὢν ἐξ ἴσου τοῖς ἀσθενεστέροις ἐσωφρόνει (Dio 57.18.7). "The ruler had to understand the secret of 'coming down to the level of the people.' Whoever did that was regarded by his supporters as possessing personal charm, and by his opponents as having *levitas popularis*" (Yavetz 1969, 139; also Wallace-Hadrill 1983, 162–66; Lana 465–87; Veyne 1990, 403).

libera ac foederata oppida sine lictoribus adibat: This is good behavior abroad (*foris civilis* above), where it was considered gracious to be attended by fewer lictors than one was entitled to (App. *BCiv.* 5.41). Germanicus toured the eastern Mediterranean before he arrived at his command in Syria (1.2; Tac. *Ann.* 2.53–54), and Tacitus writes that he visited Athens with "one lictor" (*hinc ventum Athenas, foederique sociae et vetustae urbis datum ut uno lictore uteretur, Ann.* 2.53.3), perhaps intentionally palliating the impression that he courted favor by taking no official trappings at all (*sine lictoribus*) as Suetonius asserts (Questa 1957b, 299; Marrone, 213). A common source may have included the absence of lictors in order to show Germanicus following the model of Antony, who had gone about Athens without insignia or military dress (App. *BCiv.* 5.76). There is a similar discrepancy between Suetonius and Tacitus when they write about the burial of dead at the site of the Varine disaster (below). Tacitus is the more likely to modify the flattering material (note 9). Germanicus had, in fact, no right to any lictors in a free city such as Athens, but this distinction was not always honored (Goodyear 1972–1981, 354). *Oppida* is probably a generalizing plural.

sicubi clarorum virorum sepulcra cognosceret, inferias Manibus dabat: Germanicus followed the example of Alexander the Great, who had visited the tombs of Ajax and Achilleus at Troy (Arr. *Anab.* 1.12.1; Plut. *Alex.* 15.8; Diod. 17.17.3), just as Augustus later visited the tomb of Alexander himself (Suet. *Aug.* 18.1; Dio 51.16.5). One of Germanicus' epigrams, "At the Tomb of Hector" (*Anth. Lat.* no. 708, p. 174), is referred to a visit to the site of Troy (*adito Ilio quaeque ibi varietate fortunae et nostri origine veneranda, Tac. Ann.* 2.54.2). See note 4 for the Alexander connection.

caesorum clade Variana veteres ac dispersas reliquias uno tumulo humaturus, colligere sua manu et comportare primus adgressus est: The funeral remembrances in the preceding sentence provide a transition to the story of Germanicus' visit to the battlefield in Germany where three legions under the command of P. Quinctilius Varus (*PIR¹* Q. 27) were eradicated in A.D. 9. This disaster made a deep impression on Roman consciousness (see chapter 31). The recovery of the lost legionary standards and the reestablishment of a Roman presence east of the Rhine were the necessary vengeance (on *hoste devicto*, 1.1). During Germanicus' campaign of 15, he and his legions came upon the site of the disaster and buried the remains that they found there (Tac. *Ann.* 1.61–62; Dio

57.18.1). Suetonius writes that Germanicus actually touched the bones (*colligere sua manu*) whereas Tacitus is more circumspect: *primum extruendo tumulo caespitem Caesar posuit, gratissimo munere in defunctos et praesentibus doloris socius* (*Ann.* 1.62.1). It was *nefas* for a man who performed augury (e.g., a military commander) to touch the dead (Dio 56.31.3), but the gesture of burying the bodies, *nefas* or not, was good public relations (cf. Gaius with the bones of family members, 15.1). Tacitus evidently chose to soften this image of Germanicus courting popularity, but Suetonius accepted it, just as he apparently accepted the statement that Germanicus took "no lictors" with him when he toured (above; see note 9).

3.3 *obtrectatoribus etiam, qualescumque et quantacumque de causa nanctus esset, lenis adeo et innoxius, ut Pisoni decreta sua rescindenti, clientelas di[u]vexanti:* The virtue is *lenitas*, mildness of character (Tac. *Ann.* 2.13.1; Dio 56.18.6). Suetonius' generalization implies that a number of persons (*obtrectores*) disparaged him out of envy, but he has Piso alone in mind. When Germanicus returned to Syria after visiting Egypt in A.D. 19, he found that Piso had undone arrangements that he had made (*decreta sua rescindenti*). Piso was also accused of harrying Germanicus' associates (*clientelas di[u]vexanti;* cf. Tac. *Ann.* 2.69.1, 3.13.2).

non prius suscensere in animum induxerit, quam veneficiis quoque et devotionibus impugnari se comperisset: Piso was charged with black magic as well as with poisoning (2).[5] Said to be buried beneath the floor and in the walls of Germanicus' house were body parts, lead tablets with curses and his name, objects partially burned and smeared with blood and other *maleficia* (Tac. *Ann.* 2.69.3, 3.13.2; Dio 57.18.9). All of these consecrated a person to the powers of death.

ac ne tunc quidem ultra progressus, quam amicitiam ei more maiorum renuntiaret: Only these ultimate offenses caused Germanicus to react with the reprimand of *renuntiatio amicitiae* (Tac. *Ann.* 2.70.2), perhaps the strongest censure available since *crimen maiestatis* had not yet been extended to cover so wide a range of insults as it did later (Bauman 109–13).

---

[5] "For the Romans the difference between poisoning and sorcery was, to be sure, much less apparent than it is to us, as their use of *veneficium* for both sufficiently indicates" (Goodyear 1981, 410, n. 3).

mandaretque domesticis ultionem, si quid sibi accideret: *Domesticis* =
"entourage." Tacitus expands this mandate for vengence into an elaborate
deathbed speech for Germanicus (*Ann.* 2.71).

Germanicus' *civilitas* (3.2–3) quite naturally brought him popularity. Chapter 4 is testimony from
his lifetime; chapters 5 and 6 describe his posthumous reputation.

4 ***quarum virtutum fructum uberrimum tulit, sic probatus et dilectus
a suis, ut Augustus—omitto enim necessitudines reliquas—diu
cunctatus an sibi successorem destinaret, adoptandum Tiberio dederit:***
Although here Suetonius makes Germanicus the focus of Augustus' succession
plans, in his *Life of Tiberius* he uses the correspondence of Augustus to refute the
insinuation that Augustus found Tiberius a poor second choice (*Tib.* 21.2; cf. 1.1
and Tac. *Ann.* 4.57.3). Suetonius used his information variously in order to make
the point at hand: e.g., the death of Tiberius (12.2 and *Tib.* 73.2), the bridge at
Baiae (19 and 32.1), the vows for Gaius' recovery (14.2 and 27.2). The approval
of Germanicus by other family members (*necessitudines reliquas*) can be inferred
from the way that his reputation was tapped by both Gaius and Claudius.

sic vulgo favorabilis: Parallel to *sic probatus et dilectus a suis* (above).

***ut plurimi tradant, quotiens aliquo advenierat vel sicunde discederet,
prae turba occurrentium prosequentiumve nonnumquam eum
discrimen vitae adisse:*** The plural implied by *quotiens* and *nonnumquam* is
again probably Suetonius' generalization from the single instance that follows. It
seems odd that Tacitus does not report this dramatic visit to Rome. Did he intentionally play down the prince's grandstanding as he did with the lictors and the
burial of Varus' dead (3.2)? Is Suetonius' insistence on multiple sources (*ut
plurimi tradant*) an attempt to validate this incident in the face of Tacitus' silence?
See note 9 for what seem to be similar instances.

e Germania vero post compressam seditionem revertenti: There is no
other evidence that Germanicus returned to Rome between the end of the mutiny
of A.D. 14 and his triumph in 17, although there may have been visits that went
unrecorded (note 6). Tacitus has him busy during the winters of 14–15 and 15–16
preparing for the campaigns of the summers to come (*Ann.* 1.55, 2.5–6).

***praetorianas cohortes universas prodisse obviam, quamvis
pronuntiatum esset, ut duae tantum modo exierent:*** Cf. the *universae
legiones* (1.1). At this time three praetorian cohorts were stationed in Rome and
six in outlying areas. Perhaps those along his route paid their respects (cf. 13 for
Gaius' entrance into Rome). Two cohorts normally accompanied the emperor out

of Rome (Millar 1977, 33) and seem to have made up an honor guard: two accompanied home the ashes of Germanicus, two were sent to Pannonia with Drusus, two fought in Germany with Germanicus. (Tac. *Ann.* 3.2.1, 1.24.1, 2.16.3). For praetorians with Gaius in Gaul in A.D. 39, see 43 and 45.1.

populi autem Romani sexum, aetatem, ordinem omnem: The triad of gender, age and order was commonplace for expressing universality (Tac. *Ann.* 6.19.2, 15.54.1).

usque ad vicesimum lapidem effudisse se: Milestones measured the distance from Rome. The twentieth seems to have been the psychological boundary of the city: *nos intra vicesimum lapidum, in conspectu prope urbis nostrae, annuam oppugnationem perferre piget* (Livy 5.4.12).

In chapter 5 Suetonius describes the reaction to Germanicus' death abroad, in chapter 6, the reaction in Rome. Tacitus includes this same information at *Annales* 2.72 and 2.82 respectively. He and Suetonius clearly shared a source. Posthumous honors for Germanicus (Tac. *Ann.* 2.83) are confirmed by the *Tabula Hebana* (Oliver and Palmer; Weinstock 1957, 1966) and the *Tabula Siarensis* (González).

5 *tamen longe maiora et firmiora de eo iudicia in morte ac post mortem extiterunt:* "But his reputation was far greater and better established at the time of his death and afterwards." This transition introduces the final two chapters of the Germanicus biography.

quo defunctus est die, lapidata sunt templa, subversae deum arae, Lares a quibusdam familiares in publicam abiecti: A demonstration of grief at Antioch, both public (*templa, arae*) and private (*Lares familiares,* Maurer). Anger at the gods was a possible response to disaster (Suet. *Aug.* 16.2). In contrast, temples in Rome were stormed by those eager to make thanksgiving sacrifices when they thought that Germanicus had recovered (6.1).

partus coniugum expositi: The death of Germanicus portended a deteriorating political climate, and legitimate children were exposed so that they would not be reared under unfavorable conditions. The opposite occurred under a good ruler: *tollere filios cupiunt et publicis malis sterilitas indicta recluditur* (Sen. *Clem.* 1.13.5; Plin. *Pan.* 26.4–7). This is surely rhetoric, but unwanted children might indeed be exposed for less political reasons (Harris 104–6).

quin et barbaros ferunt: Suetonius puts some distance between himself and the hyperbole that follows with *quin et...ferunt* and indirect discourse. Tacitus is more restrained when he omits the details altogether: *neque multo post extinguitur, ingenti luctu provinciae et circumiacentium populorum indoluere externae nationes regesque (Ann.* 2.72.2).

quibus intestinum quibusque adversus nos bellum esset, velut in domestico communique maerore consensisse ad indutias; regulos quosdam barbam posuisse et uxorum capita rasisse ad indicium maximi luctus: Foreigners regularly shaved their beards and heads to express mourning; Romans let theirs grow (cf. Gaius' mourning behavior at 24.2). The pattern was to do the opposite of what was usual (Plut. *Quaest. Rom.* 267a). The *reguli* were the rulers of the client states in the East with whom Germanicus had dealt. Their exaggerated mourning is flattery.

regum etiam regem et exercitatione venandi et convictu megistanum abstinuisse, quod apud Parthos iusti<ti> instar est: Eastern nobility (*megistani*) stereotypically spent its time hunting and banqueting (Tac. *Ann.* 2.2.3). The title "king of kings" was applied variously to Eastern overlords, here to Artabanus III, King of Parthia (*PIR*² A. 1155). He and Germanicus had a gracious encounter (*Ann.* 2.58), but Artabanus later came into conflict with Tiberius (Suet. *Tib.* 56; Tac. *Ann.* 6.31–37, 41–44; Dio 58.26). For his relationship with Gaius as a repeat performance, see 14.3. *Iusti<ti> instar* recognizes the fact that a *iustitium*, an official period of mourning, was a Roman concept. For Germanicus' *iustitium* in Rome, 6.2.

6.1 Romae quidem, cum ad primam famam valitudinis: Cf. a similar transition by Tacitus: *at Romae, postquam Germanici valetudo percrebuit (Ann.* 2.82.1). Suetonius drops the indirect statement of the preceding chapter, and presents the dramatic reaction at Rome as fact.

attonita et maesta civitas sequentis nuntios opperiretur: Cf. *cunctaque ut ex longinquo aucta in deterius adferebantur, dolor ira, et rumpebant questus* (Tac. *Ann.* 2.82.1).

et repente iam vesperi incertis auctoribus convaluisse tandem percrebruisset: Cf. *forte negotiatores vivente adhuc Germanico Syria egressi laetiora de valetudine eius attulere...iuvat credulitatem nox et promptior inter tenebras* (Tac. *Ann.* 2.82.4). The (false) report of Germanicus' recovery came at night. *Incerti auctores* = Tacitus' *negotiatores*.

passim cum luminibus et victimis in Capitolium concursum est ac paene revolsae templi fores, ne quid gestientis vota reddere

moraretur: Cf. *cursant per urbem, moliuntur templorum foris* (Tac. *Ann.* 2.82.4). Cf. 5 for temples at Antioch stoned out of grief.

expergefactus e somno Tiberius gratulantium vocibus atque undique concinentium: salva Roma, salva patria, salvus est Germanicus: Tacitus does not preserve this slogan verbatim, but it seems to lie beneath his *statim credita, statim vulgata sunt: ut quisque obvius...* (*Ann.* 2.82.4; cf. his paraphrase rather than quotation of the verse about Gaius, on 8.1). Suetonius reports rioting at night also for Germanicus in connection with the trial of Piso: *per noctes celeberrime adclamatum est: "Redde Germanicum!"* (*Tib.* 52.3). For the trochaic septenarius (*Salva...Germanicus*) for soldiers' songs, Suet. *Jul.* 39.2, 49.1 and 4, 51 (Guastella; Richlin 96).

6.2 *et ut demum fato functum palam factum est, non solaciis ullis, non edictis inhiberi luctus publicus potuit:* Popular demonstrations for Germanicus took place independently of the official *iustitium* (below). Tacitus writes that the display of mourning began spontaneously (*ante senatus consultum sumpto iustitio desererentur fora, clauderentur domus, Ann.* 2.82.3). In the spring of A.D. 20 Tiberius issued an edict which stated that the life of the *res Romana* should and would continue despite the loss of a leader: *monuit edicto multos inlustrium Romanorum ob rem publicam obisse.... sed referendum iam animum ad firmitudinem.... principes mortalis, rem publicam aeternam esse* (Tac. *Ann.* 3.6). Tacitus' rendering may be based on Tiberius' actual document (Koestermann 1963–1968, at Tac. *Ann.* 3.6; Syme 1958, 700–703). An edict was a communication, a statement of position, not necessarily an order (Millar 1977, 252–59). For Gaius' edicts see on 25.1.

duravitque etiam per festos Decembris mensis dies: The official cessation of business in recognition of a calamity (here the death of a prince), normally began when the death became known and lasted until the burial. The *iustitium* for Germanicus began on December 8, a two-month delay from his day of death, October 10 (*EJ* p. 41; Goodyear 1972–1981, at Tac. *Ann.* 2.82.5). Continuing through the *Saturnalia*, December 17–19 (*per festos Decembris mensis dies;* see on 17.2), it ended on December 31 (*Tabula Siarensis,* frag. 2 ll. 27–30, González). Germanicus' ashes arrived in Rome early in A.D. 20 (Tac. *Ann.* 3.1, 3–4.1), and there was another single day of mourning when they were placed in the Mausoleum of Augustus (*Tabula Hebana,* ll. 54–59, Oliver and Palmer; Fraschetti 881–82). For his *iustitium* in Parthia, see 5.

auxit gloriam desideriumque defuncti et atrocitas insequentium temporum, cunctis nec temere opinantibus reverentia eius ac metu

repressam Tiberi saevitiam, quae mox eruperit: This broad generalization is a fitting conclusion to the Germanicus portion of the text. As Tiberius
became less popular, Germanicus looked increasingly as though he would have
been the better alternative. A pervasive assessment of Tiberius' character was that
his essentially evil nature had been checked in the early part of his life but was
unveiled in his later years. An important "turning point" in this process was the
death of Germanicus (Dio 57.7.1, 13.6, 19.1; Tac. *Ann.* 6.51.3; Schwarz *RE*
3.1717; Syme 1958, 421–22; Walker 42, Questa 1963, 272–73, Gascou 432).
Suetonius subscribes to this view; Tacitus may not have (Gill 481–86; Woodman
1989; see note 10 for evidence that Tacitus modified the tradition). For Gaius'
dissimulatio, 10.2.

This chapter about Germanicus' other children, Gaius' siblings, forms a bridge between the biographies of father and son. Germanicus remains the subject of this first sentence.

7 *habuit in matrimonio Agrippinam, M. Agrippae et Iuliae filiam:*
(Vipsania) Agrippina (*PIR¹* V. 463) was the second daughter of Julia (*PIR²* I.
634), the daughter of Augustus, and of Marcus (Vipsanius) Agrippa (*PIR¹* V.
457), his long-time colleague. As Augustus' only child, Julia bore the burden of
her father's dynastic plans, and so her marriages and those of her five children
were politically significant. Agrippina's marriage to Germanicus, a cousin of several removes, was without doubt part of the succession arrangement of A.D. 4
(1.1). They were probably married by 5 (Levick 1966, 233).

et ex ea novem liberos tulit: Germanicus' image was marvelously enhanced
by his wife's production of multiple heirs, each a security for the house of
Augustus.

quorum duo infantes adhuc rapti: One of the two who died in infancy was a
Tiberius (*PIR²* I. 225). The name of the other, also male, is unknown. They must
have been born and died between A.D. 8 and 10 (Mommsen 1878, 247). Their
cremation markers have survived (*ILS* 181a, 181b).

unus iam puerascens insigni festivitate: Also a Gaius (Julius) Caesar (*PIR²*
I. 218; *ILS* 181; see on 8.2, 4). He appears to have been born in A.D. 11 and died,
an engaging toddler in his second year, not very long before Gaius Caligula's
birth on the last day of August in 12 (8.1). *Puerascere,* to become a boy, is
elsewhere unattested until late antiquity where it meant growing young again
(*repuerascere*).

***cuius effigiem habitu Cupidinis in aede Capitolinae Veneris Livia
dedicavit, Augustus in cubiculo suo positam, quotiensque introiret,***

exosculabatur: Small children were decorative objects (*deliciae,* etc.) in upper class households and sentimentalized, as was two-year-old Caligula (below, 8.1, 9, 13). They were sometimes dressed as cupids (Suet. *Aug.* 83; Plut. *Ant.* 26.2; Slater 133–40; Birt 134–64) or apotheosized as such if they died (Eitrem 1932b, 29–31). The temple of the Capitoline Venus (Venus Erycina) was the temple of Venus in Rome most closely associated with the Trojan myth and with Roman destiny (Schilling 233–66), and so the dedication of a statue of Gaius-Cupid there was consistent with the claim of the *gens Julia* that its descent was from Venus through the Trojan Aeneas. Other cupids associated with the house of Augustus were the Ascanius-Cupid of the *Aeneid* (1.658–59) and the cupids at the side of the Prima Porta statue of Augustus and in the upper ("heavenly") register of the *Grand Cameo of Paris,* both probably portraits of children of the imperial family (Studniczka 27–55; Balsdon 1936, 152–60; Hohl, 1938, 269–84; 1948–1949, 255–60; Simon 64–65).

ceteri superstites patri fuerunt: The survival of six children was very much worth noting.

tres sexus feminini, Agrippina Drusilla Livilla, continuo triennio natae: Suetonius' "continuous three-year period," if it means three consecutive calendar years, raises questions about the birthdates of these daughters. If the youngest, Julia Livilla (*PIR²* I. 674), was born in early A.D. 18 on the island of Lesbos (Tac. *Ann.* 2.54.1), then Agrippina (*PIR²* I. 641) and Drusilla (*PIR²* I. 664) could not have been born in 16 and 17 respectively because the birthday of Agrippina, evidently the eldest of the three, was November 6 (*Docs.* no. 19, p. 17; no. 21, p. 19), and the time interval between that date in 16 and the first months of 18 was not adequate for the two ensuing pregnancies. Besides, Tacitus reports five children with Germanicus at his triumph of May A.D. 17 (1.1 above; Tac. *Ann.* 2.41.3), and so two of the daughters as well as the three surviving sons (below) had been born by that date. But Suetonius' *continuum triennium* probably meant nothing more specific than a three-year interval of time (e.g., Suet. *Tib.* 15.2). Agrippina was well along in pregnancy in September of A.D. 14 (Tac. *Ann.* 2.40.2, 44.1), and this makes a baby in November of that year plausible; Livilla's birth in early 18 was thirty-nine or forty months distant, only a generous three years. Since the births had by any reckoning followed hard upon one another, they could loosely be said to have taken place within a *continuum triennium* (Fronzheim 1872, 188; Herz, 1981a, 102–4; J. Humphrey 127–28). The daughters were a trio of equals on Gaius' *securitas-concordia-fortuna* sestertius (*RIC²* Gaius 33, p. 110; *Docs.* no. 86, p. 41). The real reason for Suetonius' use of *continuum* here may be an attempt to rebut Pliny the Elder, who named Agrippina as an example of a woman who gave birth to alternating male and female children (*HN* 7.57). Her three daughters obviously came all in a row (*continuum*).[6]

totidem mares, Nero et Drusus et C. Caesar: Nero (*PIR*[2] I. 223), the oldest, was apparently born in A.D. 6. The name of Drusus (*PIR*[2] I. 220) appears on an inscription by the middle of 8 (*ILS* 107). Suetonius introduces variety with polysyndeton for the sons in contrast to asyndeton for the daughters (above).

Neronem et Drusum senatus Tiberio criminante hostes iudicavit: See on 10.2, 12.1, 15.1 for more about these brothers. Suetonius condenses a great deal of historical controversy into *senatus Tiberio criminante hostes iudicavit*. When the death of Germanicus once again destabilized Augustus' succession plans and when in A.D. 23 Drusus, the son of Tiberius, also died (Suet. *Tib*. 39, 62.1; Tac. *Ann*. 4.8.1–2; Dio. 57.22.1–4), attention focused on these two oldest sons of Germanicus, both still under twenty and vulnerable to cooption. The praetorian prefect, L. Aelius Sejanus (*PIR*[2] A. 255), who filled the power vacuum until the elderly princeps moved against him in A.D. 31 (on 12.1), was at the center of intrigue. Either through Sejanus' initiative or in his wake many lost their lives, among them both Nero and Drusus Caesar and their mother Agrippina. It remains unclear exactly who was responsible for their deaths. Nero and Agrippina were probably first arrested in 27 or 28 (on 10.1), and then exiled in 29 at the height of Sejanus' power (Suet. *Tib*. 53.2, 54.2; Tac. *Ann*. 5.3–5). Nero was forced to suicide in 31 (Suet. *Tib*. 54.2; Dio 58.8.4). Drusus was apprehended in 30 (Suet. *Tib*. 54.2; Dio 58.3.8), and both he and Agrippina died from starvation in 33 after the fall of Sejanus (Tac. *Ann*. 6.23.2–5; Dio. 58.22.4–5; Suet. *Tib*. 53.2, 54.2). At one point Suetonius writes that Tiberius accused Sejanus of ruining the brothers because he hated the entire house of Germanicus (*ausus est scribere Seianum se punisse, quod comperisset furere adversus liberos Germanici*

---

6 If, of course, the younger Agrippina was born in early November of A.D. 14 after a more or less term pregnancy, and Agrippina the Elder did not join her husband in the field until summer of that year (8.4), another problem arises, but not every visit that Germanicus made to Rome was necessarily recorded (4); there is no record of his being active in the field until the end of 14. Mommsen (1878, 254–55) solved the problem of three consecutive calendar years by assigning Livilla's birth to late 17 (making Tacitus incorrect at *Annales* 2.54.1), giving Agrippina November of 15, Drusilla 16, and positing a miscarriage for the high-profile pregnancy of late 14. A more recent solution has Drusilla as the eldest born early in 15, gives Agrippina November of 16 and trusts Tacitus on the date of Livilla's birth (J. Humphrey 132–33). But the evidence that Agrippina came first is persuasive: she was married in 28 (Tac. *Ann*. 4.75.1), five years before her sisters (Tac. *Ann*. 6.15; see on 24.1), Suetonius lists her first here (cf. the brothers in order of age below) and they are also named in this order on the sestertius. For the problem caused by Agrippina's claim that she was born at Cologne, see on 8.3 and note 7; for her whereabouts in 14, see on 8.4.

filii sui, Suet. *Tib.* 61.1). But here and elsewhere (*Tib.* 52.3, 53, 54.2, 55) he finds Tiberius at fault. Gaius barely survived this power struggle (on 10.1, 12.1; Tac. *Ann.* 6.3.4) and himself changed his mind about where responsibility lay, at first blaming Tiberius but later Sejanus for all the ills that befell his family (15.4, 30.2; Dio. 59.4.2–3, 16.1–4).

The real beginning of the *Life of Caligula,* the chronological narration that Suetonius includes in all his *Lives.* Here follow Gaius' birth, his early years in camp with his father and then the period in Rome, his entrance into public life, his marriage, all a prelude to the death of Tiberius (12.2–3) and his accession to the principate (13). Suetonius was always interested in birthplaces (*Tib.* 5; *Ves.* 1.2–4; *Vit.* 1–3.2; Steidle 68–70) as well as in ancestries, but never more than here where he evaluates primary sources. The length and detail of the discussion must stem from the fact that he saw himself breaking new ground with his confident discovery that Gaius had been born in Antium. His argument seems aimed at those (especially Tacitus?) who unthinkingly accepted the notion that Gaius was "born in the camp" from the emperor's own propaganda (8.1; Tac. *Ann.* 1.41.2; Hurley 327), a notion that had its origin in the fact that he was in the Rhine camp with his father from A.D. 14 to 16; it was part of the "Gaius, darling of the camp" motif associated with the Rhine mutiny (Tac. *Ann.* 1.41; Dio 57.5.6–7).

8.1 *C. Caesar natus est pridie Kal. Sept.:* For corroboration of August 31, Dio 59.7.3; also *CIL* 6.2298 and 6.2300.

patre suo et C. Fonteio Capitone coss.: A.D. 12 (1.1, 8.3). C. Fonteius Capito (*PIR*² F. 470) was eclipsed by his more prominent colleague (Dio 56.26.1).

ubi natus sit, incertum diversitas tradentium facit: Suetonius first presents the positions put forth by others (8.1), refutes each and then presents his own (8.2–5).

Cn. Lentulus Gaetulicus: Gaetulicus (Cn. Cornelius Lentulus Gaetulicus, *PIR*² C. 1390) was the son of Cossus Cornelius Lentulus (*PIR*² C. 1380), who fought the Gaetuli in Mauretania in A.D. 5–6 and handed on to his son the *cognomen* that memorialized the *ornamenta triumphalia* that he received for his success. Velleius describes the younger Gaetulicus as a golden youth (*adulescentis in omnium virtutum exempla geniti,* 2.116.2). His daughter had at one time been engaged to Sejanus' son (Tac. *Ann.* 6.30.2), and Tiberius gave him command of the Army of Upper Germany in 29 at the height of Sejanus' power (Dio 59.22.5). He nonetheless managed to survive the purge of 31 (Tac. *Ann.* 6.30.2–3) and was still at his post in 37 when Gaius inherited him from Tiberius. For his end, see on 24.3, 43, 44.1.

Tiburi genitum scribit: For Tibur and its significance, see 8.2, where Suetonius refutes this claim by Gaetulicus.

Plinius Secundus: Pliny the Elder presumably discussed the birthplace of Gaius in his *Libri bellorum Germanorum* (Munzer 70–71).

in Treveris vico Ambitarvio supra Confluentes: In the first century the Treveri occupied the west bank of the Rhine both north and south of the Mosel River. *Confluens,* (or *Confluentes*) was the standard name for a place that stood at the junction of two rivers, in this case the confluence of the Mosel and the Rhine. A Roman camp was there during the time when Pliny served with the German armies (ca. A.D. 46–58) and quite possibly earlier (Flor. 2.30.2; Filtzinger 168–203). It survived throughout the Empire (Amm. 16.3.1) and gave its name to modern Coblenz. The village of Ambitarvium is otherwise unknown, but *supra* locates it either in the hills above the rivers or upriver from Coblenz (Wightman, 129–30).

addit etiam pro argumento aras ibi ostendi inscriptas OB AGRIPPINAE PUERPERIUM: Pliny's knowledge of the inscription suggests personal inspection. Altars were a frequent feature at river junctions (e.g., Livy, *per.* 139; *TLL* 4.244.60–75). Suetonius answers this argument at 8.3.

versiculi imperante mox eo diuulgati: The verses that circulated when Gaius became emperor (*imperante mox eo*) are a third witness to his birth on the frontier; Suetonius will rebut them at 8.5 (*versiculorum quoque fidem*). His presence with the Rhine armies from A.D. 14 through 16 easily escalated into the allegation that he had been born there, and there was no reason for the prospective or fledgling emperor to discourage such an attractive rumor—rather motive to generate it. Because he lacked the necessary military credentials, he attached himself to his father's reputation until he could gain some of his own (43–48). In the meantime the childhood association with the legions was better than nothing. This does not mean that he liked being called by his baby name when he was emperor; he evidently found Caligula (9) beneath his dignity (Sen. *Dial.* 2.18.4; see note 106).

apud hibernas legiones procreatum: Procreatum can be either begotten or born, but neither was true for Gaius in winter quarters. *Hibernus* ("wintering") as an adjective with *legio* is unusual (*TLL:* 8.2688.67–70; Cic. *ad Att.* 4.19.2; Sternkopf 261–62).

in castris natus, patriis nutritus in armis, / iam designati principis omen erat: An elegaic distich, common for lampoons and slogans (Richlin 95–96). Note those used against Tiberius (Suet. *Tib.* 59). "Born in the camp" and "reared among his father's legions," along with the nickname Caligula (9), were allied notions which reinforced the popular image of Gaius as *legionum alumnus.* Seneca confirms the pervasiveness of this constellation: *hoc* [the nickname Caligula] *enim in castris natus et alumnus legionum vocari solebat, nullo nomine militibus familiarior umquam factus* (*Dial.* 2.18.4). Tacitus paraphrases the couplet instead of quoting it: *iam infans in castris genitus, in contubernio legionum eductus...quem militari vocabulo Caligulam appellabant* (Tac. *Ann.* 1.41.2; cf. 6.1 for his avoiding the exact transmission of a slogan about Germanicus as well). Dio omits "born in the camp" and has him reared there "for the most part:" τὸν υἱόν, ὃν Γάιον Καλιγόλαν, ὅτι ἐν τῷ στρατοπέδῳ τὸ πλεῖστον τραφεὶς τοῖς στρατιωτικοῖς ὑποδήμασιν ἀντὶ τῶν ἀστικῶν ἐχρῆτο, προσωνόμαζον (57.5.6). It is likely that he modified the story in his version because he knew Suetonius' argument.

8.2 *ego in actis Anti editum invenio:* Suetonius states the results of his own research concisely and with assurance before he refutes the other claims. The open records of state were variously the *acta publica* (Suet. *Tib.* 5) or *diurna* (Tac. *Ann.* 13.31.1) or *diurna populi Romani* (Tac. *Ann.* 16.22.3), often simply *acta*. Suetonius also used them to confirm the date and place of Tiberius' birth (*Tib.* 5). Antium (present-day Anzio) was on the coast about thirty-five miles south-southeast of Rome, a resort and a favorite retreat for the imperial family, especially the Claudian branch (Tac. *Ann.* 15.23.2). Gaius was fond of the place (8.5 and 49.2) and was married there (Dio. 58.25.2; on 12.1). Other connections of the family with this town: Suet. *Aug.* 58.2; *Tib.* 38; *Ner.* 6.1, 9, 25.1; Tac. *Ann.* 15.39.1. Similar uses of the first person singular at 19.3, 51.1, 3.

Gaetulicum refellit Plinius quasi mentitum per adulationem: Suetonius accepts Pliny's refutation of Gaetulicus before refuting Pliny in his turn; there is no evidence that he knew the work that contained this piece of flattery. Three hexameters by Gaetulius about constellations visible in Britain, perhaps in anticipation of a proposed invasion (46), were preserved by Probus (Serv. *ad G.* 1.227–29). Pliny the Younger (*Ep.* 5.3.5), Martial (*praef.* 1.11–12) and Apollinaris Sidonius (*Carm.* 9.259; *Ep.* 2.10.6) all name him among writers of lascivious epigrams (Malcovati 32–38). Gentlemen poets were versatile (e.g., Germanicus and Tiberius, 3.1; Suet. *Tib.* 70.2).

ut ad laudes iuvenis gloriosique principis: *Gloriosi* = vainglorious. Gaius is the subject of the verb *glorior* three times (12.3, 38.3 and 41.2). Suetonius anticipates the negative judgment that he will make on him soon enough (10.2–11, 22 and following).

aliquid etiam ex urbe Herculi sacra sumeret: "Herculean Tibur" (Mart. 1.12.1, 4.62.1; Prop. 2.32.5), modern Tivoli, located in the hills about twenty miles east-northeast of Rome, was, like Antium, another rural escape for well-to-do Romans (Suet. *Aug.* 72.2; *Cl.* 34.1). The worship of the emperor was connected with the worship of Hercules (Taylor 163–65), whose cult and temple dominated the town.

abusumque audentius mendacio, quod ante annum fere natus Germanico filius Tiburi fuerat, appellatus et ipse C. Caesar, de cuius amabili pueritia immaturoque obitu supra diximus: Suetonius adds the name and birthplace of the brother whom he introduced with the family of Germanicus (7; *supra diximus* is one of three cross references in this text; also 32.1 to 19, 35.1 to 26.1). Again the stress is on the child's lovability (*amabili pueritia = insigni festivitate,* 7). Both Pliny and Gaetulicus knew about this other Gaius and knew where he was born. He apparently played a larger role in family propaganda than might have been expected from him tender years.

8.3 *Plinium arguit ratio temporum:* Gaetulicus having been disposed of, Suetonius moves on to refute Pliny on grounds of chronology. His style can be brief and direct, seemingly when he was not dependent on another text (D'Anna 180–82; cf. *ego in actis Anti editum invenio,* 8.2).

nam qui res Augusti memoriae mandarunt, Germanicum exacto consulatu in Galliam missum consentiunt iam nato Gaio: A direct acknowledgement of oral tradition (cf. 19.3). Suetonius' sarcasm is directed toward those on whom the obvious did not register (Tacitus? see note 9); since Germanicus was consul and not in a military camp in A.D. 12, neither was Agrippina, and so Gaius could not have been born there. At 1.1 Suetonius writes that Germanicus was sent to Germany to command the legions but here that he was sent to Gaul. It was the same; the provinces where the legions were stationed on the left bank of the Rhine were indeed in Gaul but were called Upper and Lower Germany.

nec Plini opinionem inscriptio arae quicquam adiuuerit: The plural altars (8.1) are now only one.

Agrippina bis in ea regione filias enixa sit: In *ea regione* refers either to the general area of the northern frontier or to the region around Coblenz, although the demonstrative strengthens the argument in favor of the latter. Germanicus decided to send his wife and son from the camp near present day Cologne (Tac. *Ann.* 1.39.1) to Ambitarvium (8.1) or Trier (*in proximam civitatem,* 9) when the mutiny of A.D. 14 grew dangerous (Tac. *Ann.* 1.41.1; Dio. 57.5.6). Perhaps a villa at Ambitarvium was a regular birthing place for the imperial wives who accompanied their husbands to the North (Mommsen 1878, 252). Either Agrippina and Drusilla (7) or both could have been born there although Agrippina would later claim that she was born at Cologne (*oppidum Ubiorum, in quo genita erat,* Tac. *Ann.* 12.27.1).[7]

qualiscumque partus sine ullo sexus discrimine puerperium vocetur, quod antiqui etiam puellas pueras, sicut et pueros puellos dictitarent: Unless this pedantic discussion is an addition to the text (apparatus), it shows Suetonius mining his own work for a point about archaic feminine and diminutive forms of *puer* (*Rel.* Reiff. p. 347, no. 199 = *De institutione officiorum;* Wallace-Hadrill 1983, 77). *Puerperium* was the word in general use for childbirth (Sen. *QNat.* 3.27.2; Tac. *Ann.* 15.23.1). Pliny himself understood that it made no reference to gender (*HN* 7.3). This point does nothing further to refute Pliny's argument, and one suspects that its inclusion was an excuse for a display of erudition.

8.4 *extat et Augusti epistula:* Another use of source materials to corroborate the *ratio temporum* argument (8.3). Suetonius used the correspondence of Augustus for details elsewhere (on 4), especially in the life of Augustus himself (Aug. 7.1, 51.3, 64.2, 71.2–3, 76.1–2, 86–88, 92.2). It is uncertain to whom or in what form it was available (Wallace-Hadrill 1983, 91–96; Gascou 471–75).

ante paucos quam obiret menses ad Agrippinam neptem ita scripta de Gaio hoc—neque enim quisquam iam alius infans nomine pari tunc supererat: The letter (below) is dated May 18. Augustus died on August 19, A.D. 14 (1.1). Note is taken once again of the charming young Gaius who had died shortly before (7, 8.2). The choice of *praenomina* was limited within a given

---

7 In A.D. 50 Agrippina established a veterans' colony called *Colonia Claudia Augusta Agrippinensium* (more commonly *Colonia Agrippinensis* or some variant), modern Cologne. Tacitus writes that she founded the colony in order to "show her power to allied nations" (*quo vim suam sociis quoque nationibus ostentaret, Ann.* 12.27.1). She may have claimed that she was born there for the same reason that Caligula was happy to have been born *in patriis armis.* There was a pre-existing family association with the site since the Ubii had originally been settled near modern Cologne by her grandfather Marcus Agrippa (on 7; Tac. *Germ.* 28.4; *Ann.* 12.27.1; Strab. 4.3.4).

upper class family (Doer 99), and so there was nothing strange about the Julius Caesars continuing to try for a Gaius.

Puerum Gaium XV. Kal. Iun. si dii volent, ut ducerent Talarius et Asillius, heri cum iis constitui: Augustus decided the travel arrangements. Talarius (*PIR¹* T. 3) is otherwise unknown. A witticism is attributed to an Asillius Sabinus (*PIR²* A. 1213; Sen. *Suas.* 2.12), and Tiberius rewarded a peson of that name for a frivolous dialog (Suet. *Tib.* 42.2), quite possibly the same man. Suetonius sees these two escorting little Gaius to the frontier as proof that he was not there already (below). But why does Augustus have to write to his mother to tell her that these two will escort him? Was she already in the North, perhaps at Ambitarvium, but not with her husband? Note *pervenias* below (see note 6; J. Humphrey 126). On the other hand, it may have been a communication, a kind of formal notification of plans, to her while she was still in Rome. Cf. the correspondence from Augustus to Livia about Claudius (Suet. *Cl.* 4.1–6).

mitto praeterea cum eo ex servis meis medicum quem scripsi Germanico si vellet ut retineret: The doctor of choice for this assignment was a slave, an ordinary *medicus,* not one of the few philosopher-physicians who achieved special status in imperial households (Scarborough 111). His presence appears to be a routine precaution and need not indicate chronic ill health for Gaius (on 50.2).

valebis, mea Agrippina, et dabis operam ut valens pervenias ad Germanicum tuum: Agrippina is also joining her husband (*pervenias*). A friendly closing for a letter; cf. *sed da operam ut valeas et, si valebis...* (Cic. *Fam.* 16.12.6), less formal that the standard *s. v. b. e. e. v. = si vales, bene est, ego valeo.*

8.5 ***abunde parere arbitror non potuisse ibi nasci Gaium, quo prope bimulus demum perductus ab urbe sit:*** But since Suetonius does not demonstrate that this was Gaius' first trip (although it certainly was), the argument from the correspondence is not really an additonal proof. *Parere* = "to accede to evidence." *Bimulus,* the endearing diminutive for *bimus,* two year old, is used only with humans (*TLL* 2.1991.30–45); it reinforces the "cute child" motif of this part of the text.

versiculorum quoque fidem eadem haec elevant et eo facilius, quod ii sine auctore sunt: "These arguments also diminish the trustworthiness of the verses [the *in castris natus* couplet, 8.1], and they do so the more easily because they [the verses] are anonymous." *Eadem haec* = *ratio temporum* (8.3) the argument from chronology.

sequenda est igitur, quae sola [auctor] restat et publici instrumenti auctoritas: Instrumentum = document. After rebutting Gaetulicus (indirectly) and Pliny (directly), Suetonius returns to his own proof: he saw the record of Gaius' birth in the *acta diurna. Auctor* (*auctore, apparatus*) probably entered the text from the nearby *auctore* (*sola* perhaps confused with *sine* in *sine auctore*, above) and/or from *auctoritas* that follows. The problem in the archetype may have been deeper, for the mere omission of *auctor* (*et* must then go as well) leaves an awkward sentence.

praesertim cum Gaius Antium omnibus semper locis atque secessibus praelatum non aliter quam natale solum dilexerit tradaturque etiam sedem ac domicilium imperii taedio urbis transferre eo destinasse: For Antium, see on 8.2. After Gaius' return from the northern front in A.D. 40, he proposed a retreat from Rome, first to Antium and then to Alexandria (49.2). The plan is phrased as intention rather than fact (*tradatur...destinasse = proposuerat* at 49.2). Gaius operated one of his pleasure galleys (37.2) from there (Pliny *HN* 32.3–5).

9 *Caligulae cognomen castrensi ioco traxit:* The camp nickname Caligula, "Little Boots," from *caligae,* soldier's boots, is everywhere connected with the story about his childhood presence with his father's army (on 8.1; Tac. *Ann.* 1.41; Dio 57.5.6; Sen. *Dial.* 2.18.4) and evidently spawned a number of jokes about footwear (on 52, note 106). It is not attested epigraphically.

quia manipulario habitu inter milites educabatur: Gaius is shown dressed as a little soldier on the *Grand Cameo of Paris* (on 7 and 10.1). Cf. *tamquam... [Agrippina] filium ducis gregali habitu circumferat Caesaremque Caligulam appellari velit* (Tac. *Ann.* 1.69.4). *Manipularius,* "belonging to a common soldier," is found as an adjective only here and at Val. Max. 6.1.12 (*TLL* 7.315.47–49, 52–53), both disputed readings; Suetonius seems fond of adjectives. Note *castrensis,* above; also *hibernus* (8.1), *Syriacus* (10.1).

apud quos quantum praeterea per hanc nutrimentorum consuetudinem amore et gratia valuerit, maxime cognitum est: Gaius' mission was to acquire the "love and favor" (*amore et gratia*) of the soldiers (= *ad concilianda vulgi studia,* Tac. *Ann.* 1.41.2). The plural of *nutrimentum* = "upbringing," "rearing" (Suet. *Aug.* 6.). When Suetonius writes an awkward and involved sentence like this one, it seems likely that he is compressing information from a source. He apparently wants to hurry through circumstantial explanations in order to make his point, to get to the rubric's punch line.[8]

cum post excessum Augusti tumultuantis et in furorem usque praecipites solus haud dubie ex conspectu suo flexit: Suetonius submits this incident as proof that Gaius was successful in ingratiating himself with the legionaries. There were two distinct traditions about the end of the mutiny of A.D. 14 (1.1) when Germanicus prepared to evacuate his wife and son (on 8.3). The wagon train carrying them was apparently intercepted (*reprenso ac retento vehiculo*, below), and according to one tradition, Agrippina and Gaius were held hostage for some undetermined period of time until the pregnant Agrippina's release was negotiated (48.1; Dio. 57.5.6–7). According to another (less plausible) the pathetic sight of the two so moved the legionaries that they begged that the members of Augustus' family be allowed to stay with them and repented their entire insurrection. This second version conceded Gaius (below) but sent Agrippina away because of her incipient confinement (Tac. *Ann.* 1.44). In the first version, the mutineers are in control, but the second is reluctant to show the future emperor and his father in an embarrassing situation and favors Germanicus. Both Tacitus and Suetonius appropriated the second but Suetonius writes that it was the sight of Gaius alone (*solus*), not the sight of Gaius and Agrippina together, that turned the soldiers from their rage. His insistence (*haud dubie*) may be his response to liberties that Tacitus took by inserting Agrippina into the scenario (Hurley 316–28).[9] On this much discussed episode, Questa 1963, 165–68; Kessler 25–29; Walser 55–59; Liebenan 729–30; Burian 25–29; Frontzheim 1877, 345–46.

non enim prius destiterunt, quam ablegari eum ob seditionis periculum et in proximam civitatem demandari animadvertissent: It is Gaius alone who is about to be sent away (*ablegari eum*) to the *proxima civitas,* the territory of the Treveri (above 8.1). Tacitus stresses the fact that the blood of Augustus had to be entrusted (*demandari*) to foreigners: *pergere ad Treviros [et] externae fidei* (*Ann.* 1.41.1).

tunc demum ad paenitentiam versi reprenso ac retento vehiculo invidiam quae sibi fieret deprecati sunt: In his pathetic account Tacitus

---

[8] Similar instances of this compressed style occur at 10.1, 13–14.1, 18.3, 27.1, 38.2 and 3.

[9] Suetonius may also respond to Tacitus about the long lists of Gaius' would-be victims that were found on the Palatine (49.3, 55.2) and perhaps about Germanicus' welcome in Rome (4). Something similar may lie beneath the entire argument about Gaius' birth (8). Further comparisons between the two are drawn from Germanicus' lictors in Athens and the burial of Varus' dead (3.2).

implies an exodus on foot (*incedebat muliebre et miserabile agmen, profuga ducis uxor, parvulum sinu filium gerens* (*Ann.* 1.40.4), but Suetonius is specific about the conveyance, and it is only logical that no one was expected to walk to *Confluentes*.

Suetonius moves on more quickly with significant events of Gaius' childhood and youth. This material is essentially factual and neutral—until 10.2, where there is a foretaste of the *monstrum* to come.

10.1 *comitatus est patrem et Syriaca expeditione:* Suetonius focuses on the location of the troops and calls Germanicus' *maius imperium* in the East a "Syrian expedition." Gaius was the only one of the children who accompanied his parents from Rome (1.2; *Docs.* no. 33, p. 29), although his youngest sister Julia Livilla was born on the way (on 7; Tac. *Ann.* 2.75.1). Agrippina brought the two of them home along with Germanicus' ashes in A.D. 20 (*duobus cum liberis,* Tac. *Ann.* 3.1.4). We do not hear that Gaius was paraded before these soldiers as he had been in Germany, but the fact that he was taken along, now a winning five year old, implies a similar intention. The child wearing armor on the *Grand Cameo of Paris* (on 7, 9) is no longer a toddler, and since the gem plausibly portrays the apotheosis of Germanicus in A.D. 19 when Gaius was seven, it suggests that he continued to play the little soldier in the East.

unde reversus primum in matris...contubernio: Gaius lived in Rome with his mother for at least seven years from A.D. 20 until she was exiled (below).

deinde ea relegata in Liviae Augustae proaviae suae contubernio mansit: Suetonius seems clear about the sequence of these events, but his story differs from that of Tacitus, who writes that Tiberius did not move openly against Agrippina and her son Nero until after Livia was dead in A.D. 29 (*Ann.* 5.1, 3–5).[10] The two accounts have been rationalized by the speculation that Tiberius ordered Gaius removed to his great-grandmother's protection a year or two before Agrippina's relegation in 29 (Willrich 97; Gelzer 382; Balsdon 1934a, 13). Tension between Agrippina and Tiberius is indeed attested from 27 on (Vell.

---

10 Tacitus may have rearranged the order of events to support his thesis that Livia's death was another in the series of things that stripped away Tiberius' hypocrisy. Dio and Suetonius see the deaths of Germanicus, Drusus and Sejanus as pivotal in removing the layers of repression from Tiberius and revealing his naturally heinous character (6.2). Only Tacitus adds Livia as a fourth. He accuses her of hostility toward Germanicus and his family (*Ann.* 1.33.3, 2.82.1, 4.12.3) but at the same time says that she was a restraint on Tiberius' cruelty (*Ann.* 6.51.3) and that she protected Agrippina while she lived (*iam incolumi Augusta erat adhuc perfugium...tunc velut frenis exoluti proruperunt missaeque in Agrippinam ac Neronem litterae quas pridem adlatas et cohibitas ab Augusta credidit vulgus (Ann.* 5.3.1).

2.130.4; cf. Tac. *Ann.* 4.67.3, 70.4), and Nero was on trial in 27 or 28 (*causa Neronis,* Pliny *HN* 8.145). The move against them may have come in two phases: first a military guard (Tac. *Ann.* 4.67.4) and departure from Rome to Herculaneum (Sen. *Dial.* 5.21.5) and then, around the time of Livia's death, relegation to the Pontian Islands where they later died (14.2, 15.1; see on 7 for Nero and Drusus and more on this confusing time; Meise 237–44; Barrett 1989, 21–23). By this scenario Gaius was with Livia alone from 27 or 28 until 29. Does *mansit* imply that Agrippina and Livia had shared a household? Cf. *transit* below.

quam defunctam praetextatus etiam tunc pro rostris laudavit: If Dio is correct that Livia died at the age of 86 (58.2.1), her death occurred after her birthday on January 30, A.D. 29 but early in the year (*Docs.* no. 3, p. 10; Tac. *Ann.* 5.1; Ginsburg 21–22, 26–27). Gaius was sixteen in the first half of 29 and had not yet put on the *toga virilis* (*praetextatus etiam tunc*). Although a boy who had not been properly initiated did not normally speak in public, there seem to have been exceptions in the funeral orations that members of Augustus' family delivered: Augustus spoke for his grandmother Julia at the age of twelve (Suet. *Aug.* 8.1; Quintilian found this unusual, *Inst.* 12.6.1) and Tiberius for his father at the age of nine (Suet. *Tib.* 6.4). It seems that it was the custom for the youngest to deliver the eulogy (e.g., the Younger Drusus for Augustus, also *pro rostris,* Suet. *Aug.* 100.3). Or was Gaius already the only suitable descendant left? On his gift for public speaking, see 53.

transit ad Antoniam aviam: *Transit:* cf. *mansit* (above). Both ancient tradition and modern scholarship have decided that Antonia Minor prejudiced her grandson Gaius in favor of Antony and that she exposed him to the temptations of monarchy through her "house guests," the sons of Eastern kings, who became the companions of the impressionable young prince (Willrich 97–100; Gelzer 382; Balsdon 1934a, 13–14). He lived with Antonia for no more than two years (A.D. 29–31).

et undevicensimo aetatis anno accitus Capreas a Tiberio: The exact sequence of events for this portion of Gaius' life is unclear (see *nec ita multo post* at 12.1). In A.D. 27 Tiberius retired to Capreae (Suet. *Tib.* 40; Tac. *Ann.* 4.67.1) where he spent the rest of his life with the exception of a few trips to the mainland but never to Rome, not even for Livia's funeral (Suet. *Tib.* 51.2). He summoned Gaius to join him in the year when Gaius was eighteen (*undevicensimo aetatis anno*), the year that ended on August 31, A.D. 31. It was probably late 30 (see 12.1 on his appointment as *pontifex* for 31), the time when Sejanus was hostile toward Gaius and when Tiberius was becoming suspicious of Sejanus.

Although anecdotes about Gaius' interaction with Tiberius and his court (10.2–11) seem to imply continuous residence on Capreae from then on, this would not have been the case (12.1 on his marriage at Antium).

uno atque eodem die togam sumpsit barbamque posuit: The replacement of the *toga praetexta* by the adult toga marked a freeborn Roman male's entrance into public life. It should have preceded any offices or priesthoods that Gaius held (12.1). The first shaving of the beard was also a rite of passage but a separate ceremony, and so the fact that they occurred together was worth noting.

sine ullo honore qualis contigerat tirocinio fratrum eius: Tirocinium was a period of apprenticeship for a Roman youth but came to mean the taking of the *toga virilis* itself. Gaius' brother Nero received the adult toga in A.D. 20 at the age of 14 (Tac. *Ann.* 3.29.1; Dio 57.18.11) and Drusus in 23 at 15 or 16 (Tac. *Ann.* 4.4.1). Tiberius honored both initiations by *congiaria* (Suet. *Tib.* 54.1), but Gaius had to wait until he was emperor for his (17.2). The hurried agenda may reflect hasty plans necessary amidst political uncertainties.

The rest of this chapter and all of the next interrupt the more or less chronological narration of Gaius' early career in order to illustrate how there were already recognizable signs of his depravity. A "change" was recognized in Gaius (on 22.1), but what follows here is more in accordance with the view that personality was static and that appearances to the contrary resulted from pretense (cf. Tiberius, 6.2). This passage, along with the notice of Gaius' first marriage appended to it (12.1), has a close parallel in Tacitus' *Annales* 6.20, a chapter that seems similarly disconnected from the larger context in which it appears.

10.2 *hic omnibus insidiis temptatus elic<i>entium cogentiumque se ad querelas nullam umquam occasionem dedit:* If there were persons trying to drag Gaius into conflict, they were a faction favoring the succession of Tiberius Gemellus (Tiberius Julius Caesar Nero, *PIR*[2] I. 226), the natural son of Drusus, son of Tiberius (Tac. *Ann.* 6.46; Dio. 58.23.3; Philo *In Flacc.* 12, 22; *Leg.* 39, 41; Willrich 112; Gelzer 383–84).

perinde obliterato suorum casu ac si nihil cuiquam accidisset, quae vero ipse pateretur incredibili dissimulatione transmittens tantique in avum et qui iuxta erant obseqii ut: "Ignoring what had happened with amazing pretense, blotting out the disasters that had befallen his family and pretending that the things which he himself suffered had never happened, his behavior characterized by such deference toward his grandfather and those who were close to him that...," an awkward sentence (see note 8). This time his source is also recognized in the parallel passage in Tacitus that is strikingly similar in thought: *immanem animum subdola modestia tegens, non damnatione matris, non exitio fratrum rupta voce; qualem diem Tiberius induisset, pari habitu, haud multum distantibus verbis* (6.20.1). Like Tiberius, Gaius was a hypocrite (6.2; Philo *Leg.* 22, 36), but his decent behavior in the presence of Tiberius and his associates seemed remarkable only in the light of his later reputation. It is not possible to speculate about his real emotions. After all, if Nero and Drusus had lived, he would not have been his family's sole male survivor.

non immerito sit dictum nec servum meliorem ullum nec deteriorem dominum fuisse: Cf. Tacitus: *neque meliorem umquam servum neque deteriorem dominum fuisse* (*Ann.* 6.20.1), where the maxim is ascribed to Passienus Crispus (C. Passienus Crispus *PIR¹* P.109), consul and orator. Passienus was in favor under Gaius and to the emperor Nero (*PIR²* D. 129) he was both uncle by his marriage to Domitia (*PIR²* D. 171), Nero's father's sister (Quint. *Inst.* 6.1.50), and then stepfather because of his marriage to the younger Agrippina (Suet. *Ner.* 6.1; *Rel.* Reiff. no. 71, p. 88–89). Passienus had a reputation as a wit and a number of clever sayings are attributed to him (Pliny *Ep.* 7.6.11; Sen. *Ben.* 1.15.5; *QNat.* 4 *praef.* 6; Quint. *Inst.* 6.1.50). Gaius the slave-master surfaces again when L. Arruntius (*PIR²* A. 1130) said that he was killing himself just before Tiberius died in order to avoid servitude (Tac. *Ann.* 6.48.2; Dio. 58.27.4). Philo also makes him a slavemaster (*Leg.* 119), as does Seneca (*Apocol.* 15.2). The image persisted (Aur. Vict. *Caes.* 3.7) and has a place in the larger context of the Romans' conception of themselves. During the Empire they insisted on thinking of themselves as a free (non servile) people and used the slave-slavemaster idea as a negative metaphor for the wrong kind of political relationship between people and princeps (*ruere in servitium consules, patres, eques,* Tac. *Ann.* 1.7.1; *Hist.* 1.16.4). The assumption was that only a person willing to be a slave would wish to be a master. Augustus and Tiberius both reacted strongly against the title *dominus* (Suet. *Aug.* 31.1, *Tib.* 27). Gaius is pictured elsewhere as a slave of sorts (32.3, 35.3, 57.4) and as a slavemaster (26.2; Sen. *Apocol.* 15.2).

11 *naturam tamen saevam atque probrosam ne tunc quidem inhibere poterat:* His cruelty was innate (*saevitia ingenii*, 27.1). Just as Gaius' *dissimulatio* was a prelude to the slave-master *sententia* (10.2), so his cruelty and his predilection for base pleasures will introduce a second *sententia* (below).

quin et animadversionibus poenisque ad supplicium datorum ⸱upidissime interesset: This youthful eagerness to be present at punishments ʲicted sadism, a major theme of the *Life* (27.4, 30.1, 32.1–2, 33; cf. τῆς τοῦ ⸱ θέας ἀπλήστως εἶχεν, Dio 59.10.2; see Sen. *Dial.* 5.19). The younger

Drusus liked blood too: *vili sanguine nimis gaudens* (Tac. *Ann.* 1.76.3; also Dio 57.13.1–2).

et ganeas atque adulteria capillamento celatus et veste longa noctibus obiret: These youthful visits to low haunts in disguise prefigured licentiousness (36) and transvestitism (52) to come. Gaius' model Antony also went slumming (Plut. *Ant.* 29.1–2) as did his soul mate, the emperor Nero (*adrepto pilleo vel galero popinas inibat,* Suet. *Ner.* 26.1; Tac. *Ann.* 13.25.1), and the Caesar Gallus in the fourth century (Amm. 14.1.9). Bentley's suggestion of *lupanaria* for *adulteria* (*apparatus*) seems correct; the coupling of the concrete with the abstract (*ganeas atque adulteria*) is not to be expected, and the combination of cheap eating places and brothels was a cliché; e.g., *Nero itinera urbis et lupanaria et deverticula veste servili in dissimulationem sui compositus pererrabat* (Tac. *Ann.* 13.25.1).

ac scaenicas saltandi canendique artes studiosissime appeteret: This anticipates his later singing and dancing (54). Again like Nero, he is credited with an excessive interest in affairs of the stage as either spectator or performer, the latter more disgraceful (Suet. *Ner.* 21; Tac. *Ann.* 16.4).

facile id sane Tiberio patiente, si per has mansuefieri posset ferum eius ingenium: The *scaenicas artes* frowned on above are now deemed civilizing although still disreputable. The elderly princeps is portrayed as intending Gaius to be his successor here, but see on 14.1 and 19.3.

quod sagacissimus senex ita prorsus perspexerat, ut aliquotiens praedicaret: The predictions that follow were obviously retrojected into Tiberius' last years because they would not have been made until Gaius was known to be a disaster. For another, see 19.3; also Dio 58.23.3–4; Tac. *Ann.* 6.46.4. They all make the point that the *sagacissimus senex* did indeed know what he was letting Rome in for when he chose Gaius.

exitio suo omniumque Gaium vivere et se natricem [serpentis id genus] p(opulo) R(omano): Gaius' survival meant not only Tiberius' own destruction (for the allegation that Gaius murdered him, see 12.2–3) but also the destruction of Rome and the entire world as well. A *natrix,* a venomous water snake, represented hostile agression (Cic. *Ac.* 2.38.120; Sen. *Dial.* 4.31.8; also Luc. 9.720). Gaius poisoned Rome from within.[11]

---

[11] Gaius is often associated with poison, 12.2, 23.2–3, 29.1, 49.3, 55.2; note 111. And so is Nero, his double in infamy, Suet. *Ner.* 33.1–2, 34.2, 35.5, 36.2, 43.1.

Phaet<h>ontem orbi terrarum educare: Phaëthon, the son of Helios, drove his father's chariot, lost control of the horses, then came too near the earth and burned it (Ov. *Met.* 2.1–366; Lucr. 5.400). He is the paradigm of a youth who tackles a job beyond his capacity and causes wholesale destruction, an apt referent for Gaius. Like the slavemaster image, the image of destructive fire clung closely to him just as it did to Nero, Lucan's Phaëthon: *seu te flammigeros Phoebi conscendere currus, / telluremque nihil mutato sole timentem / igne vago lustrare iuvet* (1.48–50). Seneca taps the same motif when he writes that Gaius left the world "burned up" (*a quo imperium adustum atque eversum funditus, Dial.* 11.17.3; also *ardebant cuncta,* Juv. 6.618). Phaëthon burning the world was a Stoic metaphor for order gone awry, for an inversion of the concept that the intelligence of the sun controlled all (Degl'Innocenti 78–88). Both Agrippinas dreamed that they gave birth to firebrands for sons (Pliny *HN* 7.45). Tiberius allegedly quoted the line, "when I am dead, let the world be consumed by fire" (ἐμοῦ θανόντος γαῖα μιχθήτω πυρί, Dio 58.23.4; *TGF adespota* no. 513, vol. 2, p. 145), as did Nero, changing it to: ἐμοῦ ζῶντος, "while I'm alive..." (Suet. *Ner.* 38.1). See notes 12 and 67.

Suetonius appears to return to chronological sequence when he presents more information about Gaius at the court of Tiberius.

12.1 *Non ita multo post:* "Not much later" than what? If temporal sequence has been resumed, the phrase apparently refers to the last time marker, the summons to Capreae in A.D. 30 or 31 (10.1), and implies that Gaius was married shortly thereafter. But Dio is clear that Gaius was married in 35, and he can be trusted this once because he writes that Tiberius was at Antium for the wedding at the time of the trial of Fulcinius Trio in Rome (L. Fulcinius Trio, *PIR²* F. 517; Τιβέριος δὲ ἐν Ἀντίῳ τοὺς τοῦ Γαίου γάμους ἑώρταζεν, 58.25.2). Tacitus puts the accusations against Trio together with the visit of Tiberius to the mainland in 35 (*Ann.* 6.38.2, 39.2), but he does not mention the marriage. Instead he inserts it incidentally into the year 33 to provide context for the "good slave-bad master" aphorism (10.2; Tac *Ann.* 6.20.1). Both Suetonius and Tacitus appear to be interpolating both the aphorism and its context together from a source that had no interest in chronological accuracy but rather provided a setting for Passienus' witticism. Tacitus introduces the parallel passage with *sub idem tempus* = (?) *non ita multo post,* not a very reliable way to date anything.[12] A more defensible return to accurate temporal sequence comes with *deinde augur* (below).

---

[12] In the Tacitus passage the "good slave-bad master" *sententia* is preceeded by a statement about Gaius' sycophantic behavior in the Tiberian court just as it is here (10.2). Tacitus continues as though he were giving for the first time the information that Gaius was on Capreae, information

Iuniam Claudillam M. Silani nobilissimi viri f(iliam) duxit uxorem:
Tiberius arranged this first marriage for Gaius. Junia Claudilla (or Claudia, *PIR²*
I. 857) was the daughter of M. Junius Silanus (*PIR²* I. 832), a prominent senator
and consul suffect in A.D. 15. Silanus was being rewarded for his loyalty (Tac.
Ann. 3.24.3; 57.1; 6.2.2; Dio 59.8.5; Syme 1981, 200–201). For his end, 23.3.

deinde augur in locum fratris sui Drusi destinatus: This priesthood was a
stage on the way to *pontifex* (below). Gaius' summons to Capreae for the *toga
virilis* (10.1) prepared him to take over his public role after he fell into disfavor
in 30 (7; Dio 58.3.8). A drachma from Cappadocia (A.D. 37) shows him with an
augur's staff (*RIC²* Gaius no. 63, p. 113; Gelzer 382). There is no evidence that
Drusus was an *augur* (Dessau 110, n.1; for his other titles: *ILS* 185, 186).

*prius quam inauguraretur ad pontificatum traductus est insigni
testimonio pietatis atque indolis:* He was made *pontifex* in 31 along with
Sejanus and Sejanus' son (Dio 58.7.4) and then was quaestor in 33 (Dio 58.23.1;
ILS 189). Tiberius praised him (Dio 58.8.1), no doubt for *pietas* (toward himself,
of course), and the appointments were ostensibly a reward (*insigni testimonio
pietatis atque indolis*).

deserta desolataque reliquis subsidiis aula: Gaius was a survivor. For the
value of a recognized line of successors as *subsidia* for a reigning monarch, a
hedge against would-be challengers, 1.1 and 4, 15.2; Tac. *Ann.* 1.3.5; Dio
54.18.1; Jos. *AJ* 18.221.

*Seiano †vete suspecto mox et oppresso ad spem successionis paulatim
admoveretur:* The exact relationship between the rise of Gaius' star and the fall
of Sejanus' must remain uncertain because of the loss of the Tacitus text and the
intrinsic secrecy of court politics (10.1; Tac. *Ann.* 6.3.4; Dio 58.8.1–2). Ihm's
Seianoque tunc (*apparatus*) for *Seiano †vete* is attractive because it offers a mod-
ifier for *suspecto* (*tunc*) to balance *mox et* (= *etiam*) *oppresso*.

12.2 *quam quo magis confirmaret, amissa Iunia ex partu: Quam* = the
hope (*spem*, above) of becoming emperor. The death of Junia Claudilla is cor-
roborated by Tacitus for early 37 (*Ann.* 6.45.3) and by Philo without a date
(*Leg.* 62–63). Dio, on the other hand, writes that Gaius got rid of her: τήν τε
θυγατέρα αὐτοῦ [M. Junius Silanus] ἐκβαλὼν (59.8.7). Perhaps Dio did not

---

which should have been introduced into the lost portions of *Annales* 5 and 6. Both Suetonius and
Tacitus add a second aphorism after the slave-master example, Suetonius the aphorism about Gaius
as a viper and Phaëthon (11) and Tacitus a prediction of Galba's principate, an anecdote that appears randomly in other texts and was obviously retrojected into this context from a later period
(Suet. *Gal.* 4.1; Dio 57.19.4; Jos. *AJ* 18.216; Scott 1932, 471–73; Townend 1960, 113–19).

know or remember what had happened to Claudilla and so unburdened Gaius of her as conveniently as he could when he needed to report a second marriage; he or his source probably assumed that Gaius routinely divorced all wives (25.1–2). See notes 27 and 28 for similar errors by Dio.

Enniam Naeviam, Macronis uxorem, qui tum praetorianis cohortibus praeerat: More properly, *Enniam, Naevii Macrionis uxorem* (Causabon, *apparatus;* Ennia Thrasylla (*PIR² E.* 65). She was possibly the granddaughter of Tiberius' long time astrologer and associate Thrasyllus (*PIR¹* T. 137; see 19.3; Cichorius 390–92). Macro, Q. Naevius Sutorius Macro (*PIR¹* N. 10; *Docs.* no. 254, p. 72; Naevius Sertorius Macro for Dio, 58.9.2), a Roman knight and in charge of the watch, had been used by Tiberius to help get rid of Sejanus (Dio 58.9.2–6, 12.7; Tac. *Ann.* 6.23.2; Philo *Leg.* 37) and then became praetorian prefect himself. A powerful figure in the last years of Tiberius' reign (Tac. *Ann.* 6.29.3, 48.2, Dio 58.21.3, 27.2), he allied himself with Gaius' prospects (Tac. *Ann.* 6.45.3; Dio 58.28.4, 59.10.6; Philo, *Leg.* 32–38; *In Flacc.* 11–12), deserting the old emperor's setting sun in favor of a rising one (Tac. *Ann.* 6.46.4; cf. Dio 58.28.4).

sollicitavit ad stuprum pollicitus et matrimonium suum, si potitus imperio fuisset: Charges of sexual alliance involving members of the imperial family are usually found in contexts in which women had political cards to play. Ennia may have had a degree of influence in her own right if Thrasyllus was her grandfather (above), but real power obviously lay with Macro and Gaius. The liaison was explained in two ways: Tacitus (6.45.3) and Dio (58.28.4) write that Macro offered Gaius his wife in order to court favor with the young prince; by this interpretation, Gaius is dominant. Suetonius (here) and Philo (*Leg.* 39–40), on the other hand, write that Gaius seduced Ennia so that she would influence her husband to embrace his interests at court. In this version (more hostile to Gaius) Macro is the more powerful of the two but unable to know in what direction his fortunes lie without his wife's help, hardly likely. The fact that two versions exist seems to indicate that each man was perceived as having something to gain from the other. Adultery was frequently added to other charges or even substituted for them when convenient (on 15.4, 30.2; Bauman 176–77), and so it is quite possible that the entire story took its origin from the trial of Macro in A.D. 38 (26.1). Gaius brought a charge of adultery against him "among other charges," specifically *lenocinium,* because he had procured his wife for him (Dio 59.10.6), but see below. Sejanus was also said to have promised marriage to his paramours (Dio 58.3.8).

deque ea re et iure iurando et chirographo cavit: Gaius put his marriage proposal in writing. *Caveo,* here meaning "to provide guarantees," has legal implications (*adicit iure iurando Paeti cautum apud signa,* Tac. *Ann.* 15.16.2). *Chirographum* can be a written contract as well as handwriting (24.3). The charge against Macro in A.D. 38 may not have been *lenocinium* but rather a straightforward *accusatio adulterii* with Gaius claiming that he had been formally betrothed to Ennia (Bauman 176; cf. 25.1–2 about his treatment of the former husbands of his other wives).

per hanc insinuatus Macroni: A strong statement of the uncomplimentary judgment that Gaius was the suitor to Macro's dominance (above).

Since Gaius could only gain by Tiberius' death, stories that he murdered him inevitably appeared. Tiberius had been ill and weak for some time and the end was anticipated (Tac. *Ann.* 6.47.3, 48.2, 50.1–3; Dio 58.27.4, 28.1–2; Suet. *Tib.* 72.2–3, 73.1; Philo *Leg.* 25; Jos. *AJ* 205). With or without help, he died a natural death at the age of 78; the date was March 16, A.D. 37 (*Docs.* no. 31, p. 28; see 13). Suetonius includes several accounts in his *Life of Tiberius,* and all make the old emperor die sordidly as his character warranted. But here the manner of death emphasizes Gaius' agency (Gascou 381; Steidle 73; Mouchova 73–74).

veneno Tiberium adgressus est ut quidam opinantur: Any slow death could be ascribed to poison (cf. the death of Germanicus, 1.2), often the weapon of choice for Gaius, the poisonous snake (11; see note 11). *Ut quidam opinantur* shows Suetonius' distrust of this story; cf. *sunt qui putent venenum ei a Gaio datum* (Suet. *Tib.* 73.2).

spirantique adhuc detrahi anulum et, quoniam suspicionem retinentis dabat, pulvinum iussit inici atque etiam fauces manu sua oppresit: There are four versions of Tiberius' death in the *Life of Tiberius* (73.2): The first is that Gaius poisoned him (above); the second, that he was refused food when he was sick; the third, that he was smothered by a pillow when he demanded back the ring that had been taken from him when he fainted (the version that is repeated here); and finally, *Seneca…scribit* (which Seneca is unclear; see 53.2) that he seemed about to give his ring to someone but then changed his mind and fell dead near his couch after his attendants did not respond to his call. The hesitation with the ring is a metaphor for his indecisive choice of an heir (14.1). The neglect of his needs, the regaining of consciousness and the ring can all be derived from the Seneca report (Willrich 109; Gascou 381; Seager 245). Tacitus (*Ann.* 6.50.4–5) and Dio (58.28.3) have Macro help Gaius with the murder.

liberto, qui ob atrocitatem facinoris exclamaverat, confestim in crucem acto: Only here. Since the murder itself is problematical, so is this illustration of Gaius' gratuitous cruelty. Crucifixion, normally a punishment for slaves and non-citizens (27.3), was unusual but not unexampled for a freedman (Garnsey 127–29). Galba crucified a Roman citizen (Suet. *Gal.*9.1).

12.3 *nec abhorret a veritate, cum sint quidam auctores:* Suetonius neither verifies nor denies the tale that follows. Like other of his more colorful anecdotes, this is not told elsewhere (e.g., the poisoning of Antonia, 23.2). A similar phrase *nec abhorret a vero* introduces a climax at Suet. *Tib.* 62.3 (Mouchova 74).

ipsum postea etsi non de perfecto, at certe de cogitato quondam parricidio professum; gloriatum enim assidue in commemoranda sua pietate, ad ulciscendam necem matris et fratrum introisse se cum pugione cubiculum Tiberi[i] dormientis et misericordia correptum abiecto ferro recessisse: Gaius' own propaganda (*in commemoranda sua pietate*) may have been the origin of this story that he almost killed the old emperor. It allows him to have it two ways: He is at once the would-be avenger of his family's wrongs and at the same time he defends himself against the charge of murder and emphasizes his loyalty. But the favorable impression of *misericordia correptum* is undercut by the disparaging language of *gloriatum enim assidue* (8.2). It was easy to see Gaius' public relations efforts ironically (15.4, 16.1). For Gaius' *pietas*, see 22.1.

nec illum, quanquam sensisset, aut inquirere quicquam aut exequi ausum: The weak and devious Tiberius of tradition (Tac. *Ann.* 1.12, 6.6; Dio. 57.7.2), but who witnessed what was in his mind?

13 *Sic imperium adeptus:* *Adipiscor imperium,* standard for "becoming emperor" (e.g., *biennio continuo post adeptum imperium,* Suet. *Tib.* 38). *Sic* probably refers to the manipulations with Macro and Ennia and the murder of Tiberius, attempted or actual (12.2–3), not to his entire past history.

With great fanfare Gaius escorted the body of Tiberius from Misenum to Rome (13). This glorious beginning of his reign contrasts with its tawdry end, the "good *princeps*-bad *monstrum*" dichotomy (22.1). As the sequence of these first weeks has been reconstructed, Tiberius died on March 16 (12.2), and Gaius was named *imperator* by the senate on March 18 (14.1; *Docs.* no. 3 p. 10), although first plausibly by the military at hand in Campania (Balsdon 1934a, 25). He entered Rome on March 28 to a prearranged meeting of the senate that was attended by members of all three orders, a meeting whose ceremonial purpose is more clear than its constitutional function (14.1). The body of Tiberius was brought in, probably during the night of March 28–29, and his state funeral was held on April 3 (15.1). The most serious problem of the moment was Tiberius' will, but its nullification, like Gaius' reception in Rome, had evidently been prearranged by Macro (14.1; Dio 59.1.2.). Tiberius' heirs were Gaius, his grandson through his adoption of

Germanicus, and Tiberius Gemellus, Drusus' son, his natural grandson, each to inherit the other's portion in case of death (Suet. *Tib.* 76). In his last months Tiberius is supposed to have said, "You will kill him and another will kill you" (to Gaius about Gemellus, Tac. *Ann.* 6.46.4; Dio 58.23.3), in recognition of the potentially lethal arrangement. It is not clear why Tiberius did not make a more decisive choice; there were rumors of Gemellus' illegitimacy (Suet. *Tib.* 62.3; Dio 58.23.2) derived from the story that his mother had been involved with Sejanus (Tac. *Ann.* 4.3.3, 10.2; Dio 57.22.2, 4ᵇ).

p(opulum) R(omanum), vel dicam hominum genus, voti compotem fecit, exoptatissimus princeps: Gaius was welcome after the genuinely unpopular Tiberius. Philo's *Legatio ad Gaium* (10–11) contains similar language: ὅ τε Ῥωμαίων δῆμος ἐγεγήθει καὶ πᾶσα Ἰταλία τά τε Ἀσιανὰ καὶ Εὐρωπαῖα ἔθνη (the universality of his appeal). ὡς γὰρ ἐπ' οὐδενὶ τῶν πώποτε γενομένων αὐτοκρατόρων ἅπαντες ἠγάσθησαν (= *exoptatissimus*), κτῆσιν καὶ χρῆσιν ἰδίων τε καὶ κοινῶν ἀγαθῶν οὐκ ἐλπίζοντες ἕξειν, ἀλλ' ἔχειν ἤδη νομίζοντες... (= *voti compotem fecit*, the populace getting its wish).

maximae parti provincialium ac militum, quod infantem plerique cognoverant: Gaius had been exposed to the bulk of the legions (*maximae parti*), most of whom were stationed on the northern or eastern frontiers where he had been as a young child (8–9, 10). His father had preceded him in popularity abroad (on 3.2), and provincial inscriptions that salute him as the son of Germanicus are plentiful (Rosborough 22–23; *Docs.* no. 33, p. 29) but routine (Smallwood 1961, 161–62).

sed et universae plebi urbanae ob memoriam Germanici patris miserationemque prope afflictae domus: Roman civilians are balanced against provincials and the military (above). For the same contrast elsewhere, 5 vs. 6; 14.2 vs. 14.3. *Afflicta domus,* the ruin of the house, i.e., the deaths of Gaius' brothers as well as of his father and mother may have been a kind of slogan adopted by the faction that championed his family (cf. *suorum casus,* 10.2; Tac. *Ann.* 4.53.2). Germanicus' popularity among the *universa plebs* rubbed off on Claudius too (Suet. *Cl.* 7, 11.2).

itaque ut a Miseno movit: The beginning of a long and awkward sentence that extends through *tradantur* (14.1; see note 8). Tiberius died at his villa at Misenum (Suet. *Tib.* 72.3, 73.1; Tac. *Ann.* 6.50.1; Dio. 58.28.1; *Docs.* no. 31, p. 28) at the tip of the westernmost promontory of the Bay of Naples, the location for many luxurious country houses (Phaedrus 2.5.7–10; D'Arms 23–30, 88–89, 184–85 for detail and testimonia). He owned others (Tac. *Ann.* 4.59.1; Suet. *Tib.* 39) including twelve on Capreae (Tac. *Ann.* 4.67.3).

quamvis lugentis habitu et funus Tiberi prosequens: Wearing the *toga pulla,* the mourner's dark-colored garment, Gaius proceeded to Rome with a military escort for the body (Suet. *Tib.* 75.3), probably by way of the Via Appia (Garzetti 1974, 81). Reverence to the ashes or body of the deceased displayed *pietas;* see 15.1 for Gaius' burial of Tiberius and his mother and brother and 3.2 for Germanicus with the victims of the Varine disaster. Tiberius similarly escorted the body of Augustus back to Rome from Nola, also near the Bay of Naples, with notables from towns along the way acting as pall bearers (Suet. *Aug.* 100.2; Dio 56.31.3), and the body of his brother Drusus from Germany (Dio 55.2.1). The elder Agrippina brought back the ashes of Germanicus from Antioch (on 6.2; Tac. *Ann.* 3.1.4; cf. 24.3 for the younger Agrippina in A.D. 39).

tamen inter altaria et victimas ardentisque taedas densissimo et laetissimo obviorum agmine incessit: The funeral procession provoked comparison with a triumphal procession. Altars and sacrificial victims during the initial euphoria of the reign also appear in Philo (*Leg.* 12). Cf. Galba's welcome to Rome: *per omne iter dextra sinistraque oppidatim victimae caederentur* (Suet. *Gal.* 18.1, noted by Maurer).

super fausta nomina: Otho (M. Salvius Otho, *PIR¹* S. 109) was also hailed emperor *inter faustas adclamationes* (Suet. *Oth.* 6.3). The familiar names that follow are "extra" (*super*), beyond the usual names of good omen. *Fausta nomina* were both those derived from propitious words (*faustus, felix, valens*) and those with good associations such as *Africanus;* here they are presumably Gaius' new *cognomina, Augustus* and *Germanicus.* Persons with lucky names were chosen for ritual and other duties: *ingressi milites, quis fausta nomina, felicibus ramis* (Tac. *Hist.* 4.53.2).[13]

sidus et pullum et pupum et alumnum appellantium: The first three of these are attested as pet names, often in poetry: *sidus* (Ov. *Pont.* 3.3.2; Stat. *Silv.* 3.4.26; Hor. *Epod.* 17.41; Curt. 9.6.8); *pullus* (Pl. *Cas.* 1.50; Hor. *Sat.* 1.3.45); *pupus* (Varro *Sat. Men.* 546). Seneca uses *sidus* for Nero, a shining star of an emperor (*Dial.* 11.13.1). The phrase *alumnus legionum* was an important tag for Gaius (on 8.1: Tac. *Ann.* 1.44.1; Sen. *Dial.* 2.18.4), who called himself the "nursling" (τρόφιμος = *alumnus*) of the senate (καὶ υἱὸς καὶ τρόφιμος αὐτῶν λέγων εἶναι, Dio 59.6.1).

---

[13] Although *fausta omina* (*apparatus*) are common enough (*Aug.* 57.2, 98.2; *Cl.* 17.2; Tac. *Ann.* 1.35.3), *fausta nomina* are also attested (Cic. *Scaur.* 30; Plin. *HN* 28.22; Plut. *Cat. Min.* 57; for the collection of instances, Pease at Cic. *De Div.* 1.102). The position of *fausta nomina* within the portion of the sentence controlled by *appellantium* also favors the manuscript reading.

14.1 *ingressoque urbem:* On March 28, twelve days after Tiberius died (12.2–3, 13), ten days after his *dies imperii* (below), Gaius entered Rome: *A. d. v. K. Apriles...hoc die [C.] Caesar Augustus Germanicus urbem ingressus es[t]* (*Docs.* no. 3, p. 10). The body of Tiberius followed that night (on 15.1).

statim consensu senatus et irrumpentis in curiam turbae: Dio's description of the same meeting adds contingents from the knights and the people (παρόντων ἐν τῷ συνεδρίῳ καὶ ἱππέων τοῦ τε δήμου τινῶν, 59.6.1) and dates it to five months and four days before Gaius' twenty-fifth birthday (59.6.2), i.e., March 28, the same day on which he entered the city, Suetonius' *statim*. The crowd "breaking into the senate house" (*irrumpentis in curiam turbae*) suggests an event engineered to affirm Gaius' support by all three orders. He could not have called this meeting himself since he did not yet have *tribunicia potestas* (below on *ius arbitriumque omnium rerum*). Sources differ about whether Gaius or Macro (through intermediaries) notified the senate of Tiberius' death (Jos. *AJ* 18.234; Dio. 59.3.1).

inrita Tiberi voluntate, qui testamento alterum nepotem suum praetextatum adhuc coheredem ei dederat: Tiberius had made his will in A.D. 35, two years before his death. Macro saw to it that it was declared invalid (*inrita*) by the senate on the argument that Tiberius had shown himself of unsound mind when he made his heir a boy who was not yet of age (Dio 59.1.2). This made the legal ground for the annulment *querela inofficiosi testamenti,* the "complaint of undutiful will." Wills could be challenged when they included or excluded legatees contrary to what could be considered the reasonable "duty" of the testator (Nicholas 261–64; Crook 122–23; Buckland 327–29; Manning 63–67; Watson 62–72; for more "undutiful wills," see on 38.2, 3). If money had been the only issue, the youth of Tiberius Gemellus would not have mattered, since he, along with Gaius and his sisters, would have been an heir even if Tiberius had died intestate. But the transfer of money was clearly recognized as the transfer of power (Timpe 1962, 71–75; Levick 1976, 220; Veyne 1990, 332–33). Tiberius Gemellus (on 10.1) and his twin brother (Tiberius Germanicus Julius Caesar, *PIR*² I. 224) were born in A.D. 19 (Tac. *Ann.* 2.84.1; the brother died in 23, Tac. *Ann.* 4.15.1), a date that has been called into question because of the emphasis that the tradition places on the youth of Gemellus (*praetextatum adhuc;* ἔτι γὰρ παιδίον ἦν in A.D. 33, Dio 58.23.2; also Dio 59.1.2; Philo *Leg.* 23). But even if the correct birth date was 20 instead of 19 (Hirschfeld 366–73), Gemellus was still 16 or 17 in 37, not too young to have been given the adult toga if Tiberius had chosen to bring him forward. Nor was he too young to be a focus for the political ambitions of others—despite Philo's assertion that he could not have headed a conspiracy at his young age (*Leg.* 23). His youth is always emphasized to make him seem more helpless before the conniving Gaius (on 23.3 for his pathetic death).

ius arbitriumque omnium rerum illi permissum est: The phrase *ius arbitriumque omnium rerum*[14] seems to refer to the assumption of the powers that defined the principate, and Dio reckons Gaius' reign from the March 28 meeting (59.6.2, 30.1). Suetonius says that he reigned ten days longer (59), and this makes his *dies imperii* March 18, two days after Tiberius' death, a date that coincides with the testimony of the *Acta Fratrum Arvalium* for A.D. 38: *xv K. Apriles...hoc die C. Caesar Augustus Germanicus a senatu impera[tor appellatus est* (*Docs.* no. 3, p. 10).[15] Since Macro had already arranged the transfer of power with the army where it really counted (Tac. *Ann.* 6.50.4; Philo *Leg.* 58), the March 28 meeting evidently ratified the constellation of powers that accompanied the title *imperator* and conferred additional ones (Timpe 1962, 67–70; Barrett 1989, 55–58). A possibility is that Gaius initially made a perfunctory *recusatio imperii* to the March 18 salute and then "acquiesced" to the "persuasion" of the three orders at the meeting in Rome (Jakobson and Cotton, 497–501). This would explain Dio's assertion that at first Gaius refused imperial titles but then assumed them all on one day (59.3.1–2).

tanta publica laetitia, ut tribus proximis mensibus ac ne totis quidem supra centum sexaginta milia victimarum caesa tradantur: More public rejoicing. Philo writes that it lasted for seven months until Gaius' became ill (*Leg.* 12; see 14.2). Suetonius' precise period of a "scant three months" (*tribus proximis mensibus ac ne totis quidem*) within which the one hundred sixty thousand victims were sacrificed came to an end at some point before June 18. This rather precise time reference probably came from a source that also identified the terminus for the offerings; Gaius' first *congiarium* on June 1 is a possibility (17.2). Suetonius puts some distance between himself and this detail when he attributes it to a nameless authority (*tradantur*).

---

[14] Suetonius' language is similar to that of the *lex de imperio Vespasiani: ...utique quaecunque ex usu rei publicae maiestate divinarum hum[an]arumque publicarum privatarumque rerum esse censebit, ei agere facere ius potestasque sit...* (*ILS* 244. 17–19; Timpe 1962, 75 and n. 3).

[15] In a related error Dio gives March 26 as the date of Tiberius' death (58.28.5) and March 28 as Gaius' *dies imperii,* a two day interval as in Suetonius; he says that he reigned three years, nine months and twenty-eight days (59.30.1), a calculation that tallies closely with his accession five months and four days before his twenty-fifth birthday (59.6.2). But see on 58.1 and 59 and notes 119 and 120). Dio's account reflects confusion of some sort with the two-day interval and/or the dates of March 16 and March 18 themselves, perhaps xvii or xv before the Kalends of April was misread as vii or v at some point (Snyder 45; also Wardle 1991, 163 n. 13).

Here follow specific instances of spontaneous devotion that make particular the preceding general-ization about Gaius' popularity (13), first at Rome (14.2) and then in foreign parts (14.3). Artabanus, who furnishes the example of devotion from abroad, recalls the emotional attachment that this same King of Parthia had allegedly felt toward Germanicus some seventeen years earlier (5; Tac. *Ann.* 2.58). Gaius, like his father Germanicus, is portrayed having an excellent relation-ship with the King of Kings.

14.2 *Cum deinde paucos post dies in proximas Campaniae insulas traiecisset:* His trip was to the islands off Campania (greater detail at 15.1) to retrieve the remains of his mother and brother Nero, who had been exiled and died there (7, 10.1). This demonstration of piety was performed soon (*paucos post dies*) after Suetonius' last time marker, the meeting of March 28 (14.1), although not in fact until after the funeral of Tiberius on April 3 (15.1).

vota pro reditu suscepta sunt, ne minimam quidem occasionem quoquam omittente in testificanda sollicitudine et cura de incolumitate eius: Vows were taken for his safety both at the time of this excursion to the islands and on the occasion of his illness later in the year (below). A mishap to him at this critical time would have meant instability for Rome, and so there was an understandable concern for his safety and health as a practical matter. *Devotiones* are described below, but prayers and sacrifices for an emperor's well-being were standard (Suet. *Tib.* 38; Pliny *Ep.* 10.35). The Jews sacrificed on his behalf (Philo *Leg.* 356–57; for sacrifices on behalf of the emperor, Price 205–15).

ut vero in adversam valitudinem incidit: Philo gives the date of Gaius' ill-ness as the eighth month after the beginning of his reign, i.e., late October—early November (*Leg.* 14), and says that the news spread quickly because the sailing season was not yet over (*Leg.* 15; for the end of the season on November 11, Pliny *HN* 2.125; Casson 1971, 270). Dio writes that Gaius became ill shortly after September 12 (59.7.9–8.1; for an explanation of this date, see on his first consul-ship, 17.1; also note 32). The duration of the illness is also unclear. If the story about his being asked to choose a name for his nephew Nero is true (almost cer-tainly not, on 24.1), he was recovered by mid-December. On the other hand, he is not recorded present among the Arval Brethern on January 11 (*Docs.* no. 1, pp. 9–10), and this may indicate that he was still out of circulation at the begin-ning of the next year (Dobrowski, 162–65). Only Philo refers the deterioration of Gaius' behavior to this illness which he saw as the result of the high and loose living that the new emperor took up as soon as Tiberius was dead (*Leg.* 22). Modern scholars have seized on this and made a non-specific "nervous break-down" or some other disease a convenient rationalization for his entire reign. But it was the perception of serious illness, not the illness itself, that was important. Contingency plans (plots?) may have been formed while he was out of action, and when he recovered, he realized that he was more vulnerable than he had imagined (Dobrowski, 133–70). There is no way to know what was wrong with him or to know if this episode bore any relation to his health, physical or mental, in general.[16] See 50.2–3 for his health.

pernoctantibus cunctis circum Palatium: The Palatine hill, formerly the home of wealthy Romans, was becoming the family compound of the reigning family during this period. The faithful watched all night like lovers or sentries in an army camp (*pernoctare*).

non defuerunt qui depugnaturos se armis pro salute aegri quique capita sua titulo proposito voverent: Cf. Dio 58.8.3. Vows like these had their origins in *devotio,* the barter of a life for a life, either as a direct promise or by way of surrogate human sacrifice in the gladiatorial contests. Augustus was flattered by promises of his subjects not to outlive him (Dio 53.20.2–3). The man who promised to give his life for the emperor swore solemnly under oath (ἔνορκος, Dio 59.8.3) and advertised his piety by having a placard (*titulus*), probably a wooden tablet, carried before him in parade (Veyne 1983, 281–82). Suetonius will describe their fates later (27.2).

accessit ad immensum civium amorem notabilis etiam externorum favor: The transition from devotion in Rome to devotion abroad.

14.3 *nam Artabanus Parthorum rex, odium semper contemptumque Tiberi prae se ferens:* Artabanus III (5) held power in Parthia from A.D. 12 until he died in 38. The internal arrangement in the buffer state of Armenia affirmed by Germanicus (1.2) lasted until the Roman-friendly Artaxias III (Zeno) died, probably in 34. Soon thereafter Artabanus saw an opportunity and tried to install his own son on the Armenian throne (*odium semper contemptumque Tiberi prae se ferens = senectutem Tiberii ut inermem despiciens,* Tac. *Ann.* 6.31.1). Conflict with Rome began in 35 (Tac. *Ann.* 6.31–37, 41–44; Dio 58.26.1–4; Jos. *AJ* 18.96–102; Magie 507–9, 1364; Debevoise 157–56). *Prae se ferens* = "displaying" (the same phrase at 19.2).

amicitiam huius ultro petiit venitque ad colloquium legati consularis: The consular legate was L. Vitellius (*PIR¹* V. 500), the father of the emperor of

---

[16] A nervous breakdown due to dissipation is accepted by Gelzer (389–90), Balsdon (1934a, 36) and Garzetti (1974, 84); Willrich thought it was brought on my job-related stress (118). Sandiston argued for epidemic encephalitis (207–8), Katz for thyrotoxicosis (1972, 223–25).

A.D. 69. He was consul for the first time in 34 and legate in Syria from 35 until 39. A peace initiative was begun by Tiberius but was probably not successful until the spring or early summer of 37 after Gaius had become emperor (Garzetti 1956, 211–29). Which of the two would get credit for the end of hostilities? Dio (59.27.3) and Tacitus (by inference from his silence about it under Tiberius) concur with Suetonius that Vitellius' meeting with Artabanus took place at the beginning of Gaius' reign. If it happened before Tiberius died, it may have been transferred into that time frame by those who were unwilling to grant a foreign policy success to the unpopular Tiberius (Gelzer 398; Magie 508; Debevoise 168, n. 69) or by Gaius himself who claimed the the capitulation of Artabanus with the bridge at Baiae (19.1). Josephus, on the other hand, writes that the meeting took place under Tiberius (*AJ* 18.101–3); other revisionists may have wanted to take credit from Gaius and give it to Tiberius. Suetonius states unequivocally that Artabanus initiated the contact with Vitellius (*ultro*), but elsewhere (*Vit.* 2.4) he credits Vitellius with forcing Artabanus to terms. Dio (59.27.3), Josephus (*AJ* 18.101), and Tacitus (by inference, *Ann.* 6.32.3–4) concur with this other interpretation.[17]

et transgressus Euphraten: The portion of the Euphrates that lay between Syria and Armenia was a frontier, both real and symbolic. A conference there signified that each party was meeting the other halfway; in A.D. 18, Artabanus had offered to honor Germanicus by approaching the river (*daturumque honori Germanici ut ripam Euphratis accederet,* Tac. *Ann.* 2.58.1). By crossing to the Roman side (*transgressus*), he completed the gesture of compliance (*amicitiam huius ultro petiit,* above). Josephus' more restrained account of the meeting not only sets the incident in the reign of Tiberius (above), but also shows Artabanus and Vitellius coming together at the middle of a bridge constructed as an emblem of compromise and emphasizes the equal terms with a feast celebrated on a structure erected at the halfway point (*AJ* 18.101–2; cf. the platform on the Baiae bridge, Dio 59.17.6–7).

aquilas et signa Romana Caesarumque imagines adoravit: Cf. [Vitellius] *...Artabanum Parthorum regem summis artibus...ad veneranda legionem signa*

---

[17] In these passages (Josephus excepted), Vitellius is praised for his diplomatic achievement and at the same time criticized for his sycophancy; he was known as the first and the worst of the flatterers of Gaius and Claudius. Tacitus does not have an account of the Vitellius-Artabanus incident (presumably because Book 7 of the *Annales* is missing) but rewrites this same dual assessment of Vitellius' character (*Ann.* 6.32.3–4). Suetonius' description of the meeting in this passage in which Artabanus makes his move unasked must derive from a different interpretation of the event, one that emphasized the loyalty and friendship of an Eastern king to Gaius as the son of Germanicus (cf. 5 for the mourning of the King of Kings when he died).

pellexit (Suet. *Vit.* 2.4) and θῦσαι ταῖς τοῦ Αὐγούστου τοῦ τε Γαΐου εἰκόσιν ἠνάγκασε (Dio 59.27.3). Representations of the Caesars, here portraits of Augustus and Gaius, accompanied the legionary standards, perhaps on the *signa*, perhaps on their own poles (Campbell 96–97). This addition to the story may have been suggested by the fact that Vitellius was accused of bringing proskynesis to Rome (Suet. *Vit.* 4.5; Dio 59.27.5; Magie 1364).

After the spontaneous displays in 14.2–3, here follow Gaius' own strategies to make himself popular. Suetonius judged that successful efforts of this sort were commendable just as they had been for Germanicus (3.2–3). First come Gaius' conscious efforts to display *pietas* toward his family (15.1–3) beginning with the funeral for Tiberius and funeral honors for his mother and brother Nero (15.1).

15.1 *Incendebat et ipse studia hominum omni genere popularitatis:* Cf. *conciliandaeque hominum gratiae ac promerendi amoris mirum et efficax studium* (about Germanicus, 3.1).

Tiberio cum plurimis lacrimis pro contione laudato funeratoque amplissime: Gaius' first act of filial piety was to hold a proper funeral for Tiberius. It was a lavish and traditional ceremony (πολυτελεῖς νόμοις τοῖς πατρίοις, *Jos. AJ* 18.236; also Dio 58.28.5). This contrasts with Dio's statement that Gaius showed disrespect to Tiberius because the funeral took place with unseemly haste, his body having been brought in during the preceding night, and because he did not so much praise him in the funeral oration as use the occasion to link himself with Augustus and Germanicus (59.3.7–8). But Dio is wrong, at least about the timing. He or his sources appear to have conflated the public parade and display of the body with the funeral. Tiberius' body was in the city by March 29 (*iiii K. Apr. corpus in urbe perlatum per mili[t.]*), but the funeral did not take place until April 3 (*iii Non. Apr. f[unere] p[ublico] e[latus] e[st], Docs.* no. 31, p. 28), an interval that allowed time for proper preparations (Charlesworth 1933b, 107–8). Gaius proposed divine honors for Tiberius during these first weeks, but the idea was dropped (Dio 59.3.7). In A.D. 40 it was voted that his birthday be celebrated (Dio 59.24.7).

confestim Pandateriam et Pontias ad tranferendos matris fratrisque cineres festinavit: Cf. Dio 59.3.5. Gaius' immediate departure (*confestim*) reiterates the *post paucos dies* for the trip at 14.2. *Pontiae* is usual for Pontia, the largest of the *Pontiae insulae*, today's Ponza. Pandateria is now Ventontene. The islands are off the Campanian coast about halfway between Rome and Naples. The property of the imperial family, they were sites for genteel exile during the first century. Elsewhere, Suetonius writes that Nero's remains were scattered beyond retrieval (Suet. *Tib.* 54.2). For their exiles, see 7, 10.1. Nero was on Pontia, Agrippina on Pandateria (*Pandataria,* Suet. *Tib.* 53.2).

tempestate turbida, quo magis pietas emineret: The bad weather (severe, minimal, desirable, or possibly sought out as suggested here: *quo magis pietas emineret*), was an important element in Gaius' advertisement of himself as a dutiful son in the family of Germanicus. The outside limit of the sailing season was March 10, but the sea was not considered safe until May 27 (Casson 1971, 270). For this storm as an occasion for devotion toward Gaius, 14.2; as an excuse to kill his father-in-law, 23.3.

adiitque venerabundus ac per semet in urnas condidit: He approached the burial places of Agrippina and Nero in a spirit of reverence (*venerabundus*) and put their remains in the burial urns with his own hands. Cf. τά τε ὀστᾶ τά τε τῆς μητρὸς καὶ τὰ τῶν ἀδελφῶν τῶν ἀποθανόντων αὐτός τε πλεύσας καὶ αὐτὸς αὐτοχειρίᾳ ἀνελόμενος ἐκόμισε (Dio 59.3.5; the strong *per semet* = αὐτοχειρίᾳ and the repeated αὐτός). Once again someone who holds *augurium* (like Germanicus at the scene of the Varine disaster, 3.2) touchs a body or bones (or is said to) despite the fact that it is *nefas*. Willingness to risk pollution was a mark of piety. Since the ceremonial gestures on the islands were not witnessed by the populace, official publicity had to generate this report. The burial urns of Agrippina and Nero have been found in or near the Mausoleum of Augustus (*Docs.* nos. 84a, 85a, p. 41).[18]

nec minore scaena: *Scaena* = "theatricality." The deposit of the urns in the Mausoleum (below) was the same kind of studied production as the trip to the islands.

Ostiam praefixo in biremis puppe vexillo et inde Romam Tiberi subvectos: The nautical parade approached the city by way of the Tiber to the Campus Martius where there seems to have been a landing place. Gnaeus Piso (2) had landed at the same place when he returned to Rome after his confrontation with Germanicus in Syria (*navem tumulo Caesarum adpulerat,* Tac. *Ann.* 3.9.2). The military *vexillum* on the stern of the ship made the burial a state affair.

---

[18] Willrich (115, n. 5, followed by Barrett 1989, 58) thought that Gaius would not have dared touch the bones if he had *augurium,* and so he was not yet *pontifex maximus* on this April date in A.D. 37. But Gaius received all the titles that Tiberius collected throughout his life (except for *pater patriae*) on a single day (Dio 59.3.1–2), presumably March 28 (on 14.1), and he was clearly Augustus when he placed the ashes of Agrippina and Nero in the tomb as the inscription on Agrippina's urn shows: *ossa Agrippinae...matris C. Caesaris Aug. Germanici principis* (*Docs.* no. 84a, p. 4).

per splendidissimum quemque equestris ordinis: There was a role for knights in imperial funerals during this period (those of Drusus, Dio 55.2.3; of Augustus, Suet. *Aug.* 100.4 and Dio 56.42.2; of Germanicus, *Tabula Hebana* ll. 57–58, Oliver and Palmer 231; of Drusilla, Dio. 59.11.2). *Splendidus* was standard for an *eques* and as a superlative it anticipates the later trend toward superlatives as equestrian titles. Those who carried the urns (below) were "the most distinguished members of the equestrian order," probably chosen from among the young members of senatorial families who remained knights until they received the questorship and took their places in the senatorial order (e.g., Claudius; on 15.2). Or *splendidissimum quemque* may refer specifically to the *seviri,* the heads of the six *turmae equitum Romanorum* who were chosen from this group. Gaius was present dressed for a triumph in a purple-bordered toga and attended by lictors (Dio 59.3.5). It was, as Suetonius says, a *scaena* (above).

medio ac frequenti die: Gaius gave his piety maximum exposure by staging the funeral when the area was crowded. Piso (above) had also arrived at the Campus Martius conspicuously (*dieque et ripa frequenti,* Tac. *Ann.* 3.9.2).

duobus ferculis Mausoleo intulit: Each urn was on its own litter. The Mausoleum of Augustus on the Campus Martius (outside the *pomerium* and hence a proper burial place) was built as early as 28 B.C. (Suet. *Aug.* 100.4) as a personal memorial for Augustus and a dynastic one for his family (Strab. 5.3.8; for the possibility that Gaius was himself buried there, see 59).

inferiasque is annua religione publice instituit: Anniversary commemorations of the death dates of Agrippina and Nero are not attested epigraphically. Agrippina died on October 18, A.D. 33, the second anniversary of the death of Sejanus, and Tiberius made the annual thanksgiving for his death (*EJ* no. 52, p. 64) apply to hers as well (*Ann.* 6.25.3; Suet. *Tib.* 53.2). A sacrifice on her birthday (October 25? 26?), however, is recorded for A.D. 39 (*Docs.* no. 9, p. 13; Herz 1981a, 104).

eo amplius matri: As Gaius' most direct link to Augustus, Agrippina was central to his efforts to emphasize his family connections and legitimize his claim to the job. She appeared with increasing prominence on his coinage (Trillmich 181–84).

circenses carpentumque quo in pompa traduceretur: Circenses = ludi circenses, chariot races, opened with a *pompa circensis,* a parade from the Capitol to the race course. They could be held in honor of individuals (Suet. *Cl.* 11.2; Dio 60.5.1). A *carpentum* was a covered two-wheeled "woman's" vehicle whose use was increasingly restricted to members of the imperial family. Claudius granted a posthumous one to his mother Antonia (Suet. *Cl.* 11.2), and another conferred status on the younger Agrippina (Tac. *Ann.* 12.42.2). A dupondius of Gaius (*RIC²* Gaius no. 55, p. 112) shows Agrippina's *carpentum* with its side curtains rolled up to display her image.

The young emperor was the last surviving male among the blood descendants of Augustus in the branch of the family that mattered,[19] and as such found himself naked on the public stage. He needed as much family as he could rally to fortify his dynastic position and so utilized them, living and dead, until he could produce some children of his own (24, 1–2, 25). Suetonius runs through the contribution each member made toward strengthening Gaius' position. Agrippina was the granddaughter of Augustus (15.1), but Germanicus had the higher profile (15.2). Gaius rehabilitated the Antonian branch of his family (26.1) with honors for his paternal grandmother Antonia (15.2). Even embarrassing Claudius was drawn into public view as the brother of Germanicus (15.2). Gaius' sisters also had roles to play (15.3), especially Drusilla (24.1–2). Tiberius Gemellus was a somewhat different case (15.2); Gaius coopted him, incorporated him into his own circle either to defuse him as a rival or to add yet another body between himself and the daggers of would-be assassins, or both. Emperors were clearly conscious of their need to protect themselves with heirs, as can be seen from Augustus' repeated attempts to arrange for a long line of them (1.1 and 4 on the adoption of Germanicus; also Dio 54.18.2 on Augustus' adoption of his grandsons Gaius and Lucius Caesar). Tiberius ostensibly gave Gaius precisely this advice when he told him to care for Gemellus not only because of kinship but also because while he lived he would prove a protective "wall;" it was dangerous for the powerful to find themselves alone (ὡς τεῖχός σοι καὶ τῆς ἀρχῆς ὁμοῦ καὶ τῆς σωτηρίας περιὼν γίνοιτο ἂν Τιβέριος [Gemellus], φροίμιον δὲ τοῦ δυστυχοῦς μεθιστάμενος. αἵ τε γὰρ μονώσεις ἐπικίνδυνοι τοῖς εἰς τηλικούτων πραγμάτων ὄγκον καταστᾶσιν (Jos. *AJ* 18.221–22). Gaius later turned against these persons; 15.2–2 is reversed at 23.2–3 and 29.1.

15.2 At in memoriam patris Septembrem mensem Germanicum appellavit: It was a Hellenistic custom to honor a living ruler as a divinity by renaming a month after him. When Julius Caesar allowed the name of his birth month to be changed from *Quintilis* to *Julius*, it was one of the excesses that led to his death (Suet. *Jul.* 76.1). Augustus more tactfully honored his title and not his family when he changed *Sextilis* to *Augustus* (Suet. *Aug.* 31.2; Dio 55.6.6–7). Tiberius refused to name a month either for himself or for Livia (Suet. *Tib.* 26.2; Dio 57.18.2). Nero, on the other hand (Suet. *Ner.* 55; Tac. *Ann.* 15.74.1; 16.12.2), and Domitian (Suet. *Dom.* 13.3; *ILS* 6644) did name months for themselves.[20] These later changes did not survive, but *Julius* and *Augustus* became

---

[19] The Junii Silani, the grandchildren of the younger Julia (*PIR²* I. 635), the sister of Gaius' mother Agrippina, were also direct descendants. See on 35.1.

[20] Domitian, like Gaius, renamed September Germanicus when he took that name after his own German victories: *post autem duos triumphos Germanici cognomine assumpto Septembrem mensem et Octobrem ex appellationibus suis Germanicum Domitianumque transnominavit, quod altero suscepisset imperium, altero natus esset* (Suet. *Dom.*13.3).

permanently fixed in the calendar, evidently because Julius and Augustus became *divi*. For Gaius to insert his father into line after them (September had no special association with Germanicus) was a radical suggestion that Germanicus too was a god.[21] This change apparently never became established, for if it had, Claudius would surely have retained it since he too used his brother to validate his credentials. Months named after Gaius' family (e.g., Drusilla, Nero) did survive in Egypt for some time (Scott 1931a, 221–36).

post haec: Assuming that this temporal expression is accurate (never certain), the change of month name dates to the very beginning of Gaius' reign since the next subject is Antonia, who died on May 1, A.D. 37 (*Docs.* no. 31, p. 28), about five weeks after Gaius became emperor.

Antoniae aviae, quidquid umquam Livia Augusta honorum cepisset uno senatus consulto congessit: During her lifetime Livia had the privileges of a Vestal and became Augusta and a priestess of *divus Augustus* at her husband's death (Suet. *Aug.* 101.2; Dio 49.38.1, 55.2.5, 56.46.1–2; Tac. *Ann.* 1.8.1, 4.16.64). These are the honors that Antonia received from Gaius (Dio 59.3.4). But in his *Life of Claudius* Suetonius writes that she refused the title Augusta from Gaius and that it was Claudius who rewarded her with it (*cognomen Augustae ab viva resusantum,* Suet. *Cl.* 11.2; also Dio 60.5.1). It is true that she is merely Antonia in the *Fasti Ostienses* that record her death (Docs. no. 31, p. 28), but she is *Antonia Augusta* when sacrifices were made to her on her birthday in 38 and 39 (*Docs.* no. 3, 8, pp. 10, 13; Charlesworth 1933b, 108–9). Gaius was clearly responsible for the honorific title, but because Claudius annulled his *acta* (Suet. *Cl.* 11.3), he had to reaffirm it and when he did so he took the credit for himself. For Gaius' alleged lack of respect for her, see 23.2, 24.1, 29.1. For other actions that Claudius had to reaffirm see on the return of Commagene to Antiochus (16.3) and notes 27 and 28.

Claudium, equitem R. ad id tempus: Claudius never entered the *cursus honorum* and so remained an *eques* (15.1). His only attested public exposures were at the games he and Germanicus gave in honor of their father Drusus in A.D. 6 (Dio 55.27.3), a few priesthoods (Suet. *Cl.* 4.7, 6.2; Tac. *Ann.* 1.54.1), and as an escort of Germanicus' ashes when they were returned from Syria (Tac. *Ann.* 3.2.3). Later the knights used him as their emissary to Gaius (Suet. *Cl.* 6.1; Dio 59.6.6).

---

[21] *Mensis Germanicus* may have been part of an aborted attempt to deify him. The *divus* with the star on his forehead on the Ravenna relief has been identified as Germanicus. It is dated to the reign of Claudius (Jucker 1976, 237–67; Pollini 121).

collegam sibi in consulatu assumpsit: Claudius was 46 when he finally became consul and senator at the same time in A.D. 37 (καὶ ὑπάτευσεν ἅμα καὶ
ἐβούλευσεν, Dio 59.6.6; for this suffect consulship, 17.1).

fratrem: Tiberius Gemellus is *frater* again at 23.3 and 29.1 when his death is
described. Since he and Gaius were both "grandsons" of the emperor Tiberius (on
14.1) and enjoyed the same relationship with the head of the family, they were
brothers. But *frater* could also mean *frater patruelis,* cousin on the father's side;
they were second cousins by blood. The irony of designating their relationship as
brother is intentional: τὸν γένει μὲν ἀνεψιὸν εὐνοίᾳ δὲ ἀδελφόν (Philo *Leg.* 26)
and τὸν ἀδελφὸν ἢ καὶ τὸν υἱὸν (Dio 59.8.2).

Tiberium die virilis togae adoptavit: Cf. Dio 59.3.1, 8.1–2; Philo *Leg.* 26–
27. The adoption may not have been a legal one, either *adoptio* or *adrogatio.*[22]
Two posthumous inscriptions call Gemellus the son of Drusus, his natural father.
His cremation marker found near the Mausoleum of Augustus reads *Ti. Caesar
Drusi Caesaris f. hic situs est* (*Docs.* no. 88, p. 42); he was also *Drusi f.* when his
replacement as an Arval Brother was named on May 24, A.D. 38 (*Docs.* no. 3,
p.11). Adoption effected a permanent change, including a change of name, and so
if this one took place, it was reversed after Gemellus' death (23.3, 29.1), an action otherwise unattested in antiquity (Buckland 720). It is possible, if unlikely,
that Gaius did take the extra-legal option of reversing the adoption because he
wanted to obliterate all traces of their relationship (Willrich, 289; Smallwood
1961, at *Leg.* 27). But it was in the interest of an emperor to appear to obey the
law, and if he did want to cover over his own complicity in murder, erasing a
publicly acknowledged adoption could only call attention to the conflict between
them. According to Philo, Gaius said that the youth was still in need of a
guardian, a teacher and a tutor and that he would be all these and a father to him
as well (ἐμαυτὸν μὲν ἤδη γράφω πατέρα, υἱὸν δὲ ἐκεῖνον (*Leg.* 27). It seems a

---

22 Gemellus' status was ambiguous for either of the two forms of adoption. *Adrogatio* was for a
man *sui iuris,* no longer under his father's jurisdiction; Gemellus' *pater familias* Tiberius was
indeed dead, but he was still a minor until he received the *toga virilis* from Gaius. Was its bestowal
meant to make him eligible for this form of adoption? *Adoptio,* on the other hand, was for a man
still subject to *patria potestas* and was accomplished by "buying" a son from his father. From what
adult male relative would Gemellus have been transferred to Gaius? From Claudius perhaps?
Adrogatio required the approval of representatives of the *comitia curiata; adoptio* was more private
(Jolowicz and Nicholas, 119–20). Here the adoption is reported in connection with the introduction of Gemellus into public life and appears to be a public act; but according to Philo it seems to
have been private. He writes that Gaius promised to be Gemellus' guardian in the presense of τούς
ἐν τέλει (*Leg.* 26), presumably his *consilium* although possibly the magistrates.

kind of promise to act *in loco parentis*.[23] By taking him under his protection and providing for his future (naming him *princeps iuventutis,* below), he probably accomplished all he needed. Gemellus here between Claudius (above) and Gaius' sisters (15.3) shows that Suetonius thought that Gaius' treatment of him served a similar function in strengthening the dynasty.

appellavitque principem iuventutis: Cf. Dio 59.8.1. *Princeps iuventutis,* leader of the *equites* of military age, came to designate crown prince status after Augustus gave it to his adoptive sons Gaius and Lucius, also on the occasion of the *toga virilis* (*RG* 14; also Dio 55.9.9–10; Tac. *Ann.* 1.3.2; *EJ* nos. 61, 65, 66, 67, 75, pp. 66, 70 for inscriptions and coins). The future emperor Nero also received the title along with the adult toga in A.D. 51 at the age of 14 (Tac. *Ann.* 12.41.1; *Docs.* no. 14, p. 16; no.100, p. 44; no.104, p. 45). For Germanicus (Ov. *Pont.* 2.5.41; *Tr.* 2.167) and Drusus the Younger and for Nero and Drusus, the sons of Germanicus (for whom the evidence is inferential), the publicity was less. There is no epigraphic confirmation for Gemellus as *princeps iuventutis* and the title does not appear on his tombstone. It was not a legally ratified designation (like adoption) that needed to be undone if plans changed. Tiberius Gemellus was also honored as an Arval Brother (*Docs.* no. 3, p. 11).

15.3 *de sororibus auctor fuit, ut omnibus sacrimentis adicerentur:* Gaius was eager to call attention to his sisters. He gave them the privileges of Vestals and the right to sit with him at the circus games and included them in official prayers and oaths (Dio 59.3.4, 9.2). They were not, however, included in the first oaths taken to him in the provinces (*Docs.* nos. 32, 33, pp. 28, 29). There was an interval before this formula reached the hinterlands. The three were featured on a sestertius of A.D. 37–38 as the personifications of *securitas, concordia and fortuna* (7) and were probably named in a *sacrificium* on January 12 (?) 38 (*Docs.* no. 2, p. 10, as restored on the basis of this passage and Dio 59.9.2; Mommsen 1884, 154–58), but not later in the reign (see on 24.3). Prayers for "the emperor and his family" were routine (*tibi domuique tuae,* Suet. *Aug.* 58.2; Γαίωι Καίσαρι Σεβαστῶι καὶ τῶι σύμπαντι οἴκωι αὐτοῦ, *Docs.* no. 33, p. 29), but naming family members was not. Tiberius objected to the inclusion of Nero and Drusus in the January vows in 24 (Tac. *Ann.* 4.17.1; Suet. *Tib.* 54.1). It evidently suggested succession.

---

[23] Philo writes that Gaius wanted to adopt Gemellus in order to have *patria potestas* over him, both the right to control his wealth and the power of life and death (*Leg.* 28). But the inheritance had already been appropriated (14.1), and Gemellus' family burial (on 23.3) was incompatible with the exercise of *patria potestas.*

neque me liberosque meos cariores habebo quam Gaium habeo et sorores eius: Cf.*<neque me>* *neq[u]e liberos meos eius salute cariores habebo* (*Docs.* no. 32, p. 28, May 11, A.D. 37). The future verb is usual. Dio records the oath verbatim: ὅτι καὶ σφῶν αὐτῶν καὶ τῶν τέκνων καὶ ἐκεῖνον καὶ τὰς ἀδελφὰς αὐτοῦ προτιμήσουσιν, ὤμοσαν (59.9.2).

item relationibus consulum: quod bonum felixque sit C. Caesari sororibusque eius: Proposals brought before the senate by the consuls were routinely prefaced with a salute to the emperor (Talbert 236). Cf. *"Quod bonum...faustumque sit tibi domuique tuae, Caesar Auguste!"* (Suet. *Aug.* 58.2). The language was standard—except for the sisters.

Gaius began by implementing a general amnesty. The mechanism was the abolition of the *crimen maiestatis,* the treason law that had been extended to include defamation, written or spoken, of the emperor and his family (Bauman 205). Its growth under Tiberius is depicted (by Tacitus especially) as an immense source of mischief since it could be used in many different situations and conveniently added to other charges. It allowed the admission of evidence from the defendant's own slaves, and Gaius abolished it as a conciliatory gesture (τά τε τῆς ἀσεβείας ἐγκλήματα παύσας, Dio 59.4.3; τά τε ἐγκλήματα τῆς ἀσεβείας...κατέλυσε, Dio 59.6.2). He is credited with three self-congratulatory statements about his generous and forgiving nature: He said that he was destroying evidence about the persecution of his family so that none of the persons involved ever need fear him, that he did not fear plots against his life since no one had any reason to hate him (15.4) and finally that freedom of speech would serve his own reign well (16.1). In the context of the reputation that he left behind these words are ironic even though they may well have originated in a point of view that approved of Gaius, perhaps the product of his own establishment. See on the death of Tiberius (12.3), on Artabanus (14.3) and on his reverence toward the bones of Agrippina and Nero (15.1) for what may be traces of his own propaganda beneath the otherwise negative tradition. It is only logical that such existed. There is brief witness of it in Gaetulicus' flattery (8.1–2).

15.4 *Pari popularitate damnatos relegatosque restituit:* Political measures produced the same positive effect as did *pietas* toward his family (15.1–3). Gaius restored exiles, some friends of his family (Dio 59.3.6) but others associates of Sejanus,[24] in order to defuse potential opposition (Meise 117). Some of these same persons were executed in A.D. 39 when he reversed his policy (28; Dio 59.13.2).

---

24 One of these last was P. Pomponius Secundus (*PIR[1]* P. 563; Dio 59.6.2), whose release came six or seven years after he had been arrested for harboring a fugitive member of Sejanus' circle in A.D. 31 (Tac. *Ann.* 5.8.2). He held no particular importance for the story of Gaius' reign but was probably chosen as an example because he had command of the Army of Upper Germany under Claudius (Pliny *Ep.* 3.5.3). Dio mistook Publius for his brother Q. Pomponius Secundus (*PIR[1]* P. 564), who was *consul ordinarius* with Gaius in A.D. 41 (17.1) and in office when Gaius was killed. He may also have confused him with a senator involved in an aborted conspiracy (59.26.4; on 16.4).

criminum, si quae residua ex priore tempore manebant, omnium gratiam fecit: Gratiam fecit = "he overlooked." The only cases known to be outstanding from the time of Tiberius were those against Albucilla (*PIR²* A. 487) and some of her friends who had been accused of treason just before Tiberius died. Notable survivors of the group were C. Vibius Marsus (*PIR¹* V. 388), once companion to Germanicus and later *legatus* in Syria under Claudius, and Cn. Domitius Ahenobarbus (*PIR²* D. 127), the first husband of Agrippina the Younger and the father of the emperor Nero (on 24.1); he survived because of the change of regime (*mutatione temporum*, Suet. *Ner.* 5.2; Tac. *Ann.* 6.47–8; Dio. 58.27.1–28.1; Bauman 130–34, 204–5).

commentarios ad matris fratrumque suorum causas pertinentis: These were the official documents concerning the charges against his mother and brothers. For his brother Nero's trial (*causa*), see Pliny *HN* 8.145; also on 7 and 10.1.

ne cui postmodum delatori aut testi maneret ullus metus: An overt statement of the conciliatory motive behind the clemency. Suetonius paraphrases what Dio records more fully: "I did this so that, even if someday I wish to bear malice toward someone on account of my mother and brothers, I will not be able to punish him" (τοῦτ' ἐποίησα ἵνα μηδ' ἂν πάνυ ἐθελήσω ποτὲ διά τε τὴν μητέρα καὶ διὰ τοὺς ἀδελφοὺς μνησικακῆσαί τινι, δυνηθῶ αὐτὸν τιμωρήσασθαι, 59.6.3). Dio adds that Gaius was praised for saying this and that it was assumed that he was telling the truth because of the innocence of youth (59.6.4).

convectos in forum, et ante clare obtestatus deos neque legisse neque attigisse quicquam, concremavit: The public display symbolized the abolition of the *lex maiestatis*. But he only pretended to burn the papers or burned copies instead (Dio 59.4.3, 6.3). They reappeared in A.D. 39 (30.2; Dio 59.10.8, 16.3), and Claudius finally got rid of them (Dio 60.4.5), one of the many things he did to put the memory of Gaius to rest (τὰ μὲν δὴ οὖν ὑπό τε τοῦ Γαΐου καὶ ὑφ' ἑτέρων δι' ἐκεῖνον οὐκ ὀρθῶς γενόμενα ἀνέτρεψε, Dio 60.5.1; for the list, 60.1–8.3).

libellum de salute sua oblatum non recepit contendens nihil sibi admissum cur cuiquam invisus esset, negavitque se delatoribus aures habere: "Claiming that there was no reason for anyone to hate him, he would not listen to informants," presented as Gaius' own words. When he refused to accept the accusatory document, he refused to indict (for other *libelli*, 49.3). This may show that there was an otherwise unknown plot against him early in his reign (Meise 115, n. 147). Aurelius Victor illustrated the "good" early period of his reign with this detail and reports a conspiracy: *delataque coniuratione* (*Caes.* 3.8). But Gaius is continually drawn into parallels with Julius Caesar, who refused a *libellus* the day he was killed (Suet. *Jul.* 81.4).

Chapter 16, a rubric of "good government," is a dense collection of Gaius' good actions, most but not all of which took place near the beginning of his reign. A number of these are also found together at Dio 59.9.4–6, already gathered perhaps by a common source. Suetonius makes Gaius responsible for everything that happened on his watch, just as he does with all of the emperors. This does not necessarily mean that Gaius initiated these measures himself. The relationship between an emperor and his advisors is uncertain as is the very concept of government for the early Empire, and the question of who or what process was ultimately responsible for decisions is not limited to the reign of Gaius. It may have been Macro (12.2) who gave Gaius the benefit of his political experience during the first year (on 15.4; for his end, 26.1). Many of these measures were a response to unpopular measures of Tiberius, from whom Gaius found it desirable to separate himself. He often reverted to Augustan precedent.

16.1 *spintrias monstrosarum libidinum...urbe submovit:* The *spintriae* (*spintria* = σφίγκτης or σφίκτης = *cinaedus,* catamite) were a particular group of sodomites associated with Tiberius in his retreat on Capreae, their name, at least, a recent import: *tuncque primum ignota antea vocabula reperta sunt sellariorum et spintriarum,* Tac. *Ann.* 6.1.2). It first appears in Latin in mid-century (Petron. *Sat.* 113). The emperor Vitellius was nicknamed "Spintria" because he spent time on Capreae with Tiberius when he was young (Suet. *Vit.* 3.2). Gaius, who had been there too, was taking pains to separate himself from Tiberius whose reputation as an aged pervert was obviously well-lodged in contemporary perception (Tac. *Ann.* 6.1.2; Dio 58.22.1–3; in detail: Suet. *Tib.* 42–44);[25] if it had not been, Gaius would not have made an issue of throwing out the *spintriae. Urbe* transfers them from Capreae to Rome.

aegre ne profundo mergeret exoratus: He made himself appear a defender of antique virtue, especially if this is a reference to the *poena cullei* (Maurer), the primitive punishment in which the guilty person was sewn into a sack with an ape, a snake, a dog and a cock and thrown into the sea. For the "sack" as a threat, Suet. *Ner.* 45.2.

These authors had been proscribed during the reign of Tiberius under the provisions of the *crimen maiestatis.* Gaius' suspension of this law (15.4) brought about the relaxation of censorship. The work of these three continued in circulation; Suetonius cites two of them as a source (*Aug.* 35.2; *Vit.* 2.1).

---

25 Erotic tokens that can be dated to Tiberius' reign may give his reputation some basis (Buttrey 52–63).

Titi Labieni: *PIR*[2] L. 19. Of the family of Julius Caesar's assassin with the same name and hence an easy object of imperial suspicion, Labienus was an orator during the reign of Augustus. His sharp tongue gave him the punning nickname "Rabienus." When his histories were burned, he was supposed to have buried himself alive in the family tomb (Sen. *Controv.* 10. *praef.* 4–8). The Elder Seneca wrote that Labienus had predicted that much of his work would be read after he was dead (*Memini aliquando, cum recitaret* [Labienus] *historiam, magnam partem illum libri convolvisse et dixisse: haec quae transeo post mortem meam legentur, Controv.* 10. *praef.* 8). Seneca could not have expressed himself so freely unless censorship had indeed been relaxed.

Cordi Cremuti: Cremutius Cordus (A. Cremutius Cordus, *PIR*[2] C. 1565) wrote his histories under Augustus, was accused by allies of Sejanus in A.D. 25 and starved himself to death (Tac. *Ann.* 4.34–35.4; Dio 57.24.2–4; Sen. *Dial.* 6.1.2, 22.4–7). He had praised the assassins of Julius Caesar (*laudatoque M. Bruto C. Cassium Romanorum ultimum dixisset,* Tac. *Ann.* 4.34.1; also Suet. *Tib.* 61.3), and this implied censure for Caesar and hence for the principate itself (Bauman 101–2). His writings were burned (Tac. *Ann.* 4.35.4; Dio 57.24.4; Sen. *Controv.* 10. *praef.* 7–8), essentially a symbolic act, because not every copy could be destroyed. His daughter hid some (Tac. *Ann.* 4.35.4; Sen. *Dial.* 6.1.5; Dio 57.24.4). Tacitus composed a brave speech for his self-defense. As a source for Suetonius, *Aug.* 35.2.

Cassi Severi: *PIR*[2] C. 522. Like Labienus, Cassius Severus was an orator under Augustus with a reputation as a vitriolic speaker *plus bilis...quam sanguinis* (Tac. *Dial.* 26.4, also 19.1; Sen. *Controv.* 3 *praef.* 1–18). His attacks on distinguished persons provided an excuse to extend the charge of *maiestas* to include verbal abuse (probably in A.D. 8, Tac. *Ann.* 1.72.3; Bauman 28–30; cf. Dio 56.27.1; Suet. *Aug.* 55). After twenty-five years of exile and another trial *in absentia* he died in poverty (Tac. *Ann.* 4.21.3; *Rel.* Reiff. no. 69, p. 87). Suetonius used his writing (*Vit.* 2.1).

scripta senatus consultis abolita requiri et esse in manibus lectitarique permisit, quando maxime sua interesset ut facta quaeque posteris tradantur: Another ingenuous implicitly ironic statement like those in 15.4. In the event, it was not at all to the advantage of Gaius' reputation (*sua interesset*) that the account of his reign was handed down to posterity.

rationes imperii ab Augusto proponi solitas sed a Tiberio intermissas publicavit: More openness. The *rationes* were the accounts of public funds that had not been published while Tiberius was absent from the city. Augustus made public detailed accounts on two known occasions, once when he was ill in 23 B.C. (Suet. *Aug.* 28.1; Dio 53.30.1–2) and then again in his will (Suet. *Aug.* 101.4; Tac. *Ann.* 1.11.4; Dio 56.33.2; Brunt 1966, 88). *Solitas* may be Suetonius' generalization from these two instances, although Dio implies that it was a routine practice interrupted by Tiberius and resumed by Gaius (Dio 59.9.4). No particular occasion is noted here.

With these next items Suetonius runs through the social orders from top to bottom, an organizational principle that he chooses elsewhere (26.2–5, 30.2). First the senate:

16.2 *magistratibus liberam iuris dictionem et sine sui appellatione concessit: Tribunicia potestas* gave the emperor permanent possession of the right to hear appeals and replaced the earlier *provocatio ad populum* (Dio. 51.19.6–7; Jones 1953, 918–30; 1954, 485–88). Augustus delegated the privilege to surrogates (Suet. *Aug.* 33.3); Tiberius did hear appeals (Dio 59.8.5; Tac. *Ann.* 3.18.1, 70.3) and was perceived as inhibiting the independent action of the senatorial court (Tac. *Ann.* 1.75.1). This gesture for the benefit of the senate attempted to set Gaius apart from Tiberius, but he interfered in their cases nonetheless (53.2; Dio 59.18.2).

Next the knights: The first emperors found it difficult to stabilize a firm roll of *equites Romani* because the definition of the order was in transition. By the second century B.C. *eques Romanus* had ceased to connote military responsibility and had become a mark of status correspondent to wealth. Individual worth could change, however, and as more men met the minimum property qualification of 400,000 sesterces, a sure list of *equites* (those registered in the six *turmae* of the eighteen centuries) was difficult to determine, especially when the censorship was in disarray at the end of the Republic. Besides, there were always vacancies to be filled since membership was not inherited but had to be reestablished with each generation. A further difficulty was the apparent existence of an elite group within the larger group, the *equites equo publico,* those entitled to the "public horse," a relic of their obsolete military function. Tiberius defined the *equites* broadly, by three generations of free birth, the property qualification and entitlement to sit in the first fourteen rows of the theater (Pliny *HN* 35.32); perhaps he realized that the retention of the awkward and old-fashioned formal structure of the "public horse" was impossible in the face of the growing number of men who could meet the financial requirement. Although Gaius revived the institution (below), it had disappeared completely by the end of the century when an *eques* was defined by the census alone (Wiseman 1970, 78–82).

equites R. severe curioseque nec sine moderatione recognovit: Gaius held a formal inspection (*recognitio*) of the equestrian order in the form of a parade (*transvectio*), a kind of public roll call at which it was made clear who was on the list and who was not. In doing this he again deserted the practice of Tiberius and followed the lead of Augustus, who had tried to bring order to the rolls by reviving the old custom of the review on horseback (*post longam intercapedinem reducto more,* Suet. *Aug.* 38.3), revised the list often and called the financially qualified candidates to task for their behavior (below; Suet. *Aug.* 37, 38.3–39; perhaps = Dio 54.26.8–9; Jones 1951; also Dio 55.31.2). Tiberius, on the other hand, did not fill the vacancies (Suet. *Tib.* 41), and so Gaius consequently found their numbers low (Dio 59.9.5) and enrolled the foremost men from all over the Empire. Claudius continued the *recognitio* (Suet. *Cl.* 15.1, 16.1–2).

palam adempto equo quibus aut probri aliquid aut ignominiae inesset: It was the conferring of the horse that the emperors appear to have controlled at the *recognitiones* (Wiseman 1970, 81; Crook 64). Augustus did not compel those whose membership was challenged literally to dismount when they rode by as had been the former practice (*quod fieri solebat,* Suet. *Aug.* 38.2), but Gaius seems to have (*palam adempto equo*). The option of judging character gave the emperor control over access to the elite list (Suet. *Aug.* 39).

eorum qui minore culpa tenerentur nominibus modo in recitatione praeteritis: Gaius could chastise a knight without removing his name from the census by passing over his name in silence when the names of others were read. Augustus also had a range of punishments down to a rather similar mild one: *lenissimum genus admonitionis fuit traditio coram pugillarium, quos taciti et ibidem statim legerent* (Suet. *Aug.* 39). Claudius was soft (Suet. *Cl.* 16.1–2).

Finally the populace at large: Dio was less certain than Suetonius that appealing to the masses was a good idea. In a parallel passage he writes that returning elections to the people (16.2), doing away with an unpopular tax (16.3) and lavishing gifts (18.2) "delighted the common people but distressed thoughtful persons" (τῷ μὲν φαύλῳ ἐχαρίσατο, τοὺς δ' ἔμφρονας ἐλύπησε, 59.9.7). Suetonius was probably on his own when he reevaluated these actions; he was hard-pressed to fill out the rubrics he devoted to the laudable part of Gaius' career (on 22.1). The measures that pandered most obviously to public appeal anticipate the strategy that was left to him after he broke openly with the senate (30.2; also 48.2, 49.1; Momigliano 1932b, 215), and it was not a far reach from the remission of taxes to throwing money to the crowd (37.1).

ut levior labor iudicantibus foret, ad quattuor prioris quintam decuriam addidit: There were three *decuriae,* rolls of potential jurors, when Julius Caesar abolished the one whose members were not of the two upper orders (Suet. *Jul.* 41.2; Dio 43.25.1). Three were present again under Augustus, presumably all *equites,* and he added a fourth of less status to furnish manpower for less important juries (Suet. *Aug.* 32.3). Gaius added the fifth mentioned here, also presumably of less status (confusedly Pliny *HN* 33.30–31, 33; Jones 1955, 9–21, 41–42; Sherwin-White 1985, 129, 308 on Pliny *Ep.* 1.19.2, 4.29.1). More *decuriae* were popular because jury duty was considered onerous (Suet. *Aug.*

32.3, *Cl.* 15.1; Pliny *HN* 29.18). Jurors petitioned Galba unsuccessfully for a sixth to lighten their load (Suet. *Gal.* 14.3).

temptavit et comitiorum more revocato suffragia populo reddere: This (yet another) reversal of Tiberian policy is referred to A.D. 38 (Dio 59.9.6). In 14 Tiberius had transferred to the senate the right to select magistrates, but the formality of a vote in the popular assembly (*comitia*) was retained (Tac. *Ann.* 1.15.1; Dio 58.20.3–4, 59.9.6; Vell. 2.124.3; Jones 1955, 46–47; Syme 1958, 756–59). What Gaius altered was apparently the senators' right to make binding nominations, but the power that he restored to the people was not very substantial since the emperor's influential nominations remained (Balsdon 1934a, 152; Suet. *Jul.* 41.2; *Aug.* 56.1; Tac. *Ann.* 1.81; on the transition from imperial suasion to overt appointment, Levick 1967, 207–30). *Temptavit* implies what Dio explains, that Gaius soon (A.D. 39) removed this right from the popular assembly because the people failed to exercise their franchise in the meaningless elections whose outcomes had been prearranged in private deals (59.20.4–5).

16.3 ***legata ex testamento Tiberi quamquam abolito...cum fide ac sine calumnia repraesentata persolvit:*** Since Tiberius' will had been invalidated (*testamento...abolito*) in order to exclude Tiberius Gemellus from the succession (14.1), Gaius displayed generosity when he nonetheless fulfilled its provisions. But in a sense he revalidated the will when he performed this duty of a legal heir. Tiberius' bequests were 1000 sesterces apiece to the praetorian guard, 500 to the city guard, 300 to the night watch and the legionaries, and in addition, a total of 45 million to the people at large. Gaius gave each of the praetorians an additional 1000 of his own (Dio 59.2.1–3; Suet. *Tib.* 76). A sestertius that commemorated his address to them may have been distributed as part of this payment (*RIC*[2] Gaius no. 32, p. 110; Sutherland 1951, 109, 114; Balsdon 1934a, 34).[26] Although Claudius was the first to buy his office (15,000 to each praetorian, Suet. *Cl.* 10.4; 20,000 to each, Jos. *AJ* 19.247), Gaius' bonus was a milestone in the development of the payoff (cf. Germanicus with the legions in A.D. 14, on 1.1).

sed et Iuliae Augustae, quod Tiberius suppresserat: This too put Gaius into line with the imperial family. Tiberius' refusal to pay Livia's bequests (Tac. *Ann.* 5.1.4; also Suet. *Tib.* 51.2; *Gal.* 5.2; Dio 58.2.3[a]) was consistent with his shunning of personality cults in general (see on 6.2 for his reaction to

---

26 This coin, the "*adlocutio* sestertius," lacks the usual *S. C.* of senatorial sanction, an omission that is inconsistent with Gaius' cooperative approach to the senate at this early point but consistent with his dependence on the praetorians. It was struck again in A.D. 39 and 40 (*RIC*[2] Gaius nos. 40, 48, p. 111).

Germanicus' popularity). Only here does Suetonius call her Julia Augusta, the name she received after the death of Augustus. Her legal name is appropriate in this context of her will. Combined with the *congiaria* (17.2), it was an expensive summer for the young emperor.

ducentesimam auctionum Italiae remisit: *Ducentesimam:* sc. *partem* (1/200, i.e., 1/2 of 1%). The abolition of this tax on public sales of property (A.D. 38, Dio 59.9.6) was as welcome as a tax reduction always is, and Gaius publicized it widely on a coin of very small denomination, a *quadrans* with a *pilleus* (liberty cap) on the obverse and on the reverse *RCC* (*ducentesima remissa; CC* = 200; *RIC*² Gaius no. 52, p. 111; Sutherland 1951, 120 and n. 1). If the abolition of the tax applied only to Italy (*Italiae*), it is clear whom it was intended to please, and it was not so costly as it would have been if it had been applied generally throughout the Empire. It backfired in the end, however, when a variety of new taxes designed to replace it proved extremely unpopular (40–41.1). Augustus had established the *aerarium militare* to finance the settlement of his discharged veterans in A.D. 6 (Aug. *RG* 17; Suet. *Aug.* 49.2; Dio 55.25.2–6). Originally funded by gifts from Augustus himself and by a 5% death tax, a 1% (*centesima*) sales tax came to be its chief resource (Tac. *Ann.* 1.78.2). In 17 Tiberius halved it because of the windfall of revenues from Cappadocia which became a taxable province at that time (1.2; Tac. *Ann.* 2.42.4).[27]

multis incendiorum damna supplevit: Disaster presented the emperor with an opportunity for popular relief measures (Veyne 1990, 366; for Gaius' regret that he had too few, 31). Gaius joined the soldiers in putting out a fire and helped those who had suffered loss (Dio 59.9.4). As often, Suetonius has a generalizing plural. This was presumably a fire that occurred on October 21, A.D. 38, in the "Aemiliana" quarter of Rome (*XII K. Nov. Aemiliana arser[unt]*, *Docs.* no 31, p. 28 = *Fasti Ostienses*) where there were fires under Claudius and Nero also (Suet. *Cl.* 18; Tac. *Ann.* 14.40.2). It was apparently a poor district located at the southern end of the Campus Martius (*PA* 1; Varro *Rust.* 3.2; *RE* 1:541). For other

---

[27] The *quadrantes* were issued between March 18, A.D. 39, and Gaius' death, and this caused Willrich (424 and n. 4) to think that Dio was wrong in assigning the tax reduction to 38. The fact that Dio groups it with other popular measures does make his dating suspect, and he is definitely in error when he writes that it was a 1% tax that Gaius remitted (59.9.6). He may have confused himself from his own report that Tiberius had raised the tax from .05% to 1% again in A.D. 31 (Dio 58.16.2). If there was an increase in 31, it was lowered to .05% either by him or by Gaius before it was rescinded completely. There is no evidence for this; perhaps Dio made a mistake about Tiberius' increase in the first place. See note 28 for a way that Dio may have solved problems. Barrett (1989, 249–50) argues that RCC did not necessarily stand for *ducentesima remissa*. For the idea that *libertas* (the liberty cap) equated with the emperor's *liberalitas*, Stylow 290.

emperors fighting fires, Tac. *Ann.* 6.45.1; Vell. 2.130.2; Suet. *Cl.* 18; *Ves.* 17; *Tit.* 8.4; *Dom.* 5.

The return of Commagene to Antiochus (Antiochus IV = C. Julius Antiochus, *PIR²* I. 149), the reversal of its annexation as a province, has been taken as an example of Gaius' reversion to the policy of Antony (and perhaps Germanicus), the policy of controlling territory through friendly kings who were loyal to the emperor at Rome as their personal overlord (Willrich 299, 302; Momigliano 1932b, 220–21; Garzetti 1975, 85). Apart from referring to Antiochus as though he were one of many (*ut Antiocho Commageno*), Suetonius shows no interest in other settlements such as those for the three sons of the Thracian Cotys VIII (*PIR²* C. 1554), who received Thrace and kingdoms in Asia Minor (Dio 59.12.2); they had grown up in Rome while Thrace was under Roman regency (Tac. *Ann.* 2.67.2; *Docs.* no. 401, p. 120). Gaius gave Ituraea to Sohaemus, Pontus to Polemon II (Dio 59.12.2; Barrett 1977) and the Tetrarchies in Asia Minor to "Herod" Agrippa (M. Julius Agrippa, *PIR²* I. 131; Dio 59.8.2; Jos. *AJ* 18.237).

ac si quibus regna restituit...ut Antiocho Commageno: Commagene was northern Syria, a separate kingdom after 162 B.C. The adjective is necessary to distinguish the Antiochi who ruled there from the earlier Seleucid Antiochi. In A.D. 18, soon after the death of King Antiochus III (*PIR²* A. 741; Tac. *Ann.* 2.42.5; Jos. *AJ* 18.53), Commagene became a Roman province (Tac. *Ann.* 2.56.4) not long after Cappadocia (1.2). In 37 Gaius returned it to client kingdom status by restoring Antiochus' son as Antiochus IV, the Antiochus named here. His Roman name, Gaius Julius Antiochus, probably came from forebears who got it from Augustus (Braund 42–43, 50, n. 25). Gaius also gave him the coastal region of Cilicia which had been detached from Commagene by Tiberius (Tac. *Ann.* 2.58.1) and with that access to the sea (Dio 59.8.2). But Dio reports that at some later point Gaius took his kingdom away and that Claudius put him back on his throne in 41 (60.8.1). Gaius' *acta* were annulled (Suet. *Cl.* 11.3; Dio 60.4.1), and so Claudius gave Antiochus his kingdom a second time;[28] in fact, he maintained all of Gaius' foreign arrangements. There is no direct evidence that Antiochus spent the years between 18 and 37 in Rome, but it is probable that he did. He is depicted along with Herod Agrippa as an intimate, the two of them his "tyrant teachers," (ὥσπερ τινὰς τυραννοδιδασκάλους, Dio 59.24.1). He ruled as a

---

[28] Finding the appointment of Antiochus twice in his sources, Dio must have invented an explanation by assuming that Gaius took Antiochus' kingdom away (Barrett 1990, 285). He may have solved some other apparent discrepancies by a similar tactic (see on Julia Claudilla,12.2; the honors to Antonia, 15.2; the *ducentesima*, 16.3; the extra day for the Saturnalia, 17.2, and note 27). Claudius too had a good relationship with Antiochus and was happy to claim credit for this benefaction, but it was Gaius who first gave it back to him: the city of Germaniceia Caesarea dated its coinage from A.D. 38, and so was named after Gaius, not Claudius (Jones 1971, 264; for a summary of numismatic confirmation, Magie 1367–68, n. 49). For another possible confusion of its removal and restoration, Jos. *AJ* 19.276.

highly successful client king until 72 (*servientium regum ditissimus,* Tac. *Hist.* 2.81.1; also Jos. *BJ* 7.228–43).

adiecit et fructum omnem vectigaliorum et reditum medii temporis: *Vectigaliorum* also at Suet. *Aug.* 101.4 (but *vectigalium* at 38.1 and *Tib.* 49.2). *Vectigalia* were generally taxes on services as opposed to general tributary taxes (40–41.1), although in reference to provinces they might refer to all kinds (Brunt 1990, 426). But *reditum* refers to revenue in general, and so *vectigal* for special taxes seems correct here. Suetonius implies that Antiochus was only one of a number (*ut Antiocho Commageno*) to whom Gaius remitted everything that had been collected during the years when his country had been a Roman province, but Commagene was the only state eligible for this largesse except perhaps the Tetrarchy of Phillip, which had been annexed to Syria from A.D. 33–34 until Herod Agrippa received it back (Willrich 299, n.3). Only Suetonius reports the refund.

sestertium milies confiscatum: Elliptical for *centena milia sestertium,* a thousand times a hundred thousand sesterces, 100,000,000, a generous round number.

Suetonius closes this chapter of miscellaneous benefactions with the honors voted for Gaius' *clementia* in A.D. 39 (Dio 59.16.10). But he makes them dependent on an act of clemency that Dio and Josephus refer to the conspiracies that threatened in his final months (Dio 59.26.4; Jos *AJ* 19.32–36). This rearrangement is clearly Suetonius' own. It is not without internal logic, however, as he moves from Gaius' generosity (16.3) to his generosity in combination with clemency and finally to the reward for clemency (16.4).

16.4 *quoque magis nullius non boni exempli fautor videretur:* *Quoque magis = quo magis* and *-que,* "and so that he might seem a greater advocate of every admirable model of behavior... " editorial comment by Suetonius.

mulieri libertinae octingenta donavit, quod excruciata gravissimis tormentis de scelere patroni reticuisset: This was a bright spot in an otherwise grim period. Dio names the *patron* as Pomponius (*PIR¹* P. 516) and says that his crime was a plot against Gaius in A.D. 40 and that he was betrayed by an unnamed friend (59.26.4). Pomponius may be an error derived from the (wrong) Pomponius who was recalled from exile in 37 (on 15.4 and note 24; Dio 59.6.2). Josephus identifies him as the senator Pompedius and his accuser as Timidius (*PIR¹* T. 158) and says that his specific crime was abusing Gaius (ὡς λοιδορίᾳ χρησάμενον, *AJ* 19.33). The freedwoman was as an actress Quintilia

(*PIR¹* Q. 29),[29] whom Gaius' assassin Cassius Chaerea (*PIR²* C. 488) was forced to torture against his will (for Chaerea's softheartedness, see on 40, 56.2). As Josephus tells it, the point of the story is Chaerea's increasingly intolerable position (*AJ* 19.32–6; Timpe 1960, 494–96). But a different inference, Gaius' unpredictability, is the point for Suetonius and Dio. Only Suetonius is interested in the amount of money involved. *Octingenta* (*sc. milia*) = 800 times a thousand = 800,000 sesterces.

quas ob res inter reliquos honores decretus est ei clipeus aureus: *Quas ob res* is made to provide a logical transition, but it is inaccurate, since the *clipeus aureus* was voted in A.D. 39 (Dio 59.16.10) and was obviously not given in recognition for his generosity to Quintilia in late 40 or early 41. A *clipeus* was a medallion shaped like a round shield and decorated with the bust of the emperor, a token of honor for famous men since the fifth century B.C. (Pliny *HN* 35.12–13). Augustus had been given a golden one inscribed with the imperial virtues instead of his likeness (*RG* 34). Germanicus was voted a golden one too (on 3.1), although Tiberius reduced it to the more usual bronze (Tac. *Ann.* 2.83.3).

quem quotannis certo die collegia sacerdotum in Capitolium ferrent, senatu prosequente nobilibusque pueris ac puellis carmine modulato laudes virtutum eius canentibus: This celebration was voted to Gaius directly after he attacked the senate in a speech at some point in A.D. 39 (30.2; for more on the date, see note 39). Frightened, the senate decreed annual sacrifices τῇ φιλανθρωπίᾳ (Dio 59.16.10), to his *clementia*.[30] A golden image of him was to be carried to the Capitol and hymns were to be sung in its honor by the noblest of the Roman youth (εἰκόνος τε αὐτοῦ χρυσῆς ἐς τὸ Καπιτώλιον ἀναγομένης καὶ ὕμνων ἐπ᾽ αὐτῇ διὰ τῶν εὐγενεστάτων παίδων ᾀδομένων), both on the anniversary of the speech and "in the days (?) pertaining to the Palatine" (ἐν ταῖς τῷ παλατίῳ προσηκούσαις, Dio 59.16.10). Dio's εἰκών is Suetonius' *imago clipeata* (Scott 1931b, 105). The second occasion for festivities that Dio gives is unclear; perhaps it is a reference to the *ludi Palatini* (on 54.2, 56.2, 57.4, 58.1), perhaps an unsolvable textual problem (Boissevain at 59.16.10). The vague *certo die* seems to indicate a date other than an obvious one like his birthday. Barrett suggests that it was September 21, the anniversary of the day when Gaius received the title *pater patriae* (on 19.2). The *collegia sacerdotum* were the four

---

[29] A freedwoman more stalwart than the nobly born male conspirators reappears in Epicharis (*PIR²* E. 72), who refused to betray the conspiracy against Nero in A.D. 65 (Tac. *Ann.* 15.51, 57).

[30] This recalls the temple to the *clementia* of Julius Caesar built in 43 B.C. (Weinstock 1971, 241). See on 22.3 for Gaius' temples and for the possibility that Dio's report of a temple for Gaius voted by the senate, was derived from the vote of the *clipeus*.

major priesthoods (*RG* 9.1). A chorus of boys and girls on state occasions was not unusual (cf. the *ludi saeculares* of Augustus; *EJ* no. 32, p. 60); such a group sang at the dedication of the temple of Augustus at the end of August (21; Dio. 59.7.1). *Modulus* = "musical," "harmonius."

decretum autem ut dies, quo cepisset imperium: *Autem* makes it clear that this vote for honors for Gaius' *dies imperii* was a second vote, distinct from the vote (*decretus est,* above = ἐψηφίσαντο, Dio 59.16.10) that established the procession to the Capitoline. Dio corroborates a second vote: *decretum [est]=* αὐτῷ ἔδωκαν (59.16.11).

Parilia vocaretur velut argumentum rursus conditae urbis: The holiday called Parilia on April 21, a spring agricultural festival of purification, came to be celebrated as the birthday of Rome (Cic. *Div.* 2.98 for the first mention in this sense; Wissowa 199–201). The senate's second decree attached it to Gaius' *dies imperii,* March 18 (14.1), so that the day he became emperor was counted a symbolic new beginning (*argumentum* = symbol; Weinstock 1971, 175, 184–86, 191). Julius Caesar had used the Parilia for his own glorification when on the preceding day (April 20) in 45 B.C. games were held in recognition of his final victory in the civil war (Dio 43.42.3). His military success was combined with the idea that he was a second founder of Rome. Gaius was voted an ovation "as though he had conquered some enemies" (ὡς καὶ πολεμίους τινὰς νενικηκότι, 59.16.11) at the time that the Parilia was moved.[31]

A rubric on consulships is standard (cf. Suet. *Cl.* 14; *Ner.* 14). Although it has been argued that Gaius' choices brought in a new group of men who had been adherents of his father, the "party of Germanicus" (Colin 394–416), continuity was really more the rule. The first consuls of his reign had been chosen by Tiberius in any case (Talbert 202–4), and among the later ones for whom Gaius was responsible, several had served Tiberius. Some continued their careers under Claudius. The most striking thing about his consular appointments is not who they were but how many they were and how frequently he himself held the office. Consuls suffect who relieved the ordinary consuls on July 1 of each year had been introduced shortly before Actium (Dio 48.35.2), but Augustus then reverted to the traditional two consuls each year until 5 B.C. when *suffecti* were reintroduced, and four consuls each year became the norm. After his first turn as a *suffectus* Gaius served as *ordinarius* three times in three years but only long enough to give his name to the year. He may have appointed multiple *suffecti* for the second half of A.D. 40 (17.1), and at some point he established a pool with enough names for at least four years with the specific year for service to be chosen by lot (Suet. *Cl.* 7). This gave him the opportunity to put a large number of men under

---

31 Barrett (1989, 71–72) argues that April 21, the date of the Parilia, was used as Gaius' *dies imperii* because an interval of time was needed between his acclamation on March 18 (on 13–14.1) and the passage of a law by the *comitia* granting him special powers. But Barrett's parallel examples are for Nero and after, the evidence for March 18 is strong (*Docs.* no. 3, p. 10), and Suetonius' *vocarentur* indicates that it was a different day, not April 21, that was called Parilia.

obligation to him, a rather desperate pitch for loyalty and further evidence of how very needy of support he was (cf. on 15.2–3 for his use of his family). Claudius followed Gaius' lead in giving short consulships in order to reward more men, and under the Flavians this practice became the rule (Gallivan 1979, 66; Talbert 21).

17.1 *consulatus quattuor gessit:* Four consulships in five calender years was unprecedented.

primum ex Kal. Iul. per duos menses: The *ordinarii* for A.D. 37 were Cn. Acerronius Proculus (*PIR²* A. 32) and C. Petronius Pontius Nigrinus (*PIR¹* P. 218). Gaius tactfully (under good advice?) permitted them to fill out their terms (Dio 59.6.5). He and Claudius relieved them on July 1 (on 15.2) and then yielded quickly to the previously designated *suffecti* on August 31, Gaius' birthday. Their two month terms are confirmed by the *Fasti Ostienses* (*Docs.* no. 31 p. 28; also Suet. *Cl.* 7). Dio says that they did not resign until September 12 (59.7.9; see note 32). The suffects that followed on September 1 were A. Caecina Paetus (*PIR²* C. 103) and C. Caninius Rebilus (*PIR²* C. 393; *Docs.* no. 31, p. 28). Caecina has been tenuously connected to Germanicus as the son (perhaps) of one of two Caecinae who served with him in Germany (Colin 403–4). But these two had already been chosen by Tiberius (τοῖς προαποδεδειγμένοις, Dio 59.7.9). Gaius was not consul at all in 38, a year for which the *Fasti Ostienses* provide all four names (*Docs.* no. 31, p. 28). The *ordinarii*, M. Aquila Julianus (*PIR²* A. 982) and P. Nonius Asprenus (*PIR²* N. 121), the latter probably a member of the final successful conspiracy against Gaius (on 58.3), had also been preselected (προαποδεδειγμένων, Dio 59.9.1). But the *suffecti*, Ser. Asinius Celer (*PIR²* A. 1225) and Sex. Nonius Quinctilianus (*PIR²* N. 153) did have minimal connections with the family of Germanicus, the former as his wife's nephew, the latter as the nephew of someone who had once put in a good word for Claudius (Tac. *Ann.* 3.18.4; Colin 405). They may have been Gaius' first selections.

secundum ex Kal. Ian. per XXX dies: As *ordinarius* Gaius gave his name to the year 39 (Tac. *Agr.* 44.1) and then retired after an unprecedented 30 days. The prestige of sharing the consulship with the emperor was given to L. Apronius Caesianus (*PIR²* A. 972), who continued in office for the usual six months (59.13.2; *Docs.* no. 7, p. 13). He was the son of the Lucius Apronius (*PIR²* A. 971) who had been with Germanicus in Germany (Tac. *Ann.* 1.56.1, 72.1) but who had also been Tiberius' proconsul in Africa (Tac. *Ann.* 3.21.1) and *legatus* with the Army of Lower Germany from 28 until 34 (Tac. *Ann.* 4.73, 6.30.2, 11.19.1); his daughter was married to Gaetulicus (8.1, 24.3; Tac. *Ann.* 6.30.2), who was himself a holdover from Tiberius. His son had not surprisingly been an associate of Sejanus also, but he was spared by Tiberius (Dio 58.19.1) and was thus a conservative choice that kept power in a family that had been politically astute enough to straddle the Sejanus divide. Gaius retired at the end of January in favor of the city prefect, Q. Sanguinius Maximus (*PIR¹* S. 136; Dio 59.13.2), now suffect for the second time. His unusual second consulship may have been in return for his defense in 32 of Memmius Regulus (P. Memmius Regulus, *PIR²* M. 468; Tac. *Ann.* 6.4.3; Colin 405–9; for Memmius' relationship with Gaius, see on 25.2; also 22.2, 57.1). One of the suffects who took office on July 1 was Cn. Domitius Corbulo, either father (*PIR²* D. 141) or son (*PIR²* D. 142). Dio thought that it was the elder Corbulo and that he had been chosen so that Gaius could use him as a *delator* (59.15.3–5), but Gaius had a close connection with the younger one who was the half-brother of his last wife, Milonia Caesonia (*PIR²* M. 590; 25.3; Syme 1970, 29–30; Townend 1961, 234–37; Colin 409–11). Corbulo's colleague is unknown (Gallivan 1979, 67; J. W. Humphrey and Swan 326–27). These suffects were relieved of their offices at the beginning of September (23.1, 26.3), and one killed himself. They were replaced by the renowned orator, Cn. Domitius Afer (*PIR²* D. 126; Dio 59.20.1–3; Tac. *Dial.* 13.3, 15.3; Quint. *Inst.* 12.11.3) and by A. Didius Gallus (*PIR²* D. 70; *L'Année Epigraphique* 1973, no. 138, pp. 39–40; Gallivan 1979, 66; J. W. Humphrey and Swan 325). Afer had prosecuted friends of Gaius' family under Tiberius (Tac. *Ann.* 4.52, 66) but he flattered Gaius and made peace with him (Dio 59.19.1–7). Didius continued his career under Claudius.

tertium usque in Idus Ian.: Gaius was not in Rome on the first of January in A.D. 40, and his potential colleague had died as Suetonius will explain below (*tertium autem Luguduni iniit*). The senate was in a state of confusion because of his absence and were too frightened to convene until he sent word on the twelfth that he had resigned (Dio 59.24.2–6). January 12 may have been chosen because it was the regular day for the election of consuls (Talbert 206–7) and so appropriate for his resignation.[32] The next day the consuls suffect for the second half of the year took office and served (presumably) until the end of June (Dio 59.24.2–6). They were C. Laecanius Bassus (*PIR²* L. 30) and Q. Terentius Culleo (*PIR¹* T. 54; *Docs.* p. 2; *L'Année Epigraphique* 1982 no. 196, p. 55), both of whom had moved up from praetorships they had held under Tiberius. The names of those who filled out the second half of 40 are not known, but it is possible that Gaius brought in several pairs, each of whom served a short term (Gallivan 1979, 67–69; J. W. Humphrey and Swan 326–27).

---

[32] Dio's statement that Gaius' first consulship terminated on September 12 in A.D. 37 (59.7.9) may have been derived from this January 12 resignation. He may have confused the two consulships and referred the twelfth to the wrong month and the wrong consulship.

quartum usque septimum Idus easdem: Gaius' consulships grew shorter yet. In 41 he resigned on January 7, an important date for the imperial family. A vow for his well-being was fulfilled in the shrine of the Dea Dia on that day in 38 (on 14.2; *Docs.* no. 1, pp. 9–10; for January 7 for Augustus and Tiberius, Herz 1981a, 91; Fishwick 1987–1990, 483). His colleague in this last consulship was Cn. Sentius Saturninus (*PIR¹* S. 296; Dio 59.29.5, 30.3; *Docs.* p. 2), who came under consideration to replace Gaius as emperor because he was already in place at the time of the assassination (Jos. *AJ* 19.166). Gaius' replacement on January 7 was Q. Pomponius Secundus (on 15.4; see note 24), who was killed as part of the conspiracy against Claudius in 42 (Tac. *Ann.* 13.43.2).[33]

ex omnibus duos nouissimos coniunxit: Duos is an error since the last three, not the last two, came in consecutive years. Suetonius also reports on Claudius' and Nero's sequential consulships: *ex quibus duos primos iunctim* (Suet. *Cl.* 14); *medios duos continuauit* (Suet. *Ner.* 14). Gaius was sensitive to charges that his consulships were too many and too soon (Dio 59.13.6, 19.2). *Ex quibus* (*apparatus*) seems preferable for *ex omnibus.*

tertium autem Luguduni iniit solus, non ut quidam opinantur superbia neglegentiaue, sed quod defunctum sub Kalendarum diem collegam rescisse absens non potuerat: Gaius spent part of the winter of 39–40 in Gaul in the provincial city of Lugudunum (or Lugdunum, modern Lyon, 20, 24.3, 43– 45). The name of the consul designate who died in Rome on the last day of 39 is unknown, but his death had nothing to do with Gaius' resignation on January 12 (above), which had been preplanned. Word of his colleague's death could not have gone to Lugdunum and the response back so quickly. Dio's similar judgment is "not on purpose, as some think" (οὔτι καὶ ἐπιτηδεύσας, ὥσπερ οἴονταί τινες, 59.24.2 = *non ut quidam opinantur superbia neglegentiaue*). A common source had presumably already replied to an assumption about Gaius' arrogance and excused him this time; or Dio could have influenced by Suetonius on this point (cf. on Gaius born in his father's camp, 8.1).

The emperor was expected to demonstrate his *liberalitas* with the official largess of *congiaria* and banquets (17.2) and provide *spectacula,* gladiatorial contests and *ludi,* both *circenses* and *scaenici*

---

[33] January 7, the seventh day before the Ides, is contradicted by a wax tablet from the Naples area that states that already on the Nones (the fifth) Saturninus and Pomponius Secundus were consuls: *Q. [P.]omponio, Sencio Saturnino co(n)s(ulibus) nonas Ianuarias, Caio K.(aesari) Augusto Germanico, Sulpicius Faustus scripsi...* (*L'Année Epigraphique* 1978, no. 137, pp. 47– 48). But a number of such tablets give misinformation about Gaius' consulships (Barrett 1989, 253). *Septimum* written out is odd since elsewhere Suetonius uses numerals for dates (e.g., 58.1, *VIIII. Kal. Feb.*).

(18; Veyne 1990, 398–419). After Tiberius' disinterest, Gaius' lavish entertainments were welcome. Two occasions stand out in particular. One was the dedication of the Temple of Augustus on August 30, A.D. 37, followed by the celebration of his own birthday the next day (Dio 59.7.1–4). The other was the two-day birthday party for his deified sister Drusilla in 39, date unknown, the year after she died (24.2; Dio 59.11.3, 13.8–9). Suetonius describes neither event as a whole but as usual dissects them and distributes their parts among his rubrics. Although his shows were more elaborate and larger than those that had gone before, they were not out of line with contemporary practice—with the exception of the bridge of boats across the Bay of Naples (19). Whatever else that extravaganza was, Suetonius thought that it was a good show and as such placed it here among Gaius' positive contributions. Games that he sponsored out of Rome, anticlimactic after the description of the bridge, are tacked on at the end (20).

17.2 congiarium populo bis dedit trecenos sestertios: Confirmed by the *Fasti Ostienses: K. Iun. cong(iarium) d(ivisum) * LXXV. XIII [K.] Aug. alteri * LXXV. (Docs.* no. 31, p. 28). * = *denarius.* One *denarius* = four *sestertii*, and so 75 *denarii* = 300 *sestertii. Congiaria* were direct gifts that the emperor gave on various pretexts to all those who were enrolled for the grain dole. Tokens were distributed that could be exchanged for cash. What occasions did these two mark? Dio notes only one instance of general largesse and says that it was for the belated celebration of Gaius' *dies togae virilis* and that the gift was 240 sesterces but with 60 in interest due because of the postponement (τὰς ἑξήκοντα κατ' ἄνδρα δραχμάς, ἃς ἐπὶ τῇ ἑαυτοῦ ἐς τοὺς ἐφήβους ἐσγραφῇ οὐκ εἰλήφεσαν, μετὰ τόκου πεντεκαίδεκα ἄλλων δραχμῶν ἀπέδωκε, 59.2.2; δραχμή = *denarius*). There had been *congiaria* when his brothers Nero and Drusus came of age (10.1; Suet. *Tib.* 54.1; Tac. *Ann.* 3.29.3; also for the emperor Nero, Suet. *Ner.* 7.2; Tac. *Ann.* 12.41.1). Augustus proudly enumerated his frequent *congiaria,* sometimes giving out 250, sometimes 300, sometimes 400 sesterces (*RG* 15 ; Suet. *Aug.* 41.2). But 300 was common (Suet. *Jul.* 38.1; *Tib.* 20; *Dom.* 4.5; Tac. *Ann.* 2.42.1; Dio 60.25.7). The idea of "interest," (μετὰ τόκου) had precedent with Caesar, who promised 300 sesterces to each citizen in return for their support in his war against Pompey (Dio 41.16.1). He paid it three years later with an extra 100 for the delay (*pro mora,* Suet. *Jul.* 38.1; Dio 43.21.3; for another delayed *congiarium,* Suet. *Aug.* 42.2). Gaius may have given 240 with a bonus to round it out. If the June 1 distribution commemorated his coming of age (Balsdon 1934a, 34), it does not necessarily follow that it was the exact anniversary of the date on which he received the adult toga (for a possible sequence of events in 30–33, see on 10.1 and 12.1; for a connection of this date with thanksgiving sacrifices for him, see on 14.1). The second *congiarium* was given on July 19, the date that began the fixed (Sothic) year in Egypt, the day on which the Nile overflowed its banks and the day when Isis was reunited with her husband-brother Osiris. Given Gaius' interest in the Isiac religion (on 22.3, 54.2, 57.4) and the importance of the date (Merkelbach 9–31), he might have made some event coincide with the existing holiday. Was it possibly his sister Drusilla's marriage (on 24.1) or his own (25.1) or both?[34]

totiens abundantissimum epulum senatui equestrique ordini, etiam coniugibus ac liberis utrorumque: For more details, see 18.2. The occasions for the two *epulum publicum* (the plural *epula* never occurs; *epulis* at 27.3) were the dedication of the temple of Augustus (Dio 59.7.1) and the celebration of Drusilla's birthday (Dio 59.11.3, 13.9). Mass feedings of this sort were taking place by the end of the Republic. A parallel is the banquet that Julius Caesar included with the funeral games for his daughter Julia in 46 B.C. (Suet. *Jul.* 26.2; Veyne 1990, 220).

posteriore epulo forensia insuper viris, feminis ac pueris fascias purpurae ac conchylii distribuit: The gifts at the second feast (*posteriore epulo*), the one in honor of Drusilla's birthday (Dio 59.13.9), had precedent both as favors at dinner parties (Suet. *Aug.* 75; Suet. *Ves.* 19.1) and at the *ludi Megalenses*, a traditional time for banquets (Ov. *Fast.* 4.353–54), a feast to which Drusilla's birthday festival was likened (Dio 59.11.3). The *forensia* (sc. *vestimenta*) that the men received were garments appropriate to the Forum, i.e., *togae* (Suet. *Aug.* 73; Petron. *Sat.* 56.9; Augustus gave them also, Suet. *Aug.* 98.2). The women and young people received *fasciae,* cloth bands or ribbons. *Purpura* (πορφύρα) and *conchylium* (κογχύλιον) were shellfish whose names were used for the dye made from them and also for cloth colored by the dye, both purple but evidently different tones (together at Pliny *HN* 9.124).

adiecit diem Saturnalibus: The extra day for the Saturnalia was calculated to please slaves and the lower class (Balsdon 1965, 123–25). The holiday began on December 17 and during the Republic lasted three days (Wissowa 207, n. 7). Gaius added a fourth day and then Claudius a fifth where the number stabilized officially. In practice, however, it lasted seven. Dio writes that Gaius added the fifth day as well (59.6.4), but that it was abolished at some point and Claudius restored it (60.25.8). This seems to be another instance in which Claudius had to revalidate the measures of Gaius that he wanted to retain. Again he gets credit for something that Gaius did. See notes 27 and 28.

---

[34] Other suggestions for the July 19 *congiarium* are that it honored either his first consulship or the payment of Tiberius' legacy (Balsdon 1934a, 34, 183) or his election to his second consulship for 39 (the date for the *comitia* that ratified the selection of consuls was in July after the tenth, Herz 1981a, 100–101 and n. 69). See on 17.1 for a January date for the selection of consuls.

appellavitque Iuvenalem: This name for the extra day is unattested elsewhere, although Nero called the games that celebrated the first shaving of his beard the *Iuvenales* (Suet. *Ner.* 11.1; Tac. *Ann.* 14.15.1. 15.33.1; Dio 61.19.1). The name recognized the *collegia iuvenum,* fraternities of youths who performed ritual functions (Neraudau 371–77; Nock 354).

18.1 ***Munera gladiatoria partim in amphitheatro Tauri:*** Like Marcus Agrippa (7), T. Statilius Taurus (*PIR¹* S. 615) was a *novus homo* and Augustus' stalwart *adiutor* on his way to the top. In recompense he was invited to help beautify Rome, and a stone amphitheater that carried his name was built on the Campus Martius in 30 B.C. (Suet. *Aug.* 29.5; Tac. *Ann.* 3.72.1; Dio 51.23.1). Gaius tried to replace it with a (presumably grander) one (21, on 34.1). Gladiatorial contests were *munera* because the ancients understood them as originating in blood offerings to the dead: *officium autem mortuis hoc spectaculo facere se veteres arbitrabantur* (Suet. *Ludicra historia* = *Rel.* Reiff. no. 194, pp. 343–44; Hopkins 1983, 3–4). See 14.2 and 27.2 for the knight who offered his life for Gaius by fighting in the arena. The *amphitheatrum Tauri* was destroyed in the fire of A.D. 64 (Dio 62.18.2).

partim in Saeptis aliquot edidit: The *Saepta* was also located in the Campus Martius and was a part of the Augustan building program. Agrippa (7) was responsible for its redecoration and rededication in 26 B.C. and named it the *Saepta Iulia* in honor of Augustus (Dio 53.23.2). The *Saepta,* or "enclosures," had been the traditional voting place of the *comitia centuriata,* but as the popular franchise grew less important (on 16.2), its large space was increasingly used for shows and not for voting (Suet. *Cl.* 21.4; *Ner.* 12.4). Although gladiatorial shows might take place in the Forum (Hopkins 1983, 5), these were the only two structures available during the reign of Gaius (also named together at Dio 59.10.5). Destroyed by fire in A.D. 80 (Dio 66.24.2) and again repaired, the *Saepta* was rendered obsolete by the Colosseum, the final solution to the problem of exhibition space.

quibus inseruit catervas Afrorum Campanorumque pugilum ex utra regione electissimorum: Campania, especially the region around Capua, was a traditional source for gladiatorial talent and many of the schools for gladiators were located there (Balsdon 1969, 291–92). Africa does not seem to have been a special source. *Afer* is more common for a person from Africa, *Africanus* (18.3) for an animal.

neque spectaculis semper ipse praesedit sed interdum aut magistratibus aut amicis praesidendi munus iniuxit: The public shows became the only outlet for expression for the ordinary people of Rome after other means of political involvement disappeared with the coming of the Empire (on 16.2 for their disenfranchisement). They might use the opportunity to express opinions (on 41.1, the objection to taxes), but more importantly they were occasions for interaction between emperor and subject as patron and recipient of his largesse. He could be gracious while he shared their experience, and they could salute him in return. His personal and interested attendance was expected (Cameron 1976 157–61, 170–77; Hopkins 1983, 14–20; Veyne 1990, 398–403; Bradley 1981, 129–30, 134–35). The crowd had not liked it when Julius Caesar read and answered letters *inter spectandum,* and so Augustus was careful to give the entertainments his entire attention (Suet. *Aug.* 45.1; Tac. *Ann.* 1.54.2). Tiberius understood their importance, but he stopped attending nonetheless (Suet. *Tib.* 47; Tac. *Ann.* 1.54.2, 76.3–4; Dio 57.11.5). Claudius appears to have enjoyed them thoroughly (*Cl.* 21.5). Gaius was properly involved but he did not always behave well (26.5, 30.2–3, 35.2–3, 41.1). The presidency was not an honorary position since someone had to determine which gladiators lived or died (30.2–3, 35.2–3; Ville 401–2), and a member or the imperial family or a substitute presided at the major contests that were sponsored by the princeps. Gaius exploited the family connection with Germanicus when he sent Claudius: *praeseditque nonnumquam spectaculis in Gai vicem, adclamante populo: 'Feliciter' partim 'patruo imperatoris' partim 'Germanici fratri'* (Suet. *Cl.* 7).

18.2 *scaenicos ludos et assidue et varii generis ac multifariam fecit:* Two kinds of *ludi, ludi scaenici* and *ludi circenses,* celebrated Rome's established festivals. Stage entertainments (*ludi scaenici*) given on the first days of each holiday period outnumbered the horse races which were featured only on the final day or days. The *ludi scaenici* were mostly pantomimes (more or less serious dance performances) and less sophisticated mimes and farces (Bieber 227). Audiences might create disturbances, and for this reason Tiberius banished actors from Rome and presumably closed the theaters in A.D. 22–23 (Suet. *Tib.* 37.2; Tac. *Ann.* 1.77; Dio 57.21.3). Gaius brought them back (Dio 59.2.5) and spent much time in their company (33, 54.1, 58.1). For his irregualar behavior in relation to stage entertainments, 26.4, 27.4, 54.1. *Multifariam,* "in many places," makes reference to the permanent theaters in Rome, the theaters of Pompey (when it became available, 21) and of Balbus and Marcellus. There were possibly temporary sites as well (Dio 59.5.3).

quondam et nocturnos accensis tota urbe luminibus: Given the difficulty of providing artificial light on a large scale, *ludi nocturni* were worth noting. For other *nocturna spectacula,* Suet. *Aug.* 31.4; *Dom.* 4.1; Tac. *Ann.* 14.20.5, 21.3; and see 54.2 and 57.4 for something planned for the night that Gaius was killed.

sparsit et missilia variarum rerum: Gaius was perhaps the first to throw *missilia* on a large scale (Millar 1977, 137). *Missilia* (always plural) were *tesserae,* small cubic or spherical tokens or tickets that could be traded for gifts of grain or money or other things (*variarum rerum*). In this sense they are frequently noted in inscriptions (*TLL* 8.1139.33–49) but in literary texts only in Suetonius and once in Seneca (*Ep.* 74.6). Prizes ranged from birds and tame animals to food and farms (Suet. *Ner.* 11.2; Dio 66.25.5). Unlike the tokens that were dispersed systematically at *congiaria* (17.2), these were thrown randomly to crowds. The occasion could be any public gathering, a banquet (Suet. *Aug.* 98.3; *Dom.* 4.5), the theater (Dio 66.25.4), the circus (Dio 67.4.4) or none at all (*sparsa et populo missilia omnium rerum per omnes dies,* Suet. *Ner.* 11.2). Gaius threw them at a gymnastic contest (Dio 59.9.6; see also.26.4). For his throwing the prizes themselves, Jos. *AJ* 19.71, 93.

et panaria cum obsonio viritim divisit: Public banquets (17.2) had begun with the guests served at tables (*cenae rectae* = proper meals), but in time they became something more akin to picnics with baskets of prepared food (box lunches), and finally handouts of money, the "little baskets" (*sportella* or *sportula*) were substituted (*RE* 3A.1883–86). Tiberius gave a feast with a thousand tables (*populo mille mensis,* Suet. *Tib.* 20) to celebrate his triumph in A.D. 12, but the picnic basket was well enough established by the time of Claudius for him to call a short gladiatorial show a metaphorical *sportula* (*velut ad subitam condictamque cenulam invitare se populum,* Suet. *Cl.* 21.4). Nero gave baskets (Suet. *Ner.* 16.2) and Domitian big ones (*panaria*) to senators and knights and little ones (*sportella*) to the common people (Suet. *Dom.* 4.5), but he also restored the formal meals (*revocata rectarum cenarum consuetudine,* Suet. *Dom.* 7.1). Under Gaius the form of the public feast seems to have been in transition. *Panaria* (bread baskets) filled with prepared food (*obsonium,* ὀψώνιον, cooked food other than bread), are distributed here. But at 32.2 a slave steals a piece of silver inlay from a couch at an *epulum publicum,* and the knight eating "opposite" (*contra se,* below) also implies a more formal arrangement.

qua epulatione: A vague transition. At which of the two banquets (on 17.2) did this happen?

equiti R. contra se hilarius avidiusque vescenti partes suas misit: With whom did the emperor eat on these occasions? *Contra se* gives the impression of Gaius and the knight at a table opposite one another. Or was the knight "opposite" only in the sense that he consumed his food in Gaius' line of vision? This anecdote illustrates Gaius' perennially capricious behavior; he would sometimes bestow inappropriate largesse (εἰς οὓς ἥκιστα ἐχρῆν ἀλόγῳ μεγαλοψυχίᾳ χρώμενος, Jos. *AJ* 19.201; see 16.4 and especially 55; also Philo *Leg.* 339–43). There is nonetheless something appealing about an emperor who rewarded gusto at the table.

sed et senatori ob eandem causam codicillos: The name of this senator who also enjoyed his meal is unknown. A "little codex" was several (*codicilli*, plural) writing surfaces (wax or vellum) bound together in codex form. They were suitable for short but serious communications because they could be sealed easily. *Codicilli* from the emperor had binding force.

quibus praetorem eum extra ordinem designabat: In a political context, *designare* means "appoint" or "elect." Gaius names this man praetor, and Suetonius reveals something about the mechanism of the electoral process. Elections in the senate were not a total fiction, especially for offices below consul, despite the influence of the emperor's *commendatio* (on 16.2). Of the twelve praetors to be elected in A.D. 14, the year when Tiberius removed *suffragium* from the *comitia* to the senate, he "commended" four who were to be "elected" without "being defeated" and without "canvassing" (*moderante Tiberio ne plures quam quattuor candidatos commendaret sine repulsa et ambitu designandos,* Tac. *Ann.* 1.15.1). The other eight were apparently freely chosen by the senate and their names handed on to the *comitia* for ratification. The procedure may have been that the ones whom the emperor "commended" (nominated) were voted on *extra ordinem,* out of order (i.e., first), before the rest of the selection proceeded (*ILS* 244; Jones 1955, 34–35, 49–50; Levick 1967, 207–11). Gaius puts the unnamed senator on the preferred list.

18.3 ***edidit et circenses plurimos a mane ad vesperam:*** Gaius was a serious racing fan (55.2–3; Dio 59.14.5–7; Jos. *AJ* 19.257). He increased the number of chariot races held each day from the traditional ten (Dio 58.12.8) to twenty and then to forty, this last number on his birthday in 37 (Dio 59.7.2–3). Nero also increased their number (Suet. *Ner.* 22.2).

interiecta modo Africanarum venatione: Africanae (sc. *bestiae,* Aug. *RG* 22; Λιβυκὰ θηρία, Dio 59.7.3, 13.9; 60.7.3) were large cats other than lions, i.e., panthers or cheetahs, available for import after the Jugurthine war (Toynbee 1973, 82). *Venationes,* beast-baitings of various sorts, began in Rome in the second century B.C. but (along with everything else) became more grand and exotic during the early Empire. They were frequently held in connection with races

(Suet. *Aug.* 43.2; *Cl.* 21.2–3; Dio 60.7.3, 23.5, 61.9.1; Ville 382–83). Gaius sponsored massive *venationes* at the two extraordinary galas that he put on, the dedication of the Temple of Augustus and the birthday celebration for Drusilla. 400 bears and 400 *Africanae* were killed at the first (Dio 59.7.3), 500 bears and 500 *Africanae* at the second (Dio 59.13.9). For the punishment of "the beasts," see 27.1, 3.

modo Troiae decursione: More commonly the *lusus Troiae* (Suet. *Aug.* 43.2; *Cl.* 21.3). Suetonius may have chosen the word *decursio* (usually a miliary incursion, a military exercise only in Suetonius, *Ner.* 7.2; *Gal.* 6.3) to match *venatio* (above). Like *venationes,* the Trojan games, a kind of grand march on horseback performed by young boys of the nobility, took place in conjunction with the races (Suet. *Tib.* 6.4; *Cl.* 21.3; *Ner.* 7.1). The myth that they had been brought from Troy with Aeneas (Verg. *Aen.* 5.545–603) made them a specific interest of the *gens Iulia;* there is no record of them after their line came to an end. First presented at Julius Caesar's triumph in 46 B.C. (Suet. *Jul.* 39.2; Dio 43.23.6) and frequent under Augustus (Dio 48.20.2, 51.22.4, 54.26.1; Suet. *Tib.* 6.4), Gaius resumed them after an interruption by Tiberius, a Julian only by adoption. They are reported twice for his reign, once at the dedication of the Temple of Augustus (Dio 59.7.4) and again at Drusilla's funeral (Dio 59.11.2; see 24.2). Suetonius described them in his *Liber de puerorum lusibus* (*Rel.* Reiff. no. 197, pp. 345–46).

et quosdam praecipuos...nec ullis nisi ex senatorio ordine aurigantibus: The much-criticized participation of Roman gentry in public exhibitions may have originated in or even been limited to "special" competitions such as the one alluded to here, entertainments that allowed upper class amateurs to imitate the professionals (Veyne 1990, 385–86, 466, notes 306, 307; see 30.2 for knights in the arena). Gaius had his own spots for practicing his chariot driving, at least one of which turned into a public course (on 54.1). Private games included the *ludi Palatini* at which Gaius planned his acting debut (54.2, 56.1, 58.1) and Nero's *Iuvenalia* at which he began his performing career (Suet. *Ner.* 11.1; Tac. *Ann.* 15.33.1; Dio 62.20.1–2).

minio et chrysocolla constrato circo: *Minium* = cinnabar (mercuric sulphide) or some other substance that produced a bright red pigment. *Chrysocolla* usually = malachite (copper carbonate), a green pigment. These minerals tinted the race course the colors of Gaius' favorite racing faction, the Greens (55.2; Dio 59.14.6; Jos. *AJ* 19.257). Nero liked the Greens too and also colored a course with *chrysocolla* and wore a matching green tunic when he drove (Pliny *HN* 33.90). The other important faction was the Blues. The Reds and Whites came to function as minor league subsidiaries to the two major colors but maintained a degree of autonomy; the colors of sand suggest that the Greens and the Reds raced as a team during this period (Cameron 1976, 45–73).

commisit et subitos: Extra, unscheduled games: Cf. ὥς που καὶ ἔδοξεν αὐτῷ (Dio 59.7.3).

cum e Gelotiana: Suetonius did not feel that it was necessary for him to identify the *domus Gelotiana* to his readers.[35] It was apparently a structure on the slope of the Palatine that overlooked the Circus Maximus, either a house incorporated into the palace complex or one built for viewing the races. The Circus Maximus lay in a valley to the southwest of the Palatine, between it and the Aventine, and the topography allowed privileged spectators to watch the action from above (Suet. *Aug.* 45.1; Dio 57.11.5; see also 26.4 for the juxtapostion of Circus and Palatine). *Gelotiana* suggests laughter (γέλως), a "house of laughter," and a site on the hill devoted to pleasure. For laughter as a metaphor for elegant and sophisticated pleasure, see, e.g., *ridet argento domus* (Hor. *Carm.* 4.1.6).

apparatum circi prospicientem pauci ex proximis Maenianis postulassent: Those who asked for races were apparently in the Circus Maximus observing the preparations (*apparatum circi,* 26.4) just as Gaius was observing them from the *Gelotiana. Maeniana* were ranges of seats, a term transferred from its original meaning of balconies, good viewing places. They were named after a fourth century B.C. magistrate and architect who is credited with inventing overhanging porches (*RE* 14.249–50). *Prospicientem* is awkward as part of the double accusative with *postulo;* Suetonius tries to put more circumstantial information into the sentence than the syntax will comfortably hold (see note 8).

From the usual *spectacula,* Suetonius moves on to an affair of A.D. 39 that clearly made a strong impression on everyone. The bridge of boats across the Bay of Naples gets an entire chapter. Dio's detail is even greater (59.17). Suetonius appears to be on his own in judging the bridge as something better than irresponsible excess; he approves Gaius' creative energies (19) and separates the bridge itself from the problems that arose when the party got out of hand (32.2). At least in part (probably in large part) the show existed for its own sake (Garzetti, 91; Barrett 1989, 212). The excuse for it was the only military success that Gaius' reign had seen, the submission of Artabanus to Lucius Vitellius in the spring or early summer of 37 (14.3; Momigliano 1932b, 220; Balsdon

---

[35] But he did feel that he had to explain the structure called the *Hermaeum* in which Claudius tried to hide after Gaius' assassination (Suet. *Cl.* 10.1). Both of these places happen to be named in the same inscription, the only other evidence for either. It is a memorial from one slave of the imperial household to another: *Philodespotus ser Caesaris ex Hermaeo Symphoro tesserario ser Caesaris de domo Gelotiana* (*CIL* 6.8663).

1934a, 53). Gaius reenacted the campaign when he paraded across the bridge from one of his villas to the port of Puteoli in imitation of a military attack and made a triumphant return with his hostage Darius (*PIR²* D. 10), the son of Artabanus. The meeting that had ended hostilities quite plausibly took place on a bridge thrown across the Euphrates for that very purpose (Jos. *AJ* 18.101–2). The *spectaculum* thus took the form of a surrogate triumph over the East, unofficial and not in Rome. If this seems obvious now, it cannot have been missed by contemporaries, but everything that Gaius did was given the worst possible construction. In this case he asked for it; the bridge was an arrogant display even in an extravagant age. Furthermore, the parody of a triumph did not play well in Rome, especially if it took place shortly after an overt confrontation with the senate that had voted him an ovation (for the timing, see on 19.3 and note 39).

19.1 *novum praeterea atque inauditum genus spectaculi excogitavit:* Suetonius puts the emphasis on Gaius' ingenuity. The verb *excogitare* "invent," "devise," is picked up each time he refers to the bridge: *pontem excogitatum* (19.3); *Puteolis dedicatione pontis, quem excogitatum ab eo...* (32.1). The verb is also used with the bird sacrifices, 22.3; see the *nova* and *inaudita* taxes (40).

nam Baiarum medium intervallum †*Puteolanas moles...ponte coniunxit:* Gaius and members of the imperial family, along with other wealthy Romans, had multiple villas on the west coast of the *sinus Puteolanus,* the north-western portion of the Bay of Naples where Baiae was located (37.2; Philo *Leg.* 185; Jos. *AJ* 18.248–49; Tac. *Ann.* 14.4.2; Pliny *HN* 9.172). Dio locates the western anchor of the bridge at Bauli (59.17.1), today's Bacoli, and modern scholarship agrees (Maiuri 249–61). Tacitus identifies Bauli as a villa south of Baiae, between there and Misenum (*Ann.* 14.4.2; also Cic. *Ac.* 2.125), and Pliny (wrongly), as a location to its north (*HN* 3.61). The nomenclature of these sites is imprecise; both Baiae and Bauli were complexes of villas and estates without municipal status (D'Arms 23–26, 42, 113, 184–85). Josephus, on the other hand, says that the western end of the bridge was at Misenum (*AJ* 19.5), the Roman naval base. It was agreed that the eastern end was in Puteoli, modern Pozzuoli (Dio 59.17.1; Jos. *AJ* 19.5), originally the Greek city Dicaiarchia. Puteoli served as the port for Rome until the harbor at Ostia was improved under Claudius and Trajan, and it remained an important commercial center throughout the first century (Jos. *AJ* 18.248). Augustus had built a new breakwater, the *Puteolanae moles,* to facilitate the importation of Egyptian grain (D'Arms 81–82, 138; see note 38), and the bridge of boats probably took its start from there. This was where Augustus and Antony had concluded peace with Sextus Pompey in 36 B.C. (on 23.1). A celebratory banquet followed on Pompey's ship that was moored alongside the mole (on 32.1; App. *BCiv.* 5.69–73). The *Epitome de Caesaribus* implies matching breakwaters at either end (*quod in sinu Puteolano inter moles iacet,* 3.9; cf. ἀπ' ἄκρων ἐπ' ἄκρα, Jos. *AJ* 19.6). A parallel construction for parallel *moles* might be looked for beneath the textual crux here; on the other hand, it was Puteoli that had the significant harbor structures.

trium milium et sescentorum fere passuum spatium: 3.6 Roman miles is a neater 3 miles in the *Epitome de Caesaribus* (3.9). Dio gives 26 stades (59.17.1) and Josephus a tidy 30 (*AJ* 19.6). The ancient measurements are somewhat exaggerated. Those of Suetonius (about 3 1/3 English miles) and Dio (about 3 English miles) coincide roughly but are actually closer to the longer distance between Puteoli and Misenum than between Puteoli and Bauli (for a discussion, Barrett 1989, 212).

contractis undique onerariis navibus et ordine duplici ad anc[h]oras conlocatis: Merchant vessels were available in the harbor at Puteoli, others were hastily gathered, more yet (rafts?) were built on the spot (Dio 59.17.2). The number of boats required for a double row several miles long was obviously large and generated the idea that a sufficient number had been withdrawn from the grain transport service to cause a famine (Dio 59.17.2; Sen. *Dial.* 10.18.5–6; Vic. *Caes.* 4.3). Seneca (mistakenly) assigns the bridge to January of A.D. 41 (*intra paucos illos dies quibus C. Caesar perit, Dial.* 10.18.5), perhaps relating it to the famine of 42 (Dio 60.11.1; Suet. *Cl.* 18.2; Balsdon 1934a, 189; J. W. Humphrey at Dio 59.17.2). See 39.1 for a similar alleged result when Gaius commandeered overland transport; also 26.5 for his deliberately causing famine. Unpopular emperors were routinely accused of this (Suet. *Ner.* 45.1).

superiectoque terreno ac derecto in Appiae viae formam: Something had to be put over the vessels to form a surface that could be traversed (δίοδός τις, Dio 59.17.3; *pervium*, Aur. Vict. *Caes.* 4.3). The *Epitome de Caesaribus* is closer to Suetonius: *arenae aggestu ad terrae speciem viam solidatam* (3.9). The variant *aggere terreno* (*apparatus*) makes clearer the comparison with the Appian Way with its image of a road with a properly raised crown.

19.2 *per hunc pontem ultro citro commeavit biduo continenti:* Dio writes that Gaius made a single round trip with a day of rest in between his progress of the first day from Bauli to Puteoli and his return trip from Puteoli to Bauli on the third (κἀνταῦθα τῆς ὑστεραίας ἀναπαυσάμενος ὥσπερ ἐκ μάχης, 59.17.5). Suetonius' sentence means either that Gaius and his party went back and forth (*ultro citro*) over the bridge once or several times on each of two successive days (*biduo continenti* as ablative of duration, accepted by Balsdon 1934a, 51, and D'Arms 91, n. 92) or a single round trip over a two-day period (*biduo continenti* as ablative of time within which), a closer correspondence with

Dio's account, and undoubtedly correct since *primo die* and *postridie* (below) indicate two days with two different functions.[36]

primo die phalerato equo: The first day utilized military insignia. Gaius rushed across the bridge to Puteoli with horsemen and foot soldiers as if in battle charge (Dio 59.17.4). *Phalerae* were metal disks that decorated the heads or breasts of war horses.

insignisque quercea corona: Cf. Dio 59.17.3. The *corona civica,* the crown of oak leaves, belonged among Gaius' paraphernalia on the bridge because in subduing the Parthians (14.3) he had "saved Rome." The civic crown was granted to the Roman citizen who had saved the life of a fellow citizen. It became standard for the princeps, the *ex officio* savior of all Roman citizens (Julius Caesar, Dio 44.4.5; App. *BCiv.* 2.106; Augustus, Aug. *RG* 34; Dio 53.16.4; Claudius, Suet. *Cl.* 17.3; Maxfield 72; but not Tiberius who was out of step, Suet. *Tib.* 26.2). It may have been given him along with the title *pater patriae* in September of 37 (Barrett 1989, 70–71; Scheid and Broise 225, 240–42).

et caetra et gladio: The *caetra* was a small shield. Cf. ξίφος τε παρεζώσατο καὶ ἀσπίδα ἔλαβε (Dio 59.17.3).

aureaque chlamyde: *Chlamys* = *paludamentum,* a short military cloak associated with the triumphant general's display and thus with the princeps (cf. 25.3). Nero wore an elaborate one with golden stars (*distinctaque stellis aureis,* Suet. *Ner.* 25.1). Gaius' *chlamys* was purple silk covered with gold and precious stones. He allegedly wore the breastplate of Alexander beneath it (Dio 59.17.3), but Suetonius postpones notice of this to the rubric about Gaius' clothing (52) and carefully keeps the hubris that it represented out of this laudable part of the bridge experience.

postridie quadrigario habitu: The return trip was more imperial and Gaius became a triumphant general with his spoils. He wore the tunic of a chariot driver but triumphing generals wore tunics too; it was golden (χιτῶνα χρυσόπαστον ἐνδύς, Dio 59.17.5).

curriculoque biiugi famosorum equorum: The renowned horses, those who won the most victories for him, are a nice touch (οἱ ἀθληταὶ ἵπποι οἱ

---

[36] The discrepancy between the two and three days does not change the story in its essentials but perhaps reflects the use of different sources. Is it possible that Suetonius' *continenti* is his insistence that the account which he chose to follow on this point was correct? See on *continuo triennio* in 7 and note 9.

ἀξιονικότατοι, Dio 59.17.5). Was his favorite Incitatus among them? For his interest in racing, see 18.3 and 55.2–3.

prae se ferens Dareum puerum ex Parthorum obsidibus: Darius, the son of Artabanus III, was one of plural Parthian hostages (ἐν τοῖς ὁμηρεύουσι τότε τῶν Πάρθων ὤν), part of a train of purported spoils (ὡς καὶ λάφυρα, Dio 59.17.5). He had been sent to Rome after the settlement between Parthia and Rome in (14.3; Jos. *AJ* 18.103).[37] *Prae se ferens* = "displaying, showing off;" for the same expression applied to Artabanus, 14.3.

comitante praetorianorum agmine et in essedis cohorte amicorum: He was accompanied by his court who were eccentrically dressed (ἐν ἐσθῆσιν ἀνθιναῖς...ἰδίως πως ἕκαστοι κεκοσμημένοι, Dio 59.17.6). On the way back he stopped on the bridge, gave a post-victory harangue to the troops and added a donative before the feasting and all-night party began (32.1; Dio 59.17.6–8). For Gaius riding to battle in an *essedum*, 51.2.

19.3 scio plerosque existimasse talem a Gaio pontem excogitatum: Suetonius gives three explanations, two that he found in his sources or still circulating orally, and one to which he had private access. Dio and Josephus call the bridge pure arrogance: Gaius, they write, drove a chariot across the sea because he was tired of triremes and wanted to get the better of Neptune or Xerxes or both (Dio 59.17.1, 4, 11; 26.6; Jos. *AJ* 19.6.). Seneca calls it a perverse desire to cause a famine (on 19.1; Sen. *Dial.* 10.18.5).[38] The bridge was obviously a much discussed phenomenon. With the first person here and below, Suetonius enters the discussion himself and draws together the stories that he knows. Similarly at 8.1–2; more of his own assessment at 51.1, 3.

aemulatione Xerxis, qui non sine admiratione aliquanto angustiorem Hellespontum contabulaverit: Cf. Dio 59.17.9, 11. It is unthinkable that

---

[37] Balsdon thought that the hostages were actually received at this time and that the purpose of the display was "to advertise in Italy the success of Rome in her recent negotiation with Parthia and to impress the hostages themselves with Roman power" (1934a, 53). A reenactment is more likely not only because the hostages had been surrendered about two years earlier but also because, if they had really been received at this time, there might have been less room for the imaginative explanations of the bridge's purpose.

[38] Another (less imaginative) explanation is perhaps exposed by Suetonius' word choice at 32.1: *Puteolis dedicatione pontis*. Did it celebrate the dedication of a new (rebuilt? improved?) breakwater at Puteoli? The possibility is noted by J. W. Humphrey at Dio 59.17.11. But a *moles* at Puteoli is not found among Gaius' building projects (21). A breakwater and a thoroughfare across the sea merge in two epigrams about the harborworks at Puteoli (*Anth. Pal.* 7.379, 9.708, not however about Gaius, Cichorius 343–44; Cameron 1993, 60–61).

Gaius himself, whatever else he was doing, did not realize that he was actualizing a metaphor. Xerxes' hubris in crossing the Hellespont (Hdt. 7.36), turning the sea into land, was a pervasive cliché (for an extensive list of examples through the first century, Mayor 2.127–28 on Juv. 10.173–84; see on 37.3). Gaius' bridge crossed a body of water wider than the Hellespont and so was a valid rhetorical statement that Roman success in the East (in this case the submission of Artabanus) was greater than Eastern success against the West. Gaius must have understood this, and so the rationale is not without a kind of truth.

alios, ut Germaniam et Britanniam, quibus imminebat, alicuius inmensi operis fama territaret: This appears to date the bridge to a time not very long before Gaius departed for the German frontier in September of 39 (43). The event was staged *ante expeditionem* (52). Dio also puts it with events of 39, presumably in the summer when the sea was calm (59.17.10).[39] It was nonsense to suggest that it could be mistaken for a military structure (*opus*) intended to impress enemies in distant parts. But what could be a better prelude to his anticipated success in the West than a display that showed him master of the East?

sed: Suetonius accepts the explanation that follows by virtue of its source; privileged information was persuasive.

avum meum narrantem puer audiebam, causam operis ab interioribus aulicis proditam: The generational interval is plausible if Suetonius was born about A.D. 70 (Syme 1977, 44; Wallace-Hadrill 1983, 3). His father, Laetus Suetonius (*PIR¹* S. 691), had been an equestrian tribune under Otho in 69 (Suet. *Oth.* 10.1) and the family was on its way up. A grandfather was probably not among the inner circle of Gaius' court (*ab interioribus aulicis*), but there is no reason to doubt that Suetonius heard this story from him. Other instances of his private knowledge: *Cl.* 15.3, *Ner* 57.2, *Oth.* 10.1–2, *Dom.* 12.2; of other writers: Tac. *Ann.* 3.16.1; Plut. *Oth.* 14.1. More examples are collected by Gascou, 245.

quod Thrasyl<l>us mathematicus: To whom better could the prediction be ascribed than to the trusted astrologer and confidant of Tiberius? Thrasyllus (on

---

[39] The bridge is connected with Gaius' angry confrontation with the senate at some undetermined point within this general time frame (16.4, 30.2). In order to appease him, the senate voted him honors and an ovation "as if he had conquered some enemies" (ὡς καὶ πολεμίους τινὰς νενικηκότι, Dio 59.16.11; on 16.4), "but he did not value that kind of parade" (Γάιος δὲ ἐκείνης μὲν τῆς πομπῆς οὐδὲν προετίμησεν, Dio 59.17.1), and so he built the bridge on his own initiative instead. It was a kind of tactless declaration of independence from the senate; see on his non-triumph in 48.2. The engineering feat could not, of course, have been executed on the spur of the moment after he left Rome hastily and in anger (Dio 59.16.8). But it is easy to see why his detractors put this spin on the sequence of events.

12.2) was with Tiberius from his exile on Rhodes to the end (Suet. *Aug.* 98.4; *Tib.* 14.4, 62.3).

anxio de successore Tiberio et in verum nepotem proniori non magis Gaium imperaturum quam per Baianum sinum equis discursurum: Gaius is said to act out a second verbal expression (like Xerxes crossing the Hellespont, above). This prediction proves nothing about Tiberius' intentions for the succession (on 14.1) but only how quickly he was second guessed.

20 *edidit et peregre spectacula: Peregre* = "abroad," beyond Italy; the examples are in Sicily and Gaul. Emperors did not often sponsor games in the provinces (Balsdon 1969, 329–33).

in Sicilia Syracusis: Games may have celebrated the rebuilding to walls and temples in Syracuse (21). A precipitous trip there is reported directly after the death of Drusilla in the summer of 38 (below 24.2), but the games must have been planned in advance of that, and so it is unlikely that they were in her honor. Like Lugdunum (below) Syracuse had ample facilities for *spectacula* (Tac. *Ann.* 13.49.1). Other notices of the Sicilian trip: 51.1; Sen. *Dial.* 11.17.5; Jos. *AJ* 19.205.

asticos ludos: Astici ludi apparently featured drama on the model of the Greek festival of the City Dionysia in Athens. In Latin texts the phrase is found only here and in Suetonius' *Life of Tiberius* (6.4) where the *astici ludi* were probably part of the celebrations in 29 B.C. for Augustus' victory at Actium. *Ludi Graeci thymelici* (musical) are contrasted with *Graeci astici* in the *Acta ludorum saeculorum* (*CIL* 6.32323 ll.156–58). Either Suetonius idiosyncratically uses *astici* for *ludi scaenici,* or they were special productions that did not enjoy much popularity in the Roman world. If the latter is true, their revival in Greek Syracuse was worth noting.

et in Gallia Luguduni miscellos: For Gaius in Lugdunum on January 1, A.D. 40, see 17.1. The provincial capital's most important features were the Altar of Rome and Augustus established by Drusus in 12 B.C. (Dio 54.32.1) and the large amphitheater located nearby. The expensive games (Dio 59.22.1) may have celebrated the dedication of a temple begun there by Tiberius (Larfargues and Le Glay 407–10, 413) despite the fact that Suetonius does not mention any such building (21). *Miscellos, sc. ludos* (only here in connection with games, *TLL* 8.1978.62–73), "mixed," presumably because they included oratorical contests (below). For other activities in Gaul that winter, see 39 and probably 27.1, 41.2, and 45.2.

sed hic certamen quoque Graecae Latinaeque facundiae, quo certamine ferunt victoribus praemia victos contulisse, eorundem et laudes componere coactos: Gaius anticipated Nero's contests of rhetoric at the *Neronia* in A.D. 60 (Suet. *Ner.* 12.3; Tac. *Ann.* 14.20.4, 21.3; also Domitian, Suet. *Dom.* 4.4). For his own speaking skills, 10.1, 53. Thus far the competition seems a harmless upperclass activity and one that Suetonius thought worthy of inclusion among Gaius' neutral acts. Its purpose may have been to find an orator to deliver a panegyric for him (Fishwick 1987–1990, 573).

eos autem qui maxime displicuissent, scripta sua spongia linguave delere iussos: But, like the bridge at Baiae (19 vs. 32.1), the event had its uglier side. Gaius was evidently willing to humiliate his associates by having them erase their words with their tongues. The conjecture *lingua velut spongia* (Helmreich, *apparatus*) brings the text closer to what must have been the intent of the anecdote. Erasing with the choice of sponge or tongue (*spongia linguave*) was not really equivalent to a beating or a near drowning (below), but using the tongue as a sponge provided a choice for the losers between physical punishment and humiliation. Speaking at the altar at Lugdunum became proverbial for a fear-producing ordeal. Juvenal compared it with stepping on a snake barefoot (Juv. 1.44).

nisi ferulis obiurgari: Ferulis obiurgari = "be punished with the rod." The contest took the form of a parody of a school lesson with the master's rod as well as the eraser (Maurer).

aut flumine proximo mergi maluissent: The *flumen proximum* was either the Rhodanus (Rhône) or the Arar (Saône) at whose confluence Lugdunum stood.[40]

Public works are always an important rubric for Suetonius (*Aug.* 29, 30.2; *Cl.* 20; *Ner.* 16.1; *Ves.* 9.1; *Tit.* 7.3; *Dom.* 5). After Augustus' whirlwind of construction any successor would have seemed lethargic, and Tiberius is credited with no construction. He did, in fact, restore and build a number of structures but did not put his own name on them (Tac. *Ann.* 2.41.1, 2.49, 4.43; Dio 57.10.1–3). As often, Gaius turned back to the precedent of Augustus and exploited this

---

[40] There may be connection between *flumine proximo mergi* and the story that Claudius was thrown into the river fully clothed when he was sent to congratulate Gaius on suppressing Gaetulicus' attempt at a coup; the delegation that he headed reached Gaius at Lugdunum (on 24.3; Dio 59.23.5; Suet. *Cl.* 9.1; Charlesworth 1934, 668; Balsdon 1934a, 82–83). The rough punishments could have included one for him (Fishwick 1987–1990, 572–73). For Gaius beating him, *Cl.* 8; Sen. *Apocol.* 15.2. See 23.3. It is interesting that both kinds of physical abuse that Gaius is said to have inflicted on inarticulate Claudius are associated in this anecdote in which inadequate orators are punished.

opportunity to gain public approval—or at least he tried to. He did not have time to finish what he began (*incohavit* and *destinaverat,* below). Suetonius deals with his less attractive building projects at 37.2–3.

21 *opera sub Tiberio semiperfecta:* Tiberius did not complete the only two buildings that were credited to him, the temple of Augustus and the theater of Pompey, twin monuments to his turpitude (named together here and elsewhere: Suet. *Tib.* 47; Tac. *Ann.* 6.45.1; Vell. 2.130.1). In the case of the temple at least, *semiperfecta* must have meant almost complete, perhaps finished but undedicated, since Gaius dedicated it within six months of the time when he became emperor (Suet. *Tib.* 74; Tac. *Ann.* 6.45.1; Dio 57.10.2).

templum Augusti...absolvit: The senate voted a temple to *divus Augustus* in 14 (Dio 56.46.3). The dedication on August 30 in 37 was a massive production that, together with Gaius' birthday the next day, included a banquet, races, a *venatio,* the *lusus Troiae,* and noble boys and girls singing hymns (Dio 59.7.1–5), most of which Suetonius works into other rubrics (17, 18.2–3). For the first time, an elephant drew the vehicle that carried the image of a deified member of the imperial family (*Anth. Pal.* 9.285; Cichorius 344–46). This original temple which has disappeared beneath later construction was located northwest of the Palatine near the temple of Castor and Pollux (22.4 for the only evidence for its location). Sacrifice was made at the *novum templum* on the first anniversary of Gaius' *dies imperii* in 38 and often thereafter (*Docs.* nos. 3, 7, 21, 22, pp. 10, 13, 19, 22). A commemorative sestertius shows Gaius sacrificing at a hexastyle temple with a triumphant *quadriga* on top, *pietas* on the obverse (*RIC²* Gaius no. 36, p. 111).

theatrumque Pompei: The theater of Pompey on the Campus Martius, dedicated in 52 B.C. (Dio 39.38.1; Gell. 10.1.7), was Rome's first permanent theater. It was restored by Augustus, who preserved Pompey's name (*RG* 20), burned (at least the *scaena,* Tac. *Ann.* 6.45.1) in A.D. 21, and was worked on again under Tiberius (Tac. *Ann.* 3.72.2; Sen. *Dial.* 6.2.4). Claudius also took credit for the dedication; he put Pompey's name back onto the structure and added to the *scaena* the names of Tiberius because he had rebuilt it, and of himself because he had dedicated it (Suet. *Cl.* 21.1; Dio 60.6.8–9). The implication is that Gaius had replaced Pompey's name with his own.

incohavit autem aquae ductum regione Tiburti...quorum operum a successore eius Claudio...alterum peractum: Cf. [Claudius] *perfecit... ductum aquarum a Gaio incohatum* (Suet. *Cl.* 20.1). Claudius completed two aqueducts, the *aqua Claudia* and the *Anio novus* that Gaius had begun (Frontin.

Aq. 2.13; Tac. *Ann.* 11.13.2; Pliny *HN* 36.122; *Docs.* nos. 308–10, pp. 83–84). Water came through the *Claudia* from springs in the hills of Tibur to the east (*regione Tiburti;* for Tibur, 8.2).

et amphitheatrum iuxta Saepta...omissum alterum est: Gaius evidently found both the *Saepta* and the Amphitheater of Taurus (18.1) unsatisfactory for his *munera* and so in 38 demolished buildings and built wooden stands (Dio 59.10.5). There is evidence for building activity in the Campus Martius to the west of the *Saepta* in an inscription commemorating Claudius' restoration of the *aqua virgo: Ti. Claudius...arcus ductus aquae Virginis disturbatos per C. Caesarem a fundamentis novos fecit ac restituit* (*Docs.* no. 208b, p. 83; Balsdon 1934a, 176). Water was necessary near amphitheaters so that *naumachiae* could be presented (Frontin. *Aq.* 2.22; for Gaius flooding the *Saepta,* Dio 59.10.5). The Temple of Isis (on 22.4) was perhaps another new construction begun in the Campus Martius. 34.1 for the destruction of statues in this area.

Syracusis conlapsa vetustate moenia deorumque aedes refectae: Damage had been inflicted on Sicily and especially on Syracuse during the Civil War. Augustus reconstructed the part of the ancient walls that were adjacent to the old town (Strab. 6.2.4), and Gaius probably continued or completed this work. See 20, 24.2 and 51.1 for his trip to Sicily in the summer of 38 and the games held there.

destinaverat et Sami Polycratis regiam restituere: The "palace" of Polycrates, the sixth-century B.C. tyrant of the then powerful island of Samos. It was an attractive imperial resting place for those who had business in the East throughout the early Empire, and a decision to establish quarters there was reasonable. Augustus had used the island for his winter quarters after Actium (Suet. *Aug.*17.3, 26.3). Gaius may have intended it as his base of operations for an Eastern trip (49.2, 51.3; Willrich 421).

Mileti Didymeum peragere: The ancient temple of Apollo at the shrine of Didyma south of Miletus (on the Ionian coast opposite Samos) had been destroyed by the Persians, and a long rebuilding was begun about 300 B.C. It was a major international site, rivaled only by Delos (Strab. 14.1.5). Gaius' cult, probably established in response to his support for the temple, is epigraphically confirmed (*Docs* no. 127, p. 48; Robert 1949, 206–38). The charge was that he ordered a sacred precinct there because he wanted to appropriate Miletus for himself; Diana, after all, had her Ephesus, Augustus his Pergamum and Tiberius his Smyrna (Dio 59.28.1). Suetonius, however, indicates that he thought moderate emperor worship in the East legitimate when he puts the Didymion here among Gaius' constructive undertakings.

in iugo Alpium urbem condere: When Gaius journeyed to the Rhine frontier (43), he had to go *per Alpes* (*Schol. Juv.* 4.8.1) and perhaps got the idea of fortifying a pass (Willrich 307, n. 2). Nothing else is known of this project unless the rhetoric of *complanata fossuris montium iuga* (37.1) refers to it (doubtful).

sed ante omnia Isthmum in Achaia perfodere: The converse of turning the sea into land (19.3, 37.3) was turning the land into sea; Xerxes' canal through Athos paralleled his bridge over the Hellespont (Hdt. 7.22, 37). That the canal through the Isthmus of Corinth in the Roman province of Achaia should be called the favorite project of someone willing to bridge the Bay of Naples is logical. It put Gaius in the company of others who thought large. Pliny spells out the hubris: *perfodere navigabili alveo angustias eas tempavere Demetrius rex, dictator Caesar, Gaius princeps, Domitus Nero, nefasto, ut omnium exitu patet, incepto* (*HN* 4.10).

miseratque iam ad dimentiendum opus primipilarem: The army would provide the available manpower, hence a senior centurion (*primipilaris*) as Gaius' front man. Since military engineers had the skills (Webster 276), legionaries were sometimes called on to dig canals (Tac. *Ann.* 11.20.2, 13.53.2; Dio 60.30.6; Suet. *Aug.* 18.2.), but manual labor of this sort was unpopular (27.3, on 55.3). For Nero's praetorians and the canal (Suet. *Ner.* 19.2; Dio 62.16).

22.1 *hactenus quasi de principe, reliqua ut de monstro narranda sunt:* Arguably Suetonius' best-known sentence. *Quasi* implies that the *monstrum* was always waiting to emerge (10.2).

Despite Gaius' blatant and urgent attempts to rally support and the bravado of his bridge at Baiae, the picture of the reign to this point fits comfortably within the continuum of the early principate. Suetonius' clear dichotomy between the good *princeps* and the evil *monstrum* is the result of his organizational imperatives, but there was a general perception that Gaius "changed," that his principate had a "good" early period followed in time by a "bad" later period.[41] Change could be reconciled with the idea that Gaius was always quite dreadful (11) by the notion of *dissimulatio* (10.2; *quasi,* above). It is in fact true that most, but not all, of what Suetonius places in the rubrics of commendable or neutral activities (15–21) took place, insofar as items can be dated, in the first two years of his reign. Events nearer the end of his life, the expedition to the German frontier (43–48) and confrontations leading to his assassination (49, 56), are well placed in the *monstrum*

---

41 Philo saw the good/bad Gaius chronologically with the illness in the autumn of A.D. 37 as both the dividing line between the two periods and the cause of insanity (*Leg.* 13). Dio is not specific, but Gaius' beginnings are praised and a change is said to occur in 38 (59.2.6–3.1). Josephus thought that it came after two years of good rule (*AJ* 18.256).

section. Philo, writing not long after Gaius was killed, already makes a strong contrast between the enthusiastic reception that the new emperor received (*Leg.* 8–21) and the utter depravity that followed (22 ff.). Dio used sources that had conceived Gaius' actions in this same antithetical way and paired corresponding good and bad acts (59.3.4–4.6, 59.8)[42] that Suetonius' method forced him to detach (e.g., 15.2–3 vs. 23–4 and 29.1, 15.4 vs. 30.2). But all of what follows about the *monstrum* is not unremittingly grim. Gaius was ridiculed as well as deplored.

Suetonius runs through Gaius' character flaws systematically (22–42) beginning with arrogance (*suberbia,* recalled at 34.1) which includes his pretensions to divinity. First come the names that Gaius wanted to take for himself. They are not very different from those that other emperors assumed, but each became ironic when applied to him. Was there a line that could not be crossed or did it matter who tried to cross it?

compluribus cognominibus adsumptis: His unofficial nickname was Caligula, of course (9), but he wanted to change his image (on 52 and note 106; Sen. *Dial.* 2.18.4). The survival of these would-be *cognomina* may ultimately depend on the persistence of "Caligula" as a kind of joke; e.g., "He thinks he should be *pius, pater exercituum* and so forth, but he's nothing but a pretend soldier." For his removal of *cognomina* from others, 35.1.

pius: *Pius* proved acceptable for other emperors (Antoninus Pius, *PIR²* A. 1513) and had already been suggested for Tiberius (Suet. *Tib.* 17.2). Gaius seems to have selected *pietas* as his signature virtue: *gloriatum assidue in commemoranda sua pietate* (12.3; also 15; for *pietas* on his coinage, Sutherland 1951, 107–8). The irony of it attached to this impious emperor (23–26) was not lost.

et castrorum filius et pater exercituum: The oxymoron of "son of the camp" and "father of the armies" seems to be the point here. Gaius capitalized on the first of these when he asserted his childhood role as the *alumnus legionum* (8.1). The second should have come with his German campaign (43–48). But how could "Little Boots" (9) be *imperator?* For the similar *parens legionum,* Tac. *Ann.* 2.55.5.

et optimus maximus Caesar: *Optimus* and *maximus* were *cognomina* of Jupiter Capitolinus, and the double superlative was standard for Trajan and afterwards (Fears 66–74; Frei-Stolba 21–31). The problem seems to be that Gaius attached the divine epithets to his family name; Caesar was not yet a title and always kept private connotations (Simpson 1981, 497–98; Fishwick 1987–1992,

---

42 Dio is assumed to follow first century sources closely if with abbreviation and editing. He summarizes the reign of Gaius in 59.1–5 and then begins from the beginning again in chapter 6. If this betrays two sources (Questa 1957a, 45–47; see note 94), then both sources were schematically conceived.

333–34; Veyne 1990, 332). Gaius was charged with setting himself up as an alternate Jupiter, a rival to Jupiter Optimus Maximus on the Capitoline (22.4).

cum audiret forte reges, qui officii causa in urbem advenerant, concertantis apud se super cenam de nobilitate generis: The kings were plausibly Antiochus and Herod Agrippa, the τυραννοδιδάσκαλοι (16.3) who were with him in Lugdunum (35.1; 59.24.1) and probably in Rome too.

exclamavit: When Suetonius' emperors quote Homer, they do it with emotion (Berthet 330). But Gaius often shouted or threatened: *vox comminantis audita est* (22.4), *exclamavit* (30.2), *clamitans* (35.3), or spoke with a loud voice, *maxima voce* (49.1), *exaudiretur a procul stantibus,* (53.1), *voce clarissima* (Sen. *Dial.* 2.18.2). See on 50.2 for loud speech as a symptom of mania.

εἷς κοίρανος ἔστω, εἷς βασιλεύς: Odysseus rallied the common lot of fighters against the Trojans and advised allegiance to Agamemnon (Hom. *Il.* 2.204–5) with this line that was proverbial for validating solitary rule (Nep. 10.6.4). Domitian used the first half of it: οὐκ ἀγαθὸν πολυκοιρανίη (Suet. *Dom.* 12.7). It also provides a contrast between Gaius and his ancestor of the same name, the allegedly more reluctant Julius Caesar, who conspicuously refused the title of king: *plebei regem se salutanti Caesarem se, non regem esse responderit* (Suet. *Jul.* 79.2); ἀπεκρίνατο μὲν ὅτι "Ζεὺς μόνος τῶν Ῥωμαίων βασιλεὺς εἴη" (Dio 44.11.3). Gaius justified the death of Tiberius Gemellus (23.3) with this argument (ἀκοινώνητον ἀρχή, Philo *Leg.* 68). More Homer at 22.4 and Dio 59.19.2.

nec multum afuit quin statim diadema sumeret speciemque principatus in regni formam converteret: Diadema and *regnum* make the reference to Caesar explicit and show that the ancients (not just modern scholarship, Willrich 444–45; Balsdon 1934a, 165–66; Weinstock 1971, 191, 217, 336) thought that Gaius was following Caesar's precedent. For further analogies between the two, see 46, 57.1–3, 58.3, 60. Gaius would scarcely have decided on an open course of kingship the day he became princeps (*statim*). He tried the Augustan model with extra emphasis on measures to gain popular support, and when he failed, he was perceived as having following the Caesarian model from the beginning.

Gaius' divine pretensions are a central motif of the tradition. Dio implies that he had an official cult as a *deus praesens* when he writes that he had two temples in Rome, one of them voted him by the senate (59.28.2), that he ordered sacrifices to be made to himself (59.4.4, 26.10) and that he was named as Jupiter in documents (59.28.8). On the other hand, there are categorical statements that no temple to a living emperor was ever built in Rome (Tac. *Ann.* 15.74.3; Dio 51.20.8). The only numismatic or epigraphic evidence for his divinity comes from outside the city (*Docs.* nos. 126,

127, 361, 401, pp. 48, 92, 120–21), and Gaius was angry at the senate specifically because it did not vote him divine honors (τὰ ὑπὲρ ἄνθρωπον, Dio 59.25.5). But surrogate concepts of divinity were available. *Numen* was the manifestation of divine power, and *genius* was a guardian spirit (Fishwick 1987–1992, 375–87). Tiberius had dedicated an altar to the *numen* of Augustus after he had ruled forty prestigious years (Nock 355; Fishwick 1987–1990, 386–87). Evidently the problem was that arrogant young Gaius intiated the cult of his *numen* himself (22.3) and demanded reverence for his *genius* (27.3; Simpson 1981, 501–10). There was a distinction "between the princes who were worshipped and those who had themselves worshipped" (Veyne 1990, 313). He called attention to his religious practices by dabbling in Isiac worship (22.3, 54.2, 57.4), postured as various gods (on what occasions? 52), demanded sycophantic behavior from his associates in imitation of an Eastern (divine) monarch (56.2) and invited the accusation that he was challenging Jupiter (22.2, 4 ; also 33, 57.3). Whether or not he thought he was a god cannot be known, but he struck contemporaries as acting as though he did (Dio 59.30.1).

Much of the material in 22.2–3 is paralleled in Dio 59.28.1–7, a segment that falls chronologically within the brief period between Gaius' return to Rome on the last day of August, A.D. 40 (49.2) and his death some five months later (58.1), a period during which his excesses became a rationale for his assassination (56.1 = Dio 59.25.5[b]; Sen. *Dial.* 3.20.9). The information seems already to have been collected in a common source and had its origin over a longer period of time.

22.2 *verum admonitus et principum et regum se excessisse fastigium, divinam ex eo maiestatem asserere sibi coepit:* This generalization about Gaius testing the limits recalls Julius Caesar, who skirted divine kingship too closely for his own good. Augustus had confined the worship of himself to the provinces, especially to the East and then only in conjunction with the goddess Roma (Tac. *Ann.* 4.37.3; Suet. *Aug.* 52). Gaius' temple at Miletus was within these bounderies (21). He always refused to take advice (*admonitus*) from anyone, from Antonia (23.2, 29.1), Junius Silanus (on 23.3) or Macro (on 26.1).

datoque negotio, ut simulacra numinum religione et arte praeclara, inter quae Olympii Iovis, apportarentur e Graecia, quibus capite dempto suum imponeret: The responsibility for moving the huge and renowned Phidean statue of Zeus from Olympia was given (*datoque negotio*) to Memmius Regulus (on 17.1, 25.2; for the rest of this story, 57.1). Colossol statues were frequent for emperors (Price 187–88); one of Augustus at Caesarea was modeled on this same Olympian Zeus (Jos. *BJ* 1.414). And it was also usual for emperors to import works of art (Suet. *Tib.* 74). Gaius brought in others (Jos. *AJ* 19.7) including the obelisk for the Circus Vaticanus that was even larger than the Olympian Zeus (on 54.1; *Cl.* 20.3; Pliny *HN* 16.201); Claudius is credited with sending some of them back (Dio 60.6.8). Nor was the exchange of heads and the relabeling of statues unheard of (Dio Chrys. *Or.* 31; Price 193–94), especially the heads of emperors who suffered *damnatio memoriae;* Gaius himself lost a few in this way (Blanck 24; Jucker 1981, 254–81). But replacing the head of an emperor like Augustus was forbidden (Tac. *Ann.* 1.73.3; Suet. *Tib.* 58; Pliny *HN* 34.46, 35.94; Bauman 71–85; Jucker 1981, 236–41), and exchanging a god's head with one's own was hubris indeed. See note 43.

partem Palatii ad forum usque promovit: Pliny comments similarly on the expansion of the Palatine: *bis vidimus urbem totam cingi domibus principum Gai et Neronis* (*HN* 36.111). No building can be attributed to Gaius for certain although it should be assumed that he continued restoring and adding to the existing structures (Tamm 1963, 65–71; 1964, 151; Bellwald et al. 18). The sale of items from the *vetus aula* (39.1) seems to imply new construction.

atque aede Castoris et Pollucis in vestibulum transfigurata: An enclosed walkway (ἔσοδον, Dio 59.28.5) led down from the Palatine to the temple of Castor and Pollux which was on the south side of the Forum, and a peristyle surrounding an open water basin stood between palace and temple. But these structures were already in place. At the most, Gaius cut a back door into the middle of the temple of the Dioscuri (διατεμὼν διὰ μέσου τῶν ἀγαλμάτων), who were to be the gatekeepers (πυλωροὺς) of his *vestibulum* (Dio 59.28.5; Tamm 1963, 68–71; 1964, 150–51). When Claudius undid Gaius' damage and returned the temple to the gods (Dio 60.6.8), he reclosed the passageway. Alternatively, the Dioscuri gatekeepers may only mean that the main entrance to the Palatine was between this temple and the new temple of Augustus (Wiseman 1987, 169).

consistens saepe inter fratres deos, medium adorandum se adeuntibus exhibebat: As demigods, the Dioscuri occupied an intermediate position on the path to divinity, and it has been suggested that this and their acceptance into the cult of Isis (Witt 71) gave Gaius the incentive to join himself to them (Philo *Leg.* 78–92). But the real reason for his choice of this temple must have been its location proximate to the Palatine. Was it a statue of himself that he placed between the brothers (Simpson 1981, 501, n. 32), or did he hold court there in person? The temple was already a public meeting place (Cic. *Phil* 3.27: [M. Antonius] *audiente populo sedens pro aede Castoris dixit*). Augustus sat in the temple of Apollo on the Palatine to hear cases (Suet. *Aug.* 29.3).

quidam eum Latiarem Iovem consalutant: Were the *quidam* who saluted him as Jupiter Latieris flattering him, or were they calling him a second class Jupiter (Simpson 1981, 498 and n. 27)? During the Republic a general could make an alternate, self-proclaimed (*sine publica auctoritate,* Livy 42.21.7) triumph for himself when he did not consider the official ovation he was voted appreciative enough of his accomplishments. Such a triumphal parade ended on the Alban Mount at the temple of Jupiter Latiaris, the god of the Latin League, (Wissowa 125; Warren 50; Livy 26.21.2–6, 33.23.3, 42.21.7, 45.38.4). A general with a genuine triumph, on the other hand, dressed like Jupiter Capitolinus and became identified with him when his parade ended on the Capitoline. Gaius had ovations (16.4, 49.2, note 39), but never a triumph, except perhaps for a self-proclaimed one of a sort with his bridge at Baiae (19), and he too had a dwelling (a country house) on the Alban Mount (Sen. *Dial.* 11.17.4). His vacillation about his triumph (48.2, 49.2) was an important element in the characterization of him as capricious and plausibly prompted this joke about an alternate Jupiter on an alternate hill with an alternate triumph. Dio says that Gaius himself used the name (Δία τε Λατιάριον ἑαυτὸν ὀνομάσας, 59.28.5), although he may have been mistaken in this. See 22.4 for him as a different alternate Jupiter on the Palatine.

22.3 templum etiam numini suo proprium et sacerdotes et excogitatissimas hostias instituit: Suetonius takes up Gaius' temple, priests and sacrificial victims in the same order as they are listed in this introductory sentence. Gaius instituted a shrine to his *numen,* no doubt on the Palatine which is where Divus Augustus had his. His *templum* was probably an open air area or perhaps a preexisting building since time was short for a building project, especially if all these religious excesses are referred to the last months of his reign (Dio 59.8.1–7). Seneca mentions a mound (*tumulus*) on which daily sacrifices were made (*Dial.* 9.14.9; Simpson 1981, 489, n. 2). Dio speaks of two shrines, one voted by the senate, another built at Gaius' own expense on the Palatine (ἐν αὐτῇ τῇ Ῥώμῃ ναὸν ἑαυτοῦ τὸν μὲν ὑπὸ τῆς βουλῆς ψηφισθέντα τὸν δὲ ἰδίᾳ ἐν τῷ Παλατίῳ, 59.28.2). The one voted by the senate may be a confusion from the vote of the *clipeus* that was to be carried to the Capitol (on 16.4; Simpson 1981, 504–6) or a conflation with a different structure that Gaius is said to have begun on the Capitoline (22.4; Dio 59.28.2).

in templo simulacrum stabat aureum iconicum amiciebaturque cotidie veste, quali ipse uteretur: This statue was the replacement for the Olympian Zeus that never made it to Rome (57.1; Dio 59.28.3).[43] Gold statues were not reserved for gods (Price 186–87) but this was nonetheless extravagant; Augustus had ordered silver statues of himself melted down (Suet. *Aug.* 52). *Iconicum* = a realistic portrayal (Pliny *HN* 34.16, 35.57), and the realism increased when Gaius

---

[43] But the chronology is wrong since this "replacement statue" already stood on the Palatine while Gaius was alive and the importation of the Olympian Zeus was aborted because of events connected with Gaius' death. The grandiose project may never been much more than an intention or desire or a metaphor for his self-aggrandizement. See 22.1.

dressed it in his own clothes. For other clothed statues in Rome, Suet., *Ner.* 57.1; Pliny *HN* 8.197, 34.33; Ov. *Fast.* 6.570; Fishwick 1987–1990, 562–63.

magisteria sacerdotii ditissimus quisque et ambitione et licitatione maxima vicibus comparabant: "All the wealthiest men got the chief priesthoods in turn by competing for them with the highest bids." Gaius charged them ten million sesterces (Dio 59.28.5), and Claudius went into debt *pro introitu novi sacerdotii* (Suet *Cl.* 9.2, where the price is recorded as only eight million). In addition to Claudius, the priests were his last wife Caesonia, his horse Incitatus (55.3) and himself (Dio 59.28.5–6); the point is that he had few choices left at the end. Gaius' participation was possible in the cult of his *numen* but not in a cult for himself as a *deus praesens* (Simpson 1981, 107–8).

hostiae erant phoenicopteri, pavones, tetraones, numidicae, meleagrides, phasianae: Hostiae picks up *excogitatissimas hostias* in the introductory sentence (above); cf. *excogitare* also for the bridge at Baiae (19.1, 19.3, 32.1). Obscure rituals have been sought to explain why these particular birds were chosen. Bird sacrifices were known, especially in Egypt and the Orient (Eitrem 1932a, 53 n. 1), and if the flamingo (*phoenicopterus*) was a surrogate for the phoenix, the Egyptian bird that rose from its own ashes, the sacrifices were perhaps for a promise of resurrection or reincarnation, and Gaius was modeling the cult of his *numen* on Isis worship (Köberlein 46–49). But what these birds really have in common is the fact that they were farmed in Italy to provide luxurious dining; they were "expensive delicacies" (ὄρνιθες...ἁπαλοί τέ τινες καὶ πολυτίμηνοι, Dio 59.28.6; Sen. *Ep.* 10.12; *Dial.* 12.10.3; Juv. 11.13; Pliny *HN* 10.133; Friedländer 2.165–66). Flamingo tongues were an especially decadent treat along with pheasant and peacock brains (Suet. *Vit.* 13.2). The *tetrao*, like the *Numidica gallina,* was a guinea fowl, and so was the *meleagris,* otherwise a *gallina Africa.* Their table uses could not possibly have been overlooked by Gaius' contemporaries. Whatever he did sacrifice (perhaps indeed a flamingo, 57.4) turned into this menu-like list as a comment on his idiosyncratic excess.

generatim per singulos dies immolarentur: A different bird was sacrificed for each day of a six-day cycle: καθ᾽ ἑκάστην ἡμέραν ἐθύοντο (Dio 59.28.6). The autumn celebration for Isis lasted perhaps six days (Merkelbach 50, n. 21) and if so, may have determined the number of birds.

The climax of this rubric is Gaius' commerce with the gods themselves. He is said to have introduced foreign rites into Rome and he participated in Isiac worship (54.2, 57.4; Jos. *AJ* 19.30, 71, 104; *Suda* 1.503, Γάϊος 12). In doing this he sanctioned the religion that had made inroads into Rome despite attempts by his predecessors to hold it at bay—at least in public (Suet. *Tib.* 36; Tac.

Ann. 2.85.4; Dio 53.2.4, 54.6.6, 57.18.5; Jos. *AJ* 18.65–80), and accepted Antony's tutelary deity (Verg. *Aen.* 8.696–700; Prop. 3.11.27–46).[44] His involvement with her cult was ridiculed by the conservative elite who passed judgment on him. His religious feelings, if any, cannot be known.

22.4 *et noctibus quidem plenum fulgentemque lunam invitabat assidue in amplexus atque concubitum:* Gaius was the sun (Helios = Osiris) who enjoyed sexual intercourse with his sister the moon (Selene = Isis). An initiate of the cult of Isis was united with the goddess in her lunar manifestation, and as the full moon she was especially potent (Apul. *Met.* 11.1; Köberlein 56–57). Gaius' interest in Isis and his important relationship with his sister Drusilla (24.1) were combined in an incestuous joke that did not need explanation. A similar joke at Dio 59.26.5 and 59.27.6.

Gaius was accused of initiating a Palatine-Capitoline rivalry by setting himself up, not as an earthly counterpart of the Jupiter on the Capitoline, an acceptable posture (22.1), but as an alternate Jupiter on the Palatine. The theme is challenge, not identification. It is difficult to say where fact leaves off and ridicule begins, to what limits Gaius acted on his presumptions, and to what degree this information is a metaphor for his arrogance.

interdiu vero cum Capitolino Iove secreto fabulabatur, modo insusurrans ac praebens in vicem aurem: The intimacy with Isis (above) is paired with conspiratorial intimacy with Jupiter. Josephus writes that Gaius called him brother (*AJ* 19.4; cf. Dio 59.28.2).

***modo clarius non sine iurgiis. nam vox comminantis audita est:* ἢ μ' ἀνάειρ' ἢ ἐγὼ σέ:** Enticements alternated with noisy imprecations. This not particularly noteworthy Homeric quotation, "Either lift me or I will lift you," is a challenge from Ajax to Odysseus in their wrestling match at the funeral games for Patroclus (*Il.* 23.724). There is no evidence that it was a proverbial saying (Berthet 325). Gaius knew his Homer well if it was he who spoke it and not a literate wag who found it appropriate for him (Homer also at 22.1 and Dio 59.19.2). Dio gives more details about the circumstances: Gaius answered Jupiter's thunder and lightning with a kind of thunder machine of his own (ταῖς τε βρονταῖς ἐκ μηχανῆς τινος ἀντεβρόντα) and whenever lighting struck, he threw a javelin at a rock in return (λίθον ἀντηκόντιζεν) as he uttered this same

---

[44] A coin from Alexandria from early in Gaius' reign (A.D. 37–38) shows him radiate on the obverse, a half moon on the reverse (*Docs* no. 126, p. 48), and he was plausibly responsible for the Iseum that was built in the Campus Martius between the reigns of Tiberius and Nero (Wissowa 352–54), although Claudius would have had to sanction it too (Barrett 1989, 220). But a room decorated with Egyptian motifs in an early part of the Palatine conplex that was formerly attributed to him (Cumont 127–39) has more recently been shown to be Augustan (Tamm 1963, 60; Barrett 1989, 221, 307, n. 27).

line (59.28.6).[45] Seneca also records it when he illustrates Gaius' futile anger in lashing out at the thunder that disturbed his pantomimes and parties: *ad pugnam vocavit Iovem et quidem sine missione, Homericum illum exclamans versum* (*Dial.* 3.20.8). Once the line was attached to him, situations were invented to fit. But the idea of challenge remains central.

donec exoratus, ut referebat, et in contubernium ultro invitatus: According to Gaius (*ut referebat*), it was Jupiter Capitolinus who took the initive and invited him to share his lodging, proof of their equaliy. *Contubernium,* especially following *concubitum* in the preceeding anecdote about Isis, implies concubinage. Gaius coveted both divine females and divine males as sexual partners (36 for his tastes).

super templum Divi Augusti ponte transmisso Palatium Captioliniumque coniunxit: A bridge between the Palatine and the Capitoline over the Temple of Augustus (21) was possible since the new temple lay in the valley between the two hills. To be imagined is a causeway running across the temple roof (Stambaugh 68–69; Wiseman 1991, 44; cf. 37.1 for Gaius on top of the Basilica Julia), unless, of course, the bridge is a another metaphor for commerce between the two "gods." But the specifics (*super templum Divi Augusti*) and Pliny's comment that the entire city was surrounded by Gaius' palace suggest that something did exist (*HN* 36.111; on 22.2).

mox, quo propior esset, in area Capitolina novae domus fundamenta iecit: He constructed (or began, *fundamenta iecit*) a kind of resting place (κατάλυσίν τινα, a temporary dwelling?) so that he could live with Jupiter (ἵν', ὡς ἔλεγε [cf. *ut referebat* above], τῷ Διὶ συνοικοίη, 59.28.2; cf. *contubernium,* above). It is possible that Gaius was following the model of the *casa Romuli,* the "hut" of Romulus on the Capitoline; for "huts" on the Capitoline and Palatine, Wiseman 1981, 45; 1987, 173. For the possibility that this structure was mistaken as a second temple, see on 22.3.

Impietas, the next character flaw that Suetonius takes up, follows logically from *superbia.* Gaius showed disrespect for and cruelty toward those who deserved better from him, especially his family. This is in contrast to his initial *pietas* in chapter 15. Some of these same persons will appear again at 29.1 when his talent for verbal abuse is described. Suetonius begins with Gaius' ancestors, including Augustus, Agrippa and Livia (23.1–2), then proceeds to his "brother" Tiberius Gemellus, his father-in-law Marcus Silanus and his uncle Claudius (23.3), and finally he

---

45 A precedent of sorts can be found when Augustus built a temple to Jupiter Tonans ("the thunderer") and Jupiter Capitolinus was jealous (Suet. *Aug.* 91.2; Fears 59–60). Theaters did have thunder machines (Sall. *Hist.* 2.70.3; Phaedrus 5.7.23; Vitr. *De Arch.* 5.6.8).

elaborates on Gaius' notorious relationships with his sisters (24) and wives (25). Chapter 26 takes *impietas* further afield.

23.1 *Agrippae se nepotem neque credi neque dici ob ignobilitatem eius volebat:* For the obscure origins of Gaius' maternal grandfather Agrippa (7, 21), see Sen. *Ben.* 3.32.4; Sen. *Controv.* 2.4.12–13; Vell. 2.96.1, 127.1. Because Gaius had no credentials for his job beyond his Julian blood, he had to take his family tree seriously. But disrespect toward Agrippa was never reflected in public policy. The battle of Actium in which he played a key role continued to be celebrated on Gaius' coinage, this despite his alleged objection to the celebration of the Actian victories (below; *RIC²* Gaius no. 58, p. 112; Nicols 84–85; cf. Sutherland 1951, 102, n. 2; Tac. *Ann.* 1.41.2). Nor was Gaius ashamed to designate his mother Agrippina as *M. Agrippae [f.]* on her burial urn and *M F* on a sestertius (*Docs.* nos. 84a, 84b, p. 41; Balsdon 1934a, 30).

suscensebatque, si qui vel oratione vel carmine imaginibus eum Caesarum insererent: Note how Suetonius places *eum* (Agrippa) quite literally within the *imaginibus Caesarum*. To place his *imago* even figuratively among the death masks of the Caesars was to make him an ancestor. Agrippa's praises had been sung by the Augustan poets, notably Vergil (*Aen.* 8.682–84) and more recently by the Tiberian apologist Velleius Paterculus (2.59.5). For the allegation that Gaius denigrated Augustan authors, 34.2.

praedicabat autem matrem suam ex incesto, quod Augustus cum Iulia filia admisisset, procreatam: Not only would a union between Augustus and his daughter have kept the Julian blood pure, but an ancestor's incest would justify his own with his sisters (24.1). He thus had precedent from both Augustus and Jupiter—and from Osiris as well (22.4; noted by Dio, 59.26.5; cf. Victor 3.10; Ceausescu 272).

ac non contentus hac Augusti insectatione Actiacas Si[n]culasque victorias, ut funestas p. R. et calamitosas, vetuit sollemnibus feriis celebrari: The Actian games had been instituted by Augustus to celebrate his victory over Antony in 31 B.C. They were held on the anniversary of the battle, September 2, at Nicopolis, the city Augustus founded on the site (Strab. 7.7.6). The final battle of the war against the Sicily-based Sextus Pompeius was on September 3, 36 B.C., and Agrippa was a key figure in that victory too. Gaius broke the *fasces* (really or metaphorically?) of the consuls suffect of A.D. 39 and removed them from office for celebrating the two victories of Augustus and for recognizing his August 31 birthday inadequately (on 17.1, 26.3). This rewrote history at the expense of Augustus (and Agrippa, above) in favor of Antony. But in fact Augustus was advertised as an ancestor until the end (*RIC*[2] Gaius nos. 48, 50–54, p. 111) and he continued to be honored at regular sacrifices (*Docs*. nos. 5, 9, pp. 12, 14); Gaius dedicated his temple (21) and died in the context of the Palatine Games that had been instituted for him (56.2). The cult of Divus Augustus actually developed during Gaius' reign (Fishwick 1987–1992, 484–85). Since an attempted coup seems to have been in progress in the late summer of 39 (on 24.3), the consuls' misdemeanors with the holidays were probably only an excuse to get rid of them. Gaius would have attacked them, whichever of the two, Augustus or Antony, they had failed to honor (59.20.1–3). Claudius perpetuated the double heritage when he both swore by Augustus and honored Antony's birthday (Suet. *Cl*.11.2–3; also Sen *Dial*. 11.15.4).

23.2 *Liviam Augustam proaviam Ulixem stolatum identidem appellans:* Since Gaius had lived in Livia's house when he was young and she was very old (10.1), he probably had a vivid impression of her. Ulysses was proverbial for sly cunning (*scelerumque inventor Ulixes,* Verg. *Aen.* 2.164). *Stolatum* = wearing the *stola,* the characteristic dress of the Roman matron, of whom Livia was the paradigm. Gaius had a reputation for saying cruel and clever things (29–31) but he did not deny her official respect (*Docs*. no. 3, p. 10 for a sacrifice to her in A.D. 38). She is Livia Augusta here (also 10.1, 15.2) perhaps in order to emphasize the alleged disrespect (elsewhere Livia, 7, or Julia Augusta, 16.3).

etiam ignobilitatis quadam ad senatum epistula arguere ausus est: It was not possible to disavow the genetic contribution from the less than blue-blooded Livia without disavowing Germanicus as well, far too high a price. The context for a letter to the senate calling attention to her origins is unknown. Could it have been in regard to a proposal of deification? Her deification had been proposed under Tiberius (Suet. *Tib*. 51.2; Dio 58.2.1), and Claudius finally arranged it (Suet. *Cl*. 11.2; Dio 60.5.2). Gaius might not have wanted anyone to overshadow his sister Drusilla (24.2).

quasi materno avo decurione Fundano ortam cum publicis monumentis certum sit, Aufidium Lurconem Romae honoribus functum: Quasi: Gaius was correct, but Suetonius, with his penchant for research on families and places (8) was anxious to prove him wrong. Livia's connection with the town of Fundi is attested independently (Suet. *Tib*. 5; Linderski 463–65), and it is wholly plausible that her grandfather was a local magistrate (*decurio*). Suetonius seems to have examined the *publica monumenta* (documents) himself, and so he, not a source, has created a prosopographical problem. Livia's grandfather was an Alfidius (*CIL* 2.1667, 9.3661 = *ILS* 125 and *IGRR* 4.983), not an Aufidius. Either Gaius intentionally (Wiseman 1965) or unintentionally gave him the wrong name in his letter to the senate, or Suetonius confused two men. Since Gaius had all the argument he needed to expose Livia's humble origins in the truth, it seems more likely that Suetonius, seeking proof that the emperor was malicious, looked too creatively for evidence. A prominent Aufidius Lurco, senator and tribune of the plebs, did live in Rome in the late Republic. His name would have been recorded in the *publica monumenta* where Suetonius found it (Linderski 466–73).[46]

aviae Antoniae secretum petenti denegavit, nisi ut interveniret Macro praefectus: Antonia is the first example of those whom Gaius honored (15.2) and then rejected (Dio 59.3.3–4, 6). She asked for a private audience (*secretum petenti*). The point is made that Gaius did not take advice gracefully (on 22.2); more unwanted advice from Antonia at 29.1 and Jos. *AJ* 18.236.

ac per istius modi indignitates et taedia causa extitit mortis: Cf. Dio's "when she rebuked him, he forced her to suicide" (ἐκείνην τε γὰρ ἐπιτιμήσασάν τι αὐτῷ ἐς ἀνάγκην ἑκουσίου θανάτου κατέστησε, 59.3.6). There was a very narrow time slot in which this could have occurred since Antonia died on May 1, A.D. 37 (*Docs.* no. 31, p. 28); Gaius did not really have time to drive the seventy-three year old Antonia to her death during the first few weeks of his reign when his *pietas* was on display (Charlesworth 1933b, 108–9).

dato tamen, ut quidam putant, et veneno: Other deaths vaguely ascribed to poison are Germanicus' (1.2) and Tiberius' (12.2; see note 11). *Ut quidam putant* suggests that this detail came from a source more hostile than the one that accused him of merely insulting her to suicide.

nec defunctae ullum honorem habuit: Not true. See 15.2. Antonia was Claudius' single tenuous blood link with the *Julii,* and so he used her to validate his own claim to the principate (*RIC*² Claudius nos. 65–68, p. 124), just as Gaius had used Agrippina. Several anecdotes show Gaius rejecting her presumably healthy influence, this apparently to rescue her from the contamination of association with him (24.1, 29.1).

---

[46] There does not seem to be a corruption in the Suetonian textual tradition, because if there were, all references to a prominent Aufidius Lurco everywhere would have to be corrected or imagined away since an equally prominent Alfidius Lurco for the same period is highly unlikely. Besides, Lurco never occurs among Alfidii (Linderski 476–80).

prospexitque e triclinio ardentem rogum: Gaius looked north to the pyre on the Campus Martius from the imperial buildings in the northwest part of the Palatine (on 22.3). This funeral would seem to have been a good public relations opportunity for Gaius, and so he must have had tactical reasons for staying home. He was absent from Drusilla's too (on 24.2). Tiberius, Livia and Antonia were criticized when they were absent from Germanicus' funeral (Tac. *Ann.* 3.3.2–3).

23.3 *fratrem Tiberium...interemit:* There are two reasons why Gaius might have disposed of Tiberius Gemellus (14.1, 15.2). Either he could not keep a faction that supported him under control or he felt that he no longer needed to appease such an opposition (Willrich 112; Gelzer 384, 388; Balsdon 1934a, 37; Meise 115–19; Gatti 1057–64). A similar pattern of cooption and execution was followed by Claudius with his sons-in-law (on 35.1). The deed was quietly done. Gaius made no announcement of Gemellus' death to the senate (Dio 59.8.2), and this was consistent with his modest but proper burial as a juvenile member of the imperial family but not of an adopted heir (on 15.2). He probably died in early A.D. 38 since he was replaced among the Arval Brethern on May 24 of that year (*Docs.* no. 3, p. 11). He had been accused of praying that the emperor would die when he was sick (14.2; Dio 59.8.1; Philo; *Leg.* 22–23; *in Flacc.* 10; Jos. *AJ* 18.223). Since motives were easily imagined, Gaius was blamed for his murder, but doubt arises (below and 29.1).

inopinatem repente immisso tribuno militum: The murder was effected by mandated suicide. Since Gemellus was a member of the imperial family, it was *nefas* for anyone who had taken the oath to the emperor to harm him, and so Gemellus had to kill himself. But young and unfamiliar with violent death, he did not know how to fall on a sword and had to be taught by the tribune and centurion who were dispatched to him (Philo *Leg.* 30–31; Willrich 289). For his youthful innocence, 14.2.

Silanum item socerum ad necem secandasque novacula fauces compulit: Suetonius emphasizes intra-familial betrayal by calling M. Junius Silanus, the father of Gaius' first wife (12.1), a father-in-law despite the fact that Gaius was remarried by now (25.1; *occiderat ille socerum,* Sen. *Apocol.* 11.2). Philo says that Silanus got into trouble for giving unwanted advice (*Leg.* 63–65; on 22.1). Perhaps Gaius resented his seniority and status (*per insignem nobilitatem et eloquentiam praecellebat,* Tac. *Ann.* 3.24.3; Dio 59.8.5–6; Philo *Leg.* 75). His death probably fell within the same time frame as that of Gemellus (Dio 59.8.4), and like him he was replaced in the Arval Brotherhood on May 24, A.D. 38 (*Docs.* no. 3 p. 11). But unlike Gemellus, Silanus was eliminated publicly;

L. Julius Graecinus (*PIR²* I. 344) destroyed his own position by refusing to make a charge against him (Tac. *Agr.* 4.1).

causatus in utroque quod...cum... : Complicated parallels are constructed. Gaius' alleged reasons for the two murders are first presented and then shown to be pretexts.

hic ingressum se turbatius mare non esset secutus ac spe occupandi urbem, si quid sibi per tempestates accideret, remansisset: Hic = Silanus. This was when Gaius set out to retrieve the bones of his mother and brother early in April 37 (14.2, 15.1). He got as much favorable publicity as possible out of the stormy sea.

ille antidotum obol[e]uisset, quasi ad praecavenda venena sua sumptum: Ille = Gemellus. The prevention of poisoning, like poisoning itself, was an inexact science. Cf. *antidotum...adversus Caesarem* (29.1). This story is told only by Suetonius.

et Silanus impatientiam nauseae vitasset et molestiam navigandi: Also only here. Silanus was executed merely because he was seasick, not because he was showing disrespect.

et Tiberius propter assiduam et ingravescentem tussim medicamento usus esset: It was only cough medicine after all.[47] Gemellus may have died a natural death (Willrich 289; Balsdon 1934a, 37); Gaius would have pretended that he did in any case.

Claudium patruum non nisi in ludibrum reservavit: The entire family, including his own mother, had slighted Claudius (Suet. *Cl.* 2–4), but Gaius' treatment of him seems to have been particularly cruel (see note 40; Suet. *Cl.* 8–9; *Ner.* 6.2; Sen. *Apocol.* 15.2).

24.1 *cum omnibus sororibus suis consuetudinem stupri fecit:* Just as charges of adultery were routinely made whenever power involved a woman (on 12.2), so, when the partners were of the same family, the charge of incest was bound to follow. It is reported in passing with Agrippina and Livilla (here and 24.3; Dio 59.3.6; 11.1, 22.6; Jos. *AJ* 19.204) but emphatically with Drusilla (below).[48]

---

[47] In a variation of this theme, Nero sent Burrus (Sex. Afranius Burrus, *PIR²* A. 441) poison in the form of cough medicine (Suet. *Ner.* 35.5).

[48] Gaius' sexual alliances were particularly schematic. He had plans to make Aemilius Lepidus (below), Drusilla's husband, his successor (Dio 59.22.6–7), and they were accordingly said to be

plenoque convivio singulas infra se vicissim conlocabat uxore supra cubante: As host Gaius occupied the upper position on the lowest couch of the three at the banquet. A sister took the wife's traditional place on the same couch below him, while his actual wife reclined in the *locus consularis*, the last place on the middle couch (*supra*), the honored guest's position. The sisters rotated through the wife's position (*vicissim* = in turn).

ex iis Drusillam: All three of Gaius' sisters were important allies for the childless emperor (on 15.3), but he had a special connection with Drusilla, who, for whatever reason (sexual involvement cannot be excluded), was willing to co-operate in helping to stabilize his dynastic position. The *iustitium* at her death (24.2), her deification (24.3), the magificant celebration of her birthday in 39 (17.2, 18.2–3), and Gaius' legitimate daughter carrying on her name (25.4) are all testimony of a truly special role for this middle sister. But it was a passive one; history has given her no personality. There is no way to know whether or not Gaius had sex with Drusilla or any of his sisters. An Isis-Osiris model (on 22.4) and a desire to husband the trickle of Julian blood could have rationalized it, and his reaction to Drusilla's death was certainly intense (24.2), although that can be explained otherwise. But the earliest witnesses about Gaius, the very hostile Seneca and Philo, do not mention incest (Willrich 291). Much modern scholarship considers it a rumor (Meise 99, n. 46, for a summary). See below for Agrippina who wanted Drusilla's job. See 36.1 for more about Gaius' sexual activities.

vitiasse virginem praetextatus adhuc creditur atque etiam in concubitu eius quondam deprehensus ab Antonia avia, apud quam simul educabantur: Drusilla was about four years younger than Gaius (on 7), who lived with Antonia for a year to two before he joined Tiberius on Capreae (10.1). This anecdote gives the grandmother the opportunity to disapprove of him, and she is again divorced from responsibility in rearing the *monstrum* (23.3, 29.1). Suetonius hesitates to give this story full factual status (*creditur*).

mox Lucio Cassio Longino consulari conlocatam abduxit: Drusilla was married to L. Cassius Longinus (*PIR² C.* 503) in 33 at the same time that her sister Julia Livilla was married to Marcus Vinicius (*PIR¹ V.* 445; Tac. *Ann.*

---

lovers (36.1; Dio 59.11.1). After Drusilla died, Lepidus seems to have refocused his ambition through the other two sisters and was accused of adultery with either the ambitious Agrippina or with both her and Julia Livilla (on 24.3; Dio 59.22.6–7). Something similar seems operational with Nero and his mother Agrippina; she provided access to power for her son, but when her influence diminished, the texts become unsure of who took the initiative in their sexual relations (Tac. *Ann.* 14.2; cf. Suet. *Ner.* 28.2).

6.15.1; Dio 58.21.1). Both men had been consuls in 30 when Sejanus was at the height of his power, but they survived by virtue of their prestige (Syme 1958, 384 n. 8, 385), and Tiberius rewarded their political agility with the two princesses. Gaius divorced Drusilla from Longinus in order to marry her to M. Aemilius Lepidus (*PIR²* A. 371), who came from a family with a history of political ambition; he was a nephew of the husband (L. Aemilius Paulus, *PIR²* 391) of the younger Julia (Syme 1955, 22–33; Hayne 497–506).

et in modum iustae uxoris propalam habuit: Gaius and Drusilla remained coupled both before and after she died and was deified (24.2; e.g., an undated coin from Smyrna with Gaius on the obverse, Drusilla as Persephone on the reverse, *Docs.* no. 222, p. 65). *Propalam:* there was nothing secret about her importance.

heredem quoque bonorum atque imperii aeger instituit: To inherit the emperor's wealth was to inherit the Empire (14.1). Gaius was still childless when he was ill in 37 (14.2). If he died, Drusilla would inherit the money and Lepidus would exercise regency and be his successor (Dio 59.22.6–7; Meise 108–9). Lepidus was allowed to stand for office five years before the legal age (Dio 59.22.6), a clear sign that he was an heir designate (1.1). The arrangement was a variation on the tactic of adoption that placed a body between the emperor and potential assassins (15.2 for the "adoption" of Tiberius Gemellus). The blue Julian blood was programmed, temporarily at least, to continue through Drusilla (with or without Gaius' genetic contribution). The prestige that the *mater principis* (e.g. Livia) enjoyed is illustrated by a story told about another of Gaius' sisters, the ambitious Agrippina. In December of that year (A.D. 37) Agrippina gave birth to the first child of the new generation, the future emperor Nero. She asked Gaius to choose a name for him, presumably hoping that he would choose his own, an indication that he would adopt him. When he suggested Claudius, she knew that she would not be matriarch of the imperial house (Suet. *Ner.* 6.2; noted by Willrich 291; Balsdon 1934a, 42). Drusilla was presumably more tractable.

24.2 *eadem defuncta:* Drusilla died on June 10, A.D. 38 (*Docs.* no. 31, p. 28), quite possibly in childbirth or from complications of pregnancy. Eutropius ascribes a daughter to Gaius' union with one of the sisters (*ex una etiam natam filiam cognovit,* 7.12), no doubt a doublet of the daughter that he did have with Caesonia (25.3–4).

iustitium indixit, in quo risisse lavisse cenasse cum parentibus aut coniuge liberisve capital fuit: Cf. Dio: Gaius punished anyone who feasted or even bathed during the *iustitium* (εἴ τις εἰστίασεν ἢ ἠσπάσατό τινα ἢ καὶ

ἐλούσατο ἐν ταῖς ἡμέραις ἐκείναις, ἐκολάζετο, 59.10.8; also 59.11.6; and
Seneca: *eos qui parum maesti fuerant crudelissima adficiebat animadversione*).[49]
The *iustitium* was in effect in Alexandria as well (Philo *in Flacc.* 56) and presumably lasted from June 10 (*Docs.* no. 31, p. 28) until Drusilla was deified (cf. the
iustitium for Germanicus, 5, 6.2). Disrespect for her (an insult to the emperor
and his family) could fall under the jurisdiction of the *crimen maiestatis* even
through the law was supposed to have been in abeyance at this time (15.4, 30.1);
perhaps it never was (Bauman 105–6). Gaius may have been genuinely fond of
his sister (Willrich 295; Gelzer 392; Balsdon 1934a, 42–43; Meise 103), but the
fact remains that her death undermined his already insecure position. She had a
public funeral which Gaius did not attend. Lepidus was still in the plan and delivered the oration (Dio 59.11.1–2; Sen. *Dial.* 11.17.4). Gaius continued to need her
support dead as well as alive and so arranged her deification (below) and her
massive birthday celebration the next year (17.2, 18.2–3). Note the rhetorical
variation in the two triplets: *risisse lavisse cenasse* with asyndeton, *parentibus aut
coniuge liberisve* with varied connectives.

*ac maeroris impatiens, cum repente noctu profugisset ab urbe
transcucurrissetque Campaniam Syracusas petit:* After Drusilla died,
Gaius departed mysteriously from Rome, and left his behavior open to speculation.[50] Seneca says he spent his time playing dice *in Albano suo,* his *praedium*
near the city, and calls his activity during this crisis a cardinal instance of his
erratic inconsistency: *furiosa inconstantia...numquam satis certus utrum lugeri
vellet an coli sororem* (Sen. *Dial.* 11.17.5; note 49). Similar ambivalence occurred when citizens were punished both for failing to mourn her as a mortal and
for failing to rejoice in her godhead (below; Dio 59.11.5). Gaius may have fled
Rome until he could get the deification program in order. But the Sicilian trip

---

[49] Seneca's entire passage is pertinent; he uses Gaius' behavior at the death of Drusilla as an ex-
emplar of improper mourning: *C. Caesar amissa sorore Drusilla, is homo qui non magis dolere
quam gaudere principaliter posset, conspectum conversationemque civium suorum profugit,
exequiis sororis suae non interfuit, iusta sorori non praestitit, sed in Albano suo tesseris ac foro †et
pervocatis et† huiusmodi aliis occupationibus acerbissimi funeris elevabat mala. Pro pudor imperii!
principis Romani lugentis sororem alea solacium fuit! Idem ille Gaius furiosa inconstantia modo
barbam capillumque summittens modo Italiae ac Siciliae oras errabundus permetiens et numquam
satis certus utrum lugeri vellet an coli sororem, eodem omni tempore quo templa illi constituebat ac
pulvinaria eos qui parum maesti fuerant crudelissima adficiebat animadversione* (*Dial.* 11.17.4–5).

[50] Köberlein envisions Gaius acting out the search of Isis for Osiris, first mourning his loss and
then rejoicing in finding him (62–67). Gelzer (395–96) postpones Gaius' trip to early 39, because
of another sudden departure to Campania that spring (Dio 59.13.7) and the statement that he toured
Italy and Sicily while he was preparing a temple and divine honors for her, i. e., after her deification (Sen. *Dial.* 11.17.5).

with the games in Syracuse (20, 21) must already have been planned since it does not seem to have been hurried or spontaneous (cf. 51.1; Jos. *AJ* 19.205).

rursusque inde propere rediit barba capilloque promisso: Cf. Seneca: *modo barbam capillumque summittens.* Among the normally clean-shaven, unkempt hair and beard were standard manifestations of neglect at times of crisis (Suet. *Jul.* 67.2); it was the opposite for the bearded (cf. the mourning for Germanicus in Parthia, 5).

nec umquam postea quantiscumque de rebus, ne pro contione quidem populi aut apud milites, nisi per numen Drusillae deieravit: Drusilla was the first imperial woman to become a goddess but not the last, notably Livia (Suet. *Cl.* 11; see on 23.2), Nero's daughter Claudia (*PIR²* C. 1061) and his wife Poppea Sabina (*PIR¹* P. 630; Tac. *Ann.* 15.23.1, 16.21.2; Herz 1981b, 326). Her elevation evidently took place on September 23, A.D. 38, the birthday of Augustus (*Docs.* no. 5, p. 12; Herz 1981a, 101; cf. *ILS* 197). Since Suetonius is interested in Gaius and not in his sister, he confines the notice of her deification to this. But Dio furnishes details: she was voted all Livia's honors, one statue of her was to be set up in the senate house and another in the temple of Venus, she was to have a shrine and a priesthood of twenty individuals (both male and female), her birthday would be an important festival, her new name was to be Panthea and she was to have divine honors throughout the Empire. A Roman senator (Livius Geminus, *PIR²* L. 296) swore that he saw her ascend to heaven and was paid a million sesterces for his acute vision (Dio 59.11.2–4; Sen. *Apocol.* 1.2–3; for epigraphical confirmation of her godhead, *Docs.* no. 128a, 401, p. 49, 120). Like Gaius himself, women were to swear by her *numen* whenever they took an oath (Dio 59.11.3). All this for a young woman so recently come onto the scene must have struck many as quite inappropriate; she was not Livia.

24.3 *reliquas sorores nec cupiditate tanta nec dignatione dilexit, ut quas saepe exoletis suis prostrav<er>it:* Cf. 24.1 and note 48. The idea is that if Gaius could control his sisters' sexual favors, he could control an access to power.

Suetonius' biographical method does not allow him to relate systematically the crisis that is touched on here, the plot or plots that culminated in the deaths of Lepidus and of Lentulus Gaetulicus (8.1, 2) and in the exiles of Agrippina and Julia Livilla (29.1, 39.1). Gaius had evidently learned about a conspiracy by September 1, A.D. 39, when he eliminated the consuls suffect (on 17.1, 23.1, 26.3) and hastily left Rome (43), but the causal relationships among these actions are unclear. Gaetulicus as long-time commander of the Army of Upper Germany controlled the requisite military manpower for a coup. Evidence for his death is the thanksgiving sacrifice by the Arval Brotherhood on October 27, A.D. 39: *A.d. VI K. Novembr. ob detecta nefaria con[silia in C. Germani]cum Cn.*

Lentuli Gaet[ulici...] (*Docs.* no. 9, p. 14; also Dio 59.22.5), the fact that he was indeed replaced by Galba (on 44.1) and an Alpine pass to be held for him (Sen. *QNat.* 4a. *praef* 15). As for Lepidus, with Drusilla dead, his projected route to the principate disappeared, and he seems to have alienated Gaius by being on the wrong side of the latter's disagreement with A. Avillius Flaccus (*PIR²* A. 1414), the equestrian prefect of Egypt who was exiled and killed in the fall and winter of 38–39 (Philo *in Flacc.* 10–23, 151, 180–81; on 26.1).

When Gaius finally found a wife to produce a child for him, probably in the summer of 39 (25.4), Lepidus' ambition was further frustrated. This child would also have discouraged Agrippina, who must still have hoped to inherit Drusilla's role with her son Nero (on 24.1). She and Lepidus may have planned to see Gaius murdered and then marry; they are linked by a charge of adultery (Dio 59.22.6; Tac. *Ann.* 14.2.2). Her own elderly husband (on 15.4) was ill and died the next year (Suet. *Ner.* 5.2). After Lepidus was executed, she was forced to carry his ashes back to Rome (Dio 59.22.8) in parody of her mother's return with the ashes of Germanicus (Tac. *Ann.* 3.1.4). Julia Livilla was apparently less involved (Dio 59.22.6), but both sisters were sent to the place of imperial exile, the Pontian islands (29.1; Dio 59.3.6, 22.8). It is uncertain where the trial and execution of Lepidus took place, from where Agrippina returned with his ashes (43), where Gaetulicus was intercepted, the temporal relationship among events and even if it was a single conspiracy.[51] The fates of Lepidus and Gaetulicus are juxtaposed (Dio 59.22.5–7), but a conspiracy involving the two of them is mentioned only once (*cum vero detecta esset Lepidi et Gaetulici coniuratio,* Suet. *Cl.* 9.1). This affair left Gaius in total isolation from the family whose support he needed so badly (Meise 112, 120). He no longer trusted anyone, including Claudius (on 20; Dio 59.23.2).

quo facilius eas in causa Aemili Lepidi condemnavit quasi adulteras et insidiarum adversus se conscias ei: For meager evidence for the trial (*causa*) and execution of Lepidus and other conspirators, Sen. *Ep.* 4.7; Suet. *Ves.* 2.3; Dio 59.22.7. *Quasi:* Suetonius' skepticism is echoed by Dio, who writes that Gaius reported the execution of Gaetulicus to the senate "as if he had escaped a serious plot" (ὡς καὶ μεγάλην τινὰ ἐπιβουλὴν διαπεφευγώς, Dio 59.23.1; cf. 59.16.11). His detractors were careful to deny that plots existed in order to make his reprisals appear cruel and unjustified. An emperor could never prove that one was real unless it was successful and he was dead (Suet. *Dom.* 21; also Tac. *Ann.* 15.73.2).

nec solum chirographa omnium requisita fraude ac stupro divulgavit: Handwriting samples are noted only here. *Chirographa* = "contract" at 12.2. In both cases *chirographa* were signed papers that could be presented as evidence at a trial.

sed et tres gladios in necem suam praeparatos Marti Ultori addito elogio consecravit: Dio calls them daggers (59.22.7; for other consecrated

---

51 Willrich 297, 307–9; Gelzer 402–3; Balsdon 71–76; Stewart 75–77; Meise 108–22; Faur 1973b, 22–36; Simpson 1980, 347–66; Barrett 1989, 104–12.

weapons, Suet. *Vit.* 10.3; Tac. *Ann.* 15.74.2; for the two kinds of weapon, 49.3 and note 97). The temple of Mars Ultor had been an Augustan project in response to the assassination of Julius Caesar (*RG* 21; Suet. *Aug.* 29.2; Dio 55.10.2–5). Triumphant generals (now only emperors) were to place their trophies there. Gaius sent these legitimate spoils of (civil) war ahead to Rome since he himself would not return for another ten months (49.2). The *elogium* was the inscription which would be hung with them (cf. a different kind of *elogium* at 27.1).

Suetonius makes his marriage rubric fit beneath the larger umbrella of *impietas*—inappropriate behavior to close associates. Because Gaius went through wives quickly in his quest for legitimate heirs, he provided more material for this rubric than did most of the other emperors, but Claudius and Nero did well too (Suet. *Cl.* 26; *Ner.* 35.1–2). The three wives identified in this chapter must be added to the one whom he had married in 35 (12.1). As in the *Life of Nero*, Suetonius reports the first marriage in its proper chronological place (12.1; Suet. *Ner.* 7.2) and the later ones in a rubric here among *vitia* (Suet. *Ner.* 35; Mouchova 30–31). Gaius' failure to father children readily may have prompted a charge of "uncertain virility" (Meise 104, n. 80; Tac. *Ann.* 6.5.1).[52]

25.1 *Matrimonia contraxerit turpius an dimiserit an tenuerit, non est facile discernere:* Multiple marriages were as much the rule as the exception in the early Empire, but Suetonius judged the institution from his vantage point in the next century (Bradley 1985, 77–95; Balsdon 1934a, 40).

Liviam Orestillam C. Pisoni nubentem: Livia Orestilla is Cornelia Orestilla (or Orestina) for Dio (59.8.7; cf. 59.3.3). Perhaps she was Livia Cornelia Orestilla (*PIR²* C. 1492). Unless she had connections with the Cornelii Lentuli (see Gaetulicus, 8.1), it is difficult to see why she was chosen to be the mother of Julian heirs. The reason was probably the man to whom she was already betrothed, C. Calpurnius Piso (*PIR²* C. 284) of prominent family. When Cornelia Orestilla was transferred to the emperor, Piso was enrolled among Gaius' intimates, not really so odd an occurrence in the Roman world of marriage for political alliance.[53] Piso became an Arval Brother as the replacement for M. Junius Silanus, Gaius' first father-in-law (12.1, 23.3), on May 24, A.D. 38, at what seems to have been a time of realignments (*Docs.* no. 3, p. 11; see 23.3 for the replacement of Tiberius Gemellus on this date). He later became the eponymous leader of the Pisonian conspiracy against Nero (Suet. *Ner.* 36.1; Tac. *Ann.*

---

[52] *Incerta* in the Tacitus manuscript, emended to *quasi incestae virilitatis* (Rhenanus, Nipperdey) or *incertae* (Lipsius, Halm).

[53] According to Plutarch, Quintus Hortensius asked for the wife of Cato the Younger and Cato gave her away as his bride. The object was probably to cement the family alliance through the sharing of heirs (*Cat. Min.* 25.2). There would have been special status for a husband, ex-husband or ex-fiancé of a prospective mother of Julian offspring, e.g. Aemilius Lepidus (24.1).

15.48–72; Dio 62.24) and in a curious inversion of this story himself stole a bride from a friend (Tac. *Ann.* 15.53.4, 59.5).

cum ad officium et ipse venisset, ad se deduci imperavit: The story was told that the bride was snatched from the altar, and so Piso was rescued from a charge of collaboration, something that he did not want to be burdened with after Gaius was dead.

intraque paucos dies repudiatam biennio post relegavit: The marriage took place at some point in 37 (Dio 59.8.7); July 19 is possible (on 17.2 for the *congiarium* on that date).[54] Although *paucos dies* is an exaggeration, they were not married very long since Gaius married his next wife in the autumn of 38 (25.2). Piso was still in Rome meeting with the Arval Brothers in early June of 40 (*Docs.* nos. 4, 5, 10, pp. 11, 12, 14). Exile at some point after that is more or less consistent with Suetonius' *biennium* if the divorce took place in 38. Dio mistakenly says that they were banished within two months instead of two years (Dio 59.8.7).

quod repetisse usum prioris mariti tempore medio videbatur: The prohibition of future sexual intercourse to his divorced wives made her (not his) infertility appear the grounds for the divorce (Meise 103–5). Besides, a child born not too long thereafter could resurface as a pretender.[55]

alii tradunt adhibitum cenae nuptiali mandasse ad Pisonem contra accumbentem: noli uxorem meam premere: For *premere* as a sexual euphemism, Adams 182. Suetonius shares with Dio the preceding less hostile version of the story but not this one.

statimque e convivio abduxisse secum ac proximo die edixisse: matrimonium sibi repertum exemplo Romuli et Augusti: When Augustus, the "second founder" of Rome, preempted Livia (Suet. *Aug.* 62.2; Dio 48.44.1–5), he repeated the deed of the first founder Romulus, who had led the abduction of the Sabine women from a banquet (Livy 1.9). The scene also recalls the charge that Augustus removed a woman (not Livia) from table to cubicle under the eyes of her husband (Suet. *Aug.* 69.1). For Gaius doing it habitually, 36.2. Based on Gaius' edict, the circumstances of this wedding may not be

---

[54] The prominence of the three sisters in the oath at the opening of the year 38 might suggest that he had no wife at that time (Willrich 294, n. 3), but Gaius would not have waited so long. His sisters were given prominence at his dinner table despite his having a wife (24.1).

[55] A less pragmatic explanation has been that a consort of a god (i.e., Gaius) was forbidden other partners (Köberlein, 68–69; Eitrem 1932b, 22).

completely fabricated; on the other hand, it may have been the edict that prompted the story. Edicts were the emperor's own words and thought to be indicative of his personal style (Millar 1977, 253-54). Other tactless edicts from Gaius at 30.3, 42, 45.3, 49.1 and 53.2, all probably authentic; if he made sensible ones, they did not survive.

25.2 *Lolliam Paulinam, C. Memmio consulari exercitus regenti nuptam, facta mentione aviae eius ut quondam pulcherrimae:* Lollia Paulina (*PIR²* L. 328) was from a wealthy consular family (Pliny *HN* 9.117–18; Syme 1966, 59). Later she was a candidate to become Claudius' wife (Suet. *Cl.* 26.3; Tac. *Ann.* 12.1.1–3) and was eventually killed by the younger Agrippina (Tac. *Ann.* 12.22; Dio 60.32.4). The identity of her grandmother is unknown, but she may have been the wife of M. Lollius (*PIR²* L. 311), the consul of 21 B.C. Gaius seems to have known Lollia Paulina by reputation rather than by sight, but as with Piso (25.1), it was the alliance with Memmius that was important. Memmius Regulus (on 17.1; Publius, not Gaius, was his *praenomen*) had been consul in 31 during the crisis with Sejanus and remained loyal to Tiberius (Tac. *Ann.* 5.11.1, 6.4.3; Dio 58.9.3–13.3). He was proconsular commander of the troops in Moesia, Macedonia and Achaia (*exercitus regenti,* Dio 58.25.5). Like Piso's, his career continued under Claudius and Nero.

subito ex provincia evocavit ac perductam a marito coniunxit sibi: This third marriage took place a few days after the consecration of Drusilla on September 23, A.D. 38 (on 24.3; Dio 59.12.1). Memmius was present in Rome from the late summer or early autumn of 38 until at least mid-40 (*Docs.* nos. 5, 8, 10, pp. 12, 13, 14; see 57.1 for his location in 41). Since Gaius forced him to betroth Lollia Paulina to him, i.e., to act the role of the father (Dio 59.12.1), it is possible that she was not yet his wife but rather his ward in an arrangement made by Tiberius (Oliver 150–53).

brevique missam fecit interdicto cuiusquam in perpetuum coitu: *Missam fecit* = "abandoned." Gaius divorced her quickly, probably in the spring of 39 (see 25.3 for his next marriage) on the excuse of infertility (Dio 59.12.1, 59.23.7). Again future mates were prohibited. Lollia Paulina did remarry but never had children (Tac. *Ann.* 12.2.2).

25.3 *Caesoniam neque facie insigni neque aetate integra:* For Caesonia see also on 17.1, 33, 38.3, 50.2, 59. Born in perhaps A.D. 5 (Syme 1970a, 31), she was older than Gaius. They were married before he went north in September of 39 (43) since he was still in Rome when their (?) baby was born (below; Meise

106–8). If she is the imperial woman whose birthday was celebrated near the first of June (*Docs.* no. 10, p. 14), they were married by then.

matremque iam ex alio viro trium filiarum: The three offspring by another man are ironic in the face of the perpetual chastity mandated for his other wives. But her fertility was a given; Gaius took no chances this time.

sed luxuriae ac lasciviae perditae, et ardentius et constantius amavit: He was married to Caesonia somewhat less than two years but longer than to his other wives. Popular judgment considered it only a matter or time; he would have tired of her too if he had lived longer (Dio 59.3.3). In the meantime his extraordinary constancy had to be explained (see 33 for his torturing her to find out why and 50.2 for the love potion; Meise 105). Any woman with whom he stayed was naturally described as *luxuriae ac lasciviae perditae.*

ut saepe chlamyde peltaque et galea ornatam ac iuxta adequitantem militibus ostenderit: This only in Suetonius. A general's wife might curry favor for her husband by dressing her child in military garb (e.g., Agrippina with little Caligula, 8.1, 9), but when the wife of someone less prominent played soldier, it suggested usurpation; e.g., Cornelia (*PIR*² C. 1479), the wife of the Calvisius Sabinus (*PIR*² C. 354), legate in Pannonia, who was evidently suspected of treason by Gaius (Dio 59.18.4; for other examples, see Tac. *Ann.* 2.55.6; *Hist.* 2.63.2, 3.77.3). Dressing the wife of a Roman general (or would-be general) as an Amazon seems to send an odd message, plausibly a parody. Nero dressed concubines like Amazons when he planned to take them with him to suppress the revolt in Gaul: *concubinasque...tondendi ad virilem modum et securibus peltisque Amazonicis instuendi* (Suet. *Ner.* 44.1). A *pelta*, a small shield, was specific for an Amazon (Pliny *HN* 12.23; Mart. 9.101.5). For the *chlamys,* see 19.2.

amicis vero etiam nudam: Nudity was the proper attire for a woman *lasciviae perditae.* If Gaius dressed her as a soldier, gossip clothed her differently; see note 104 for a connection between her nakedness and the love potion (50.2).

uxorio nomine dignatus est †quam enixam, uno atque eodem die professus et maritum se eius et patrem infantis ex ea natae: "He did not honor her with the name of wife before she gave birth, claiming that on one and the same day he became her husband and the father of her baby daughter."[56]

---

[56] Reading *uxorio nomine non prius dignatus est quam,* suggested by Roth (*apparatus*). The problem is that although *non prius...quam* seems required by the sense of the sentence, a direct object for *dignatus est* (other than *enixam*) is wanting; as a relative pronoun *quam* would serve as object and make a connection with the preceding sentence as some manuscripts have it (*apparatus*).

Gaius took pride in this miraculously short and felicitous gestation (δαιμονίως, Dio 59.28.7). Dio calls this much desired heir a one-month child instead of a baby born on the wedding day (Dio 59.23.7). There is a parallel with the lucky child Drusus who was born to Livia and Augustus after only three months: Τοῖς εὐτυχοῦσι καὶ τρίμηνα παιδία (Suet. *Cl.* 1.1). Gaius acknowledged the baby as legitimate which implies that Caesonia had been his mistress (42; Dio 59.23.7). Her actual paternity was irrelevant.

25.4 *infantem autem, Iuliam Drusillam appellatam:* His deified sister continued to play her dynastic role by this name choice (cf. Dio 59.28.7). Drusilla was Livia's name too (1.1).

per omnium dearum templa circumferens Minervae gremio imposuit alendamque et instituendam commendavit: The special child would be nourished by the gods. Other versions have him give her to Jupiter (Jos. *AJ* 19.11) or place her first on the knees of Jupiter and then give her to Minerva (Dio 59.28.7). In fact, the temple of Jupiter on the Capitoline was dedicated to Minerva as well, and both gods had statues there (*PA* 298). Isis as a mother-nurturer was assimilated to all the anthropomorphic goddesses including Minerva-Athena (Witt 19–20; L'Orange 105–16; Köberlein 58–61), but a god's lap as a fortunate resting place was not exclusive with the Egyptian cult, and there was Etruscan precedent for a nurturing Minerva (Enking 111, 221–24). Augustus found himself in the lap of Jupiter in a dream (Suet. *Aug.* 94.8).

nec ullo firmiore indicio sui seminis esse credebat quam feritatis, quae illi quoque tanta iam tunc erat, ut infestis digitis ora et oculos simul ludentium infantium incesseret: Like father like daughter. If she was born in the summer of 39 (25.3), she was old enough to have these playmates before she was killed along with her mother and father in January of 41 (59).

Suetonius treats of Gaius' more distant relations and associates (26.1), and then goes further afield, moving down the orders systematically, first the senate (26.2–3), then the *equites* and the populace at large (26.4–5); the same order of treatment occurs in 16.2–3. Although the actions described here are cruel, they are not placed under the larger rubric of cruelty (27–33) because they make a point about Gaius' class inappropriate treatment. The subject is still *impietas,* disrespect.

26.1 *leve et frigidum sit his addere, quo propinquos amicosque pacto tractaverit:* Leve et frigidum = "meaningless and dull." Suetonius will now move on more quickly. He tells what happened to Macro and Ennia here but the fate of Ptolemy (*PIR¹* P. 764) in his rubric on envy (34–35); see also 55.1.

Ptolemaeum regis Iubae filium, consobrinum suum—erat enim et is M. Antoni ex Selene filia nepos: The ancients also found the Julian clan confusing, for Suetonius feels it necessary to explain the complicated family tree that had branches all over the Roman world. Ptolemy, King of Mauretania from 23 to 40, was the son of King Juba of Mauretania (*PIR²* I. 65) and Cleopatra Selene (*PIR²* C. 1488), the daughter of Antony and Cleopatra. He and Gaius were thus *consobrini,* cousins through the daughters of Antony, but a generation apart. Juba's connections with the Roman world had been long and thick. The son of the conquered king of Numidia, he was reared in Rome, made a Roman citizen, and installed as a client king in Mauretania in 25 B.C. where he served as a loyal ally. Ptolemy continued his father's Rome-friendly policy.

et in primis: In primis = imprimis = "above all" (60) as well as "among the first" = κἀκ τούτου καὶ ἕτεροι πολλοί, "after this many others..." (Dio 59.10.7). Does it mean that the deaths of Macro and Ennia (below) were the most important or the first in order of time? Perhaps both. Dio says that theirs were preliminary to a number of other executions that took place at some point in 38 (Dio 59.10.7–8) evidently fairly early in the year, for word of their deaths had reached Flaccus (on 24.3) in Alexandria by summer (Philo *In Flacc.* 16; Smallwood 1981, 236; Barrett 1989, 78).

ipsum Macronem, ipsam Enniam, adiutores imperii: Cf. 12.2, 23.2. Macro was probably a major example of the problem Gaius had sustaining relationships (φιλίας ἀμνήμων, Jos. *AJ* 19. 203; also Dio 59.10.6; Philo *Leg.* 32–41, 59–61; *in Flacc.* 12, 14). The charge brought against him was adultery, either that he was a procurer for Ennia or that he had committed adultery with his own wife because she was betrothed to Gaius (12.2; Bauman 176). Their children were also killed (Philo *in Flacc.* 14); because of the adultery charge, they might be pretenders one day (on 25.1–2, 59). Tradition, however, held that Gaius wearied of Macro's unwanted advice (Philo *Leg.* 41–61; *in Flacc.* 14–15), just as he had wearied of Antonia's (23.2, 29.1) and M. Junius Silanus' (on 23.3), and this may be true in a general way. Or the *adiutor* may have given up on the emperor first, quickly deciding that the rising sun (on 12.2) to whom he had linked his hopes was not likely to guarantee him (or anyone) much of a future. He possibly saw the next rising sun in Gemellus when Gaius was sick, but whether or not he was part of a larger opposition (*in primis* above; Gelzer 394; Stewart 75–76; Barrett 1989, 78), the example of Sejanus was precedent enough for distrusting a lone and powerful praetorian prefect. For two replacements for Macro, see on 56.1. Gaius allegedly appointed him prefect of Egypt, perhaps to put him off his guard (Balsdon 1934a, 39), perhaps as a demotion (Willrich 288), before he

forced him to suicide (Dio 59.10.6). The replacement of Flaccus, the current
Egyptian prefect, a Tiberian appointee, would have taken place sooner or later in
any case (Smallwood 1981, 236); he was relieved of the position in the autumn of
38 (on 24.3; Philo *in Flacc.* 11, 16, 158). If it was Macro who provided the political sense behind Gaius' initial attempts to show himself *civilis* (15.4–16; Meise
145–52), his departure was a disaster of major consequence for the inexperienced
young princeps.

*quibus omnibus pro necessitudinis iure proque meritorum gratia
cruenta mors persoluta est:* Pro necessitudinis iure refers to Ptolemy, *proque
meritorum gratia* to Macro. Paired concepts are especially common in this chapter: *leve ac frigidum, propinquos amicosque, ipsum Macronem, ipsam Enniam*
(above), *reverentior leniorve* (26.2; Mouchova 48).

26.2 *Nihilo reverentior leniorve erga senatum:* Suetonius next moves to
the senate. Gaius did not respect its *dignitas.*

*quosdam summis honoribus functos ad essedum sibi currere togatos
per aliquot passuum milia...passus est:* This anecdote illustrates Gaius' arrogant lack of consideration, but the same story is told differently elsewhere to
show the hardihood of the future emperor Galba: *campestrem decursionem scuto
moderatus, etiam ad essedum imperatoris per viginti passuum milia cucurrit*
(Suet. *Gal.* 6.3; Charlesworth 1933b, 110). The setting is the camp of the Army
of Upper Germany when Gaius visited in the winter of 39–40 (on 44.1). The
twenty-mile march was standard in a military training maneuver, in the later
Empire in any case (Veg. 3.4). In this version Galba's shield has disappeared and
the senators (now plural) wear togas.[57]

et cenati modo ad pluteum modo ad pedes stare succinctos linteo: This
anecdote appears to be a metaphor for the detested slave-master relationship and
as such implicates Gaius as a *dominus* again (10.2). Senators wait on him, standing sometimes at the head of the couch (*ad pluteum,* the headboard),[58] sometimes
at its foot (*ad pedes*). *Succinctos linteo* parallels *togatos* above. *Linteum*, a linen
cloth, implies a slave's garment, and *passus est* for both this anecdote and the preceding one blames the emperor for permitting senators to perform demeaning
services; volunteers were evidently not lacking.

---

[57] This kind of attendance on an emperor could be used either to show the courtier making a
grand gesture (Amm. 14.11.10) or the emperor humiliating his courtier (Plut. *Luc.* 21).

[58] Or "behind" if *pluteum* means the "back" of the couch, a furniture innnovation in this period
(Ransom 34). But the contrast with *ad pedes* suggests "head" here (cf. Prop. 4.8.68, and less
clearly, Mart. 3.91.10, 8.44.13).

alios cum clam interemisset, citare nihilo minus ut vivos perserveravit, paucos post dies voluntaria morte perisse mentitus: Claudius reportedly did the same as a way of avoiding responsibility (Suet. *Cl.* 39.1; Levick 1990, 59).

26.3 *consulibus oblitis de natali suo edicere abrogavit magistratum fuitque per triduum sine summa potestate res p.:* This was in A.D. 39, at the same time when Gaius blamed the consuls for celebrating Augustus' victory over Antony (on 23.1). The problem was not that they forgot his birthday but that they celebrated it only in a routine fashion (Dio 59.20.1). The three days when Rome was without consuls were logically just after September 2, the date of the incorrectly celebrated Actian celebration. For the replacement of these consuls, 17.1.

quaestorem suum in coniuratione nominatum: Gaius is seen in conflict with another person close to him. "His" quaestor, a *quaestor Augusti,* was a young man of good family chosen by the emperor himself. Among his other duties he acted as the emperor's spokesperson (Suet. *Aug.* 65.2; Tac. *Ann.* 16.27.1; Dio 60.2.2; Talbert 67, 167, 313).

flagellavit veste detracta subiectaque militum pedibus, quo firme verberaturi insisterent: Cf. Dio 59.25.6. The quaestor was Batilienus Bassus (*PIR²* B. 114). He and his father Capito (*PIR²* B. 116) were one of several father-son pairs whom Gaius punished sadistically (27.4; also 32.1, 56.1, notes 62, 68). *Verberatio* was a heavy beating, a punishment usually reserved for slaves and aliens (Garnsey 136–39). It took place in the Garden of Agrippina, probably in the summer of 40 (Sen *Dial.* 5.18.3, see on 32.1, 49.2). See on 27.3 for class-inappropriate punishments.

26.4 *Simili superbia violentiaque ceteros tractavit ordines: Ceteros...ordines:* Suetonius moves down the social scale.

inquietatus fremitu gratuita in circo loca de media nocte occupantium, omnis fustibus abegit: The three types of *spectacula* were first covered in chapter 18, but this time Gaius' failure with each is pointed out. Life next door to a major gathering place had disadvantages as well as advantages (18.3), and Gaius could easily hear the din from the Circus Maximus (cf. 55.3 for his concern about his horses' rest). He himself might arrive before daylight (Dio 59.13.2), but the fans were there even earlier (*de media nocte* = in the middle of the night; cf. *de die,* 37.2), at least those who wanted to secure the free seats or standing room slots (*loca gratuita*) which seem to have been in short supply.

Senators, Vestals, knights, and quite probably those entitled to a grain allowance, were eligible for free places; others were evidently sold. But this did not mean that a place was guaranteed for every entitled person since there were a larger number in each category than there was room for (cf. Sen. *Ben.* 7.12.3–6; Bollinger 17–18). It was probably early arrivals like these who were ready to demand extra races (18.3); this time Gaius' response lacked *civilitas*.

elisi per eum tumultum viginti amplius equites R., totidem matronae, super innumeram turbam ceteram: Elisi = "removed forcibly." This incident is reported only here. Large public gatherings always held potential for riots such as the one at Pompeii (Tac. *Ann.* 14.17; Veyne 1990, 392).

scaenicis ludis, inter plebem et equitem causam discordiarum ferens, decimas maturius dabat, ut equestri<a> ab infimo quoque occuparentur: Equestria = the first fourteen rows of the theater set aside for the knights. But there was not room for all of them at once (above on the *gratuita loca*), and interlopers could also cause problems (Sen. *Ben.* 7.12.3–6; Sen. *Controv.* 7.3.9). Whatever it was that Gaius did too hastily (*maturius*) made him responsible for the lowest social elements (*infimo*) of the crowd taking the knights' places. Perhaps the populace was routinely allowed into the *equestria* after as many knights as wished had entered the theater; if the special section was opened up too soon, there was a disorderly fracas (Funke 252). *Decimas...dabat,* a reference to some otherwise unknown procedure must have had something to do with the allotment of seats (Bollinger 18 and n. 139).[59]

26.5 *gladiatorio munere reductis interdum flagrantissimo sole velis emitti quemquam vetabat:* The practice of protecting the audience from the sun of the Roman summer had begun in the late Republic (Pliny *HN* 19.23–24) and came to be expected (Balsdon 1969, 257–58). During the first summer of his reign Gaius had graciously allowed the senators to wear sun hats into the theater or had the performances transferred under cover (Dio 59.7.8). The summer of 39 was especially hot and awnings were stretched even across the Forum (Dio 59.23.9).

remotoque ordinario apparatu tabidas feras, vilissimos senioque confectos gladiatores: Gaius put on second-rate *spectacula*. *Apparatus* =

[59] An emendation of *decimas* to *quattuordecim* (from XIV or XIIII to X in an early manuscript) would show him giving out the fourteen rows too quickly. Or perhaps he threw *missilia* before the tenth hour of the day (*decima [hora]*, Casaubon, *apparatus,* accepted by Rolfe 1913–1914), and the ensuing scramble put the common people where they did not belong (Sen. *Ep.* 74.6–7). Or Gaius began the show too early (*decimas* = *mimos*, Bentley, *apparatus*).

"elaborate arrangements;" cf. *apparatum circi* (18.3; also *ludi...magno apparatu,* Liv. 32.7.14; *maximo ludorum apparatu,* Cic. *Tusc.* 5.9).

†*quoque paegniaris patres familarum notos in bonam partem sed insignis debilitate aliqua corporis subiciebat:* "...and as comic gladiators he used heads of household of good reputation but conspicuous by some physical weakness."[60] *Paegniarius* = a toy (παίγνιον), a mock gladiator, a gladiatorial clown; they fought during the midday intermission, perhaps with non-lethal weapons, perhaps in costume (Suet. *Cl.* 34.2; Sen. *Ep.* 7.2; Ville 394; Friedländer 4.179; Déchelette 315; see 30.3 for the *retiari tunicati*). The objection is not to the mock contests but to honorable men (*in bonam partem*) in dishonorable roles.

ac nonnumquam horreis praeclusis populo famem indixit: The grain supply was kept in storehouses (*horrea*). It is doubtful that an emperor would intentionally cause a famine but true that any shortage would be blamed on him (Suet. *Ner.* 45.1). Claudius credited himself with securing the grain supply (Suet. *Cl.* 18.1), perhaps in deliberate contrast with Gaius, who plausibly neglected the issue (Ramage 204). For Gaius and other famines, see 39.1 and on 19.1.

This extensive rubric of *saevitia* (chapters 27–33) provides a degree of insight into the acceptable limits of cruelty in a harsh world. Some of the grotesque deeds in these chapters are standard tyrant tricks, but others are more particular to Gaius. The ones that can be identified seem to have occurred in the latter part of his reign after the reinstatement of the *crimen maiestatis* and at a time when he was indeed threatened. But they are presented bereft of context and made to appear totally unmotivated. His specialty was a sadistic desire to witness suffering (27.4, 30.1, 32.1, 33). Cruelty rubrics in other *Lives: Tib.* 57–62; *Cl.* 34; *Ner.* 33–38; *Gal.* 12; *Vit.* 14; *Dom.* 10–11 (Mouchova 43–48).

27.1 *Saevitiam ingenii per haec maxime ostendit:* This topic sentence will be followed by two others that will introduce "subrubrics" on cruelty in speech (*immanissima facta augebat atrocitate verborum,* 29.1) and cruelty of both deed and speech while at leisure (*animum quoque remittenti ludoque et epulis dedito eadem factorum dictorumque saevitia aderat,* 32.1). Gaius' cruelty was innate (*saevitiam ingenii*) and anticipated in his early life: *naturam tamen saevam atque probrosam ne tunc quidem inhibere poterat* (11).

cum ad saginam ferarum muneri praeparatarum carius pecudes compararentur: Dio puts this incident with events of the winter of 39–40 at

---

[60] Bücheler's *proque* (*apparatus*) seems the best suggestion. *Quoque* rarely serves Suetonius as a substitute for a simple connective but instead introduces a supplementary idea usually with its own verb (e.g., 24.1, 32.1, 39.1; exception, 20.1), and it rarely appears first in its own clause (exception, 16.4).

Lugdunum where extensive games caused financial strain (20; Dio 59.22.1, 3). It was necessary to keep the animals alive and healthy for the arena (but hungry at the end), and this, along with the expense of capturing and transporting them, made *munera* high-expense entertainments (Hopkins 1983, 11–12).

ex noxiis laniandos adnotavit, et custodiarum seriem recognoscens, nullius inspecto elogio, stans tantum modo intra porticum mediam: It was considered cruel (and no doubt illegal) to feed men to the beasts outside of the arena, a distinction that may not have meant much to the prisoners involved. The emphasis is on Gaius' arbitrariness; he did not examine the prisoners who had been "condemned to be torn apart" (*ex noxiis laniandos*) or even pretend to assign only those guilty of the most serious crimes to premature punishment. Would he have been less culpable if he had selected the beasts' early dinner more conscientiously? Suetonius writes as though it is clear to his readers what *porticus* he is talking about. The awkward compactness of the sentence suggests that he was condensing an account that provided more careful circumstantial details than he transmitted (see note 8). Details of the architecture of ancient Lyon are not particularly suggestive (Audin 1979). *Elogium* is the written report of the particulars of the criminal charge (cf. 24.3 for *elogium* as a placard in a temple). *Custodiarum,* "those under guard," often the word for prisoners in Suetonius (29.2, 32.1; *Tib.* 61.5; *Ner.* 31.3; *Dom.* 14.4).

a calvo ad calvum duci imperavit: He selected those who stood between two bald-headed men, proof of his arbitrariness, or maybe he chose all of them, from one end of the line to the other (Balsdon 1934a, 217). According to Dio, the expression was proverbial (τοῦτο δὴ τὸ λεγόμενον, 59.22.3) meaning perhaps "from the cradle to the grave," from the hairless infant to the hairless old man, i.e., everyone (*TLL* 3.194.61). But more may be involved when these words are put into Gaius' mouth: He was himself balding and sensitive about it (35.1–2; 50.1), and baldness was thought to result from excessive sexual activity (Suet. *Jul.* 51). The adjective *calvus* was "something approaching an obscenity, part of the coarse language of soldiers and satirists" (Wiseman 1974, 148).

27.2 *votum exegit ab eo, qui pro salute sua gladiatoriam operam promiserat:* Gaius called in the pledges that had been made for his life when he was ill (14.2). The two men may have expected monetary rewards for their grand and flattering gestures (Dio 59.8.3), but since they swore under oath, fulfillment could be exacted. This first man was a knight, Atanius Secundus (*PIR²* A. 1273, Dio, 59.8.3); he was plural when first introduced (*non defuerunt qui depugnaturos,* 14.2).

spectavitque ferro dimicantem nec dimisit nisi victorem et post multas preces: The fight to the finish (*sine missione*, i.e., with one or occasionally both of the combatants dead or dying on the ground) was not usual. Normally one of the two could signal that he was beaten and appeal for *missio* (dismissal) from combat. It was at this point that whoever was presiding over the games (on 18.1), following the lead of the crowd if he wanted to appear *civilis,* could order him released (*missus*) or dispatched (*iugulatus*) at once. It is not clear how Atanius' adventure in the arena fits into the standard procedure (Ville 403–6). If it was either a fight *sine missione* as Suetonius seems to imply, or if he won, the wishes of the crowd (*multas preces*) seem irrelevant. The point may be that Gaius forced a serious fight of doubtful outcome for a knight, an unusual and nasty thing to do. For knights in the arena, see on 30.2. Dio writes that Atanius was killed (59.8.3).

alterum, qui se peritum ea de causa voverat, cunctantem: Cf. *quique capita sua titulo proposito voverent* (plural at 14.2). He was a plebean, P. Afranius Potitus (*PIR*[2] A. 445; Dio 59.8.3), who stalled for time before fulfilling his vow. Gaius punishes him for delaying (*cunctantem*); similarly Apelles (33; for an impatient Gaius, see 37.3). Like Atanius (above), he is known only in this connection.

pueris tradidit, verbenatum infulatumque votum reposcentes per vicos agerent, quoad praecipitaretur ex aggere: Slaves (*pueri*) drove him through the neighborhoods of Rome (*per vicos*). He wore or carried branches (*verbenatum*) and wore a headband (*infulatum*) until he was forced off the rampart (*ex aggere*), the remnant of the ancient Roman fortifications (*PA* 350–55). The *infula* shows that he was *sacer,* the property of the god and a surrogate victim for Gaius, but he was also *sacer* because he refused to fulfill his vow.[61] Cf. Colosseros led through Rome before his execution (35.2).

27.3 *multos honesti ordinis:* Distinctions between the *honestiores* (senators, knights and provincial gentry) and the *humiliores* (the mass of the free populace)

---

[61] The scapegoat pattern is perhaps pertinent. Specifics of this incident have suggested the expulsion from Rome of Mamurius Veturius (Old Mars) on March 14 every year (Lugend 9–10). Mamurius was the vegetation god of the preceeding year driven out of the city to make room for the new one (Frazer 9.229–34). If the festival existed in A.D. 38, unfortunate Afranius might have been chosen as the scapegoat for that year, but Frazer's evidence is late and the festival is not in Ovid's *Fasti* (Wissowa 147–48; Latte 117, n. 1). The little understood *regifugium* (February 24) and *poplifugia* (July 5), with their reminiscences of human sacrifice, might also have provided occasions. For Gaius' interest in ancient gods and foreign cults, Balsdon 1934a, 149–50, Bernardi 273–87, Aiardi 102–8. See on the *rex Nemorensis* at 35.3.

became codified by the second century, but class-appropriate punishments were rooted in aristocratic values that had long been honored. It is thus not anachronistic to find the concept operational earlier. The two groups received different punishments for comparable offenses. Corporal punishment (with the exception of decapitation for treason and parricide) was not properly applied to the first group, thus the impropriety of Batilienus Bassus' beating (26.3). The "beasts," the "best" of the low-status punishments (below and 27.1, 4), crucifixion (12.2), forced labor (below), and burning (27.4) were essentially slave punishments that were thought appropriate for the second group. Gaius is faulted for failing to honor traditional values (Garnsey 105–11, 129–31, Levick, 105–15).

deformatos prius stigmatum notis ad metalla et munitiones viarum: Harsh assignments to the mines or to road work were the very worst of the lower-class punishments. They effectively, and often legally as well, made the condemned man a slave (Garnsey 131–36; Tac. *Agr.* 32.4). The mines were usually imperial possessions. For road work (*munitiones viarum*): *solent* [older criminals] *et ad balineum, ad purgationes cloacarum, item munitiones viarum et vicorum dari* (Pliny *Ep.* 10.32.2). *Stigma* = the brand given a slave or, as here, a criminal.

ad bestias condemnavit aut bestiarum more quadripedes cavea coercuit: Gaius treated men like the beasts that were kept in *caveae* (low cages) before they were let loose in the arena (Sen. *Dial.* 4.11.5). The father of a knight who was forced to fight as a gladiator (on 30.2) was put into one (Dio 59.10.4). The paradigm for this punishment was Lysimachos, the successor to Alexander, who did it to Telephores of Rhodes (Sen *Dial.* 5.17.3; also *Ep.* 70.6; Plut. *De exil.* 16 [606B]; Ov. *Ib.* 517–18). It was something that any tyrant might do.

aut medios serra dissecuit: A tyrant might also cut someone apart with a saw; it was much more painful than a clean blow (Ov. *Ib.* 496).

nec omnes gravibus ex causis: Gaius overreacted; cf. Jos. *AJ* 19.203.

verum male de munere suo opinatos: Objection to the quality of his shows has already been implied (26.5).

vel quod numquam per genium suum deierassent: This should not have been a serious offense because swearing by the living emperor's *genius* was a common and ostensibly freely willed act of devotion (Bömer 120; Fishwick 1987–1992, 377 n. 6, 381). The problem was Gaius' enforcement. Perhaps the *crimen maiestatis* was extended to cover it (Guastella). Note that Gaius' concern is for his *genius* and not for himself as a *deus praesens* (on 22.3).

27.4 *parentes supplicio filiorum interesse cogebat:* It was another "time-worn trick of tyrants, the practice of torturing the feelings of a father during, or shortly after, the execution of his son, or vice versa" (Balsdon 1934a, 98; Charlesworth 1933b, 110–11). Augustus did it too (Suet. *Aug.* 13.2; Ap. *BCiv.* 4.4.20, 6.42). Gaius was associated with three father-son pairs: First, Betilienus Bassus and his father Betilienus Capito (26.3, and see on 32.1). According to Dio, Capito pretended to turn informer and fabricated accusations about the conspiracy in which Bassus was implicated. When he was caught lying, he was himself executed (Dio 59.25.6; see 56.1). But according to Suetonius and Seneca, it was Bassus who was tortured (Sen. *Dial.* 5.18.3). The second pair were Sextus Papinius (*PIR¹* P. 75) and his natural father C. Anicius Cerialis (*PIR²* A. 594). When Papinius and Cerialis were tortured, the son turned informer on grant of immunity. Gaius was supposed to have killed them both anyway (Dio 59.25.5ᵇ; Sen. *Dial.* 5.18.3). But this is not true since Cerialis turned up again later when it was he and not his son who is said to have talked. Accused as an enemy of Nero, he killed himself but was little mourned, *quia proditam G. Caesari coniurationem ab eo meminerant* (Tac. *Ann.* 16.17.6). The third pair were an otherwise unknown Pastor (*PIR¹* P. 113) and his unnamed son (Sen. *Dial.* 4.33.3–6). Suetonius apparently elaborates on these two in his examples below. Pastor may or may not have been related to a Junius Pastor (*PIR²* I. 794) whom the younger Pliny defended *contra potentissimos civitatis atque etiam Caesaris amicos* (*Ep.* 1.18.3).[62]

quorum uni valitudinem excusanti lecticam misit: This is reported only here, but dragging a sick man out to face unpleasantness had precedent (Tac. *Ann.* 2.29.2). For *lecticae* for the ill, see on 58.3. This sick father may be a doublet for gouty Pastor (*podagricus,* below).

alium a spectaculo poenae epulis statim adhibuit atque omni comitate ad hilaritatem et iocos provocavit: The focus is on the father both here and above. Seneca describes Pastor's behavior at the table in some detail. Invited to dine with Gaius on the night of his son's execution, he concealed his grief and laughed and drank in order to save the life of a second son: *duci* [the son] *protinus iussit...ad cenam illum* [i. e., Pastor] *eo die invitavit. Venit Pastor vultu*

---

62 Because the first two of these three pairs are presented together both by Dio (59.25.5ᵇ–7) and Seneca (*Dial.* 5.18.3), they appear to have been thought of together. Suetonius specifically mentions two aborted conspiracies in the last months of Gaius' reign, one of which seems to be the one that involved Bassus and Capito (56.1).

nihil exprobrante. Propinavit illi Caesar heminam et posuit illi custodem: perduravit miser, non aliter quam si fili sanguinem biberet. Unguentum et coronas misit et observare iussit an sumeret: sumpsit. Eo die quo filium extulerat, immo quo non extulerat, iacebat conviva centesimus et potiones vix honestas natalibus liberorum podagricus senex hauriebat (*Dial.* 4.33.3–4).

curatorem munerum ac venationum: The *curator munerum ac venationum* (only here) probably = the *procurator a muneribus,* whose function was to oversee the production of the imperial *munera* (Ville 285, n. 137). He had ample opportunity to displease an emperor.

per continuos dies in conspectu suo catenis verberatum non prius occidit quam offensus putrefacti cerebri odore: A vile detail but not without a touch of realism; the man's head wounds had turned gangrenous. Gaius had already enjoyed executions in his youth (*animadversionibus poenisque ad supplicium datorum cupidissime interesset,* 11; also Dio 59.10.2, 25.5ᵇ; Sen. *Dial.* 4.18.4). But other emperors did too (Suet. *Cl.* 34.1; *Vit.* 14.1).

Atellan[i]ae poetam ob ambigui ioci versiculum: The stage was the one place where criticism of the emperor was usually possible. In Atellan farces (*fabulae Atellanae*), the actors' lines might carry double meanings (*ambigui ioci*) and political allusions. An emperor ignored them or at most exiled the offending actor (Suet. *Tib.* 45; *Ner.* 39.3; Cameron 1976, 160–61), and so Gaius' punishment was exceptional. For what he may have said that angered Gaius so much, see 50.1. Domitian also killed a writer (*poeta*) because of a farce (Suet. *Dom.* 10.4), and Gaius banished Carrinas Secundus (*PIR*² C. 449) for delivering an practice oration against tyrants (Dio 59.20.6).

media amphitheatri harena igni cremavit: *Crematio,* originally intended as an execution for arsonists, was another slave punishment (on 27.3). There is no earlier report of its use in Rome than this,[63] but it was applied to Christians in A.D. 64 for their alleged burning of the city (Tac. *Ann.* 15.44; Juv. 1.155, 8.235; Sen. *Ep.* 14.5; Garnsey 125–26). It had barbaric associations (Caes. *BGall.* 6.19.5).

---

[63] The *Acta Alexandrinorum* may accuse Gaius of burning an informer to death: Γαῖος Καῖσαρ ἐκ[έ]λευσεν τὸ[ν] κατήγορον καῆναι (3.3.24–25, Musurillo 14). καῆναι has been interpreted as branding (Bell 30) because there is no other evidence for *crematio* in Rome this early (Musurillo 112–14). But it is equally possible that it either does refer to *crematio* or has been retrojected onto the *Acta* from an assumption that Gaius really did execute persons by burning them. This Suetonius passage strengthens the argument that καῆναι refers to *crematio.*

equitem R. obiectum feris, cum se innocentem proclamasset, reduxi abscisaque linqua rursus induxit: A knight should not have been thrown to the beasts in any case (27.3), but here he protests his innocence, not the illegality of the punishment. In a variant Dio writes that Gaius cut out the tongues of innocent bystanders whom he ordered to the beasts when there was a shortage of criminals available for public execution (Dio 59.10.3). The people were not to be denied their show. Tyrants traditionally did this to innocent victims so that they could not complain about their punishment (Sen. *Dial.* 5.18.1). Senaca describes in some detail a grisly method that Gaius also used for the same end, stuffing the mouth (Sen. *Dial.* 5.19.3–4).

28 *revocatum quendam a vetere exilio:* Presumably one of those who were exiled under Tiberius and whose recall is noted at 15.4 (Dio 59.13.2; also Philo *Leg.* 340 for reimprisonment and Gaius' inconsistent policy).

sciscitatus, quidnam ibi facere consuesset, respondente eo per adulationem: deos semper oravi ut, quod evenit, periret Tiberius et tu imperares, opinans sibi quoque exules suos mortem imprecari: Herod Agrippa was also caught expressing the wish that Tiberius would die (Jos. *AJ* 18.187), and Tiberius Gemellus was allegedly executed for the same sentiment about Gaius (23.3). A despot's perennial problem was the precedent that one reign set for another. For Claudius' treatment of the assassins of Gaius, see on Chaerea, 56.1 and 59.

misit circum insulas, qui universos contrucidarent: Just when people began to relax in exile, their sentences were changed (Dio 59.18.3; Sen. *Dial.* 11.13.4; Philo *Leg.* 342; *in Flacc.* 183–85; Oros. 5.7.9). Flaccus (on 24.3, 26.1), first exiled to Andros and then executed there, was a case in point (Philo *in Flacc.* 185–89), and Suetonius may have him in mind; see on 58.3 for another victim. Other emperors did the same thing: Agrippa Postumus (1.1) and Nero, the son of Germanicus, were forced to suicide in exile (Tac. *Ann.* 1.6; on 7). *Contrucidare,* "butcher in quantity," also at 48.1 and *trucidare* at 29.1; perhaps the word had special associations with Gaius: *de toto senatu trucidando cogitabat,* Sen. *Dial.* 5.19.2; see also Philo: ἀθρόους ἀνῄρει, *Leg.* 342. Gaius threatened his sisters too (29.1).

cum discerpi senatorem concupisset, subornavit qui ingredientem curiam repente hostem publicum appellantes invaderent: The setting of the senate house makes this ambush reminiscent of Caesar's murder. Suetonius' plural (*qui...appellantes invaderent*) is the single quintessential *delator* Protogenes (*PIR¹* P. 757), who helped Gaius do his dirtiest deeds and kept his victim lists for

him (49.3). He was later punished by Claudius (Dio 60.4.5). The murdered senator was Scribonius Proculus (*PIR¹* S. 215). Protogenes accused him of being
hostile to Gaius (μισῶν οὕτω τὸν αὐτοκράτορα, Dio 59.26.2) and hence a enemy of the state (*hostem publicum*) and forfeit of his rights as a citizen. Dio
assigns this violent anecdote a place among the conspiracies discovered in late 40,
a context that gives it plausibility since Gaius' relationship with the senate reached
its nadir at that time (on 49.1–2). *Discerpere*, "tear to pieces," another violent
word (= διέσπασαν, Dio 59.26.2).

graphisque confossum lacerandum ceteris traderent: A *graphium*, a
sharpened stylus, could become the weapon at hand, as it was for Julius Caesar
when he tried to defend himself (Suet. *Jul.* 82.2). Claudius had one thrown in his
face (*Cl.* 15.4), and once a crowd used them to attack a knight who had beaten his
son to death (Sen. *Clem.* 1.15.1). Claudius subjected his callers to stylus searches
(Suet. *Cl.* 35.2). It suggests an *ad hoc* attack despite the fact that Gaius "desired"
(*concupisset*, above) this outcome.

**nec ante satiatus est quam membra et artus et viscera hominis tracta
per vicos atque ante se congesta vidisset:** The mutilated body attracts the
story into the cliché that tyrants took pleasure in gloating over the remains of
their conquered rivals, especially their severed heads; Galba's was presented to
Otho (Tac. *Hist.* 1.44.1; Suet. *Gal.* 20.2), Cicero's to Antony (Dio 47.8.3; Sen.
Suas. 6.17, 20), and Pompey's to Caesar (Luc. 9.1020–1108). This casts
Scribonius as a challenger to Gaius.

Cruel speech; verbal abuse is salt on the wounds of chapters 27–28. Gaius' *atrocitas verborum*, his
acerbic wit, was an important feature of his personality. He may not have said everything ascribed
to him, but his reputation was no doubt earned.

**29.1 immanissima facta augebat atrocitate verborum. nihil magis in
natura sua laudare se ac probare dicebat quam...ἀδιατρεψίαν:** A
Greek word leads off the list. ἀδιατρεψία occurs nowhere else, but its form is
typical of abstractions formed as alpha-privative compounds.[64] The corresponding verb, διατρέπω, "turn away from, waver," makes the meaning of
ἀδιατρεψία clear. It was "steadfastness" if taken positively, or if taken pejora-
tively, "stubbornness," the trait illustrated in the next anecdote about Gaius'
obdurate refusal to heed Antonia. At the same time, the happier construction of
"sure purpose" becomes ironic when applied to this most capricious of emperors.

---

[64] The restoration of ἀδιατρεψία is, however, correct. It comes from τρέπω with the noun
ending -σια; ἀδιατρεφία of the archetype is linguistically possible only for a noun formed from
τρέφω, "nourish," not plausible in this context .

Steadfastness (i.e., *disciplina*, see *apparatus*) was the precise quality that Gaius did not have; see 16.4, 18.2, 27.1, 51, 55 for his inconsistency.

ut ipsius verbo utar: A similar reference to Gaius' idiosyncratic use of Greek is made in chapter 47: *ut ipse dicebat*, ἀξιοθριάμβ⟨ε⟩υτον (also found only in this text). Gaius seems to have known it well, especially if he coined these words as is possible (see his Homeric quotations at 22.1 and 4; 53.1 for his education). In contrast, Suetonius chooses his own words when he says of Claudius: *vel ut Graece dicam*, μετεωρίαν *et* ἀβλεψίαν (*Cl.* 39.1).

hoc est inverecundiam: In favor of judging this a gloss (*apparatus*) is the *hoc est* formula, the fact that ἀξιοθριάμβευτον (47) is left unexplained and the fact that there is no other classical evidence for *inverecundia*, "shamelessness" (*TLL* 9.162.25–55), which does not translate ἀδιατρεψία in any case. But Suetonius made a point of choosing this example of Gaius' cruel language to lead off this rubric, and it may have been he who wanted to make its significance clear.[65] If so, *inverecundia* was not an unstudied translation, since he too knew Greek well, but rather an ironic comment on the double meaning of the word as Gaius applied it to himself. Both Gaius' stubbornness and his characterization of himself as steadfast could be considered "shameless," and he could be accused of outrageous language (*atrocitas verborum*) whichever way it was taken.

Antonia, Tiberius Gemellus and Gaius' sisters appear once again to complete the stories begun about them at 15.2–3 and continued at 23.2–3 and 24.

monenti Antoniae aviae tamquam parum esset non oboedire: memento, ait, omnia mihi et <in> omnis licere: "I can do anything I want to anyone I want," the ultimate statement of arrogance and without doubt the attitude that he was perceived as taking. But did he really say this to Antonia in the few weeks during which her life overlapped his reign? The message is the same as before: she tried to guide him but was rebuffed and was thus not responsible for his deficiencies (cf. 23.2, 24.1).

trucidaturus fratrem, quem metu venenorum praemuniri medicamentis suspicabatur: antidotum, inquit, adversus Caesarem?

---

[65] An explanatory *hoc est* appears three other places in the *Lives*. In each case it introduces an amplification of information necessary in the context. *Tib.* 24.1: *statione militum, hoc est vi et specie dominationis assumpta; Gal.* 8.2: *interpretarentur significari rerum mutationem successurumque iuveni senem, hoc est ipsum Neroni; Ves.* 11: *neve filiorum familiarum faeneratoribus exigendi crediti ius umquam esset, hoc est ne post patrum quidem mortem.* Only in the Vespasian *Life* has there been a suggestion that the *hoc est* is a later gloss (*apparatus, ad Ves.* 11), but this case does not seem to be any different from the others.

This complements the story that Tiberius Gemellus took cough medicine that Gaius mistook as an antidote to poison (23.3). For *trucidaturus,* cf. *contrucidare* (28, 48.1).

relegatis sororibus non solum insulas habere se, sed etiam gladios minabatur: The threat of capital punishment was added to relegation for Agrippina and Julia Livilla. For their exile, see on 24.3; for their return, 59. See 28 for the execution of exiles.

29.2 *praetorium virum ex secessu Anticyrae, quam valitudinis causa petierat, propagari sibi commeatum saepius desiderantem cum mandasset interimi:* This man was probably trying to stay out of Gaius' way. Ten days was the maximum time that a praetor could be absent from Rome during the year in which he held office (Cic. *Phil.* 2.13; Mommsen 1871–1888, 2.195), and so he made taking the cure his excuse for a longer absence. He had gone to Anticyra, a popular spa on the coast of Phocis on the Gulf of Corinth (ἀποδημεῖν δεῦρο πολλούς, καθάρσεως καὶ θεραπείας χάριν, Strab. 9.3.3). Perhaps he was the praetor Junius Priscus (*PIR*² I. 801), who was accused on various charges in A.D. 39 but was killed because he was mistakenly thought wealthy (Dio 59.18.5; for other threatened praetors, Dio 59.23.8).

adiecit necessariam esse sanguinis missionem, cui tam diu non prodesset elleborum: Bloodletting (*missio*) as a cure for illness is found only here in non-medical writing (*TLL* 8.1140.10–12). It is a pun on a less salutary sort of bloodletting. *Prodesse* = "be beneficial," standard for describing curatives (*eaque missio sanguinis adeo non prodest,* Cel. 2.10.17). The medicinal herb black hellebore that was supposed to cure insanity and many other ailments as well (Pliny *HN* 25.54) grew at Anticyra in such abundance that the name of the town became a synonym for the drug (Pers. 4.16).

decimo quoque die: After A.D. 21 there was a mandatory ten-day delay between the passing of a death sentence and the implementing of it in order to allow time for second thoughts. But Gaius possessed ἀδιατρεψία (above) and did not change his mind. Nor had Tiberius in 21 (Tac. *Ann.* 3.51.2; Suet. *Tib.* 75.2; Dio 57.20.4).

numerum puniendorum ex custodia subscribens rationem se purgare dicebat: When Gaius signed their sentences at the end of the waiting period, he claimed that he was "clearing his accounts" (Rolfe 1913–1914), "balancing his books," an unfeeling thing to say. *Custodia* = "those in prison" once again; cf. 27.1 and 32.1.

Gallis   Graecisque   aliquot   uno   tempore   condemnatis   gloriabatur
Gallograeciam se subegisse: Gallograecia = Galatia in central Asia Minor, so
called because it had been settled by Celts in the third century B.C. This is clever
for several reasons. A punning juxtaposition of Greeks and Gauls seems to have
been common: *Graeci se in Galliam inmiserunt, in Graeciam Galli* (Sen. *Dial.*
12.7.2). In addition, it was a recollection of the paradigmatically cruel human
sacrifice of a Gallic and a Greek couple buried alive in 226 B.C. (Dio 12, frg. 47,
Boissevain; Plut. *Marc.* 3.4) or 216 B.C. (Livy 22.57.6) in order to fulfill and
thus render benign a prophecy that the Gauls and Greeks would possess Rome.
And finally, *subigere* means "dominate sexually" as well as "overcome" in a more
general sense (Adams 154–55). The idea in a verse about Caesar (*Gallias Caesar
subegit, Nicomedes Caesarem,* Suet. *Jul.* 49.4), was applied to Gaius: ἐκ δὲ τῶν
μοιχειῶν ὡς καὶ τὴν πᾶσαν Κελτικὴν καὶ Βρεττανικὴν κεχειρωμένος,
αὐτοκράτωρ τε πολλάκις καὶ Γερμανικὸς καὶ Βρεττανικὸς ἐπεκλήθη (Dio
59.25.5ᵃ). The boast is ironic both in the light of his reputation as a catamite
(36.1) and in view of his cheap military success. He was proclaimed *imperator*
seven times without fighting a battle (Dio 59.22.2). For *glorior,* 12.3, 38.3, 41.2.

30.1 *non   temere   in   quemquam   nisi   crebris   et   minutis   ictibus
animadverti passus est, perpetuo notoque iam praecepto: ita feri ut se
mori sentiat:* "Strike so that he can feel that he is dying," did indeed circulate
widely (*perpetuo notoque iam praecepto*). It reappears in the story of his assassination when it was said that the first blow struck against him was intentionally not
mortal so that now he would be the one to feel that he was dying (φασίν τινες
προνοίᾳ τοῦ Χαιρέου γενέσθαι τοῦ μὴ μιᾷ πληγῇ διεργάσασθαι τὸν Γάιον,
ἀλλὰ τιμωρεῖσθαι μειζόνως πλήθει τραυμάτων, Jos. *AJ* 19.106; see on 58.2).
For some sadistically slow deaths, see 27.3–4.

*punito   per   errorem   nominis   alio   quam   quem   destinaverat,   ipsum
quoque paria meruisse dixit:* This seems to have been Julius Sacerdos (*PIR²*
I. 538), a moderately wealthy Gaul whom Gaius killed for his money, mistaking
him for a very wealthy Gaul with a similar name (Dio 59.22.4).[66] If this error
occurred in connection with the uncertainties of 39–40, the charge was probably
maiestas, and Gaius made money from the confiscation of his property (on 38.2–
3; Balsdon 1934a, 76; Faur 1973b, 37–38; cf. on 29.2, Junius Priscus, also killed

---

66 Julii were the local leaders of Gaul from the time of Julius Caesar until A.D. 70. They served
as priests of altars such as the one at Lugdunum. A certain C. Julius Rufus of the tribe of the
Santones, *sacerdos* of the cult of Rome and Augustus, was responsible for the construction of the
Lyon amphitheater in 19. The wealth of such men was real (Audin and Guey; Fishwick 1987–
1990, 133–34; Drinkwater 192).

for being thought wealthier than he was). For Dio, the mistaken identity illuminated Gaius' carelessness (οὕτως ἀκρίτως πάντα ἐγίγνετο, 59.22.4); for Suetonius, his arbitrariness (cf. *a calvo ad calvum*, 27.1). See on 41.2 for another story touching on Julius Sacerdos' execution.

tragicum illud subinde iactabat: oderint, dum metuant: The substantive *tragicum illud* = "that line from tragedy." It is from Accius' *Atreus* (*TRF nos.* 203–4, p. 187) where it had apparently referred to Sulla (Sen. *Dial.* 3.20.4–5) but it came to typify a generic tyrant's attitude (Cic. *Off.* 1.28.97; *Sest.* 48.102; *Phil.* 1.14.34; Sen. *Clem.* 1.12.4). Seneca uses it as a caution to Nero (*Clem.* 2.2.2), and Suetonius applies it to Tiberius in a modified version: *oderint, dum probent* (Suet. *Tib.* 59.4). Gaius supposedly shouted it at frequent intervals (*subinde*), but since it was a cliché, it is doubtful that he did.[67]

30.2 saepe in cunctos pariter senatores ut Seiani clientis, ut matris ac fratrum suorum delatores, invectus est: Suetonius illustrates Gaius' hostility toward the three orders again in sequence of their diminishing importance (cf. 26.2–5). Gaius confronted the senate at some point in 39 at the time when he reversed his negative judgment on Tiberius and restored the *crimen maiestatis* (16.4). He now claimed that it was the senators who were the *delatores* and that Tiberius' actions had been justified (Dio 59.16.1–8), and early the next year he ordered Tiberius' birthday celebrated in the same manner as Augustus' (Dio 59.24.7). *Saepe* seems the familiar Suetonian generalization since a single hostile speech is introduced here. It may have been given during the summer shortly before he left Rome for his pseudo-triumph at Baiae (Dio 59.16.8–17.1; note 39 on 19.3), or perhaps it was connected with the crisis of early September (on 24.3). Dio describes Gaius, easily angered, storming out of the city on three separate occasions in 39 (59.13.7, 16.8, 21.2; for the particularly unreliable chronology at this point in his text see note 94). This frontal attack was a vastly different approach from the non-confrontational manipulation of potential opposition that his two predecessors managed. From this time on, a realistic relationship with the

---

[67] Clichés like this were reused, reworked and combined with others. Seneca plays with the Accius line: *'Oderint.' Occurrit illi futurum ut execrentur insidientur opprimant: quid adiecit? Di illi male faciant, adeo repperit dignum odio remedium. 'Oderint'—quid? 'dum pareant'? Non. 'dum probent'? Non. Quid ergo? ' dum timeant'. Sic ne amari quidem vellem* (Sen. *Dial.* 3.20.4); this is in the same passage in which he records Gaius' Homeric challenge to Jupiter (ἤ μ᾽ ἀνάειρ᾽ ἤ ἐγὼ σέ, *Dial.* 3.20.8) to illustrate the difference between hubris and greatness (see 22.4). In *De clementia* he applies it to Nero, combining it with the Greek verse that Suetonius associates (in a different version) with Tiberius' prediction that Gaius would set the world on fire after he was gone (11): *"Oderint dum metuant," cui Graecus versus similis est, qui se mortuo terram misceri ignibus iubet* (*Clem.* 2.2.2).

senate (if it had ever existed) was replaced with servility on the one side and distrust on the other. The actual deterioration in relations may not, of course, have been quite so dramatic—unless a widespread conspiracy suddenly opened his eyes (on 23.4). For more hostility to the senate as a body (*in cunctos pariter senatores*), see 49.1–2.

prolatis libellis, quos crematos simulaverat: These are the papers that he supposedly burned at the beginning of his reign to show that his clemency toward the old enemies of his family was genuine (15.4). The first ones had been copies. Dio refers to them at four points: 59.4.3, 6.3, 10.8, 16.3.

defensaque Tiberi saevitia quasi necessaria, cum tot criminantibus credendum esset: *Defensaque...saevitia quasi necessaria* expands *oderint, dum metuant* (30.1). Dio's much greater expansion of Gaius' speech (59.16.2–7) reaches a climax with this same Thucydidean idea; "No one is ruled willingly, but obeys the stronger to the extent that he fears him" (οὐδεὶς γὰρ ἀνθρώπων ἑκὼν ἄρχεται, ἀλλ᾽ ἐφ᾽ ὅσον μὲν φοβεῖται, θεραπεύει τὸν ἰσχυρότερον, Dio 59.16.7).

equestrem ordinem ut scaenae harenaeque devotum assidue proscidit: The Roman upper classes were ambivalent about their own participation in the games and on the stage. Repeated legislation was intended to keep them away from the arena, but the desire to display military prowess in public was seductive, and money may sometimes have been a factor (Suet. *Ner.* 12.1). Since the crowd preferred free gladiators to slave, it was perhaps less dangerous for knights to participate than might at first appear (Levick 1983; Ville 260–62; Hopkins 1983, 21–22; see on Atanius, 27.2). On the other hand, the arena could be a punishment; *damnatio ad gladium* or *in ludum gladiatorum* seems to have begun under Gaius (Ville 233). Dio writes that having first secured the senate's sanction to circumvent the law, Gaius executed a large number of persons, including twenty-six knights, by forcing them to fight as gladiators (59.10.1–2). Examples are the knight whose father was put into the cage (27.3) and possibly the Atanius who vowed his life for Gaius' (on 27.2) and Colosseros (35.2).

infensus turbae faventi adversus studium suum: Gaius insisted that the crowd conform to his own enthusiasms (cf. 35.3, 55.1; also Dio 59.13.5). For the importance of the emperor's interactions with the people at *munera* and games, see on 18.1. Gaius was a *parmularius,* one of those who favored the Thracian gladiators (35.2, 54.1, 55.2, also 32.2) who fought with a short curved swords (*sicae*) and used small shields (*parmae* or *parmulae*) to protect themselves.

Domitian liked the Thracians too (Suet. *Dom.* 10.1). Comparable was Gaius' bias toward the Greens (18.3, 55.2).

exclamavit: utinam p. R. unam cervicem haberet!: This statement was his signature aphorism. Its announcement, "I am an executioner," may or may not have been his own; it could have been assigned to him by those who thought him impatient to inflict capital punishment. Similar impatience is found in his boast that he condemned forty persons while his wife was taking a nap (38.3; also 37.3). Seneca explains the saying as Gaius' wanting to serve his own convenience: *[Gaius] optabat ut populus Romanus unam cervicem haberet, ut scelera sua tot locis ac temporibus diducta in unum ictum et unum diem cogeret* (*Dial.* 5.19.2). The outburst is referred to games early in 39 (Dio 59.13.6). "One neck" reappears neatly reversed in the story of his assassination when the populace noted that it was now the emperor who had the single neck whereas they had many hands: ἐπιδεικνύντες αὐτῷ ὅτι ἐκεῖνος μὲν αὐχένα ἕνα σφεῖς δὲ δὴ χεῖρας πολλὰς ἔχοιεν (Dio 59.30.1ᶜ; cf. the other reversed aphorism, 30.1; note 123). For Gaius the executioner executed, see on 58.2 and also 32.3; for his shouting (*exclamavit*), 22.1. Vulnerable necks also at 32.3 and 33.

cumque Tetrinius latro postularetur, et qui postularent, Tetrinios esse ait: If the crowd were *Tetrinii* they were outlaws like Tetrinius (*PIR¹* T. 95). They either asked for his death (*iugulatus,* on 27.2) or simply asked for him to appear. *Postulare* is a neutral verb (18.3). It was perhaps not Tetrinius' first fight since he was notorious enough to have captured the popular imagination.

30.3 *retiari tunicati quinque numero gregatim dimicantes sine certamine ullo totidem secutoribus succubuerant; cum occidi iuberentur, unus resumpta fuscina omnes victores interemit:* This passage deals with a little understood aspect of the gladiatorial contests. *Retiari* were armed with three-pronged spears (*fuscina*) and with nets for entangling their opponents. They fought in a group (*gregatim*). *Secutores,* lightly armed with sword, shield, helmet and one greave, were their opponents. If this was a serious contest, the incident bears on the question of whether the denial of *missio* permitted the resumption of combat rather than inevitable execution (on Atanius Secundus, 27.2; Ville 416–17). The *retiari* declared themselves beaten (*succubuerant* = surrender) and this must have included the laying down of arms since the *retiarius* took his weapon up again (*resumpta fuscina*). But *retiari tunicati*, without armor and wearing a unisex undergarment instead of the gladiator's usual loin cloth, apparently fought in the mock contests featured between the shows (cf. the *paegniarii,* 26.5); they were degraded as effeminate and shameful (Juv. 6.365

[O1–13] 366; Cerutti and Richardson 589, 593–94; Friedländer 4.171–74). If this was a mock contest, then the very act of inficting capital punishment on one group (*cum occidi iuberentur*), despite the fact that they had fought an uninteresting contest (*sine certamine ullo*), was cruel and evidently on the hands of Gaius, who was presiding. Claudius was blamed for ordering *retiari* killed when they fell accidentally, these presumably also some who fought only to entertain (Suet. *Cl*. 34.1).

hanc ut crudelissimam caedem et deflevit edicto et eos, qui spectare sustinuissent, execratus est: The point is again (as in the two preceeding anecdotes) the anger that Gaius felt when he was crossed. When the *retiarius* killed the *secutores*, he was not playing by the rules, abiding by the decision of the president of the games, but the crowd, treated to a little action at last (*sine ullo certamine*, above), loved it. Gaius' edict was another inappropriate verbal response. The irony of cruel Gaius calling it cruel slaughter (*crudelissimam caedem*) is not lost. For his other edicts, see 25.1.

31 ***queri etiam palam de condicione temporum suorum solebat, quod nullis calamitatibus publicis insignirentur:*** Although the implication is that Gaius simply wanted to witness mass suffering, disaster would have provided opportunity for him to respond to a crisis with *liberalitas*. Cf. on 16.3, the fire in the Aemiliana.

Augusti principatum clade Variana, Tiberi ruina spectaculorum apud Fidenas memorabilem factum: The loss of the three legions under the command of Varus in A.D. 9 (3.2) was the signal tragedy of Augustus' reign (Suet. *Aug*. 23.1, 49.1; *Tib*. 17.2, 18.1; Tac. *Ann*. 2.7). For Tiberius is was the collapse of a poorly constructed wooden amphitheater at Fidenae near Rome in 27. This was a spectacular catastrophe with 20,000 (Suet. *Tib*. 40) or 50,000 (Tac. *Ann*. 4.63.1) dead. Tacitus likened the scene to the aftermath of war (*Ann*. 4.62.1–3). There may be an aphorism lurking behind this idea: Augustus had his Varine disaster, Tiberius his Fidenae, but "Gaius' entire reign was a disaster" (*Gaianae cladis magna portio*, Sen. *Dial*. 9.14.10).

suo oblivionem imminere prosperitate rerum; atque identidem exercituum caedes, famem, pestilentiam, incendia, hiatum aliquem terrae optabat: Tiberius was fortunate to have experienced this entire assortment: *fames* (Tac. *Ann*. 6.14), *pestilentia* and *hiatus terrae* (*Ann*. 2.47.1), *incendium* (Suet. *Tib*. 50.3; Tac. *Ann*. 6.45.1). Nero was accused of making his own pyrotechnic excitement (Suet. *Ner*. 38.1; Tac. *Ann*. 15.38.1).

Just as cruel deeds (27–28) and cruel words (29–31) have been paired, so now Gaius' cruelty while "at leisure" is handled in the same sequence: deeds (32), words (33).

32.1 *Animum quoque remittenti ludoque et epulis dedito eadem factorum dictorumque saevitia aderat:* The mixture of cruelty and pleasure is noted by Seneca also: *deinde adeo inpatiens fuit differendae voluptatis, quam ingentem crudelitas eius sine dilatione poscebat, ut...* (*Dial.* 5.18.4).[68] Similar impatience is implied in the "single neck" aphorism (30.2).

saepe in conspectu prandentis vel comisantis seriae quaestiones per tormenta habebantur, miles decollandi artifex quibuscumque e custodia capita amputabat: Only slaves were supposed to be interrogated under torture, but traitors were apparently an exception, even in the late Republic (Garnsey 143–45). Gaius, according to Seneca, tortured persons simply out of pique (*torsit, non quaestionis sed animi causa, Dial.* 5.18.3); in actual fact, they were probably accused of *maiestas* (27.4, 30.1, 38.3, 41.2). Suetonius keeps Gaius at the table, while Seneca has him watch the decapitations while he walks back and forth in the Gardens of Agrippina, which was across the Tiber and outside the *pomerium* (possibly during the summer of 40; see 49.2). *Quibuscumque e custodia* = "anyone at all from among the prisoners," implying random executions (cf. 27.1); cf. *quosdam ex illis cum matronis atque aliis senatoribus ad lucernam decollaret* (Sen. *Dial.* 5.18.4).

Puteolis dedicatione pontis, quem excogitatum ab eo significavimus: The unique nature of the bridge at Baiae continues to be emphasized (*excogitare,* 19.1, 3). Other cross references within the text are 8.2 to 7 and 35.1 to 26.1.

cum multos e litore invitasset ad se, repente omnis praecipitavit, quosdam gubernacula apprehendentes contis remisque detrusit in mare: Suetonius describes what happened after the ceremonial activities on the bridge (19) were finished; more fully in Dio: The feast lasted into the night. Gaius was on the bridge but others were on boats anchored nearby in the water.

---

[68] The entire passage of Seneca is pertinent for what Suetonius writes below. It has already been noted in connection with the beating of Batilienus Bassus (26.3) and the killing of sons before the eyes of their fathers (27.4). After citing Sulla and Catiline as precedents for Gaius, he writes, *modo C. Caesar Sex. Papinium, cui pater erat consularis, Betilienum Bassum quaestorem suum, procuratoris sui filium, aliosque et senatores et equites Romanos uno die flagellis cecidit, torsit, non quaestionis sed animi causa; deinde adeo inpatiens fuit differendae voluptatis, quam ingentem crudelitas eius sine dilatione poscebat, ut in xysto maternorum hortorum (qui porticum a ripa separat) inambulans quosdam ex illis cum matronis atque aliis senatoribus ad lucernam decollaret. Quid instabat! Quod periculum aut privatum aut publicum una nox minabatur? Quantulum fuit lucem expectare denique, ne senatores populi Romani soleatus occideret!* (*Dial.* 5.18.3–4).

He became drunk and threw some of his companions into the sea and then rammed and sank them with ships. Fortunately the sea was quiet and most survived (Dio 59.17.8–10). The party evidently deteriorated, and some drowned in a melee. See on 19.1 for the victory party on Sextus Pompey's boat at Puteoli that Augustus and Antony attended.

32.2 *Romae publico epulo servum ob detractam lectis argenteam laminam carnifici confestim tradidit:* Cf. on 17.2 and 18.2 for the public banquets of 37 and 39. *Coetus epulantium* (below) suggests a reasonably large number of diners. This banquet seems to have had a table and couches, at least for some. *Argentea lamina* was decorative silver plating on a *lectus,* a dining couch, a form of decoration that became relatively common for luxury pieces in the early Empire (Pliny *HN* 33.144; Ransom 56). It seems odd that a slave would be so obtuse as to strip metal from couches while persons were lying on them, but that is what *confestim* implies.

ut manibus abscisis atque ante pectus e collo pendentibus, praecedente titulo qui causam poenae indicaret, per coetus epulantium cicumduceretur: Mutilation, especially the amputation of limbs, was a military punishment (Frontin. *Str.* 4.1.16, 42). A fine was an equivalent for civilians during the Empire (Mommsen 1899, 981–83, 982, n. 2). Claudius and Galba were thought excessive when they cut off the hands of thieves and forgers (Suet. *Cl.* 15.2; *Gal.* 9.1), but since this thief was a slave, the punishment may have been routine; the bloody display is the reason for the opprobrium. It was common for placards to announce the punishments of condemned men (Suet. *Dom.* 10.1; Quint. *Declam. Min.* 302; Dio 54.3.7; Veyne 1983, 282); cf.14.2, *titulo proposito.*

murmillonem e ludo: Murmillones (*myrmillones*), also called *Galli,* were gladiators who probably took their name from the fish insignia (μορμύλος or μορμύρος) on their helmets (Friedländer 4.176–77). They fought with a sword and had a large shield (*scutum*), and those who favored them were apparently *scutarii* (Ville 444); cf. the *parmularii,* on 30.2. This one was training in a gladiatorial school (*ludus gladiatorius*), probably in Gaius' own establishment which allegedly had 20,000 trainees (Pliny *HN* 11.144, 245). Another *murmillo* at 55.2.

rudibus secum battuentem et sponte prostratum confodit ferrea sica: Since his opponent was a *murmillo* (above), Gaius probably fought as one of his favorite Thracians (on 30.2). They were sparring with the *rudis,* the wooden sword used in practice fights, when the professional tactfully surrendered. Gaius played it seriously with a real (*ferrea*) weapon. This excursion into the arena was private like his chariot racing (18.3). *Battuere* = "beat" or "pound" and apparently "fence" when used intransitively as here.[69]

ac more victorum cum palma discucurrit: Victorious gladiators received the palm and, based on the evidence of this sentence, made a circuit of the arena (Ville 444).

32.3 *admota altaribus victima succinctus poparum habitu elato alte malleo cultrarium mactavit:* Suetonius classifies religious ritual among leisure activities (*animum...remittenti,* 32.1). In the early Empire the actual business of animal sacrifice was left to attendants or *victimarii* (*popae*), professionals who had their own *collegium* (*ILS* 4963; Wissowa 417–18, 498; Latte 383). All the *victimarii* wore the *limus,* a linen cloth wrapped (*succincti*) around the waist (Prop. 4.3.62; Ov. *Fast.* 1.319; Serv. at *Aen.* 12. 120; Ryberg 46 and passim; cf. 26.2 for the senators *succincti* like slaves). The *popa* with the mallet[70] first stunned the animal so that it would not show unseemly reluctance in dying, and then the *victimarius* dispatched it with the ritual knife (*culter*); he is designated as a *cultrarius* only here in a text (*TLL* 4.1320.55–58; otherwise in two inscriptions, *ILS* 7642 = *CIL* 10.3984 and *CIL* 10.3987; Latte 383–88). Gaius' mallet came down on his fellow attendant and made him the sacrificial victim instead. He would have presided at sacrifices, but it is highly unlikely that he ever really killed an animal. Besides, this seems absurdly inept. The anecdote nonetheless makes the point that Gaius could not be trusted, that no one close to him was safe—neither a gladiator (above), nor his consuls (below). It is true that a large number of persons who were close to him did become his victims: M. Junius Silanus, Tiberius Gemllus (23.3), Ptolemy (35.1), as well as Macro (26.1), Lepidus (24.3) and his quaestor (26.3).[71]

---

[69] The word had obscene connotations as well (Cic. *Fam.* 9.22.4; Adams 147), and it is possible that there is an innuendo about sexual activity with gladiators (*battuentem* [intransitive] = ? *mutuum struprum,* 36.1). The intransitive verb is repeated at 54.1 where Gaius again plays the *Thraex.* The two instances are plausibly the same.

[70] It is unclear whether *popa* was a popular name for any *victimarius* (Latte 384) or was the particular *victimarius* who had the task of stunning the animal with a mallet before it was killed with a knife (Ryberg 35 and passim).

[71] By analogy those who performed sacrifices were executioners because of the image of the outstretched neck (Sen. *Controv.* 2.3.19); Gaius claimed the role for himself when he wished that the Roman people had a single neck (30.1). He and his prefect Macro could have been thought of as a pair of executioners (= *victimarii*) and so could he and Aemilius Lepidus. Gaius got them both before long (*Gaius Caesar iusset Lepidum Dextro tribuno praebere cervicem, ipse Chaereae praestitit,* Sen. *Ep.* 4.7). The danger of proximity is made specific for his assassin Cassius Chaerea (16.4), who was vulnerable because he saw Gaius on a daily basis: τὸ ἐφ᾽ ἡμέρᾳ κινδυνεύειν φιλίᾳ καὶ θεραπείᾳ (Jos. *AJ* 19.21). And Gaius himself is portrayed as a sacrificial

lautiore convivio effusus subito in cachinnos consulibus, qui iuxta cubabant, quidnam rideret blande quaerentibus: quid, inquit, nisi uno meo nutu iugulari utrumque vestrum statim posse? The consuls reclining on either side were as close as it was possible to be. The threat to them is, as elsewhere, expressed as the slitting of multiple throats (30.2, 33).

33 *inter varios iocos:* More of Gaius' nasty tongue, but now in a more private context.

cum assistens simulacro Iovis...consuluisset uter illi maior videretur: There are three versions of this anecdote; in each case Gaius asks that someone recognize him as a god, and each time the answer frustrates him. A Gallic shoe-maker (a Platonic joke?) answered that he was a large piece of nonsense (μέγα παραλήρημα, Dio 59.26.9), and Lucius Vitellius, when asked if he could see Gaius speaking with the moon, thought fast and answered that only the gods could see one another (Dio 59.27.6). Gaius' question here, whether he or Jupiter appeared the greater, continues the theme of divine challenge (22.4).

Apellen tragoedum...cunctantem flagellis discidit: Apelles (*PIR²* A. 907), the most famous of the tragic actors of the time, was a constant companion to Gaius, an example of the men who were his advisors: actors, gladiators and charioteers (ἐδούλευε δὲ καὶ τοῖς ὀρχησταῖς καὶ τοῖς ἄλλοις τοῖς περὶ τὴν σκηνὴν ἔχουσι, Dio 59.5.2; cf. Mnester on 36.1; see 54.1). The verbal wit here is the pun on the name Apelles that mixes Greek and Latin: *pellis* and the alpha-privative prefix = "skinless;" Gaius tore his skin off with the whipping (Barrett 1989, 217). Philo confirms the torture of Apelles but does not give the reason for it (ἐφ᾽ ἑτέραις αἰτίαις, *Leg.* 206).

conlaudans subinde vocem deprecantis quasi etiam in gemitu praedulcem: Apelles said nothing (*cunctantem,* above). Cf. 27.2 for P. Afranius Potitus delaying. Gaius was impatient; see 37.3.

quotiens uxoris vel amiculae collum exoscularetur, addebat: tam bona cervix simul ac iussero demetur: Necks again (cf. 30.2, 32.3). This wife is probably Caesonia who appears in the next anecdote. *Amicula* is a generic girl friend, but see the *prostituta Pyrallis* (36.1).

quin et subinde iactabat exquisiturum se vel fidiculis de Caesonia sua, cur eam tanto opere diligeret: He would "make inquiry with the cords"

victim when he was assassinated (57.1, 4; 58.2), killed by Chaerea, another "assistant" (*victimarius*); praetorian tribunes were apparently executioners for the upper classes.

(*fidiculis*) as to why he loved her so. There had to be an explanation for his seemingly inexplicable passion (25.3, 50.2). It is uncertain whether the cords were a torture instrument for binding (Suet. *Tib.* 62.2) or, because of their association with the rack, for stretching (Sen. *Dial.* 5.3.5, 19.1; Val. Max. 3.3.5). *Quin et* introduces a climactic example at 5 and 37.1 as well.

The cruelty of the last seven chapters is fairly typical of all tyrants, but envy and spite are specific for Gaius. These faults resonate with his unwillingness to take advice or to be crossed in any way.

34.1 *Nec minore livore ac malignitate quam superbia saevitaque:* The transition sentence picks up the *superbia* of chapter 22 and the *saevitia* of 27–33.

paene adversus omnis aevi hominum genus grassatus est: He was jealous of the dead as well as the living. *Grassor* is a strong verb with overtones of lawless brigands in search of random victims. Suetonius makes two emperors its subject, Gaius (here and 56.1) and Nero (*Ner.* 36.1).

statuas virorum inlustrium ab Augusto ex Capitolina area propter angustias in campum Martium conlatas: The precinct of the temple of Jupiter on the Capitoline became crowded with trophies, votive offerings and free-standing statues (*PA* 47–50). They were removed in 179 B.C. and again by Augustus when he refurbished Rome. The Campus Martius also became crowded as time passed (Livy 40.51.3; Strab. 5.3.8). *Angustiae* = a narrow place; cf. 51.2.

ita subvertit atque disiecit ut restitui salvis titulis non potuerint: When Gaius began a new amphitheater in the Campus Martius he evidently disturbed both the *Aqua Virgo* which Claudius restored (21) and the statues that were there. The implication is that the disarray was such that Claudius could not reerect them even though their bases were intact (*salvis titulis*). For Claudius' policy on statues, Dio 60.25.2–3.

vetuitque posthac viventium cuiquam usquam statuam aut imaginem nisi consulto et auctore se poni: All emperors controlled the messages conveyed by statues of the living or recently dead, e.g., Drusilla's statue in the temple of Venus (Dio 59.11.2). Claudius had Gaius' statues quietly removed (Dio 60.4.5).

34.2 *cogitavit etiam de Homeri carminibus abolendis, cur enim sibi non licere dicens, quod Platoni licuisset, qui eum e civitate quam constituebat eiecerit?* This is Suetonius' only notice of Plato or his works (Gascou 715, n. 20). Plato's *Republic* outlines the ideal city state and finds no place in it for narrative poets like Homer (*Rep.* 377–393). But there is no reason to think that Gaius really disliked or distrusted Homer's poetry; note the Homeric quotations at 22.1 and 22.4. The point is, if Plato could refashion the city, why not Gaius? This is a prelude the main point of the story, the rejection of Vergil and Livy (below).

sed et Vergili[i] ac Titi Livi scripta...paulum afuit quin...amoveret: The visions of Rome that Vergil and Livy (below) championed paralleled Homer's epic vision for Greece. The *Aeneid* ratified and popularized the Augustan interpretation of the war against Antony as a foreign war between East and West (especially at *Aen.* 8.671–713), and Livy also took the Augustan line (Syme 1959, 60). The threat to ban their writings is related to the charge that Gaius rejected his Augustan heritage (23.1, 26.3). But how might anyone know what Gaius "almost" did (*paulum afuit quin,* see 48.1)? He quoted Vergil (45.2).

imagines...ex omnibus bibliothecis: Likenesses of authors, always or usually portraits on medallions, were placed in the public libraries of which there were four or five in Rome (16.4 on the *clipeus* of Gaius; on 3.1 for the portrait of Germanicus).

quorum alterum ut nullius ingenii minimaeque doctrinae, alterum ut verbosum in historia neglegentemque carpebat: All poets needed *ingenium* and *ars* (Ov. *Tr.* 2.424; Cic. *Orat.* 1.45.198; Goodyear 1984, 608–9). Livy's wordiness was proverbial but not necessarily considered a fault (*Livi lactea ubertas,* Quint. 10.1.32). Carelessness is otherwise unattested. *In historia* seems superfluous unless his history is being contrasted with his dialogues and philosophical writings (Sen. *Ep.* 100.9; Goodyear 1984, 608).

de iuris quoque consultis, quasi scientiae eorum omnem usum aboliturus, saepe iactavit se mehercule effecturum, ne quid respondere possint praeter eum: *Responsa* were the answers (*respondere*) of the jurists (*iuris consultis*) who were consulted on legal decisions. Augustus singled out some who had the privilege of responding in his name (Nicholas 31). Gaius was jealous of their prestige.

Three persons are named in a clever comment on Gaius' hostility to two distant cousins who were potential competitors and thus legitimate objects of his envy. The first was Torquatus, perhaps L. Junius Silanus (*PIR²* I. 829),[72] and the other was Magnus, Pompeius Magnus (*PIR¹* P. 477). Shortly after Claudius became emperor, he attempted to neutralize the potential opposition by marrying these two to his daughters (Syme 1958, 385–86; Levick 1990, 57–61); both accompanied

---

[72] Not D. Junius Silanus Torquatus (*PIR²* I. 837), the traditional identification (Mommsen 1903, 126, n. 4; Willrich 462, n. 1; below).

him to Britain in A.D. 43 (Dio 60.21.5). But his cooption failed and he found it necessary to kill Magnus and both his parents in 46 or 47 (Dio 60.31.8; Tac. *Hist.* 1.48.1; Suet. *Cl.* 27.2, 29.1–2; Sen. *Apocol.* 11.5) and to force Lucius to suicide in 49 (Suet. *Cl.* 29.2; Tac. *Ann.* 12.3; Dio 60.31.8; Sen. *Apocol.* 8.2, 10.4, 11.5). It was the same pattern of attempted cooption and elimination that Gaius followed with Tiberius Gemellus (15.2, 23.3). The appearance of these sons-in-law in this story suggests that it formed early in Claudius' reign when they were still in his good graces. Sandwiched between them is a joke, a hypothetical Cincinnatus, a "curly head," whom the balding Gaius envied.

35.1 *vetera familiarum insignia nobilissimo cuique ademit:* Here follows a conflation of *cognomina* and the physical objects or qualities from which they might be derived. Romans wore their *insignia* as their names, not on their persons.

Torquato torquem: Torques, originally barbarian ornaments, were twisted metal collars regularly awarded as military decorations by the late Republic. They were decorations for soldiers of the rank of centurion and below and were worn as shoulder ornaments and not around the neck (Maxfield 86–88). But Augustus awarded what was evidently an old-fashioned torque to the upper-class C. Nonius Asprenas (*PIR²* N. 126) after he was hurt in the *Lusus Troiae* (Suet. *Aug.* 43.2), probably a gesture to validate the *cognomen* Torquatus that he gave to him and his descendants.[73] The Torquatus in this passage has been identified as D. Junius Silanus Torquatus (notes 72 and 77, a son of M. Junius Silanus (Torquatus) (*PIR²* I. 839), *consul ordinarius* in 19, and Aemilia Lepida (*PIR²* A. 419), daughter of the younger Julia (note 19). But the Torquatus named here may not be Decimus but rather Lucius Junius Silanus (above), to whom Claudius betrothed his daughter Octavia (*PIR²* C. 1110; Suet. *Cl.* 24.3, 27.2; Tac. *Ann.* 12.3.2; Dio 60.5.7)[74] because he fills out the symmetry of the anecdote so nicely.

---

[73] Augustus thus revived a Republican *cognomen* that had first appeared in the fourth century B.C. among the Manlii (Livy 7.10.11–13).

[74] D. Junius Silanus Torquatus, L. Junius Silanus (above) and M. Junius Silanus (*PIR²* I. 833) were great-great-grandsons of Augustus, second cousins at one remove to Gaius, possessors of Julian blood and a threat to a reigning princeps. Decimus became consul in A.D. 53 (Tac. *Ann.* 12.58.1) and was eventually killed by Nero (Tac. *Ann.* 15.35; Dio 62.27.2). Neither Marcus nor Lucius nor their father is known to have been a Torquatus, but an inscription refers to a sister Junia Lepida (*PIR²* I. 861) as the daughter of Torquatus (*IG* 2–3².4242), and there was a L. Junius Silanus Torquatus (*PIR²* I. 838) in the next generation (Marcus' son). The *cognomen* seems to have been available in this family whether attested for individuals or not. The father perhaps received it because of his proconsulship in Africa (A.D. 30–35, Dio 59.20.7 vs. Tac. *Hist.* 4.48.1; Syme 1981, 197–98). The C. Nonius Asprenas who received the torque from Augustus (above) was probably a son of L. Nonius Asprenas (*PIR²* N. 118), consul in A.D. 6 and also proconsul in Africa for three years under Tiberius. Was "Torquatus" a kind of trophy for the African command? Was its removal related to Gaius' division of Africa and the disappearance of this last senatorial military responsibility (Tac. *Hist.* 4.48; Dio 59.20.7)?

There is no other witness that Gaius forbid anyone to use the name Torquatus—let alone remove an improbable torque from his person.

Cincinnato crinem: According to popular belief, the original Cincinnatus (L. Quinctius Cincinnatus), the fifth century B.C. dictator, got his *cognomen* from his curly hair (Dio 5. frg. 23.2, Boissevain). The Quinctii used Cincinnatus into the next century when it was replaced by Crispinus (curly hair again), a name still found in the patrician *gens Quinctia* in the early Empire. Accordingly, a specific person might be sought from among the Quinctii Crispini, a youth to match Torquatus and Pompeius Magnus.[75] But no hypothetical Quinctius had the prestige to compete with a Junius Silanus and Pompeius Magnus as an equal third. Gaius could forbid Pompeius to use Magnus and in some figurative sense take a torque from Torquatus (i.e., regret the additional prominence that the *cognomen* bestowed on the already powerful Junii Silani), but taking curly hair away from a Crispinus or a Cincinnatus makes the point that Gaius' jealous nature was particularly vulnerable before men with handsome heads of hair (35.2). He took exception to the son of the *eques splendidus* Pastor (*munditiis eius et cultioribus capillis offensus,* Sen. *Dial.* 4.33.3; cf. 27.4). In the very unlikely event that a real person is to be sought behind "Cincinnatus," it might be he.

Cn. Pompeio stirpis antiquae Magni cognomen: Dio writes that Gaius almost killed Pompeius Magnus but contented himself with taking his *cognomen.* Claudius restored it in A.D. 41 and married him to his daughter Antonia (*PIR²* A. 886; Dio 60. 5.8–9; also Suet. *Cl.* 27.2; Sen. *Apocol.* 11.2). Magnus was a distant cousin to Gaius because he was the son of M. Licinius Crassus Frugi (*PIR²* L. 191; 37.1) and Scribonia (*PIR¹* S. 221), the great-granddaughter of the Scribonia (*PIR¹* S. 220), who was Augustus' first wife, and a direct descendent of the original Pompey the Great. He was born about A.D. 24 and seems to have been the only living bearer of this promising name,[76] a deliberate political statement since it came from his mother's rather than his father's family. Gaius was understandably suspicious; hence a command that he revert to the more usual patrilineal naming system. Besides, how could anyone be Magnus other than himself? Pompeius still had his *cognomen* in A.D. 40,[77] which means that if this story is

---

[75] Suggested has been an unknown son of T. Quinctius Crispinus Valerianus (*PIR¹* Q. 38; *RE* 24.1019), consul suffect in A.D. 2 and prominent under Tiberius. He was himself the adopted son of T. Quinctius Sulpicianus (*PIR¹* Q. 37), consul in 9 B.C. and alleged adulterer of the daughter of Augustus. The Quinctii were not without ambition.

[76] Tiberius took on the restoration of the Theater of Pompey which burned in A.D. 21 because there was no Pompeius to do it (cf. 21; Tac. *Ann.* 6.45.1).

[77] Pompeius Magnus was still Magnus at the time when he became a *Salius* during Gaius' third consulship (January 40). Two Junii Silani (one a Torquatus) had already been made *Salii Palatini*

more than a metaphor for Gaius' anxiety about Magnus' potential, the stripping of it took place in the last year of his reign (Charlesworth 1933b, 109–10).

Ptolemaeum, de quo ret\<t\>uli: Suetonius refers his readers to 26.1 where Ptolemy's relationship with Gaius is made clear. Other cross references at 8.2 and 32.1.

et arcessitum e regno et exceptum honorifice: Once again Gaius honors a relative before he turns against him. It is unclear when Ptolemy was summoned and whether it was to Rome or Lugdunum (below). If to the latter in the winter of 39–40, he joined two other client kings, Antiochus and Herod Agrippa (16.3; Dio 59.24.1, 25.1). A cryptic anecdote places him still in Mauretania at some point when Gaius was in Rome (55.1).

non alia de causa repente percussit, quam quod edente se munus ingressum spectacula convertisse hominum oculos fulgore purpureae abollae animadvertit: Ptolemy's death is placed among the events of early 40 (Dio 59.25.1) probably at Lugdunum (20 and 27.1 for Gaius' games there). Although client kings could wear the purple, many tactfully did not (Suet. *Aug.* 60; Balsdon 1934a, 193). The *abolla* was a long garment, a dramatic statement under the circumstances, and Gaius would not allow himself to be upstaged. Both this explanation for the execution and Dio's, that Gaius killed Ptolemy for his money (59.25.1), seem inadequate. Better perhaps is the argument that he fell under suspicion in the general uneasiness that followed the threats of 39 when Gaius trusted no one, least of all his family. Ptolemy died because of "who he was," *pro necessitudinis iure* (26.1; Fishwick 1971, 471–73).[78] In favor of a Roman rather than a Gallic setting for his death is a statement of Seneca's: *Ptolemaeum Africae regem, Armeniae Mithridaten inter Gaianas custodias vidimus (Dial.* 9.11.12). If *vidimus* is taken literally, then Seneca personally saw the two kings imprisoned in Rome, a scenario that can be rationalized if Ptolemy was summoned to Rome by 39 where the scene in the amphitheater and his imprisonment took place and was then removed under guard to Lugdunum where he was killed (Fishwick 1971, 467–71). Easier is a figurative reading of Seneca's *vidimus*. His execution was a prelude to several years of fighting in Mauretania

---

by Gaius, probably in 37 (*ILS* 9339; Mommsen 1903, 125–28). This inscription is the basis of Mommsen's identification of Torquatus as Decimus (above). The *Salii Palatini* were a priesthood whose membership was composed of patrician youths, often very young (Levick 1990, 17).

[78] If he was himself involved in Gaetulicus' plot, it may have been because he came to know him when Gaetulicus' father, Cossus Cornelius Lentulus (*PIR*[2] C. 1390), campaigned with his own father Juba against the Gaetulians (Fishwick and Shaw 1976, 491–94; Faur 1973a, 264–67).

after it was annexed as a Roman province in 40 (Dio 59.25.1; 60.8.6; Pliny *HN* 5.2, 5.11).

35.2 *pulchros et comatos, quotiens sibi occurrent, occipitio raso deturpabat:* His own hair loss was an embarassment, and so he humiliated others (for his baldness, 27.1, 35.1, 50.1). Tiberius was also ridiculed for baldness (Dio 58.19.1–2).

erat Aesius Proculus patre primipilari: The proper name (Aesius Proculus, *PIR²* A. 431) and the detail of his father's rank seem to give legitimacy to the anecdote. A *primipilaris* was a retired *primus pilus,* first centurion of the first cohort of the first century of a legion. The position was well paid and the discharge grant substantial enough to secure equestrian status (Dobson 426; see 38.2 and 44.1 for their retirement benefits).

ob egregiam corporis amplitudinem et speciem Colosseros dictus: Gaius was jealous of more than hair (above). The name *Colosseros,* from κολοσσός and ἔρως, means "Giant Cupid" (Rolfe 1913–1914), and it should be wondered if an inference about the size of his genitals could be avoided by Suetonius' readers. Gladiators sometimes had names that were suggestive of the sexuality with which their occupation was linked (e.g., *Kallimorphos, Pulcher, Nympheros,* Hopkins 1983, 21–22; Robert 1940, 301). Cf. the gladiator Columbus at 55.2.

hunc spectaculis detractum repente et in harena deductum: See on 30.2 for knights in the arena voluntarily or otherwise. For Gaius dragging bystanders casually to punishment, Dio 59.13.4; also Suet. *Cl.* 34.2; *Dom.* 10.1. But it is difficult to believe that Aesius Proculus was not a professional if his fighting name was already so well-known.

Thr<a>eci et mox hoplomacho comparavit: Colosseros' first opponent was one of Gaius' own favorites, an indication that he was an enemy, but his second was a *hoplomachus,* heavily armed like a *murmillo* (30.2, 32.2) and also an opponent of a *Thraex.* The *hoplomachus* (probably the same as a Samnite) had a large shield and a helmet with visor, neck-protector and crest (Robert 1940, 65–66; Ville 419, n. 139; 48, n. 128). *Thraex* and *hoplomachus* seem to have formed a proverbial contrast: *quidam cum hoplomachis, quidam cum Thraecibus optime pugnant* (Sen. *Controv.* 3. *praef.* 10, as an example of different persons of different persuasions).

bisque victorem constringi sine mora iussit et pannis obsitum vicatim circumduci ac mulieribus ostendi, deinde iugulari: Colosseros won both matches. Double jeopardy on a single day was cruel and unusual (Pliny *Ep.* 8.14.21; Ville 397, n. 108), but since his death was intended from the beginning, the detour through the arena was irrelevant. Now no threat to Gaius' virility, he was shown to the women of the city bound and in rags that may have displayed his new impotence. Cf. Afranius led through the city (Guastella).

35.3 *nullus denique tam abiectae condicionis tamque extremae sortis fuit, cuius non commodis obtrectaret Nemorensi regi:* Gaius envied the lowest sorts. The *rex Nemorensis* was a runaway slave (*tam abiectae condicionis tamque extremae sortis*) who had the job of being "king of the grove" (*nemus*), the priest of Diana at Aricia. The temple of Diana and its sacred grove were on the Alban Mount, also the site of the temple of Jupiter Latiaris and the location of estates of wealthy Romans (Suet. *Jul.* 46; Cic. *Att.* 15.4.5 = 4a, *Att.* 115.6.1), including Gaius himself (on 22.2). Each new king challenged the previous king by plucking a bough from a tree in the grove (Frazer 1.1–43). For Gaius and archaic ritutals, see note 61; for his playing the slave: 10.2, 32.3, 57.4.

quod multos iam annos poteretur sacerdotio, validiorem adversarium subornavit: The change of priests was not spontaneous but had become a kind of delayed death sentence for the slave who got his job when he killed his predecessor; he would be killed by his successor in turn. What could be a more apt analogy for Gaius, the "best of slaves and the worst of masters" (10.2), who was accused of killing Tiberius and was living on borrowed time? It is a variation on Tiberius' prophecy, "You will kill him and another will kill you" (on 13). According to this, the primitive custom had been allowed to slide; it was, however, in effect in the second century (Paus. 2.27.4).

cum quodam die muneris essedario Porio post prosperam pugnam servum suum manumittenti studiosius plausum esset: An *essedarius* fought from a chariot with a driver. The slave freed by the otherwise unknown Porius (*PIR¹* P. 650) was plausibly his attendant, an arms bearer, a "second" as at a duel, a pall bearer as necessary, certainly his driver (Ville 376).

ita proripuit se spectaculis, ut calcata lacinia togae praeceps per gradus iret, indignabundus et clamitans dominum gentium populum ex re levissima plus honoris gladiatori tribuentem quam consecratis principibus aut praesenti sibi: Gaius' envy of the applause for Porius leaves the reader with the image of him rushing from the games in anger—but foolishly tripping over the hem of his own clothing, a perfect climax for this rubric of *livor* and *malignitas*. For other angry exits, 48.2 and Dio 59.13.7, 16.8, 21.2. He did not like to be crossed (30.2–3, 55.1).

The irony of Gaius dismissing Tiberius' *spintriae* (16.1) becomes overt in the context of his own sexual excesses. Other emperors earn similar rubrics: Julius (Suet. *Jul.* 49–52), Augustus (*Aug.* 68–69), Tiberius (*Tib.* 44–45), Nero (*Ner.* 28–29).

36.1 Pudicitiae <neque suae> neque alienae pepercit: Cf. *neque suae neque aliorum pudicitiae parcens* (Aur. Vict. 5.5). Very similarly about Nero: *suam quidem pudicitiam usque adeo prostituit, ut...* (Suet. *Ner.* 29).

M. Lepidum: This charge of sexual liaison followed naturally from their political involvement. See 24.1, 24.3 and note 48 for the role of Aemilius Lepidus in the family.

Mnesterem pantomimum: Handsome Mnester (*PIR²* M. 646; also 55.1, 57.4) was one of the entertainers with whom Gaius consorted (cf. Apelles, 33). He later became the paramour of Claudius' wife Messalina (Valeria Messalina, *PIR¹* V. 161; Dio 60.22.3–5, 28.3–5) and was put to death along with her and her party in A.D. 48 (Tac. *Ann.* 11.36.1; Dio 60.31.5; Sen. *Apocol.* 13.4).

quosdam obsides: It was standard that the children of client kings be "educated" in Italy (on 16.3), a euphemistic description of a status somewhere between friendly visitor and hostage. None is known for this period except for the Parthian prince Darius (14.3, 19.2–3). Ravenna was the usual holding ground for such youths (Braund 11–17).

dilexisse fertur commercio mutui stupri: The active (male) role in homosexual intercourse was considered acceptable whereas the passive (female) one was degrading and a standard insult (Richlin 220–26). Gaius played both. The phrase *mutuum stuprum* occurs only in Suetonius, once here and once in reference to Otho's relations with Nero (*Oth.* 2.2). A variant is applied to Vitellius: *hunc adulescentulum mutua libidine constupratum* (*Vit.* 12).

Valerius Catullus, consulari familia iuvenis, stupratum a se...etiam vociferatus est: Since this young man played the acceptable role (above) in their sexual union, he did not hesitate to brag about it (*vociferatus est*) and attach his name to the relationship. Valerius Catullus (*PIR¹* V. 35, perhaps = *PIR¹* V. 36) is otherwise unknown, but he may have been the son of the Valerius Catullus who was consul suffect in 31 (*PIR¹* V. 37, perhaps = Sextus Tedius Valerius Catullus, *PIR¹* T. 38). This would account for the *familia consularis*. Valerii Catulli remained prominent (L. Valerius Catullus Messallinus, *PIR¹* V. 41, consul

73; L. Valerius Catullus, *PIR¹* V. 39, honored by a statue in Athens under Trajan); perhaps that is why Suetonius preserved his name.

latera sibi contubernio eius defessa: Gaius was insatiable. *Latera* = "loins," the "general site of the exhaustion that might follow intercourse" (Adams 49). For *latus* and *latera* as male genitalia, Catull. 6.13; Petron. *Sat.* 130; Mart. 7.58.3; Apul. *Met.* 8.26. The active partner was wearied.

super sororum incesta: Cf. 24.1.

notissimum prostitutae Pyrallidis amorem: Pyrallis (*PIR¹* P. 819), probably a freedwoman (cf. the *amicula* in 33 and Nero's Acte, *PIR²* C. 1067; Suet. *Ner.* 28.1, 50; Tac. *Ann.* 13.12–13; Dio 61.7.1). Gaius was supposed to have visited prostitutes (Tac. *Ann.* 15.72.2; see on 50.1).

non temere ulla inlustriore femina abstinuit: Gaius worked up the social scale. His brothel held *matronae* (41.1).

36.2 quas plerumque cum maritis ad cenam vocatas praeterque pedes suos transeuntis diligenter ac lente mercantium more considerabat, etiam faciem manu adlevans, si quae pudore submitterent: The generalization that follows is very reminiscent of charges that Antony made about the licentious behavior of Augustus, who had his friends inspect wellborn women for him as though they were merchandise: *condiciones quaesitas per amicos, qui matres familias et adultas aetate virgines denudarent atque perspicerent, tamquam Toranio mangone vendente* (Suet. *Aug.* 69.1).

quotiens deinde libuisset egressus triclinio, cum maxime placitam sevocasset, paulo post recentibus adhuc lasciviae notis reversus vel laudabat palam vel vituperabat, singula enumerans bona malave corporis atque concubitus: This may be the frequent Suetonian pluralization of an event involving the wife of Valerius Asiaticus (*PIR¹* V. 25), whose talents Gaius announced: *huic* [Asiaticus] *in convivio, id est in contione, voce clarissima qualis in concubitu esset uxor eius obiecit* (Sen. *Dial.* 2.18.2). But the brief retreat into an adjoining room seems to have been a standard charge. Gaius removed Livia Orestilla from bridegroom and table (25.1) and Augustus did something similar: *feminam consularem e triclinio viri coram in cubiculum abductam, rursus in convivium rubentibus auriculis incomptiore capillo reductam* (Suet. *Aug.* 69.1).

quibusdam absentium maritorum nomine repudium ipse misit iussitque in acta ita referri: *Repudium* = notification of divorce. The births, marriages, divorces and deaths of prominent persons were carried in the *acta diurna* (for the birth of Gaius, 8.1). For the frequency of divorce notices, *tamdiu istuc* [divorce] *timebatur, quamdiu rarum erat; quia nulla sine divortio acta sunt, quod saepe audiebant, facere didicerunt* (Sen. *Ben.* 3.16.2).

A rubric of extravagance, the object of Stoic attack (e.g., Sen. *Ep.* 122) and attempts at legislative control (Tac. *Ann.* 2.33; Dio 57.15.1). Its most important marker was "unnaturalness." Although there is exaggeration and typological anecdote in this chapter, the early Empire was a luxurious time, especially judged from the vantage point of the relatively more puritanical time when Suetonius wrote. Tiberius' parsimony would have made Gaius' free spending ways seem outrageous no matter what the facts. With the exception of the story that Gaius threw coins from the rooftop (37.1) and the money that he went through so quickly (37.3), Dio does not record this material whose highly rhetorical character suggests that Suetonius used a source other than the first century histories. The sequence of vices is similar in other biographies where life style (extravagance, moderation or stinginess) also follows lechery (36; *Jul.* 53; *Aug.* 70–78; *Tib.* 46–48; *Ner.* 30–31).

37.1 *Nepotatus sumptibus omnium prodigorum ingenia superavit, commentus novum balnearum usum, portentosissima genera ciborum atque cenarum:* "In his extravagance he surpassed the prodigality of all other spendthrifts in ingenuity," a condensed opening for a long and rhetorically self-conscious sentence. *Nepotatus* = "prodigality," elsewhere only in Pliny (*HN* 9.114, 14.57), each time with the same negative implications as here. *Commentus* = "contriving" amplifies the cleverness (*ingenia*) of the introductory clause. *Portentosissima* = "very peculiar," unnatural, the marker for indecent extravance: *hoc est luxuriae propositum, gaudere perversis nec tantum discedere a recto, sed quam longissime abire, deinde etiam e contrario stare* (Sen. *Ep.* 122.5). The novelties of baths, food and feasts (*balnearum, ciborum, cenarum*) are explained separately in the three balanced parts of the purpose clause that follows. *Genera ciborum atque cenarum* plays on the difference between "food" and "feast" (cf. Apul *Met.* 10.13, 15).

ut calidis frigidisque unguentis lavaretur: Cf. Pliny *HN* 13.22. Hot and cold baths were usual, but the addition of perfume was worth comment. Trimalchio washed his hands in it (Petron. *Sat.* 47.1), a private citizen sprayed it on his walls (Pliny *HN* 13.22) and Nero rigged the dining room of his golden house so that guests could be sprinkled while they ate (Suet. *Ner.* 31.2). He followed Gaius' example: *qui exemplo Caii Caligulae calidis et frigidis lavaret unguentis* (Eutropius 7.14.1; also Oros. 7.7.3).

pretiosissima margarita aceto liquefacta sorberet: Pretiosissima picks up *portentosissima* (above) to connect bath and table. Just as perfume was the paradigm of luxury (Pliny *HN* 13.20), so pearls were the most precious of jewels: *principium ergo columenque omnium rerum preti margaritae tenent* (Pliny *HN* 9.106, also 37.62); they covered Gaius' third wife Lollia Paulina at her betrothal banquet (Pliny *HN* 9.117). But Gaius was not the only one to dissolve them in vinegar. Pliny tells the story that Cleopatra bet Antony that she could spend an amazing ten million sesterces on a single banquet, indeed, on her own dinner alone. She won by taking off one of her extraordinary pearl earrings and dissolving it in a container of strong vinegar. When she started to repeat the proceedure with the second earring, the referee of the contest stopped her; she had made her point (*HN* 9.119–21; retold by Macrobius, *Sat.* 3.17.16–18). Cleopatra's pearl is transferred to Gaius along with the ten million sesterces, a figure that was apparently proverbial for his extravagant feasts: *C. Caesar...centiens sestertio cenavit uno die; et in hoc omnium adiutus ingenio vix tamen invenit quomodo trium provinciarum tributum una cena fieret* (Sen. *Dial.* 12.10.4).[79] It was clearly not easy for anyone to spend that much, hence the need for *ingenium* (above). Nor was it cheap for others to entertain Gaius (Pliny *HN* 14.56; Philo *Leg.* 344).

convivis ex auro panes et obsonia apponeret: If liquefied pearls were a strange food (*cibum*), this describes an odd banquet (*cena*) with golden food for table decorations. The extravagance of Trimalchio's dinner party comes to mind (Petron. *Sat.* 31–41). Vitellius and Domitian were also undisciplined hosts (Suet. *Vit.* 13; Dio 67.9.1–5); Trajan, on the other hand, was praised for his simple and tastefully set table: *ergo non aurum nec argentum nec exquisita ingenia cenarum, sed suavitatem tuam iucunditatemque miramur* (Pliny *Pan.* 49.7; also Sen. *Ep.* 119.13.1; Tac. *Ann.* 2.33.2, where the sumptuary law of A.D. 16 attacks table furnishings specifically: *vasa auro solida ministrandis cibis*).

aut frugi hominem esse oportere dictitans aut Caesarem: No doubt true enough, but this was a pun that could have been included among Gaius' clever sayings (29–31; Barrett 1989, 216). Crassus Frugi, the father of Pompeius Magnus, if not terribly bright (Sen. *Apocol.* 11.2), was nonetheless close to the throne. Both Gaius and Claudius had to reckon with the family (on 35.1).

---

[79] Pearls proved tasty when dissolved in vinegar by persons other than Cleopatra and Gaius (Hor. *Sat.* 2.3.239–42; Pliny *HN* 9.122). Crushed pearls will dissolve but not so dramatically; they release bicarbonate of lime (= bicarbonate of soda? Ullman). Much of chapter 10 in Seneca's *Consolatio ad Helviam matrem* expands on Gaius' extravagant feasting: *O miserabiles, quorum palatum nisi ad pretiosos cibos non excitatur! Pretiosos autem non eximius sapor aut aliqua faucium dulcedo sed raritas et difficultas parandi facit...* (*Dial.* 12.10.5; *sestertium centiens* four times in 9 and 10 of this chapter).

quin et nummos non mediocris summae e fastigio basilicae Iuliae per aliquot dies sparsit in plebem: This shower of gold and silver coins took place after Gaius returned to Rome at odds with the senate in A.D. 40 (49.1–2). He had thrown *missilia* before (18.2). Suetonius is content to report it as an act of extravagance, but Dio contributes the detail that Gaius threw pieces of iron along with the coins; some died scrambling for the money (59.25.5). It was scarcely necessary to include lethal objects in order to cause a riot (cf. on 26.4 for the greedy melees that accompanied the throwing of *missilia* to crowds; *circa praemium rixa est,* Sen. *Ep.* 74.8).[80] The Basilica Julia was located in the Forum between the Palatine and the Capitoline, just to the north of the new temple of Augustus. The structure had an inside gallery (Pliny *Ep.* 6.33.4; *PA* 79), but all the reports make it clear that Gaius was in a position high above the ground, plausibly on the roof. Cassius Chaerea let slip this opportunity to push him to his death (Jos. *AJ* 19.71). There may be some relationship between this vantage point and the bridge or causeway from the Palatine to the Capitoline (22.4). For *quin et,* see 5, 33.

37.2 *fabricavit et deceris Liburnicas:* A Liburnian galley was the Rome's light, fast warship with two banks of oars, but a *deceris* (δεκήρης), a "ten-fitted ship," was large and awkward.[81] *Deceres Liburnicae* is thus an oxymoron, an "unnatural" vessel, another illustration of this rubric's theme. More may be involved if this is a pun on the litters sometimes called *liburnae* (Juv. 3.240; *Schol. Juv.* 3.240; for litters, 43, 58.3). Pleasure craft were frequent at Baiae: *ut praenavigantes adulteras dinumeraret et tot genera cumbarum variis coloribus picta et fluvitantem toto lacu rosam, ut audieret canentium nocturna convicia* (Sen. *Ep.* 51.12; also Nero, Suet. *Ner.* 27.3). Gaius had two pleasure boats or floating shrines on Lake Nemi that were not unlike the ones described here (on 35.3; Ucelli 286–92) and a *quinquiremis* at Antium (Pliny *HN* 32.3–5). As precedent there were the houseboats of Cleopatra (Suet. *Jul.* 52.1), Ptolemy Philopater and Hiero of Syracuse (Athen. 5.204b–209e), the last a "twenty-fitted ship."

---

[80] The fourth century *Chronica Urbis Romae* (*Chron. Min.* 141–48) chose this incident as emblematic for Gaius' reign: *de basicila Iulia sparsit auros et argeneos, in qua rapina perierunt homines xxxii, [mulieres] ccxlvii et spado* (145).

[81] Each section held ten rowers who could be arranged in a number of different ways. The more elaborate the structure, the less seaworthy the boat. But this was moot since the larger boats in the imperial navy were essentially floating platforms for ship-to-ship boarding that rarely got out of the sight of land (Casson 1971, 103–7, 141–42). *Deceris* seems to be otherwise unknown in Latin (*TLL* 5.139.27–28) although familar enough in Greek and certainly a known type of Roman ship (e.g., at Actium, Plut. *Ant.* 64.1).

gemmatis puppibus, versicoloribus velis: Cf. Athen. 5.205a and 207d for gems and mosaics on ships. Gaius' own Nemi barges had mosaics and bronzes. *Versicoloria vela* were probably not sails but awnings on the model of the colored awnings used for shade in Roman theaters (26.5; Plut. *Luc.* 7.5; Athen. 5.205f, 206a; Casson 1971, 164–65, n. 41).

magna thermarum et porticuum et tricliniorum laxitate magnaque etiam vitium et pomiferarum arborum varietate: The parallel phrases, each enclosing several genitives, present an elaborate balanced construction similar to the *portentosissima...pretiosissima* structure of 37.1. *Laxitas* ("great spaciousness") is used elsewhere for extravagant houses: *tanta laxitas, ut porticus triplices miliarias haberet* (Suet. *Ner.* 31.1; also *Aug.* 72.1). For porticoes and dining rooms on shipboard, Athen. 5.204f, 205a; for baths, Plut. *Luc.* 7.5; Athen. 207e. Trees were "unnatural" when they grew where they did not belong, e.g., in roof gardens: *nulla culminibus meis / imposita nutat silva* (Sen. *Thy.* 464–65); *in summis culminibus mentita nemora* (Sen. *Controv.* 5.5, also 2.13; Sen. *Ep.*122.8). Hiero's ship had them (Athen. 5.207d–e).

quibus discumbens de die: *De die* = "from daybreak, and thus, "all day long" (*TLL* 5.1043.23–30), especially for a *convivium* (*convivia 'de die' duc[eb]antur a primo mane coepta,* Porph. at Hor. *Epod.* 13.4; also Catull. 47.6; Curt. 5.7.2, 8.3.8). "In daylight hours" (Rolfe 1913, 7–10). Cf. *de media nocte, 26.4.*

inter choros ac symphonias: A contrast between vocal and instrumental music is implied here, but elsewhere the distinction is less clear: *symphoriarum cantibus* (Sen. *Ep.* 51.4); *per symphoniarum cantum* (Sen. Dial. 1.3.10). *Ad symphoniam* = background music at banquets (Petron. *Sat.* 32, 36, 43; Sen. *Ep.*12.8).

litora Campaniae peragraret: Gaius "coasted the Campanian shore." His un- wieldy pleasure craft did not go far out to sea (note 81). After the death of Drusilla, he "wandered" randomly along the coasts of Italy and Sicily (*Italiae ac Siciliae oras errabundus permetiens,* Sen. *Dial.* 11.17.5; see 24.2). This probably refers to an interlude on his ships.

in extructionibus praetoriorum atque villarum omni ratione posthabita: Both *praetoria* and *villae* designate country houses, but the former were larger. Gaius had houses at Baiae (19.1; Jos. *AJ* 18.248–49; Phil. *Leg.* 185), the Alban Mount (22.2, 35.3; Sen. *Dial.* 11.1.4), Antium (8.5, 49.2), Mevania (43) and probably Velitrae, Augustus' birthplace (*in Veliterno rure,* Pliny *HN* 12.10). There would have been others.

nihil tam efficere concupiscebat quam quod posse effici negaretur:
The desire for the impossible (Guastella); grandiosity was an important aspect of his personality (on 50.2).

Suetonius embarks on the standard diatribe against the unnaturalness of making the sea into land, the land into sea, raising plains into mountains and leveling mountains to the plains. It had its origin in Xerxes bridging the Hellespont and digging a canal through Mount Athos and has already been met in Gaius' bridge at Baiae (19) and his intention of digging through the Corinthian isthmus (21). Here the bridge is a villa built out over the sea and the canal lets water into the land to enhance the landscape and build the famed fishponds at Baiae. Xerxes' hubris was applied to Lucullus in this same way: *quem ob iniectas moles mari et receptum suffossis montibus in terras mare haud infacete Magnus Pompeius Xerxem togatum vocare adsueverat* (Vell. 2.33.4).[82] The language was pervasive: *montes perfossos, convalles aequatas,* applied to Claudius' aquaducts: (Pliny *HN* 36.12.3).

37.3 *et iactae itaque moles infesto ac profundo mari et excisae rupes durissimi silicis:* A sentence crafted from clichés. *Moles* = breakwater often and at 19.1, but here it refers to the pilings on which expensive villas were built out over the sea, an "unnatural" act that indicated the hubris of the leisure class: *contracta pisces aequora sentiunt / iactis in altum molibus* (Hor. *Carm.* 3.1; also 2.20–21; Sen. *Controv.* 2.1.13, 5.5; Sen. *Thy.* 459–60; for building on the water at Baiae, D'Arms 126–33). *Durissimi: silex* was quintessentially hard rock.

et campi montibus aggere aequati et complanata fossuris montium iuga: Although Suetonius seems to extend his topic into the larger geography of plains and mountains, this is no more than a grandiose variation on what has preceded. The *moles* are now *aggera* as high as mountains, and in order to bring the villas into juxtaposition with the water, cuts are made through *iuga*. Velleius uses similar language for Lucullus' seawater sluices (*suffossis montibus,* 2.33.3), and Plutarch says that when Lucullus did his landscaping, he left ridges (*iuga*) hanging over his trenches (λόφους ἀνακρεμαννύντος αὐτοῦ μεγάλοις ὀρύγμασι, *Luc.* 39.3); also *alii fossis inducunt mare* (Sen. *Controv.* 2.1.13). It is highly doubtful that any of this refers to an *urbs in iugo Alpium* (21) or to harbor improvements at Rhegium (Jos. *AJ* 19.205) or to breakwaters at Puteoli (19.1; Willrich 420–21).

incredibili quidem celeritate, cum morae culpa capite lueretur: Cf. *ac ne paululum quidem morae patiens,* 38.3. Gaius was characterized as impatient of delay (*impatiens morae,* 51.2). He rushed from the games (35.3), was intolerant

---

82 Plutarch also describes Lucullus as a "Xerxes in a toga" but ascribes the aphorism to a Stoic instead of to Pompey: ὁ Στωϊκὸς Τουβέρων θεασάμενος Ξέρξην αὐτὸν ἐκ τηβέννου προσηγόρευσεν (*Luc.* 39.3).

of those who "hesitated" (*cunctantem,* 27.2, 33), had difficulty waiting for those
who left him money to die (38.2) and desired to punish as many as possible at one
time (30.2, 38.3).

immensas opes totumque illud T<i>. *Caesaris vicies ac septies milies*
sestertium non toto vertente anno absumpsit: This is 2,700,000,000 sesterces; *milies* with *sestertium* = 100,000,000, i.e., a thousand times a hundred
thousand sesterces. Dio gives two variants: 2,300,000,000 and 3,300,000,000
(59.2.6), evidently from two sources. Cf. on 43 for Dio offering another choice
of figures for the muster in Gaul. Interesting is Suetonius' confident choice of a
single figure. For the expensive first summer, see 16.3, 17.2. Suetonius writes
here that the money was gone before the first year was out, but Dio, that it lasted
for two years (οὐδὲ ἐς τὸ τρίτον ἔτος, Dio 59.2.6), a time period more or less
consistent with the money-driven executions in Gaul (on 30.1, 41.2) and the
auctioning of family property (on 38.4–39.1) in A.D. 39.[83] Josephus also claims a
two year period of moderation (μέτριον παρέχων, *AJ* 18.256). It is specifically
stated that it was Tiberius' (i.e., family) money that he spent.[84] Claudius seems
nonetheless to have found ample funds on hand when he became emperor
(Balsdon 1934a, 187–89; Willrich 431). Nero admired his uncle for his ability to
spend lavishly: *laudabat mirabaturque avunculum Gaium nullo magis nomine,
quam quod ingentis a Tiberio relictas opes in brevi spatio prodegisset* (Suet. *Ner.*
30.1). This final item in the rubric doubles as an introduction to the next, ac-
quisitive greed (38–42).

A spendthrift emperor found destitution his reward, and so the rubric of greed logically follows
that of extravagance. Suetonius uses this sequence for other emperors: *destitutus atque ita iam
exhaustus et egens ut...* (Suet. *Ner.* 32.1); *exhaustus operum ac munerum inpensis stipendioque...*
(*Dom.* 12.1; also *Tib.* 49; Gascou 749, n. 261; Mouchova 49). These chapters (38–42) are well
organized: first come Gaius' manipulations of the laws of inheritance (38.1–3), then the auctions
of all manner of things, including himself (38.4–39), and special taxes (40–41). Chapter 42 holds
the leftovers.

---

[83] Elsewhere Dio seems to say that the treasury was exhausted in 38, although this in a passage
that appears to be a summary of events from different periods (59.10.7).

[84] The relationship between public and private funds in the Empire is somewhat uncertain. "But
in the end the distinction between the two may not have been of great practical importance, because
the emperor subsidized the public treasuries with his own steadily increasing private wealth, and
was empowered to draw on funds from the public treasuries for the administration of his
provinces" (Garnsey and Saller 1987, 24). The distinction "depended ultimately on the needs of
the individual emperor and on his sense of the proper" (Jolowicz and Nicholas 328, n. 7). Gaius is
portrayed as having a personal stake in all manner of revenues (38–42). If he considered this
proper, others did not.

38.1 *exhaustus igitur atque egens ad rapinas convertit animum:* The language is similar in parallel rubrics about other emperors: *procedente mox tempore etiam ad rapinas convertit animum* (Suet. *Tib.* 49.1); *calumniis rapinisque intendit animum* (*Ner.* 32.1). *Rapinae* for imperial pillage also at *Jul.* 54.3; *Ves.* 16.3.

vario et exquisitissimo calumniarum et auctionum et vectigalium genere: The topic sentence outlines the next four chapters. Cf. *vectigalium* vs. *vectigaliorum* at 16.3.

Calumniae (above) are false reports, and here follow Gaius' attempts to rescind citizenship, to invalidate wills and to influence the outcome of trials. His strategy was to make wealth forfeit to him through manipulation of the legal system. The *crimen maiestatis* was a useful mechanism for this since the goods of persons convicted under its provisions were confiscated (Garnsey 112, 116–17; see on 15.4, 30.2, 38.2–3).

negabat iure civitatem Romanam usurpare eos, quorum maiores sibi posterisque eam impetrassent, nisi si filii essent, neque enim intellegi debere posteros ultra hunc gradum: Since children at birth took the citizenship status of their fathers and since there were no legal distinctions between naturalized peregrines and born citizens, disallowing Roman citizenship to the grandchildren of the persons to whom it had originally been granted was seriously illegal. The question is relevant to Gaius' avarice since peregrines could not inherit under Roman wills and this allowed estates to default to the state, either the *fiscus* (Tac. *Ann.* 2.48.1) or the *aerarium* (Tac, *Ann.* 3.25.1; Watson 26–27; Buckland 319–20, 330, 334–38; Crook 120–27; Brunt 1966, 79–81; note 84).

prolataque Divorum Iuli et Augusti diplomata ut vetera et obsoleta deflabat: *Diplomata honestae missionis* were legal proofs of discharge that granted citizenship and the right to marry to provincials who served twenty-five years in the non-citizen *alae;* they were so called because they were folded tablets, usually made of bronze (Suet. *Aug.* 50; *Oth.* 7; also *Ner.* 12.1). They began with the name of the living emperor who made the grant but not, of course, with *divus,* the honorific for deified dead emperors. Its inclusion here has the effect of showing Gaius disrespectful toward his predecessors. Although the point is that he deliberately misinterpreted precedent which was long established by Suetonius' time, there was not, in fact, a long tradition of granting citizenship to discharged auxiliaries when Gaius came to power. Evidence is sketchy but Julius and Augustus evidently rewarded individual soldiers occasionally. Grants of citizenship to entire auxiliary units are not attested until the reign of Claudius (*diplomata* are collected in *CIL* 16 and Roxan; Sherwin-White 1973, 245–49).[85] And so by implication, Claudius' consistency and generosity are contrasted with Gaius' illegal action. *Deflare* = "blow away," used figuratively only here (*TLL* 5.361.25–26).

38.2 *arguebat et perperam editos census, quibus postea quacumque de causa quicquam incrementi accessisset:* *Perperam* (sc. *viam*) = "in an erroneous fashion." *Quibus postea quacumque de causa quicquam incrementi accessisset* = "...to which any addition at all was added later for any reason." Gaius wanted the citizenship lists closed for the same reason that he wanted to invalidate the *diplomata* (38.1), so that inheritances would fall to him.

testamenta primipilarium, qui ab initio Tiberi principatus neque illum neque se heredem reliquissent, ut ingrata rescidit: Wills might be declared void and an estate forfeit under a charge of *querela inofficiosi testamenti* if the testator was of unsound mind; this had been the case with the will of Tiberius (14.1). In a convenient piece of circularity, the failure to name a person who might reasonably be expected to be a legatee could serve as evidence of the mental incapacity of the testator. Although *primipilares* had a reasonable amount of money to dispose of (on 35.2, 44.1), Gaius was still going far down the social scale in search of monetary gratitude (Veyne 1990, 437 n. 129). Their wills were "ungrateful" (*ingrata*) if they did not include their commander-in-chief presumably because, in theory at least, these senior career soldiers owed their lucrative promotions to him. It was not unreasonable for them to acknowledge their special relationship by such a gesture, and indeed it had become a regular practice over the previous twenty to twenty-five years. "At that time [A.D. 39]," writes Dio, "[Gaius] seized for himself without the sanction of a vote absolutely all the property of the ex-centurions [i.e., *primipilares*], who left it to anyone other than the emperor after the time of Germanicus' triumph" (ἐν δὲ τῷ παρόντι πάσας ἁπλῶς τὰς τῶν ἐν τοῖς ἑκατοντάρχοις ἐστρατευμένων οὐσίας, ὅσοι μετὰ τὰ ἐπινίκια ἃ ὁ πατὴρ αὐτοῦ ἔπεμψεν ἄλλῳ τινὶ αὐτὰς καὶ μὴ τῷ αὐτοκράτορι κατελελοίπεσαν, αὐτὸς ἑαυτῷ καὶ ἄνευ ψηφίσματος ἐσέπραξε, 59.15.2). Germanicus' triumph in 17 (1.1) fell within the same time frame as the beginning of Tiberius' reign (*ab initio Tiberi principatus*). Although by civil law a will was also void when the legatee (Tiberius is this case) died before the testator, emperors became an exception, and the inheritance was thought of as falling to the

---

85 Inherited citizenship for this group was not a permanently closed issue, however, for after A.D. 139–44 the children of auxiliary veterans had to earn it a second time by serving in the army themselves. On the question of privileges for legionaries as well as auxiliaries and other military units, see Alföldy 225–26, Nesselhauf 438–42, Campbell 439–45.

office instead of to the individual (Brunt 1966, 78; see below on *derisores vocabat*). This issue is not in question here.[86]

item ceterorum ut irrita et vana, quoscumque quis diceret herede Caesare mori destinasse: Understand *rescidit* (above) again. Suetonius insists on compression and balance at the expense of clarity (*primipilarium...ceterorum; ingrata...irrita et vana; qui...quis,* see note 8). If someone could be found to bear witness that a testator had at any time made a verbal statement (*diceret*) that he intended to name Gaius in his will (*herede Caesare mori destinasse*) but did not do it, the will that he actually wrote was nullified. Domitian is said to have used the same tactic: *confiscabantur alienissimae hereditates vel uno exsistente, qui diceret audisse se ex defuncto, cum viveret, heredem sibi Caesarem esse* (Suet. *Dom.* 12.2). The grounds were arguably *querela inofficiosi testamenti* once again (on the *testamenta primipilarium* above and 14.1) or possibly *crimen maiestatis,* because the persons who changed their minds were guilty of disrespect toward the emperor and consequently of a kind of posthumous treason (Bauman 138–41). The practice of naming Rome's leaders as legatees along with family members predated the Empire and had begun as a relatively innocent gesture of respect to a patron (Rogers 140–58). But it had dangerous potential, and it became unwise to tempt a greedy emperor to seek reasons why a will might be *irritum et vanum* and risk having the entire estate fall forfeit. Gaius provides the first evidence of attacking wills in this way (Bauman 138, n. 25); for Nero, Suet. *Ner.* 32.2.

quo metu iniecto: The fear, that is, that a witness could be produced who would swear that the testator had voiced an intention to make Gaius his heir.

cum iam et ab ignotis inter familiares et a parentibus inter liberos palam heres nuncuparetur: Another balanced sentence. Gaius considered the wealthy elderly his family: πατέρας τε καὶ πάππους μητέρας τε καὶ τήθας σφᾶς ὀνομάζων (Dio 59.15.6). The more politic emperors (including Claudius)

---

[86] Dio writes, "It had been voted earlier [i.e., before A.D. 39] that whoever was willing to leave anything to Tiberius but survived him should give it to Gaius when he did die" (ὅσοι τινὰ τῷ Τιβερίῳ καταλιπεῖν ἐθελήσαντες περιῆσαν, τῷ Γαΐῳ αὐτὰ τελευτῶντες χαρίσωνται· ἵνα γὰρ δὴ καὶ παρὰ τοὺς νόμους καὶ κληρονομεῖν καὶ δωρήματα τοιαῦτα λαμβάνειν, ὅτι μήτε γυναῖκα τότε γε μήτε παῖδας εἶχε, δύνασθαι δοκῇ, δόγμα τι προέθετο, 59.15.1). The vote was necessary because the childless Gaius could not have inherited without it. Dio is quite clear about the legal point involved. He objects to the unmarried and childless Gaius as an heir, but the fact that the legacies originally intended for Tiberius were to pass on to Gaius did not create a problem for him.

refused to receive legacies from strangers or from persons with children (Dio 60.6.3).[87]

derisores vocabat, quod post nuncupationem vivere perseverarent et multis venenatas matteas misit: More impatience (on 37.3) and Gaius' sharp tongue again. He called such persons "mockers" (*derisores*) and hence treasonous because after announcing that they would leave money to the emperor in their wills (*nuncupatio*), they did not die. *Mattea* (ματτύη) was a cooked delicacy, "candy," a reasonably convenient vehicle for poison. The word is largely confined to the first century (*TLL* 8.491.10–21; Sen. *Controv.* 9.4.20; Petron. *Sat.* 65; Mart. 10.59.4, 13.92.2). For Gaius and poison, see note 11.

38.3 *cognoscebat autem de talibus causis: Talibus causis* applies to all the questioned wills that have been described to this point. Conducting the trials personally (*cognoscebat*) was a way of calling attention to his close interest in the outcome (cf. Dio 59.18.2).

taxato prius modo summae ad quem conficiendum consideret, confecto demum excitabatur: According to this, the legality of wills was predicated on the amount of money the emperor needed, a fact that assumed that appropriate *delatores* could always be produced as required. An apparent attempt to create rhetorical balance has produced another awkwardly compressed sentence (cf. *item...destinasse*, 38.2); literally, "the total amount [of money] that he went to court (*consideret* = "sit to try a case") to raise (*ad quem conficiendum*) having been determined (*taxato*) first, [this amount] having been raised (*confecto*), he finally left the court (*excitabatur* = "be roused into activity"). *Consideret* and *excitabatur* are paired both by (contrary) meaning and in relation to the ablative participles that introduce the two portions of the sentence (*taxato, confecto*) but they are not parallel grammatically. This disturbs what seems to be the self-conscious symmetry of the sentence. See note 8.

ac ne paululum quidem morae patiens: Impatience again; cf. *morae culpa capite lueretur* (37.3).

super quadraginta reos quondam ex diversis criminibus una sententia condemnavit gloriatusque est expergefacta e somno Caesonia quantum egisset, dum ea meridiaret: This anecdote could easily have been placed among the examples of Gaius' cruel and arrogant speech (29–31). The reference

---

[87] Domitian failed to understand: *tam caeca et corrupta mens adsiduis adulationibus erat, ut nesciret a bono patre non scribi heredem nisi malum principem* (Tac. *Agr.* 43.4).

to Caesonia dates to the end of Gaius' reign, his most threatened period. She is the only one of his wives granted a shred of personality (25.3, 33, 50.2, and see especially on her death, 59). For *glorior*, 12.3, 29.2 and 41.2.

Suetonius follows his outline (38.1) and now describes Gaius' auctions (*auctiones*, 38.4–39). This is not a unique instance of an emperor auctioning off family possessions; note also Nerva (Dio 68.2.2), Antoninus Pius (*SHA* 7.10), Marcus Aurelius (*SHA* 17.4–5), Pertinax (*SHA* 7.8–8.7). The younger Pliny approved when Trajan sold excess estates and other items (*Pan.* 50.5). The problem with Gaius was the greed with which he did it.

38.4 *Auctione proposita reliquias omnium spectaculorum subiecit ac venditavit:* This took place in Rome in A.D. 39 (Dio 59.14.1–4; see on 37.3 for Gaius needing money). *Subiecit* = "put up for auction," more fully, *praeconi* or *hastae subiecit*, i.e., placed in the charge of an auctioneer or beneath the spear stuck into the ground, the standard under which these sales took place because of their origin as the sale of war booty. *Munera* were expensive and gladiators were recycled (Fishwick 1987–1990, 580). Those from the imperial stables often appeared in entertainments not sponsored by the princeps, perhaps hired out, seemingly sold on this occasion (Ville 290). Gaius controlled a large number (on 32.2). What is noteworthy here is his greedy desire for profit.

exquirens per se pretia: "Determining the sale price himself," i.e., bidding up the price: αὐτός τε ἐπὶ τοῦ πρατηρίου καθεζόμενος καὶ αὐτὸς ὑπερβάλλων (Dio 59.14.2). An emperor would not be imagined present at so a mundane an event. In contrast, Nerva, when he sold his household gold and silver and furniture, did not quibble about the price: οὐ μέντοι καὶ περὶ τὰς τιμὰς αὐτῶν ἐμικρολογήσατο (Dio 68.2.2).

et usque eo extendens, ut quidam immenso coacti quaedam emere: Under Augustus two praetors chosen by lot had given two public shows annually, partly at state expense, partly at their own (Dio 54.2.4). Tiberius cut back on the scale (Suet. *Tib.* 34.1). This story appears to recover the details of the Augustan arrangement: "for he ordered two praetors to be chosen by lot for the gladiatorial games, as had once been the case" (δύο γὰρ στρατηγοὺς ἐς τοὺς ὁπλομαχικοὺς ἀγῶνας, ὥσπερ ποτὲ ἐγίγνετο, λαγχάνειν ἐκέλευσε, Dio 59.14.2).

ac bonis exuti venas sibi inciderent: Dio, on the contrary, writes that they saved their lives by spending their money freely (59.14.4).

nota res est, Aponio Saturnino inter subsellia dormitante, monitum a Gaio praeconem ne praetorium virum crebro capitis motu nutantem sibi praeteriret: An illustration (*nota res*) of the general topic of greedy acquisition. The scene includes the auctioneer's platform (πρατήριον, Dio 59.14.2) and benches (*subsellia*) for the buyers. One of the two praetors (above) was Aponius Saturninus (*PIR²* A. 936, probably = M. Aponius Saturninus, *PIR²* A. 937), a wealthy senator and a member of the senatorial delegation to Claudius in the praetorian camp after the assassination of Gaius (Jos. *AJ* 19.264). It was probably his son, another M. Aponius Saturninus (*PIR²* A. 938) who was consul suffect under Nero (Tac. *Hist.* 3.11), and as legatus in Moesia, deeply involved in events of A.D. 69 (Tac. *Hist.* 1.79.5, 2.96, 3.9–11, 5.26). The later prominence of the family may have played a part in the preservation of his name in this incident (cf. Valerius Catullus, 36.1), but it would be interesting to know why he was seen as a particular dupe. This anecdote bears witness to the very great antiquity of the notion that a buyer could nod off at the auction and wake to find himself committed beyond his depth.

nec licendi finem factum, quoad tredemim gladiatores sestertium nonagies ignoranti addicerentur: He nodded thirteen times. 9,000,000 sesterces for thirteen gladiators was more than excessive. Games were expensive, but perhaps 2,000,000 (?) would put on a show in this period (Hopkins 1983, 8, n. 12; Duncan-Jones 245–46).

39.1 in Gallia quoque: Suetonius' auction rubric pairs the sale of family heirlooms in Lugdunum in the winter of 39–40 (59.21.5–6) with the sale of gladiators in Rome (38.4).

cum damnatarum sororum ornamenta et supellectilem et servos atque etiam libertos immensiis pretiis vendidisset: See 24.3 and 29.1 for the relegation of Agrippina and Julia Livilla because of their complicity with Aemilius Lepidus. It is uncertain how far the sisters accompanied Gaius when he left Rome for Gaul and the German frontier (on 24.3 and 43), but he apparently confiscated their movable property on the spot and so had it with him when he spent the winter in Lugdunum; it was thus booty from a conquered (domestic) enemy (Cic. *Phil.* 2.64–5; Sen. *Dial.* 6.20.5, for goods seized in civil conflict). Their equipage for the road would have included not only personal possessions (*ornamenta*) but also tableware, bedding and the like (*supellectilem*) and a staff (*servos atque etiam libertos*) since wealthy travellers either stayed on their own estates along the way or carried their accommodations with them (for Gaius' baggage train to Gaul, Dio 59.21.2; Casson 1974, 180). The obligations to which freedmen were liable could be passed on to heirs or sold (Treggiari 76), and in this sense Gaius gained possession of his sisters' *liberti*. The freedmen themselves, of course, could not be sold like slaves; hence the emphasis of *etiam*.

invitatus lucro, quidquid instrumenti veteris aulae erat ab urbe repetiit: Invitatus lucro = "enticed by the profits;" *instrumenta* = "possessions" in general. *Veteris aulae* = "the old palace" (Rolfe 1913–1914) seems to refer to modifications of the buildings on the Palatine (on 22.2).

comprensis ad deportandum meritoriis quoque vehiculis et pistrinensibus iumentis, adeo ut et panis Romae saepe deficeret: "Hired" (*meritoriis*) wagons were available for intercity transportation and presumably for the transport of goods as well (Friedländer 1.279–80). *Pistrinensia iumenta* were the beasts who turned the millstones to grind wheat for bakeries (Apul. *Met.* 9.10–11). They are introduced here so that Gaius can be charged with striking a blow at the heart of Roman sustenance, the bread supply (26.5). The accusation is the same as the one made about the ships accumulated for the Baiae bridge (19.1).

et litigatorum plerique, quod occurrere absentes ad vadimonium non possent, causa caderent: The litigants could not present themselves in court on their appointed dates (*occurrere ad vadimonium*) because of lack of transportation and so lost their cases (*causa caderent*). A *litigator,* a person involved in a civil suit, posted a bond (*vadimonium*), with or without money, to guarantee his appearance on the specified day (Buckland 613–14).

39.2 *cui instrumento distrahendo nihil non fraudis ac lenocinii adhibuit, modo...increpans...modo paenitentiam simulans:* Cf. Gaius' alternating threats and cajolements with Jupiter (*modo insusurrans...modo clarius nec sine iurgiis,* 22.4).

modo avaritiae singulos increpans et quod non puderet eos locupletiores esse quam se: Gaius put pressure on potential customers by accusing wealthy individuals of not being ashamed to have more money than he, the emperor. Dio writes that he goaded them into buying by telling them that they should no longer pretend to be poor (59.21.6).

modo paenitentiam simulans quod principalium rerum privatis copiam faceret: He sold the reputation of three generations of his family (τὴν δόξαν τῶν ποτε χρησαμένων αὐτοῖς συμπωλῶν σφισιν, Dio 59.21.5). The objects from the *vetus aula* (39.1) had belonged to Germanicus, the elder Agrippina, Agrippa and Augustus and included booty from Antony (Dio 59.21.6).

compererat provincialem locupletem ducenta sestertia numerasse vocatoribus, ut per fallaciam convivio interponeretur, nec tulerat moleste tam magno aestimari honorem cenae suae: This "wealthy provincial" is a Gaul since the context remains the auction at Lugdunum (*sedenti in auctione,* below). *Vocatores* were hospitality stewards whose duty it was to extend invitations to banquets and help arrange the guests at table; the places had to be filled and the host might not always know who had been invited (Sen. *Dial.* 5.37.4; Balsdon 1969, 33–34). The situation lent itself readily to stories and jokes about wrong identifications and gate crashing (Mart. 7.86.11; Sen. *Dial.* 2.14.1– 2; Pliny *HN* 35.89). The favor of dinner with Gaius was prized: *egit* [Vespasian] *et gratias ei apud amplissimum ordinem, quod se honore cenae dignatus esset* (Suet. *Ves.* 2.3). The bribe of 200,000 sesterces (*ducenta sestertia,* sc. *milia*) was less than Gaius was supposed to have spent to feed his guests (on 37.1 and note 79; Sen. *Ep.* 95.41).

huic postero die sedenti in auctione misit, qui nescio quid frivoli ducentis milibus traderet diceretque cenaturum apud Caesarem vocatu ipsius: Gaius, now reduced to the level of his bribe-taking staff, auctions off the pleasure of his own company. The trifle (*nescio quid frivoli*) is a pretense that the Gaul's cash outlay was for merchandise, not for an invitation.

The third of Gaius' money-raising measures, the *vectigalia.* After getting rid of the *ducentesima rerum venalium* (16.3), Gaius found that he had to substitute new sources of revenue. *Vectigalia* were a great variety of indirect taxes to which Roman citizens in Italy were subject. Examples were taxes on services, inheritance or port taxes, and sales taxes of various sorts, such as on the sale of slaves. They were in contrast to the *tributum,* the direct tax paid only by provincials during this period.

40 *vectigalia nova atque inaudita:* These taxes were apparently new in Rome itself, at these rates in any case (Brunt 1981, 163). They and the opposition to them (41.1) are assigned to the last months of his reign (Dio 59.28.8–11; Jos. *AJ* 19.24–27). Claudius undid them one by one as opportunities presented (Dio 60.4.1). Cf. the novelty of the Baiae bridge expressed in the same terms: *novum praeterea atque inauditum genus spectaculi excogitavit* (19.1).

primum per publicanos, deinde, quia lucrum exuberabat, per centuriones tribunosque praetorianos exercuit: The perennially unpopular *publicani* were tax farmers, contractors responsible for the collection of *vectigalia* and also for direct taxes before the time of Augustus and in some provinces. They filled the gap left by the absence of a civil service and remained necessary into the second century or later. "The collection of indirect taxes remained a weak point in the financial administration of the Empire" (Rostovtzeff

389; see Crook 233–36; Jones 1974, 165–67; Brunt 1990, 360–86). Although Gaius was not the first to use soldiers for tax collection, the assignment of the task to the praetorians, in Rome at least, appears to be an early example of the trend away from the *publicani*. The military remained intermittently responsible, especially in the provinces (Tac. *Ann.* 4.72.1; Brunt 1990, 390; McGinn 87–89). Gaius' assassin, Cassius Chaerea, as a praetorian tribune, was one of those saddled with this unpopular task. He pitied the people from whom he had to collect and was consequently less than diligent; his dereliction angered Gaius. Or so it was reported. Chaerea had to remain untainted because of his hero's role, and Gaius' anger increased the number of reasons for his involvement in the conspiracy (on 16.4, 56.2; Jos. *AJ* 19.28–29).

nullo rerum aut hominum genere omisso, cui non tributi aliquid imponeret: The taxes covered a wide area. Dio's list is almost the same as Suetonius' (below): τις τά τε ὤνια καὶ τὰ καπηλεῖα τάς τε πόρνας καὶ τὰ δικαστήρια τούς τε χειροτέχνας καὶ τὰ ἀνδράποδα τὰ μισθοφοροῦντα τά τε ἄλλα τὰ τοιαῦτα, ἐξ ὧν οὐδὲν ὅ τι οὐκ ἠργυρίζετο, παραλείπῃ (Dio 59.28.8).

pro edulibus, quae tota urbe venirent, certum statumque exigebatur: Pro = "on." Suetonius' foodstuffs are Dio's taverns (τὰ καπηλεῖα). It seems to have been a fixed tax (*certum statumque*), not a percentage.

pro litibus ac iudiciis ubicumque conceptis quadragesima summae, de qua litigaretur: Dio's τὰ δικαστήρια. *Ubicumque* implies that the percentage levied on court cases was in effect throughout the Empire. This was in contrast to the tax on restaurant fare limited to Rome (*tota urbe*). *Quadragesima* (sc. *pars*), a tax of one fortieth or two and one-half per cent of the value of the property under contention.

nec sine poena, si quis composuisse vel donasse negotium convinceretur: One could not avoid the tax by "settling out of court" (*negotium composuisse*) or conceding the suit (*negotium donasse*). Something similar with the prostitutes (below).

ex gerulorum diurnis quaestibus pars octava: The porters (*geruli* = sedan chair carriers) are apparently Dio's τὰ ἀνδράποδα τὰ μισθοφοροῦντα, wage-earning (*diurnis quaestibus*) slaves. The tax of twelve and one half per cent seems quite high.

ex capturis prostitutarum quantum quaeque uno concubitu mereret: The interval at which the tax on prostitutes (Dio's τάς τε πόρνας) was collected from one customer (*uno concubitu*) is unclear, but the parallel with the porters above (*ex gerulorum diurnis quaestibus* vs. *ex capturis prostitutarum*) invites the assumption that it was daily. If so, like the *octava* (above), it seems high. Since Claudius undid Gaius' taxes (Dio 60.4.1), no inference can be made from this for similar taxes in other places or at other times during the Empire (Bagnall 5–12; despite McGinn 90–93, 95–98). For the imperial brothel, 41.1.

additumque ad caput legis, ut tenerentur publico et quae meretricium quive lenocinium fecissent: Caput legis = a paragraph of the law (Cic. *Fam.* 8.8.3). *Publicum* = "tax collection;" *ut tenerentur publico* = "were subject to the collection of this tax." *Meretricium* and *lenocinium,* a natural pair (Cic. *Verr.* 2.3.6); note the gender specific occupations (*quae* vs. *qui*). *Lenocinium* ("enticement" at 39.2) is brothel keeping here, often with *facere* in this sense (*TLL* 7.1153.19–21).

nec non et matrimonia obnoxia essent: The *infamia* of prostitution (and the attendant tax liability) could not be erased by an expeditious marriage, just as the tax on law cases could not be avoided by failing to follow through with the suit (above). It was also forbidden to cross the line between prostitute and wife in the other direction; under Tiberius a married woman of equestrian family was not allowed to register as a prostitute in order to avoid the punishment for adultery to which she would otherwise have been subject (Tac. *Ann.* 2.85.1–2; Suet. *Tib.* 35.2).

41.1 *eius modi vectigalibus indictis neque propositis, cum per ignorantiam scripturae multa commissa fierent:* The new taxes were proclaimed aloud but not posted, at least not in the beginning. But ignorance of the law was no excuse, and so Gaius saw to it that the people remained ignorant, and fines incurred by non-compliance were added to the revenues (Dio 59.28.11).

tandem flagitante populo proposuit quidem legem: The crowd complained vociferously at the *ludi circenses,* and Gaius responded without the proper imperial *civilitas* (on 18.1), conduct that came home to haunt him soon enough. Some persons were killed (Dio 59.28.11; Jos. *AJ* 19.24–26). The date of the riot is not known except for the fact that it served as a prelude to his assassination (see 49.2 on *intraque quartum mensem periit;* Jos. *AJ* 19.27; Balsdon 1934a, 103). The crowd surely called for the abolition of the new taxes (Jos. *AJ* 19.24) and not merely for their publication as is implied here. For other instances of Gaius' bad behavior at games, 30.2, 3; 35.2, 3.

sed et minutissimis litteris et angustissimo loco, uti ne cui describere liberet: Posting the taxes (*proposuit*) represented a kind of compromise. There is a parallel in Nero's behavior in similar circumstances in A.D. 58 when the populace complained about the *publicani*. Nero considered rescinding the taxes but he chose to restrain the tax farmers instead. It may have been they who did not want the exact terms of the law known and their own profits made explicit (Furneaux at Tac. *Ann.* 13.51.1; also 13.50.3).

ac ne quod non manubiarum genus experiretur: Manubiae = the general's share of the booty, an appropriate word for profit skimming.

lupanar in Palatio constituit: His reputation for debauchery (36), his extravagant entertainments (37.1–2) and his tax on prostitutes (40) generated the story of an imperial brothel. Messalina (on 36.1) also turned the Palatine into a brothel, a metaphor for her promiscuity (Dio 60.31.1; also 60.18.1–2), and Nero did something similar (Suet. *Ner.* 27). The *lupanar* finds a place here in the rubric of greed and not in the rubric of sexual excess because it shows Gaius taking measures to increase the base for this *vectigal;* i. e., he provided his own opportunities, the same point that is made about the court cases (38.3) and in the gambling incident that follows (41.2).

districtisque et instructis pro loci dignitate compluribus cellis, in quibus matronae ingenuique starent: Similarly in Dio: ἀλλὰ τά γε οἰκήματα τὰ ἐν αὐτῷ τῷ παλατίῳ ἀποδειχθέντα, καὶ τὰς γυναῖκας τὰς τῶν πρώτων [= *matronae*] τούς τε παῖδας τοὺς τῶν σεμνοτάτων [= *ingenuique*], οὓς ἐς αὐτὰ καθίζων ὕβριζεν (Dio 59.28.9). Prostitutes were available for inspection (*starent*) before their services were purchased. They did business in *cellae,* small rooms for menials (Sen. *Controv.* 1.2.5, 10; Petron. *Sat.* 8).

misit circum fora et basilicas nomenculatores ad invitandos ad libidinem iuvenes senesque: Fora are plural because new imperial ones had been built to complement the original Republican one (on 44.2, 60). *Basilicae* were also places for public assembly, indoor extensions of the *fora. Nomenculatores* were slaves or freedmen who announced the names of persons whom their master met.

praebita advenientibus pecunia faenebris appositique qui nomina palam subnotarent, quasi adiuvantium Caesaris reditus: A final turn of the screw of avarice comes when Gaius' guests turn into customers and he collects interest on the money he lends to be spent on his own taxable enterprise.

41.2 *ac ne ex lusu quidem aleae compendium spernensplus mendacio atque periurio lucrabatur:* He cheated. Dicing was illegal but the law was ignored (Balsdon 1969, 154–59), most notably by Augustus (Suet. *Aug.* 70.2, 71) and Claudius (*Cl.* 5, 33.2; Sen. *Apocol.* 14.4–15.1), but also by Nero (Suet. *Ner.* 30.3), Vitellius (*Vit.* 4) and Domitian (*Dom.* 21). Gaius played at dice when he should have been mourning his sister (on 24.2; Sen. *Dial.* 11.17.4).

et quondam: At this point Suetonius adds a story that Dio places in the winter of 39–40 in Lugdunum (Dio 59.22.1–4).

proximo conlusori demandata vice sua progressus in atrium domus: Gaius gave his turn in the game to the player next to him. *Demandata* = "handed over" (cf. *in proximam civitatem demandari,* 9). But in the courtyard (*in atrium*) of what home? Suetonius appears to take an incident from a detailed source that assumed the audience recognized the setting. Cf. *stans tantum modo intra porticum mediam,* also apparently about Lugdunum (27.1).

cum praetereuntis duos equites R. locupletis sine mora corripi confiscarique iussisset: Dio's parallel: "Once when he was playing dice and realized that he had no money, he demanded the census lists of the Gauls and ordered the wealthiest of them to be killed; he returned to his fellow gamblers and said, 'You are playing for a few drachmas but I have taken in a hundred and fifty million' " (κεβεύων δέ ποτε, καὶ μαθὼν ὅτι οὐκ εἴη οἱ ἀργύριον, ᾔτησέ τε τὰς τῶν Γαλατῶν ἀπογραφάς, καὶ ἐξ αὐτῶν τοὺς πλουσιωτάτους θανατωθῆναι κελεύσας, ἐπανῆλθέ τε πρὸς τοὺς συγκυβευτάς, καὶ ἔφη ὅτι "ὑμεῖς περὶ ὀλίγων δραχμῶν ἀγωνίζεσθε, ἐγὼ δὲ ἐς μυρίας καὶ πεντακισχιλίας μυριάδας ἤθροισα," Dio 59.22.3–4). Of the two knights, one was Julius Sacerdos, the Gaul killed because of mistaken identity, probably on a charge of *maiestas* (on 30.1).

exultans rediit gloriansque numquam se prosperiore alea usum: *Glorior* again (12.3, 29.2, 38.3). Suetonius, who is usually eager to quote Gaius directly (29–31 and elsewhere), here uses indirect statement whereas Dio retains the quotation (above). Suetonius keeps the emphasis on the greedy dicing instead of the verbal wit.

42 *Filia vero nata paupertatem nec iam imperatoria modo sed et patria conquerens onera conlationes in alimonium ac dotem puellae recepit:* According to this, Gaius' money troubles had begun even before the birth of Drusilla, who was born (on 25.4) at roughly the time to which his money-grabbing schemes are referred (Dio 59.14.1–4, 15.1–6, 21.1–6, 22.3–4).

edixit et strenas ineunte anno se recepturum stetitque in vestibulo aedium Kal. Ian. ad captandas stipes: When the new year began in the spring, *strenae* (New Year's Day good luck gifts) had been tree branches, but they had long since turned into cash (Sym. *Relat.* 15.1–2; Ov. *Fast.* 1.189–92). Augustus diplomatically used the money to buy statues for the city (Suet. *Aug.* 57.2). Stingy Tiberius forbade the giving of them after January 1 since they required him to reciprocate fourfold all month (Suet. *Tib.* 34.2). Gaius is shown culpable not because he took the *strenae* but because he sollicited them by imperial edict (*edixit*) and because he did nothing *civilis* with them. The *vestibulum aedium* where he stood was the porch of the temple of Jupiter Capitolinus (*in Capitolio,* Suet. *Aug.* 57.2).

quas plenis ante eum manibus ac sinu omnis generis turba fundebat. novissime contrectandae pecuniae cupidine incensus, saepe super immensos aureorum acervos patentissimo diffusos loco et nudis pedibus spatiatus et toto corpore aliquamdiu volulatus est: The final image in this rubric of greed is Gaius rolling in money. Dio writes that it was collected from the Palatine brothel and that the populace loved the idea (τὸ πλῆθος... ἔχαιρον ὁμοῦ οἱ τῇ τε ἀσελγείᾳ αὐτοῦ, 59.28.10).[88] The crowds (*omnis generis turba*) were not altogether displeased with him in this final period; slaves, women, children (or those who resembled them) and some of the army remained happy until the end (Jos. *AJ* 19.129–31).

A return from rubrics of character traits to a rubric of quasi-narration about Gaius' activities in Gaul and on the German frontier between September of 39 and spring of 40. Suetonius' point with these chapters (43–48) is, however, not to present a clear historical picture of the campaign but to show Gaius interested only in receiving the rewards for a military enterprise portrayed as absurd and accomplishing nothing. The account of it may have been taken from the *tantorum dedecorum rumores* that preceded him to Rome (48.2); there is no evidence that anything objective ever existed. Reconstructions have been difficult because Dio's chronology and his selection of subject matter for the winter of 39–40 are more confused than usual (59.21–25.5ᵃ; see note 94).

The following seems certain: A large military force was gathered before Gaius departed Rome (43); he put an end to the *Lepidi et Gaetulici coniuratio* (on 24.3, 43, 44.1); he spent part of the winter in Lugdunum (20, 27.1, 30.1, 40.2) but was at some point present with both German armies on the Rhine (26.2, 44.1, 45.1–2, 48, 51.2); after he replaced Gaetulicus with Galba as commander of

---

[88] It has been suggested that the source of this odd behavior was an ancient Egyptian (not Isiac) tradition that allowed gold to kings alone; Gaius was trying to impregnate his flesh with it (cf. his golden statue, 22.3; his golden beard, 52) and thereby assimilate himself into divine royalty in preparation for his removal to Alexandria (49.2). It is further suggested that Suetonius found fault with Gaius because he did not understand this ritual ("Suétone toutefois n'a pas compris...le sens de l'acte de Caligula," Guey 443–45). It was not because Suetonius and his predecessors failed to understand Gaius that they ridiculed him.

the Army of Upper Germany, Galba restored the lax discipline of the troops (24.3, 26.2, 44.1); some sort of exercise took place on the shore of the English Channel (47). Much less certain are Gaius' military objectives, in particular the seriousness of his intention to invade Britain (43, 44.2, 46) and the timing of his visits to the legions in both Upper and Lower Germany and what took place while he was with them (45, 48). Behind it all was his desire to acquire the military credentials that he lacked. Even if a serious campaign had to be postponed or cancelled, he could at least make himself present with the Armies, and a less hostile jury might have interpreted his progress through Gaul as a reasonably successful venture. As it was, he succeeded only in exposing himself to an unfavorable comparison with Germanicus, Julius Caesar and even Claudius, who would soon invade Britain.

Suetonius begins by describing the muster of troops.

43 *Militiam resque bellicas semel attigit:* Suetonius calls attention to the fact that Gaius had not had a military apprenticeship before he set out on campaign. Youths from senatorial families (including imperial princes) served as legionary tribunes before they began political careers (e.g., Gaius and Lucius Caesar, Dio 55.6.4, 10.17–19, 10ª.9; Germanicus, Dio 55.31–32, 56.15.1–17.2).

neque ex destinato: "Not according to plan," but not true since the assembly of troops (below) had obviously begun earlier, and the Baiae bridge extravaganza was called (in retrospect at least) a preliminary display (19.3, 52). Gaius' own departure may, however, have been precipitous, and his seeming whimsicality provided an excuse for the lack of results from the massive effort. For a possible relationship between his abrupt departure and the replacement of Gaetulicus with Galba, see on 23.1, 24.3, 26.3, 44.1; Balsdon 1934a, 70; Barrett 1989, 103–10.

sed cum ad visendum nemus flumenque Clitumni Mevaniam processisset: Mevania, on the Via Flaminia about a hundred miles north of Rome, was an upper class watering spot. Pleasant villas stood on the banks of the river Clitumnus that flowed past the town known for its temple and oracle (Pliny *Ep.* 8.8.5–6; Sherwin-White 1985, *ad loc.*). Gaius may have detoured to Mevania to wait until Gaetulicus was eliminated or to intercept Lepidus there (Barrett, 1989, 105–7; on 23.3); or perhaps a stop had been preplanned. Dio writes that Gaius did not announce his expedition beforehand but first went to a "suburb" from which he suddenly set forth for Gaul: οὐ μέντοι καὶ ἄντικρυς τὴν ἔξοδον προεπήγγειλεν, ἀλλ' ἐς προάστειόν τι ἐλθὼν εἶτ' ἐξαίφνης ἀπῆρε (59.21.2). Dio's προάστειον quite probably comes from *suburbanum* in a Roman source = an area near Rome but also a country house, such as one at Mevania.

admonitus de supplendo numero Batavorum, quos circa se habebat: The oracle at Mevania told Gaius to fill out the number of the *Batavi,* the German bodyguard of the imperial house, who were trusted to be completely loyal to the persons of the imperial family because as foreigners they were beyond the corruption of Roman politics (Tac. *Ann.* 15.58.2). The German guard were largely Batavians, inhabitants of the *insula Batavorum*, a large island between outlets of the Rhine. Recruits were supplied by prisoners, and so the need to fill their ranks rationalizes and demeans the excursion to the North. The point is also made that Gaius was heavily dependent on these, his only allies, who did prove reliable when he was assassinated (58.3; for the Batavians, Bellen 1–57). Dio gives another reason for the expedition—Gaius' greed (59.21.1–2).

expeditionis Germanicae impetum cepit: But a major campaign could not have begun in the autumn. Here Germany is the stated objective (cf. 45, 47). Elsewhere Germany and Britain are a double objective, although Germany is always mentioned first (19.3; Dio 59.21.3, 25.1; also Suet. *Ves.* 2.3; Pers. 6.44), and Tacitus understood it as primary: *ingentes adversus Germaniam conatus frustra fuissent* (*Agr.* 13.2; also *Germ.* 37.4). Other evidence for a German enemy, Philo *Leg.* 356; *ILS* 8791; Mommsen 1888, 19–20.

neque distulit, sed legionibus et auxiliis undique excitis, dilectibus ubique acerbissime actis, contracto et omnis generis commeatu quanto numquam antea: Cf. *contractasque ex omnibus provinciis copias,* Suet. *Gal.* 6.3; further testimony of a large force, Tac. *Agr.* 13.2; *Germ.* 37.4. The total number is given at 200,000 or 250,000 (Dio 59.22.1; see on 37.3 for another choice of figures by Dio). Since even the smaller number was more than twice the normal strength for both the German Armies combined, the figures are not plausible (Barrett 1989, 125; Faur 1973b, 27–30; Balsdon 1934b, 16). But recruitment (*dilectibus...actis*) is confirmed by the fact that Galba was busy training new troops in the winter of 39–40 (*veteranum ac tironem militem opere assiduo corroboravit;* Suet. *Gal.* 6.3) and by the circumstantial evidence that two new legions were raised by Gaius.[89] Note the stylish alliteration in the three ablative absolutes modified by the parallel *undique* and *ubique* reaching a climax in *quanto numquam antea.*

Gaius' journey to the North: But what was his immediate destination? Suetonius' *postquam castra attigit* (44.1) and the fact that Gaetulicus was relieved of his command by October 39 (on 24.3, 45) has suggested that Gaius headed directly for Mogontiacum (Mainz), the headquarters of the Army

---

[89] The argument is that the legions XV and XXII Primigeniae did not exist in A.D. 23 (Tac. *Ann.* 4.5.1) but did in 69 (*Hist.* 1.55.2–3). Since Tacitus can probably be trusted to have noted their formation and since the *Annales* are missing between 37 and 47, they must have been raised during this period. Dio makes no mention of Claudius having to increase manpower for his invasion of Britain (Ritterling *RE* 12. 1244–49; seconded strongly by Balsdon 1934b, 13–16). The evidence is summarized by Barrett (1989, 126).

of Upper Germany, for a showdown with its disloyal commander (Balsdon 1934a, 71–72). This makes him leave Rome shortly after the first of September (on 23.1, 26.3), detour hastily to Mevania, arrive on the frontier in time to remove Gaetulicus and have the news of his execution reach Rome by October 27 (*Docs.* no. 9, p. 14; cf. 24.3), a trip that was just barely possible (Balsdon 1934b, 16–17). But would Gaius and his relatively small entourage have confronted the popular Gaetulicus (Tac. *Ann.* 6.30.2) in his own camp where he was backed with his own legions? Gaius plausibly went directly to Lugdunum (only about three-quarters the distance to Mogontiacum) where he intended to spend the winter. Gaetulicus may have been summoned there and executed (Faur 1973b, 32–35; Barrett 1989, 104–6). In Suetonius' *Life of Galba*, Gaius does not appear at Mogontiacum until after Galba has had time to reintroduce some discipline (on 44.1; Suet. *Gal.* 6.2–3). Galba took command on the day before a ceremony of some sort: *a Gaio Caesare legatus Germaniae superioris in locum Gaetulici substitutus, postridie quam ad legiones venit, sollemni forte spectaculo plaudentes inhibuit* (Suet. *Gal.* 6.2), perhaps the day before the *armilustrium*, October 19, the traditional date when campaigning ended. The celebration featured a review and a purification of arms (on 44.1).

iter ingressus est confecitque modo tam festinanter et rapide: Speed is consistent with Gaius' sudden departure (*neque ex destinato,* above) and suggests urgency. Because of the crisis with Gaetulicus, haste would have been in order wherever he was headed.

ut praetorianae cohortes contra morem signa iumentis imponere et ita subsequi cogerentur: Praetorians had the reputation of being soft and unaccustomed to hard marches (Tac. *Hist.* 1.23.2, 2.19.1). Their standards were much more elaborately decorated than those of other units (Durry 198–99) and therefore probably heavier as well. Two praetorian cohorts routinely accompanied the emperor when he was away from Rome.(4).

interdum adeo segniter delicateque, ut octaphoro veheretur: *Segniter delicateque* balances *festinanter et rapide* (above). Gaius was being inconsistent again, speeding up and then slowing down. An *octaphorus* was inappropriate transportation for an emperor in Rome (see on Gaius' *lecticari,* 58.3), much less on the way to the field. It was an elegant sedan chair carried by eight bearers and always tokened oriental luxury (e.g., Cic. *Verr.* 2 5.27; Mart. 6.8). No emperor, of course, made a journey without conveniences (Suet. *Vit.* 10.2; Millar 1977, 33–36). Gaius' party included actors, gladiators, his beloved horses, and women (Dio 59.21.2), the groups that always surrounded him (on 33, 54.1; Dio 59.2.5). He needed the performers for games he evidently underwrote himself at Lugdunum (20; Willrich 306; Fishwick 1987–1990, 580). Known companions were Passienus Crispus (on 10.2; *Schol.* Juv. 4.81) and the freedman Claudius Etruscus (*PIR²* C. 860; Stat. *Silv.* 3.3.71).

atque a propinquarum urbium plebe verri sibi vias et conspergi propter pulverem exigeret: Street cleaners at work. An imperial progress through the countryside created extra work and expenditure for local inhabitants (Millar 1977, 32–33). Gaius' projected trip to the East was planned well in advance (on 49.2), and it is difficult to imagine that this one to the North was not—whether or not the departure itself was sudden.

Gaius undertook severe disciplinary measures with the army at the *castra* at Mogontiacum, headquarters of the Army of Upper Germany (Suet. *Gal.* 6.2–3), which he visited in November or December of 39 or not until after he had seen the new year in at Lugdunum (17.1). See 26.2 for an incident associated with his visit. The *ludibria* of chapter 45 evidently took place there too.

44.1 *Postquam castra attigit:* Following as it does the description of the journey north, *postquam castra attigit* makes it appear as though Mogontiacum was Gaius' first destination, but all transitional sentences in this portion of the text are vague. In addition, there is no mention of the confrontation with Gaetulicus which would be expected if Gaius had gone directly there before Galba had already taken his place (on 43).

ut se acrem ac severum ducem ostenderet: Galba is described as *severus* but not overly severe or harsh, i.e., *acer* (Suet. *Gal.* 9.1 for an exception), and he is credited with disciplining troops under his command well (Suet. *Gal.* 6.3, 7.1; Tac. *Hist.* 1.5.2, 18.3). The soldiers' jingle was *disce miles militare; Galba est, non Gaetulicus* (*Gal.* 6.2); Gaetulilcus had been lax and hence liked by his troops (Tac. *Ann.* 6.30.2). In this passage Gaius is credited with doing Galba's work (*se...ostenderet*), especially the portions of it that were most unpopular.

legatos, qui auxilia serius ex diversis locis adduxerant, cum ignominia dimisit: Cf. *legionibus et auxiliis undique excitis* (43). *Serius* suggests that the troops had been due to assemble at some specific date for which they were "too late," possibly October 19, the date of the *armilustrium* (above; Faur 1973b, 30–35). Since commanders of the *auxilia* were *praefecti*, not *legati*, Suetonius is either imprecise, or the auxiliaries were brought into place under the command of legionary *legati*.

at in exercitu recensendo plerisque centurionum maturis iam et nonnullis ante paucissimos quam consummaturi essent dies, primos pilos ademit, causatus senium cuiusque et imbecillitatem: "And when he reviewed the army and saw that many of the centurions were already elderly and some within a few days of serving out their time, he removed the head centurions [*primos pilos*], charging that they were old and weak." Military service had been extended to twenty years under Augustus (Dio 55.23.1) but was often prolonged beyond that, even until the legionaries reached the age of sixty, and this was the cause of much complaining (Suet. *Tib.* 48.2; Tac. *Ann.* 1.17.2–3, 35.2, 36.3; Dio 57.5.3; Juv. 14.196–98). Early retirement for the centurions just before they reached their time of discharge was nasty but cost effective for the regime; retirement benefits, especially for *primi pili,* (35.2, 38.2) were expensive.

ceterorum increpita cupiditate commoda emeritae militiae ad †sescentorum milium summum recidit: The *emeritae militiae* were those who had served out their time and were eligible to receive the usual retirement bonus of 12,000 sesterces (Dio 55.23.1). The crux of *sescentorum milium* is sensibly read as 6000 sesterces, a reduction to half (Balsdon 1934a, 77; Barrett 1989, 130). Annual pay was only 900 (Tac. *Ann.* 1.17.4).

Suetonius does not supply a time relationship between Gaius' dealings with the army at Mogontiacum (above) and his single accomplishment that is described here, the taking of Adminius hostage. There is no way to know when Adminius presented himself, but his surrender was apparently acted out in the early spring of A.D. 40 (on 46).

44.2 *nihil autem amplius quam Adminio Cynobellini Britannorum regis filio, qui pulsus a patre cum exigua manu transfugerat, in deditionem recepto:* Adminius (or Amminus; Barrett 1989, 287, n. 48, for the spelling) was one of the sons of Cynobellinus (Cunobelinus), scarcely king of all Britain, but chief of the expansionist Catuvellauni, the dominant tribe in the southeast. Why father and son were at odds is not known, but political upheavals in Britain sometimes spilled over into Gaul to affect the Romans. A similar incident gave Claudius his excuse to invade the island a few years later, *tunc tumultuantem ob non redditos transfugas* (Suet. *Cl.* 17.1; also Dio 60.19.1). Cynobellinus was dead by 43 when two other sons, the anti-Roman Caratacus and Togodumnus, opposed Claudius (Dio 60.20.1; Salway 55–61, 70).

quasi universa tradita insula: Cf. *quasi perpetraturus bellum* (46). Suetonius is clear about the pretense of it all.

magnificas Romam litteras misit: Magnificae litterae = *litterae laureatae,* the missive encircled with laurel with which the triumphant general announced his victory to Rome. Tacitus judged them immodest self-advertisements (*Agr.* 18.6). Persius writes that the *laurus* announced a German, not a British, victory: *missa est a Caesare laurus / insignem ob cladem Germaniae pubis* (6.43–44). The "non-triumph" (47, 49.2) is always German except here and with the *spolia* from Britain (46).

monitis speculatoribus, ut vehiculo ad forum usque et curiam pertenderent nec nisi in aede Martis ac frequente senatu consulibus traderent: Once spies or scouts, *speculatores* became an elite group within the praetorians who were assigned special tasks such as transmitting the watchword (Tac. *Hist.* 1.25.1), performing executions (Sen. *Ben.* 3.25) or acting as courtiers as here (Durry 108–10). Like little Caligula (9), they wore *caligae* (cf. 52). Since vehicular traffic was illegal in Rome during the daytime, even for emperors (Mommsen 1871–1888, 1.393–96; Friedländer 4.28–31), the dispatch of *speculatores* into the city in a chariot was massively arrogant. The *Curia Julia* adjoined both the Republican forum and the imperial *Forum Julium.* The temple of Mars Ultor where tokens of victory were received (on 24.3) and the senate voted on triumphs (Suet. *Aug.* 29.2; Dio 55.10.3) was in the second imperial forum, the *Forum Augustum.* Without qualification, *forum* usually meant the Republican forum. *Frequente senatu* = with a quorum present (Talbert 137).

A rubric of mock sorties against the Germans. Both of these anecdotes (are they doublets?) describe military farce in the context of an interrupted meal and appear to comment ironically on the edict with which the chapter closes, a communication from Gaius chastising those in Rome for enjoying elaborate banquets while he suffered hardship and danger at the front (45.3). These stories make the point that Gaius suffered mock (not genuine) hardships while he (not those back in Rome) enjoyed the pleasures of the table. His gastronomic excess has already been commented on (22.3, 37.1, 58.1; Philo *Leg.* 14) and for pleasures of the table combined with cruelty, see 32.1–2. The edict probably influenced the way these stories were told, although Gaius plausibly did ride with the troops in one or several carefully staged (*mimo,* 45.2) "safe battles" (Barrett 1989, 134) just as Claudius rode at the head of a force in Britain (Dio 60.21.3–4); [Claudius] *expeditionem unam omnino suscepit eamque modicam* (Suet. *Cl.*17.1). Balsdon (1934a, 79–81) interpreted these incidents as a misunderstanding of training exercises at Mogontiacum (Suet. *Gal.* 6.3, accepted by Davies,125–26). Emperors did participate in maneuvers: Trajan (Plin. *Pan.* 13.1); Hadrian (Dio 69.9).

45.1 *mox deficiente belli materia:* An unreliable transition.[90] Suetonius often uses *mox* as a vague connective that does not imply a close temporal relationship (e.g., 8.1, 24.1, 49.3).

---

[90] Orosius also has the phrase *deficiente belli materia* to supply a reason for Gaius' return home: *hic siquidem magno et incredibili apparatu profectus quaerere hostem viribus otiosis, Germaniam Galliamque percurrens, in ora Oceani circa prospectum Britanniae restitit. cumque ibi Minocynobelinum Britannorum regis filium, qui a patre pulsus cum paucis oberrabat, in deditionem recepisset, deficiente belli materia Romam rediit* (7.5.5). *Minocynobelinum* is evidently corrupted from Suetonius' (or Tacitus' ?) *Adminio Cynobellini* (44.2). Abridged as his account is, Orosius may be more cogent than either Suetonius or Dio about events in the North. He takes Gaius on a circuit of Germany and Gaul, has him on the Channel coast receiving Adminius into surrender and then sends him home. This is similar to Barrett's reconstruction (1989, 136–38) that connects the exercise on the coast (46) with the surrender of Adminius (44.2). Orosius may have been using Tacitus' much-missed chronological account as he does elsewhere in the portion of his

paucos de custodia Germanos traici occulique trans Rhenum iussit:
German prisoners imply relatively recent military action. The newly appointed
Galba had inherited problems (*matureque barbaris, qui iam in Galliam usque
proruperant, coercitis,* Suet. *Gal.* 6.3) and was still fighting in 41 (51.3; Dio
60.8.7; Tac. *Hist.* 4.15.2; Barrett 1989, 131–32). There was a bridge at
Mogontiacum from the first century (von Petrikovits 28; Jullian 4.162), but at
this time it was probably still temporary. For another Rhine crossing and further
notice of a bridge, 51.2. *Custodia* = prisoners also at 27.1, 29.2, 32.1.

ac sibi post prandium quam tumultuosissime adesse hostem nuntiari:
Post prandium = "after lunch." The sortie is made trivial both by the context of
the meal and by the casual period of time allotted to it. The point is that Gaius'
meals took precedence over his military objectives.

*quo facto proripuit se cum amicis et parte equitum praetorianorum in
proximam silvam: Cum...parte:* not all accompanied him and so not all were
rewarded (below). For his praetorian escort and *amici,* see on 43. Each century
of praetorians had an attachment of fifteen *equites praetoriani.*

truncatisque arboribus et in modum tropaeorum adornatis: They presumably killed the prisoners who had been set up across the river (cf. the
prisoners irregularly executed at 27.1). Gaius' victory monument had a human
shape, tree limbs clad in enemy armor; cf. *tu quoque nunc stares immanis truncus
in armis* (Verg. *Aen.* 11.173). Trophies could take many forms (e.g.,
Germanicus' pile of armor, Tac. *Ann.* 2.18.2, 22.1).

*ad lumina reversus, eorum quidem qui secuti non essent timiditatem
et ignaviam corripuit:* Following Gaius "into battle" was optional (*qui secuti
non essent*). *Ad lumina,* by lamplight; they returned after dark (Suet. *Jul.* 37.2;
Pliny *HN* 33.70).

*comites autem et participes victoriae novo genere ac nomine
coronarum donavit:* Gaius' crown begs contrast to Claudius' serious one. The
as coined by Gaius (on 23.1) and continued by Claudius shows Agrippa wearing
the prestigious *corona navalis,* a crown that Claudius made an emblem of his
victory over Britain. It honored the fact that he had passed beyond and thus conquered the Ocean: *inter hostilia spolia navalem coronam fastigio Palatinae domus
iuxta civicam fixit, traiecti et quasi domiti Oceani insigne* (Suet. *Cl.* 17.3;
Maxfield 75–76; on 46).

---

history in question. This sequence of events does not, however, allow for a visit to the Army of
Lower Germany on the way home after he left the coast (48).

quas distinctas solis ac lunae siderumque specie exploratorias appellavit: Coronae exploratoriae = "scouting" crowns, trivial indeed when compared with genuine crowns for significant accomplishments (*obsidionales, civicae, vallares,* Gell. 5.6.24–26). One job for an *explorator* might be to clear the path ahead for the emperor (about Tiberius: *in quodam itinere lectica, qua vehebatur, vepribus impedita exploratorem viae, primarum cohortium centurionem, stratum humi paene ad necem verberavit,* Suet. *Tib.* 60). Sun and moon were associated with Isis (22.4), who was also *mater siderum* (Apul. *Met.* 11.7). Whether or not Gaius awarded this crown either seriously or in jest, it is presented as an Isiac aberration.

45.2 *rursus obsides quosdam abductos e litterario ludo:* From the context the hostages seem to be German, more *custodia* (45.1), possibly the children of German chieftains already beginning their Romanization in an elementary school (*ludus litterarius*) in the provinces (on 16.2, 36.1) before being taken to Rome for the imperial triumph. Dio describes this among incidents that took place in the relative civilization of Lugdunum (59.22.2), but its military aspect suggests Mogontiacum. Even very recently subdued areas might have schools (Tac. *Agr.* 21.2).

clamque praemissos, deserto repente convivio, cum equitatu insecutus veluti profugos: Elements of the preceding anecdote reoccur: *clamque praemissos...profugos = paucos...traici occulique trans Rhenum; deserto repente convivio = post prandium...quam tumultuosissime; cum equitatu = cum...parte equitum praetorianorum* (45.1).

ac reprehensos in catenis reduxit; in hoc quoque mimo praeter modum intemperans, repetita cena renuntiantis coactum agmen sic ut erant loricatos ad discumbendum adhortatus est: Gaius was *intemperans praeter modum* because he invited the messengers who brought the news that the hostages had been recaptured to join him at the table in full armor. The pursuing force resumed the banquet that it had left (*deserto repente convivio*), and the message was brought that the last of the mock hostages had been rounded up (*agmen cogere* = "bring up the rear," i.e., the pursuers had finished with their task). Dio provides less detail: ἐκείνων μὲν γὰρ ὀλίγους ποτὲ ἀπάτῃ τινὶ συλλαβὼν ἔδησε (59.22.2). *In hoc quoque mimo* both points out a parallel between this anecdote and the preceding one (45.1) and calls attention to Gaius' interest in show business (Guastella), not only his associations with entertainers (33, 36.1, 54.1; Dio 59.5.2) but also such things as the *scaena* when he brought home the ashes of his mother and brother (15.1) and the *spectacula* at Baiae and on the Channel coast (19, 46).

monuit etiam notissimo Vergili versu durarent secundisque se rebus servarent: A rendering into indirect command of *durate, et vosmet rebus servate secundis* (Verg. *Aen.* 1.207), the emphatic last line of the dramatic speech with which Aeneas encouraged his followers to bear up and look to better times in the future as they were about to begin their first meal after being stranded on the Libyan coast. Its new context is the meal resumed after the "arduous" capture of the escapees from the *ludus litterarius*. It was a joke, but whose is uncertain; perhaps it is an example of Gaius' sense of humor to which readers have already been treated (29–33). Other emperors who quoted Vergil were Augustus (Suet. *Aug.* 40.5) and Domitian (*Dom.* 9.1; Berthet 322, n. 8). Note the inconsistency between this Vergilian quotation and Gaius' alleged desire to eliminate Vergil from the Roman canon (34.2).

45.3 atque inter haec absentem senatum populumque gravissimo obiurgavit edicto: Imperial edicts were regarded as examples of an emperor's personal style (Millar 1977, 253–56), and if what follows is an accurate transmission of one that Gaius actually wrote, it is small wonder that it was difficult to take him seriously. The "great weight" of the *gravissimum edictum* is ironic. For his other edicts see on 25.1.

quod Caesare proeliante et tantis discriminibus obiecto tempestiva convivia, circum et theatra et amoenos secessus celebrarent: *Tempestiva convivia* = long and luxurious feasts associated with pleasant places (Cic. *Mur.* 13; Sen. *Dial.* 4.28.8). They began at a "timely" (*tempestiva*) or early hour and implied inappropriate excess. Dio notes this edict more generally: "he pretended to be in danger and to be living wretchedly" (προσεποιεῖτο ἐν δεινοῖς τε εἶναι καὶ ταλαιπώρως διάγειν (59.23.1).

If Gaius had realized the Roman dream of British conquest, it would have been a very useful success, but a genuine invasion attempt was not really possible because in order to be back near Rome at the end of May of 40 (on 49.2), he had to have left the North by the end of March at the latest when it was still too early in the year to set out on the North Sea. Caesar and Claudius made their crossings in mid- and late summer (Caes. *BGall.* 4.23, 5.8; Dio.19.3). The large troop buildup (43) indicates plans for a significant action somewhere, but it is not really clear whether Gaius intended to limit himself to Germany or to invade Britain too, and, if so, when. Tacitus writes that it was commonly understood that Gaius did intend an invasion: *agitasse Gaium Caesarem de intranda Britannia satis constat, ni velox ingenio mobili paenitentiae, et ingentes adversus Germaniam conatus frustra fuissent* (*Agr.* 13.2). Most modern historians agree and think that it was called off, either at the last minute (Balsdon 1934a, 90–92; Phillips 372) or earlier (Bicknell 1968, 498; Barrett 1989, 129). Willrich thought that Gaius changed his mind because he felt threatened by political instability in Rome (314), Gelzer, that Britain had become unified against him (405–6). Davies, on the other hand, thought that the absurd business on the coast was never intended to be more than a training maneuver (126–28). It has been explained variously as a mutiny when the troops refused to embark as happened in A.D. 43 (Dio 60.19.2–3; Balsdon 91–92; Phillips 372; similarly but at the mouth of the Rhine, Bicknell 1968, 504–5). More plausibly, some sort of ceremonial display is described, like that with the bridge at Baiae (19). Just as Gaius had reenacted the acceptance of the Parthian hostage Darius into custody, here he may have acted out the acceptance of Adminius (Barrett 1989, 137–38), the sequence followed by Orosius (note 90). The theatrics were described as farce since it was imperative that Claudius' own successful crossing to Britain a short three years later be separated from his nephew's ersatz "victory." It was, after all, ridiculous to claim that the surrender of Adminius was the same as the conquest of Britian (*quasi universa tradita insula*, 44.2).

46 *postremo quasi perpetraturus bellum:* Cf. *quasi universa tradita insula*, 44.2. Like *mox deficiente belli materia* at the opening of the preceding rubric (45.1), this transition cannot be relied on to provide a trustworthy logical or temporal link.[91]

derecta acie in litore Oceani: The battle line drawn up on the shore (πάντας τοὺς στρατιώτας ἐν τῇ ἠόνι παρατάξας, Dio 59.25.1) was not part of an invasion in progress. Troops board ships before they cross into enemy territory; they deploy in battle formation only after they arrive. Dio adds that Gaius sailed out a short distance in a trireme and then sailed back (τριήρους τε ἐπέβη καὶ ὀλίγον ἀπὸ τῆς γῆς ἀπάρας ἀνέπλευσε, 59.25.2). Was this to dramatize the capture of Adminius just as the parade across the bridge at Baiae dramatized the defeat of the Parthians? It is possible that Adminius handed himself over at sea (Barrett 1989, 137–38). For triremes in Gaius' triumph, see 47.

ac ballistis machinisque depositis: *Ballistae* were weapons for throwing projectiles against the enemy. The more generic *machinae* were contrivances with which an investing army broke down defensive walls (Tac. *Hist.* 4.23.3, 4.28.3). These engines had no more practical function on a beach than did the battle line (*derecta acie*, above). Gaius was parading his artillery.

---

[91] *Perpetraturus bellum* has been read to imply that the events described in this chapter took place, not on the Channel coast where Dio puts them (ἐς δὲ τὸν ὠκεανὸν ἐλθὼν ὡς καὶ ἐν τῇ Βρεττανίᾳ στρατεύσων, 59.25.1; ὁρμήσας ὡς καὶ ἐς τὴν Βρεττανίαν στρατεύσων ἀπ' αὐτοῦ τοῦ ὠκεανοῦ ἀνεκομίσθη, 59.21.3), but on the North Sea coast near the mouth of the Rhine as a prelude to a campaign into Germany by sea in imitation of Germanicus. Bicknell (1968, 500–505) points out that the only *bellum* that Gaius could carry further (*perpetraturus*) was the one against Germany (45.1), that Gaius visited the Army of Lower Germany (48), that the Canninefates who lived on the North Sea were involved with a *ludibrium* of Gaius (Tac. *Hist.* 4.15.1), and that Victor writes *contractis ad unum legionibus spe in Germaniam transgrediendi conchas umbilicosque in ora maris oceani legi iussit* (3.11.12; see note 93).

nemini gnaro aut opinante quidnam coepturus esset: The Baiae bridge
was a novelty too (19.1, 3, and 32.1).

repente ut conchas legerent galeasque et sinus replerent imperavit,
spolia Oceani vocans Capitolio Palatioque debita: According to Dio
Gaius gave the order from a high platform (as if reviewing the troops), urged the
soldiers into battle with trumpets and then suddenly (ἐξαίφνης = *repente*) ordered
them to pick up shells (59.25.2). There have been numerous rationalizations of
this strange action: Balsdon thought that Gaius ordered the men to pick up
musculi, military contrivances that protected soldiers besieging a city and that this
was misunderstood by Roman writers (1934a, 92; 1934b, 18); or Gaius intended
his order as an intentional insult to his troops in return for their mutiny (Balsdon
1934a, 92; 1934b, 18; Bicknell 1968, 505; Phillips 373; Flory, 500–501); or the
soldiers threw the shells at one another in simulated missile attacks (Davies, 127);
or they were being asked to imitate a Celtic custom of wading in and fighting the
sea with swords, taking *spolia* of pearls (Bicknell 1962, 72–74); or (as the texts
claim) they would be part of his triumph (Barrett 1989, 138). Whether or not
Gaius really gave such an order, the reference is to pearls, the gift from the sea
washed up on the beach (*gemmas margaritasque mare litoribus infundit,* Curt.
8.9.19), always a necessary part of British conquest. They were not only very
precious (37.1) and emblematic of victory over the sea (below) but an item associated quite specifically with avarice, Julius Caesar and Britain (Flory 499–502),
where they could be found on the shore. Julius Caesar had allegedly gone there in
search of them (*Britanniam petisse spe margaritarum,* Suet. *Jul.* 47)[92] and marked
his success with the pearl breastplate that he dedicated to Venus Genetrix on his
return (Pliny *HN* 9.116), a symbol of victory over the sea. But Gaius' booty
(*spolia*) for his triumphal parade (Dio 59.25.3), came from the wrong side of the
Channel, and this made him a poor imitation of his ancestor. Conquering Ocean,
the final frontier, the end of the earth, was standard rhetoric for great achievement, best left to a real Julius Caesar (Tandoi 1967, 31–37). In A.D. 43 Claudius'
legions balked because they did not want to fight beyond the civilized world (ἔξω
τῆς οἰκουμένης στρατεύσοντες, Dio 60.19.2). Gaius had already been accused
of competing with Neptune with his Baiae bridge (Dio 59.17.4, 11). For

---

[92] Suetonius writes this about Caesar in a rubric about his luxurious taste. Tacitus also
comments on British pearls and avarice together: *gignit et Oceanus margarita, sed subfusca ac*
liventia. quidam artem abesse legentibus arbitrantur; nam in rubro mari viva ac spirantia saxis
avelli, in Britannia, prout expulsa sint, colligi. ego facilius crediderim naturam margaritis deesse
quam nobis avaritiam (Tac. *Agr.* 12.6). Pliny agrees about the poor quality of British pearls
(*parvos atque decolares, HN* 9.116). Balsdon suggested that "Gaius might well have had the
pearls of Julius Caesar in mind" but dropped the idea in favor of *musculi* (1934b, 18).

Claudius' *corona navalis,* see on 45.1 (also Sen. *Apocol.* 12.3; Pliny *Pan.* 81.4–82.2). For more comparison between the two Gaius Julius Caesars, see 22.1, 57.1–3, 58.3, 60.

et in indicium victoriae altissimam turrem excitavit, ex qua ut Pharo noctibus ad regendos navium cursus ignes emicarent: An ancient lighthouse stood until modern times on the French coast at Boulogne, the site of Gesoriacum, the major point of embarkation for Britain (Suet. *Cl.* 17; D'Erce 1966, 89–96). Whether or not it was built by Gaius, the tower long continued to be useful for the trade which had already been established between Britain and Gaul (Strab. 2.5.8, 4.5.3). But the practice of setting up a marker at the limit of forward progress as a victory monument (Drusus on the Elbe, Dio 55.1.3; Tandoi 1967, 35) was assimilated with the idea of Gaius' lighthouse. Pharos, both the island off Alexandria and the lighthouse that stood there, became a generic word for lighthouse (Suet. *Tib.* 74; *Cl.* 20.3; Juv. 12.76; Pliny *HN* 36.83); no Egyptian connection need be imagined.

pronuntiatoque militi donativo: Cf. καὶ τοῖς στρατιώταις πολλὰ ἐδωρήσατο (Dio 59.25.3). Donatives, gifts that served as salary supplements for the military, were given to commemorate special occasions, including the assumption of the principate (on 16.3; Dio 59.2.1; Suet. *Cl.* 10.4; Jos. *AJ* 19.247; Tac. *Ann.* 12.69.2; Dio 61.3.1), or as rewards or bribes for loyalty (Veyne 1990, 341, 344). The donative on the occasion of the Baiae bridge suggests a parallel for this one (καὶ χρήματά τε διὰ τοῦτ' [crossing the sea on foot] αὐτοῖς ἔδωκε, Dio 59.17.8). He validated ceremonial occasions as actual accomplishments.

centenis viritim denariis, quasi omne exemplum liberalitatis supergressus: Gaius was stingy. *Centenis viritim denariis* = four hundred sesterces apiece. Germanicus had defused the mutiny on the Rhine with six hundred to each soldier (Dio 57.5.3; Tac. *Ann.* 1.36.3), Tiberius gave the praetorians each four thousand for not siding with Sejanus (Suet. *Tib.* 48.2), and Gaius' own supplement to the praetorians on his accession had been one thousand (Dio 59.2.1). For a major act of loyalty, such as really following him across awe-inspiring Ocean (above), four hundred seems small.

abite, inquit, laeti, abite locupletes: Gaius' words of abrupt dismissal are another example of his swift and insulting speech (29–31). Was his sarcasm for the fact that they had found only shells and not pearls (Flory 501)? Was it gratuitous because he had been cheap? *Abite* and *abi* were simple commands but also particles of indignation (*TLL* 1.67.2–20).

Plans for the triumph that never happened: Gaius' indecision or change of mind about it (49.1) appears to have been a major subject for speculation and at the center of the characterization of him as capricious. The whole point in this chapter is the juxtaposition of his grandiose plans with his feeble achievements (cf. on Jupiter Latiaris, 22.2). But Gaius was not alone in seeking a false triumph with fake captives celebrated for a non-victory. Domitian was accused of celebrating his two triumphs (A.D. 83 and 84) with *falsae simulacra victoriae and mimici curri* (Pliny *Pan.* 16.3; also Dio 67.4.1–2; Tac. *Agr.* 39.1; Suet. *Dom.* 6.1). The fact that Domitian's achievements were real (Frontin. *Str.* 2.23, 11.7; Ogilvie and Richmond at Tac. *Agr.* 39.1) did not keep demeaning stories from being told.

47 *conversus hinc ad curam triumphi:* Another vague transition. Despite the implied relationship between the triumph and the affair on the Channel (46) and the capture of Adminius (44.2), it was apparently conceived as one over the Germans (*ludos extraordinarios pro victoria eius Germanica depoposcit,* Suet. *Ves.* 2.3; *insignem ob cladem Germanae pubis,* Pers. 6.43–44).

praeter captivos ac transfugas barbaros Galliarum quoque procerissimum quemque...ac nonnullos ex principibus legit ac seposuit ad pompam: Captives were the single most necessary element (Tac. *Ann.* 2.41.2; Strab. 7.1.4), good-looking ones like the proverbially tall Germans being especially desirable (Jos. *BJ* 7.118, 138; Tac. *Hist.* 4.1, *Germ.* 20.1; Strab. 7.1.2). Chieftains too were a plus (Strab. 7.1.4; Jos. *BJ* 7.118–52). Selecting them from among Gauls seems particularly unwise, however, since Rome wanted the cooperation of Gallic leaders. The *transfugas barbaros* were possibly Adminius and his associates (44.2).

et, ut ipse dicebat, ἀξιοθριάμβ⟨ε⟩υτον: ἀξιοθριάμβευτον = "worthy of being led in triumph," from θριαμβεύω = "triumph" or "lead in triumph" is included here as an example of Gaius' verbal dexterity. Cf. 29.1: *ut ipsius verbo utar,* ἀδιατρεψίαν, in each case, the only recorded use of the word. Note Suetonius' emphasis on the fact that both were Gaius' own words, apparently coinages, but neither he nor a commentator saw any need to translate this one.

coegitque non tantum rutilare et summittere comam: Both Germans and Gauls were notorious for their long red or red-blond hair, natural or dyed: *promissae et rutilatae comae* (Liv. 38.17.3; Tac. *Hist.* 4.61.1; Amm. 27.2.2; Plin. *HN* 28.191). Back in Rome, Gaius' wife was busy getting the yellow wigs ready (*lutea gausapa captis...locat Caesonia,* Pers. 6.46–47; Conington at Pers. 6.46). Domitian was accused of similar arrangements: *emptis per commercia quorum habitus et crines in captivorum speciem formarentur* (Tac. *Agr.* 39.1).

sed et sermonem Germanicum addiscere et nomina barbarica ferre:
More evidence that the projected triumph was strictly a German one (44.2). Since
it is Gauls who are being given peculiar German names (*nomina barbarica*), did
Romans by now consider Gallic nomenclature familiar?

praecepit etiam triremis, quibus introierat Oceanum, magna ex parte
itinere terrestri Romam devehi: Ships might be part of a triumphal parade
(Jos. *BJ* 7.147). Dio, not Suetonius, reports a single trireme in the affair on the
coast (59.25.2; see on 46). The overland route was probably from Gesoriacum
south until the Rhone became navigable and the ship or ships could be sent down
river to the Mediterranean. Claudius journeyed in the other direction in 43 when
he travelled along the coast from Ostia to Massilia (Marseilles) near the mouth of
the Rhone and from there on land and by rivers to the Channel (Dio 60.21.3).

scripsit et procuratoribus, triumphum appararent quam minima
summa, sed quantus numquam alius fuisset, quando in omnium
hominum bona ius haberent: This sentence illustrates Gaius' constant
predicament: the conflict between his desire for self-aggrandizement and his need
for the money to serve it (39–42). The private communication to his personal
staff (*procuratoribus*) shows him by-passing the senate who still had to vote the
triumphs now reserved for the emperor and his family (48.2).

This next episode takes place with the Army of Lower Germany on the left bank of the Rhine, presumably at Vetera, its headquarters. Gaius had run into difficulty with these same legions with his
father as a small child (9). The causal relationship between this incident and his return home (48.2)
suggests that he went to Vetera after leaving the Channel coast where he was last located (46), but
the connections that Suetonius makes between episodes of the expedition not temporal ones, and it
difficult to infer the order of events from them. He may have visited these legions before he went
to the coast and then departed for Rome directly from there (see note 90). He was associated with
some sort of military enterprise in Lower Germany (*Gaianarum expeditionum ludibrium,* Tac.
Hist. 4.15.1), perhaps staged expeditions like those near Mogontiacum or perhaps what is described in chapter 45 really took place farther north. But this is an anecdote of a different sort. The
description is of a *contio,* a formal review of the military by its commander, at which something
unpleasant and humiliating, perhaps even threatening, is reported. Some of the details do not seem
very likely (Barrett 1989, 138–39) and are in Gaius' mind in any case. The epitome of Dio does
not deal with it.

48.1 *prius quam provincia decederet: Provincia* makes it seem that the setting here is the same as the preceding one (46). Gesoriacum was in the province
of Belgica, but Lower Germany was a province too.[93]

---

[93] It can be assumed that the confrontation took place at Vetera unless, of course, Gaius took the
legions in question to the Channel coast with him. Bicknell (1968, 501–2) thinks that *prius quam*

consilium iniit nefandae atrocitatis legiones, quae post excessum Augusti seditionem olim moverant, contrucidandi: *Contrucidare* = "butcher, slaughter in mass" (cf. *qui universos contrucidarent,* 28). With what force could he have annihilated two entire legions? But then he only "thought about it" (*consilium iniit*). The legions who had offended after the death of Augustus were the First and Twentieth. Since the mutiny (*seditio*) had taken place twenty-six years earlier, not very many of the same individuals were in the ranks, despite the long length of military service (on 44.1).

quod et patrem suum Germanicum ducem et se infantem tunc obsedissent: The memory (or rather the story—Gaius was too young to remember) of Germanicus' confrontation with these legions rankled. Gaius and his mother Agrippina had been present during the mutiny and at one point were seriously threatened (Tac. *Ann.* 1.41–44; Dio 57.5). Although apologists interpreted the incident to the glory of Germanicus (on 9), it was also remembered as an embarrassment or worse.

vixque a tam praecipiti cogitatione revocatus: Who knew his thoughts? Cf. *consilium iniit* (above). This desire to put things into Gaius' mind probably shows that his behavior at Vetera was perceived as highly irregular and inappropriate; cf. the *rumores,* 48.2.

inhiberi nullo modo potuit quin decimare velle perseveraret: He could not be "kept from continuing to want to" decimate the legions. Decimation, when legionaries killed each tenth man chosen by lot from among themselves, was an old-fashioned punishment for treason or desertion but employed as recently as the Civil War by both Augustus and Antony (Dio 41.35.5, 49.27.1, 38.4). When a disobedient cohort was decimated during the fighting in Africa in A.D. 20, Tacitus judged it harsh and no longer in much use (*raro ea tempestate et e vetere memoria facinore, Ann.* 3.21.1).

vocatas itaque ad contionem inermes, atque etiam gladiis depositis, equitatu armato circumdedit: Perhaps the *contio* followed the *ludibrium* that Tacitus mentions (*Hist.* 4.15.1). A review was routine, but the legions would normally have been armed (Tac. *Ann.* 1.35.4). Was the *imperator* too unsure of himself to face them with their weapons? The unfavorable comparison between Gaius and the model of the "good general" is implicit. And what *equitatus armatus* should be thought of here? His *equites praetoriani* (45.1), perhaps one hundred eighty strong, were a small force with which to surround two legions.

---

provincia decederet proves conclusively that the entire incident on the beach took place on the North Sea at the mouth of the Rhine instead of farther west opposite Britain (on 46; see note 91).

48.2 *sed cum videret suspecta re plerosque dilabi ad resumenda si qua vis fieret arma, profugit contionem:* This scene is vaguely reminiscent of Germanicus' humiliation in the A.D. 14 mutiny. Then, amidst shouts that he seize power himself, Germanicus jumped down from the platform and dramatically, perhaps foolishly, threatened to kill himself with his sword before he was disloyal to Tiberius. A soldier insultingly offered his own sharper one (Tac. *Ann.* 1.35.4; for a reading of the incident that is hostile to Germanicus, Ross 211–20). Although Germanicus gained control of the volatile situation after a time, Gaius seems to have found himself in something that he could not handle. Perhaps he insulted the legions by reminding them of their behavior in the mutiny. Did he, unlike his father, go off in a rage (*profugit contionem*) as soon as he was challenged? He lacked patience, had a short temper and did not tolerate contradiction. His storming out of the *contio* has a parallel in his storming out of the games (*proripuit se spectaculis*) when the crowd applauded too vigorously against his wishes (35.3).

Gaius' journey home to a hostile Rome and the tension between him and the senate in the last months of his reign is the next theme (through 49.1). When he had left the preceding year, he must surely have intended to return with the desired triumph, but at some point this ceased to seem like a good idea. Considering the embarrassing stories (*rumores*) about his campaign that reached Rome before he did (below) and the atmosphere of total distrust that met him (48.2–49.2 56.1; Dio 59.25.5ᵇ–8, 26.3), the decision not to make himself conspicuously ridiculous seems only sensible. It was not necessarily a commendable refusal to take credit for military activity only just begun in Germany and Britain (Balsdon 1934a, 94; Barrett 1989, 138).

confestimque urbem †omnem petit, deflexa omni acerbitate in senatum, cui ad <a>vertendos tantorum dedecorum rumores palam minabatur: Gaius' haste is an attempt at damage control; it was not wise for an emperor to be out of Rome too long unless his rear was secured. The sequence of events implies that the stories that preceded him (*tantorum dedecorum rumores*) were those concerned with his confrontation with Legions I and XX (48.1), but they may refer to his entire expedition. The *rumores* are made an excuse for his belligerence toward the the senate (cf. 30.1). Cf. 16.4 where Sueonius makes a false causal sequence of events leading to the shield for Gaius' *clementia*. On whatever date Gaius started back to Rome, whether he left from Belgica (46) or from Lower Germany (48.1), he must have proceeded with reasonable dispatch to arrive by the end of May (on 49.2), since such a journey took about two months (Davies 126, n. 16; Barrett 1989, 136). *†omnem:* possibly from *Romam* as a gloss on *urbem*.

querens inter cetera fraudatum se iusto triumpho, cum ipse paulo ante, ne quid de honoribus suis ageretur, etiam sub mortis poena denuntiasset: Gaius does not seem to have given clear signals to the senate about his triumph (49.2). Dio' description of his behavior at this juncture serves as a generalization about his character: Gaius received nothing graciously and always suspected that he was being insulted whenever he was being honored. Small distinctions annoyed him, but he thought that large ones precluded additional rewards. He did not want to accept anything from the senate since that implied that it was superior to him, but he was angry if he felt that he was honored less than he deserved (59.23.3–4; also 59.19.2–3, 25.4).

49.1 *aditus ergo in itinere a legatis amplissimi ordinis ut maturaret orantibus:* This was a senatorial delegation,[94] i.e., from the *ordo amplissimus* = "very distinguished order." Cf. *splendidissimus,* 15.1; also Suet. *Oth.* 8.1, *Ves.* 2.3; Pliny *Ep.*10.3.

quam maxima voce: veniam, inquit, veniam, et hic mecum, capulum gladii crebro verberans, quo cinctus erat: Another example of Gaius' wit and another noisy outburst (*maxima voce;* see 22.1). Striking the hilt of his sword anticipated the executions that would follow his return (49.2; Dio 59.25.5b–26.2; cf. his list headed *gladius,* 49.3); he continued to wear his weapon while he was in the city (Dio 59.25.8). But might not contemporaries have seen a double meaning in his threat? *Capulus* meant handle (sword hilt) but sometimes phallus (Plaut. *Cas.* 909; Priap. 25.7). Cf. the double-entendre about "subjugating" whole peoples (29.2).

edixit et reverti se, sed iis tantum qui optarent, equestri ordini et populo; nam se neque civem neque principem senatui amplius fore: Cf. *deflexa omni acerbitate in senatum* (48.2). Gaius' distrust of the senate was overt by 39 (on 30.2). This degree of hostility written into an openly circulated edict seems exceptional, but it was perhaps just the unwise and tactless sort of thing that Gaius was capable of. A reconciliation of sorts came later (Dio 59.25.9, 26.3–4). The mention of the other orders shows him looking for other bases of support, but nothing could replace the senate. Favor toward the *equites* also at 53.2; disfavor toward them, 26.4, 30.2. For other edicts, see 25.1.

---

[94] This delegation was just possibly the one that Dio says replaced the delegation headed by Claudius that went north to congratulate Gaius on his deliverance from the plot against his life in 39 (on 20 and 24.3). Dio adds about the second delegation that "this happened later" (καὶ τοῦτο μὲν ὕστερον ἐγένετο, 59.23.6–7). On the other hand, Gaius' threat here does not correspond to Dio's report that Gaius received the second delegation graciously. Dio presents extremely confused chronology for 39–40 (59.21–25.4). "This happened later" is followed by a description of events that took place in the summer of 39; the account then continues through the winter and into the spring of 40 a second time. For more on source conflation in Dio, note 42.

49.2 *vetuit etiam quemquam senatorum sibi occurrere:* Out of fear of assassination. He was to sit on a high platform in the senate house and have a military guard (ὥστε μηδένα ἐξικνεῖσθαι, Dio 59.26.3), not really so outrageous a defensive posture since a similar guard had been suggested for Tiberius (Dio 58.17.4, 18.5; Tac. *Ann.* 6.15.2). Gaius was the first actually to employ one; Claudius, as often, followed his precedent (Suet. *Cl.* 12.1).

atque omisso vel dilato triumpho ovans urbem...ingressus est: Ovans urbem ingreditur was the standard idiom for entering the city with an ovation (Liv. 5.31.4; also Suet. *Aug.* 22; *Tib.* 9.2), a compromise between a triumph and nothing at all, granted for minor wars or bloodless victories or for wars against lesser (domestic) enemies (Gell. 5.6.21; Pliny *HN* 15.125). The senate voted Gaius one for eliminating Lepidus and Gaetulicus in 39 (Dio 59.23.2; on 24.3); this apparently followed a first ovation that came after he chastised them and restored the charge of *maiestas* earlier in the year before he built his bridge at Baiae (Dio 59.16.11; on 16.4 and 30.2). These two (?) ovations have in common the containment of enemies of the state, defined during the Empire as enemies of the princeps. The ovation with which he entered the city was presumably the one voted for the suppression of the plot. See on 22.2 for Jupiter Latiaris and the ovation-triumph substitution.

natali suo: He timed his entry for August 31, his birthday. In 37 he had dedicated the Temple of Augustus on that date (16.4, 17.2, 18.3, 21, Dio 59.7.2). In 38 the birthday sacrifice by the Arval Brethren was no more than routine, ostensibly because of Drusilla's recent death (Scheid and Broise 240), but his irritation with the consuls for failing to celebrate it adequately in 39 implies that he had a perennial interest in glorifying the date (on 26.3). He had returned to the neighborhood of Rome by the end of May, however, because he was present among those making the annual sacrifice to the Dea Dia at her nearby shrine on May 29 (*Docs.* no. 10, p. 14; Scheid and Broise 230–31).[95] He seems to have spent part of the summer in the Vatican Gardens (the gardens of Agrippina) across the Tiber and outside the *pomerium* where the Jewish delegation from Alexandria first met him (Philo *Leg.* 181) and where he watched an execution (on 26.3, 32.1; Sen. *Dial.* 5.18.4). He then went to his houses on the bay of Naples (Philo *Leg.* 185).[96]

---

[95] The evidence for dating the pertinent fragment of the *Acta Fratrum Arvalium* to 40 is summarized by Barrett (1989, 167–68).

[96] The reconstruction of where and when he traveled that summer depends on when he met with Philo's delegation (Balsdon 1934a, 140–41; 1934b, 19–24).

intraque quartum mensam periit: Actually within the fifth month after his return since the assassination took place on January 24, A.D. 41 (58.1). If the text is not in error (*apparatus*), Suetonius may have appropriated this countdown, not from Gaius' return, but from some specific event that a source recorded, perhaps from the riots in the circus over his new taxes (41.1; Dio 59.28.11; Jos *AJ* 19.24–27), perhaps from the uncovering of the "first phase" of the final conspiracies (56.1; Barrett 1989, 155). Cf. the very precise but unspecified time limit within which the large number of sacrifices took place when he became emperor (14.1).

ingentia facinora ausus et aliquanto maiora moliens: Cf. Dio at the same point in the narrative: "living in this way, he was bound to be plotted against" (τοῦτον δὲ τὸν τρόπον βιοὺς πάντως ἐπιβουλευθήσεσθαι ἔμελλε, 59.25.5ᵇ).

siquidem proposuerat Antium, deinde Alexandream comigrare: Cf. 8.5, 51.3. Gaius was both born (8.2) and married (on 12.1; Dio 58.25.2) at Antium (Strab. 5.3.5; Pliny *HN* 32.4). A retreat there could be compared with Tiberius' retreat to Capreae (on 7, 10.1). Gaius planned to make an Eastern progress with Alexandria as his destination, first coasting the eastern end of the Mediterranean where vast preparations were made to receive him on shore (Philo *Leg.* 250–53; e.g., at the palace of Polycrates on Samos, 21). The possibility of permanent removal to Alexandria created another parallel with Julius Caesar (*quin etiam varia fama percrebuit migraturum Alexandream vel Ilium,* Suet. *Jul.* 79.3) and with Antony and Germanicus as well (Jos. *AJ* 19.81; cf. Philo *Leg.* 338); also Nero (Suet. *Ner.* 47.2; Tac. *Ann.* 15.36.1).

interempto prius utriusque ordinis electissimo quoque: *Electissimus* = "choice, select," often of persons (cf. *pugilum ex utraque regione electissimorum,* 18.1), but not particularly associated with the upper classes as were *splendidissimus* (15.1) and *amplissimus* (49.1). He did not keep his promise to favor the *equites* (49.1) whom he attacked along with senators (Dio 59.25.5ᵇ–26.2; Jos. *AJ* 19.2). But see 53.2 for partiality toward them.

When someone survived an evil emperor and wanted to save his reputation as well as his neck, he could say that his name had been "on the list," that the emperor would have killed him if only he had lived a little longer. The idea is also expressed in the stories of persons who were allegedly summoned to Rome for execution but arrived to their good fortune after Gaius was dead (57.2, 3 and notes 107, 117; Barrett 1989, 237) and in the posthumous detachment from him of his wives' ex-husbands (25.1–2).

49.3 *quod ne cui dubium videatur:* "...and so that it not seem doubtful to anyone." Suetonius does not doubt that the lists of marked men (below) really did exist, but his insistence here and in reference to the poisons found with them (*sic* *certe* at 55.2) seems to indicate that others may have. Cf. the A.D. 14 mutiny (9) where he is similarly defensive about the central role of little Gaius. Was Tacitus skeptical about the lists? In the *Annales* he often focused on the sycophantic behavior of the senate, and this kind of hypocrisy seems the sort of thing that would have caught his attention (see note 9).

in secretis eius reperti sunt duo libelli: *Secreta* = "private affairs," here, "private papers." *Libellus* was standard for a written denunciation such as might warn an emperor of his own danger (15.4) or make other charges (30.2). The younger Pliny reports a very similar situation for himself after the death of Domitian when his own name was found in a denunciation discovered in the emperor's writing case (*nam in scrinio eius datus...de me libellus inventus est, Ep.* 7.27.14).

diverso titulo, alteri gladius, alteri pugio index erat; ambo nomina et notas continebant morti destinatorum: *Index* = title. *Notae* placed against names were marks of degradation (Suet. *Vit.* 8.1; Tac. *Hist.* 1.52.1), here marks for the punishment to come. The "sword" was plausibly for those who could be accused of *maiestas* and would be tried, convicted and executed by decapitation, the capital punishment of choice for the upper classes (on 32.2, 58.2; Jos. *AJ* 19.20; Sen. *Dial.* 5.18.4). The "dagger," on the other hand, was the weapon of suicide or assassination (12.3; Suet. *Cl.* 13.1), and the persons listed under *pugio* were logically those whom Gaius either chose to or had to get rid of privately or by imperial privilege.[97] The keeper of these books was Protogenes, the freedman of evil repute (28; Dio 59.26.1). Claudius killed him and destroyed the *libelli* (Dio 60.4.5).

inventa et arca ingens variorum venenorum plena, quibus mox a Claudio demersis infecta maria traduntur non sine piscium exitio, quos enectos aestus in proxima litora eiecit: Claudius disposed of this chest of poisons also. They were allegedly found in Gaius' dwelling on the Palatine (ἐν τοῦ Γαΐου, Dio 60.4.5). It seems that a tyrant was supposed to have such a horde (e.g., Nero, Suet. *Ner.* 47.3). The point is that Gaius' supply of poison was ample for a very, very long list of potential victims, a comment on his cruelty but also ironic notice of the large number who wanted to be known as his

---

97 A dagger was the emblem of proconsular power and the right of life and death over citizens; to take it was to assume *imperium* (*velut ius necis vitae civium,* Tac. *Hist.* 3.68.2; also Suet. *Vit.* 15.4). Galba travelled to Rome with one hanging around his neck (Suet. *Gal.* 11.1). Gaius dedicated three daggers (Dio 59.22.7) or swords (24.3) to the temple of Mars in token of his own escape from assassins. Which they were probably made a difference in the interpretation of the executions.

enemies once it became safe. With *traduntur* Suetonius puts some distance between himself and the fish story, although he accepts the lists themselves and the chest of poisons as fact (above and 55.2 for speculation on what Tacitus did with it). Orosius also writes about the fish, but for him they are a metaphor the large number of souls saved by the death of the *monstrum* Gaius (7.5.10). For Gaius and poison, note 11.

Suetonius interrupts Gaius' march to a violent end (*intraque quartum mensem periit,* 49.2) in order to generalize about his character and to describe some of its most outrageous manifestations. "Narration" will return at 56.1. Much of this material coincides closely with passages of Dio where it is assigned to the period between Gaius' return to Rome and his death.

He begins with Gaius' physical appearance which should not have been pleasing even though surviving statues suggest that he was the best-looking in his family (Couissin 249). It was generally assumed that a well-balanced mind could be found in a well-proportioned body and that facial expression, especially the look from the eyes, betrayed character. This could be analyzed even without reference to the more technical aspects of physiognomy, the popular art of reading character from physical traits. The pseudo-Artistotelian *Physiognomonica* circulated in Suetonius' day, and his own Περὶ βλασφημιῶν shows that he was familiar with this "science."[98] But if he was influenced by the physiognomical handbooks, so were others, since the portrait of Gaius was inherited (Sen. *Dial.* 2.18.1). Suetonius has a rubric about the physical appearance of each emperor (*Jul.* 45.1–2; *Aug.* 79–80; *Tib.* 68; *Cl.* 30; *Ner.* 51; *Gal.* 21.2; *Oth.* 12.1; *Vit.* 17.2; *Ves.* 20; *Tit.* 3.1; *Dom.* 18), but none is so particular as this.

50.1 *statura fuit eminenti:* Nymphidius (*PIR*² N. 250), praetorian praefect under Nero and Galba, claimed that he was Gaius' illegitimate son because he had inherited his stature (*habitu procerus,* Tac. *Ann.* 15.72.2). Plutarch shows that Nymphidius was wrong (*Gal.* 9).

colore expallido: **Expallidus** (only here) = very pale and probably unhealthy. Since one might grow pale from fear, pallor was a sign of cowardice (51; Evans 1935, 68). But Seneca calls it a symptom of madness: *tanta illi palloris insaniam testantis foeditas erat* (*Dial.* 2.18.1). Julius, Augustus and Tiberius had good color (Suet. *Jul.* 45.1; *Aug.* 79.2; *Tib.* 68.2).

---

[98] *Id verbum* [physiognomy] *significat, mores naturasque hominum coniectatione quadam de oris et vultus ingenio deque totius corporis filo atque habitu sciscitari* (Gell. 1.9.2). Suetonius' *De vitiis corporalibus* (*Rel.* Reiff. nos. 170–72, pp. 272–73) demonstrates an interest in details of physical description, and his Περὶ βλασφημιῶν (Περὶ δυσφήμων λέξεων ἤτοι βλασφημιῶν καὶ πόθεν ἑκάστη) was a compilation of pejorative terms, many related to body parts. For the idea that the portrait of Gaius was driven by physiognomy, Evans 1935, 43–84; 1969, 54–65 and Couissin 1953, 234–56. A practitioner of a similar skill, a *metoposcopus* ("brow-reader"), was summoned to see if Claudius' son Britannicus (T. Claudius Caesar Britannicus, *PIR*² C. 820) had the mark of an emperor upon him; his companion, the future emperor Titus (on 56.1) passed the test instead (Suet. *Tit.* 2; *metoposcopus* also at Pliny *HN* 35.88).

corpore enormi, gracilitate maxima cervicis et crurum: Good proportions were consonant with good character (Evans 1935, 63–64), and the leading
determinant of physiognomy. Augustus passed the test (*commoditate et aequitate
membrorum,* Suet. *Aug.* 79.2), but Gaius' skinny neck and legs did not fit his
body mass. Nero and Domitian had thin legs (Suet. *Ner.* 51; *Dom.* 18.1) and so
did Germanicus, the only defect of his otherwise fine form (3.1). Seneca confirms them for Gaius and adds disproportionately large feet (*exilitatem crurum et
enormitatem pedum, Dial.* 2.18.1).

oculis et temporibus concavis, fronte lata et torva: Eyes and brow were
the most telling features; *neque ulla ex parte maiora animi indicia cunctis
animalibus, sed homini maxime* (Pliny *HN* 11.145). Gaius' eyes were "staring"
(*Gaio principi rigentes,* Pliny *HN* 11.144) from beneath an old woman's
(evidently wrinkled) forehead (*tanta oculorum sub fronte anili latentium torvitas,*
Sen. *Dial.* 2.18.1). Nymphidius (above) claimed that he had inherited Gaius' grim
expression as well as his height (*torvo vultu erat,* Tac. *Ann.* 15.72.2).

capillo raro at circa verticem nullo: Baldness had been a token of ugliness
ever since Homer described Thersites (*Il.* 2.219), and Gaius was sensitive about
the fact that he was on his way (35.1). Cf. Seneca, *tanta capitis destituti et
†emendacitatis† capillis adspersi deformitas* (*Dial.* 2.18.1). Other balding emperors were Julius, Otho and Domitian (Suet. *Jul.* 45.2; *Oth.* 12.1; *Dom.* 18.1–2).
Gaius' semi-idealized statues show, however, a full head of hair (Brilliant 15–17).

hirsutus cetera: After the string of descriptive ablatives (above), the construction changes to a nominative modified by an accusative, a syntactical variation
that emphasizes the climax—Gaius looked like a goat. The hair that should have
been on his head was inappropriately abundant elsewhere. It was a physiognomical thesis that animal characteristics had correspondences among humans, and
goats were lecherous and insane (Evans 1935, 48–51, 64–68; Couissin 251).[99]
Seneca gives Gaius a hairy neck, skinny legs and big feet (above; *obsessam saetis
cervicem, Dial.* 2.18.1; *saetae* = animal hair specifically).

*quare transeunte eo prospicere ex superiore parte aut omnino
quacumque de causa capram nominare, criminosum et exitale
habebatur:* Gaius did not want anyone to look down on him and see his thinning
hair from above. The writer of an Atellan farce who was burned to death *ob*

---

99 Hairiness might connote any number of things: excessive sexuality, immodesty, cowardice,
changability and general malfeasance (Couissin 250). The problem with physiognomic analysis
was that one characteristic might denote many different and even opposite character traits. It was
not only an illegitimate science but an imprecise and contradictory one as well.

ambigui ioci versiculum (27.4) had in all likelihood called him a goat (Couissin 247–48); lecherous Tiberius had been called one from the stage: *in Atellanico exhodio...percrebruit, "hircum vetulum capreis naturam ligurire"* (Suet. *Tib.* 45; also *Tib.* 43.2). Which came first, the impression that Gaius looked like a goat or that he acted like one (Gascou 609)? See on 50.2 and note 100 for a connection between goats and epilepsy.

vultum vero natura horridum ac taetrum etiam ex industria efferebat componens ad speculum in omnem terrorem ac formidinem: The image of Gaius practicing his scowl in front of the mirror is rather engaging.

50.2 *valitudo ei neque corporis neque animi constitit*: His health, physical and mental.

Gaius' physical condition has been of special interest because of the problem posed by his personality. His serious illness in 37 (14.2) was not necessarily related to any underlying problem and is in any case beyond knowing; among the ancients only Philo thought that it precipitated his aberrations (*Leg.* 14). Most modern scholarship, insofar as it has looked for a medical cause for his behavior, has preferred a chronic condition. Suggestions are alcohol (Jerome, 420–21), hyperthyroidism (Katz 1972, 223–25; 1977, 451; refuted by Morgan 1973, 327–29; 1977, 452–53) or epilepsy, this last attested by Suetonius and so to be taken seriously.

puer comitiali morbo vexatus: Only Suetonius witnesses childhood epilepsy (*comitialis morbus*) for Gaius. It was traditionally the "sacred disease" because of its mysterious nature and awesome manifestation (Hippoc. Περὶ ἱερῆς νούσου), and the Latin name came from the fact that an attack during a meeting of the *comitia* indicated a divine message that postponed elections (Fest. p. 234 M). It is not likely that he suffered *grand mal* seizures (dramatic attacks) when he was emperor, for if he had, *morbus comitalis* would have found a larger place in his story. The ancients thought that it often disappeared with puberty (*puer;* Cel. 3.23.1). In spite of Suetonius' straightforward assertion, Gaius did not necessarily suffer from epilepsy during his childhood. The relatively common seizures brought on by high fever could have been mistaken or the diagnosis influenced by the tendency to draw Gaius into a parallel with Caesar (22.1, 46, 57.1–3, 60), who was supposed to have suffered from it (Suet. *Jul.* 45.1; Plut. *Caes.*17.2) as did Claudius' son Britannicus (*Ner.* 33.3). Another possible explanation is the belief that epilepsy was transmitted by goats and was a punishment for offending the goddess of the moon (Plut. *Quaest. Rom.* 290A; Hippoc. Περὶ ἱερῆς νούσου 2;

Temkin 11). Since Gaius was a goat (50.1) who consorted with the moon (22.4), the diagnosis might follow.[100]

in adulescentia ita patiens laborum erat, ut tamen nonnumquam subita defectione ingredi, stare, colligere semet ac sufferre vix posset: "In his youth he possessed endurance except that sometimes he could scarcely walk, stand, collect his thoughts or support his weight." These could be fainting spells of any sort, but the inability to collect his thoughts and to control himself (*colligere semet ac sufferre vix posset*) does fit the transient seizures caused by temporal lobe epilepsy, which (unlike *petit mal* attacks) leave the subject confused for a period of time directly afterwards. Temporal lobe epilepsy is also a culprit because of the high incidence of associated behavioral disturbance.[101] But as with childhood epilepsy (above), it is impossible to say with what accuracy the details of the description of these episodes (found only here) are valid for Gaius.

Although the ancient lay judgment that Gaius was a madman cannot be transformed into a modern psychiatric disorder (not for lack of trying),[102] it must be taken seriously for what it is, an indication that Gaius impressed his contemporaries as behaving in a fashion that lay outside of expected or acceptable norms. Many of his affects can indeed be found among diagnostic criteria for modern categories of disease, both clinical syndromes and severe personality disorders.[103] Although

---

100 Benediktson has argued moon-goat-epilepsy in the opposite direction: Gaius was sensitive about being thought a goat (50.1) because he was defensive about his disease, and he courted the moon (22.4) in an attempt to ward off her anger (1992, 162–63). But Gaius probably did not as an adult suffer conspicuous attacks that he felt he had to treat. For the history of speculation about Gaius' epilepsy (Benediktson 1989, 370 n. 3, 371 n. 5).

101 Sharbrough 282–86; Sherwin et al. 621. Temporal lobe epilepsy, so called because it involves a single part of the brain instead of the whole, has been suggested by Benediktson (1989). The psychotic symptons most commonly reported are changed patterns of agression, changes in sexual behavior (usually hyposexuality), inability to maintain social relationships, hypergraphia and preoccupation with religion, but many other psychotic affects may also be present (Lyketsos et al. 19–21).

102 The first psychoanalysis put forth in a burst of Freudian enthusiam the idea that an egoless young Gaius had assumed the ego of his "father" Tiberius (Sachs 1931). Other explanations are schizophrenia secondary to epilepsy (Esser 1958, 133–39), psychopathy (Lucus 1967), childhood experiences contributing to an anxiety condition or mania (Massaro and Montgomery 1978). For physical problems as possible contributors, see on epilepsy (above) and notes 16 and 101.

103 He fits the configurations for mania or a narcissistic personality reasonably well. Symptoms of mania include hyperactivity and expansiveness (16.4, 18.2, 19?), speech that is loud and filled with jokes and word play (29–31), inflated self-esteem (22 and passim) and a decreased need for sleep (below). A manic's mood is usually elevated, but he can be irritable instead, especially when thwarted (30.2–3, 35.2–3, 48.2; *DSM-III-R* 214–18). If Gaius suffered from bipolor disorder as is often the case with manics, a corresponding depression would not have been attracted the same kind of attention. But see his threat to retreat (below). Mania has been suggested by Massaro and Montgomery (1978, 907–9; also Moss 166). Symptoms of a narcissistic personality disorder include grandiosity (19, 46), exaggerated reactions to criticism (35.3, 48.2) and envy (34–35; *DSM-III-R* 349–51).

madness was convenient for Claudius when he wanted to put space between himself and his predecessor (Jos. *AJ* 19.284–85), the portrait of Gaius is too particular and pervasive to have been simply invented. His personality was a serious handicap.

mentis valitudinem: Only Suetonius uses this phrase. Other choices: Josephus, μάνια (*AJ* 19.1, 5, 39, 50, 193), τὸ μανικόν (19.11), παραφροσύνη (19.284, 285); Seneca, *furiosa inconstantia* (*Dial.* 11.17.5), *dementia* (*Dial.* 3.20.9; *Dial.* 9.14.5); Tacitus, *turbata mens* (*Ann.* 13.3.2), *turbidus animi* (*Hist.* 4.48.1), *ingenium mobile* (*Agr.* 13.2). Gaius' capriciousness: οὕτω γὰρ καὶ πρὸς πάντα ἐναντίος ἐπεφύκει ὥστε... (Dio 59.4.1); οὕτω που ἔμπληκτος ἦν... (Dio 59.23.4); ἡ...ἀνωμαλία πρὸς ἅπαντας (Philo *Leg.* 346). *Constantia* was a coin legend for Claudius, plausibly to separate himself from this central feature of the characterization of Gaius (Ramage 204–5).

et ipse senserat ac subinde de secessu deque purgando cerebro cognitavit: If this is true, Gaius was aware of his own problems. Depression may be described. Cf. his not knowing how to react to his sister's death, alternately playing dice and going into deep mourning (24.2; Sen. *Dial.*11.17.4–5).

creditur potionatus a Caesonia uxore amatorio quidem medicamento, sed quod in fororem verterit: Caesonia's love potion is significant for two reasons. First, it explained why Gaius quite amazingly stayed with this wife when he had not stayed with the previous ones (25.3, 33). Magic was thought to blame whenever a man showed extraordinary devotion (as Antony to Cleopatra, Dio 49.34.1; Plut. *Ant.* 37, 60). Secondly, the misfiring of the *amatorium medicamentum* rationalized her death. Some of the conspirators thought it cruel to kill her subsequent to the assassination of her husband (59), but others blamed her for Rome's suffering because she had given him the potion that made him mad (Jos. *AJ* 19.193) and set the world on fire: *avunculus ille Neronis, / cui totam tremuli frontem Caesonia pulli / infundit. quae non faciet quod principis uxor? / ardebant cuncta et fracta conpage ruebant* (Juv. 6.615–18; cf. 11 for Gaius the firebrand).[104] For other men made mad by female ministrations, see Tac. *Ann.* 4.22.3, 12.66.1; Ov. *Ars Am.* 2.106; Plut. *Luc.* 43; Pliny *HN* 25.25.

---

[104] Caesonia's choice was *hippomanes*, a distillation of a growth from the forehead of a new-born colt. It was meant to transfer to its recipient the amatory madness (ἵππου μανία) of a female horse (*cum tibi flagrans amor et libido, / quae solet matres furiare equorum,* Hor. *Carm.* 1.25.13–14; also Pliny *HN* 8.165; Verg. *Aen.* 4.515–16). *Totam frontem...pulli* implies an overdose (Courtney on Juv. 6.616). The love potion was related to the story that Gaius showed Caesonia naked to his friends (25.3): *quem adeo medicatis potionibus uxor Caesonia in amorem suum deduxit, ut de nimia inpotentia furens saepe eam nudam amicis ostenderet* (*Schol. Juv.* at 6.615).

50.3 *incitabatur insomnio maxime; neque enim plus quam tribus nocturnis horis quiescebat:* Manics do not sleep much, but this is not a necessary explanation since Gaius had perfectly good reasons to rest uneasily. And see below for the constellation of anxiety, nightmares and sleeplessness. For Gaius using these periods of wakefulness productively, see 53.2. *Insomnia* (*apparatus*) is probably correct since *insomnium* means sleeplessness only in the plural.

ac ne iis quidem placida quiete, sed pavida miris rerum imaginibus, ut qui inter ceteras pelagi quondam speciem conloquentem secum videre visus sit: Who could know the contents of his dreams unless he told? *Inter ceteras,* i.e., among the *mirae imagines* of his dreams. This conversation is suspiciously like his conversation with Jupiter and his intimacy with the moon (22.4). A special relationship with the sea is implied in the *spolia* of pearls for his non-triumph (46) and with the challenge to Neptune at Baiae (on 19.3; Dio 59.17.4, 11; 59.26.6; Jos *AJ* 19.6). Nightmares were associated with madness, a guilty conscience, and premonitions of disaster (Verg. *Aen.* 4.465–73; Sen. *Ep.* 56.6; Sen. *Controv.* 7.7.15), and like sleeplessness, they were consistent with a general nervous condition (*exercent rabidam truculenta insomnia mentem,* Sil. 10.357; *furibunda insomnia,* 11.102; Massaro and Montgomery 1979, 700).

ideoque magna parte noctis vigiliae cubandique taedio nunc toro residens, nunc per longissimas porticus vagus: "The image of the tormented prince wandering down the enomous porticoes is not easily forgotten" (Lounsbury 105). Long porticoes are appropriate for elegant buildings like those on the Palatine but are also reminiscent of a Vergilian image of wandering alone and in pain: *Polites / ...porticibus longis fugit et vacua atria lustrat / saucius* (*Aen.* 2.526–29).[105] Tacitus describes the emperor Vitellius' isolation at the end in somewhat similar terms: *in Palatium regreditur vastum desertumque...terret solitudo et tacentes loci; temptat claustra, inhorrescit vacuis* (*Hist.* 3.84.4).

invocare identidem atque expectare lucem consuerat: Perhaps another reference to his devotion to Isis as he summons forth the light of the sun (Ceausescu 277).

Suetonius apparently credits himself (*attribuerim,* 51.1) with recognizing the relationship beween Gaius' contradictory behavior and his mental state and chooses to illustrate one aspect, his arrogant boasting that was a sham in the face of his actual cowardice. Note *glorior* and *gloriosus* at 8.2,

---

[105] Long and lonely wanderings and empty porticoes were a kind of nightmare image for Vergil: *porticibus vacuis* (*Aen.* 2.761; also 12.476), and [Dido] *semper longam incomitata videtur / ire viam* (*Aen.* 4.467–68).

12.3, 29.2, 41.2, and *contemneret, irrisis* (51.1) and *minicissimus* (52.2). Nothing in this chapter has a parallel in Dio.

51.1 *non inmerito mentis valitudini attribuerim diversissima in eodem vitia, summam confidentiam et contra nimium metum:* *Mentis valitudini* is picked up from 50.2. *Attribuerim:* cf. *credo* at 51.3. The first person also at 8.2, 19.3.

nam qui deos tanto opere contemneret: He may have blasphemed by boasting that he was the equal of the traditional Roman gods (22.2–4, 33), but proprieties were always observed as the records of the Arval Brethren show (*Docs.* nos. 1–11, pp. 9–14; Scheid and Broise 217–25).

ad minima tonitrua et fulgura conivere, caput obvoluere, at vero maiore proripere se e strato sub lectumque condere solebat: Gaius' challenge to Jupiter the Thunderer (22.4) is contrasted with his groveling fear of him. Pertinent are his thunder machine on the Palatine (Dio 59.28.6) and the thunderstorms that interrupted his parties (Sen. *Dial.* 3.20.8). But fear of lightning and thunder was not unusual in a pre-scientific age. Augustus hid underground, and Tiberius wore a laurel wreath to protect himself (Suet. *Aug.* 90; *Tib.* 69).

peregrinatione quidem Siciliensi: This trip took place between the death of Drusilla on June 10 and the ceremony for her deification on September 23 in A.D. 38 (24.2); it included games at Syracuse (20, 21).

irrisis multum locorum miraculis: Sicily offered mythological riches for the traveller; *multa habeat Sicilia in se circaque se mirabilia* (Sen. *QNat.* 4A.1.1, also *Ep.* 79.1). An ancient Baedeker would have directed the sightseer to the meadow from which Proserpina had been abducted and to Arethusa now become the Alpheus. Scylla and Charybdis were offshore and Etna provided range for the imagination (below, Verg. *Aen.* 3.570–77). Strabo (6.2.4), like Gaius (*irrisis... miraculis*), was skeptical of the island's wonders.

repente a Messana noctu profugit: Messina (Messana) remains the Sicilian end of the crossing between mainland and island. Gaius planned harbor works for the strait (Jos. *AJ* 19.205).

Aetnaei verticis fumo ac murmure pavefactus: Not surprisingly, volcanic eruptions inspired the ancients to fanciful explanations, as when Vesuvius loosed giants to stalk the earth in A.D. 79 (Dio 66.21–23). Seneca, on the other hand, was capable of objective observation (*Ep.* 79.2–3).

51.2 *adversus barbaros quoque minacissimus, cum trans Rhenum inter angustias densumque agmen iter essedo faceret:* A third example of failed bravado. For corroboration for a brief trip across the Rhine, see 45.1; also, ὀλίγον ὑπὲρ τοῦ Ῥήνου προχωρήσας ὑπέστρεψε (Dio 59.21.3) and *ingressus Suebiam, nihil strenue fecit* (Eutrop. 12.7). The *essedum,* originally a Gallic war chariot and a vehicle that an emperor might use for military exercises (19.2; Suet. *Gal.* 6.3), was also generic for a light carriage, one in which he could travel comfortably (Suet. *Aug.* 76.1; *Cl.* 33.2; cf. 35.3 for an *essedarius*). *Angustiae,* normally plural for a pass or defile, is a tight place (cf. 34.1). *Barbaros:* cf. the German *nomina barbarica* (47).

dicente quodam non mediocrem fore consternationem sicunde hostis appareat: The enemy was not expected. Gaius participated only in safe battles (on 45.1–2).

equum ilico conscendit ac propere <re>versus ad pontes: A horse was faster and more mobile. The singular and plural of *pons* were apparently interchangeable (Tac. *Ann.* 2.8.2, 13.7.1; Goodyear 1972–1981 at *Ann.* 2.8.2; note Cic. *Fam.* 10.18.4 vs. 10.23.3 for the same bridge denoted by both numbers), or the plural may mean that it was a bridge of several spans. See on 45.1 for the possibility of a bridge at Mogontiacum.

ut eos calonibus et impedimentis stipatos repperit, impatiens morae per manus ac super capita hominum translatus est: The bridge was clogged with the ubiquitous camp followers and baggage. A service settlement existed at Mogontiacum by the middle of the first century (von Petrikovits 28), but tradespeople were never absent from an army. Gaius had made a similarly undignified retreat from the games, tripping over his toga as he went (35.3; also see 48.2). Note that he is impatient once again (on 37.3).

51.3 *mox:* The transitional adverb makes a purely mechanical connection. There is no temporal and little logical connection between the incursion into Germany (above) with the threat from Germany that prodded Gaius to escape abroad (8.5, 49.2).

etiam audita rebellione Germaniae fugam et subsidia fugae classes apparabat uno, solacio adquiescens transmarinas certe sibi superfuturas provincias: Cowardice alone is now the theme. New or continued fighting on the frontier is attested by the fact that Galba subdued the Chatti in 41 (Dio 60.8.7), but action in Germany had no connection with the well-prepared trip that had already been anticipated in the previous summer (Philo *Leg.* 185,

250, 338; Jos. *AJ* 19.81). The threat to take the center of government East and leave the difficult senate behind was always possible. Even Tiberius had a fleet ready for an escape from Capreae in case his confrontation with Sejanus did not end successfully (Suet. *Tib.* 65.2), and Julius Caesar and Nero contemplated flight to Egypt (Suet. *Jul.* 79.3, *Ner.* 47.2; Dio 63.27.2b; Plut. *Gal.* 2.1; see 49.2).

si victores Alpium iuga, ut Cimbri, vel etiam urbem, ut Senones quondam, occuparent: The enemies of the moment were not the Cimbri and Senones but the Chatti on the southern portion of the Rhine frontier and the Chauci and the Canninefates on the northern (Dio 60.8.7; Tac. *Hist.* 4.15.2). The Cimbri had penetrated beyond the Alps near the end of the second century B.C. before Marius stopped them, and the memory of their prowess was kept alive. Tacitus describes them as *parva nunc civitas sed gloria ingens* (*Germ.* 37.1); their remnant lived near the North Sea (Pliny *HN* 4.96). The Senones were the Gauls who were held responsible for the sacking of Rome in 390 B.C. (Livy 5.35.3; Gell. 17.21); they like the Cimbri were prototypical invaders (Pliny *HN* 3.116; Stat. *Silv.*1.624; Juv. 8.234). Together they were a cliché: *nos primi Senonum motus Cimbrumque ruentem / vidimus* (Luc. 1.254–55).

unde credo: Cf. *attribuerim* (51.1). The first person singular also in reference to Gaius's birthplace (8.2), and in the rationale for the Baiae bridge (19.3).

percussoribus eius postea consilium natum apud tumultuantes milites ementiendi, ipsum sibi manus intulisse nuntio malae pugnae perterritum: This ploy of Gaius' assassins to take blame from themselves is found only here. *Percussores* = Gaius' assassins. The *tumultuantes milites* were the German body guards who rallied to his corpse (58.3; οἱ δὲ στρατιῶται... ἐθορύβουν τε καὶ ἐστασίαζον, Dio 59.30.1b; also Jos. *AJ* 19.119–26).

A rubric of clothing that includes Gaius dressing like gods. What he wore was inappropriate for an adult Roman male and thus "unnatural" (see 37). He was changable in this as in all else, alternately masculine and feminine, human and divine, domestic and military. There seems to have been particular interest in his shoes, almost certainly because of his childhood nickname "Little Boots" (9).

52 *vestitu calciatuque et cetero habitu neque patrio neque civili ac ne virili quidem ac denique humano semper usus est:* A topic sentence that includes all the categories that will follow. *Calciatus* (*calceatus*), footwear, is often found paired with *vestitus,* clothing (e.g., Gell. 13.22; Apul. *Flor.* 8. [28]). In contrast to *vestitus patrius* and *civilis* (i.e., Roman dress, the toga, a mark of alliance with the senate), Gaius' public attire was Eastern, regal and effeminate (below), the sort of apparel in which invective traditionally clothed political enemies (Cic. *Verr.* 3.5.31, *Cat.* 2.22; Weinstock 1971, 324–25). Transvestitism (*ne virili quidem*) was "contrary to nature" (on 37; *non videntur tibi contra naturam vivere qui commutant cum feminis vestem?* Sen. *Ep.* 122.7) and had been anticipated in the youthful Gaius (*capillamento celatus et veste longa... obiret,* 11). For Julius Caesar's clothing, Suet. *Jul.* 45.3.

saepe depictas gemmatasque indutus paenulas, manuleatus et armillatus in publicum processit; aliquando sericatus et cycladatus: He often appeared in public (*in publicum processit*) in triumphal dress during his final months (Dio 59.26.10). The *paenula* was a sleeveless cloak worn against bad weather by both men and women, normally dark and heavy, but occasional examples might be elegant (Mart. 2.57.4, 5.26.1, 14.145; Kolb 73–116). The embroidery and precious stones belonged on the *chlamys* with which it is conflated (19.2; Dio 59.17.3; Val. Fl. 6.226). Sleeves (*manuleatus* = wearing a sleeved garment) were effeminate (Sen. *Ep.* 33.2; Cic. *Rab. Post.* 26; *Cat.* 2.22; Gell. 6.12; for Julius Caesar, Suet. *Jul.* 45.3), and bracelets (*armillatus* = wearing bracelets) were for women (Pliny *HN* 12.88) or foreigners (Suet. *Ner.* 30.3). Silk (*sericatus* = wearing silk, only here), the epitome of luxury, was also feminine and foreign (Dio 59.26.10; Tac. *Ann.* 2.33.1). Seneca describes Gaius as *perlucidus* (transparent, i.e., wearing light garments, *Dial.* 2.18.3), silk's primary association (Sen. *Ep.* 114.21; Pliny *HN* 11.78; Juv. 2.78). A *cyclas* (*cycladatus* = wearing a *cyclas*, also only here; ἡ κυκλάς [ἐσθής] or ἔγκυκλον) was a lightweight circular garment with a decorated border (described by Servius at *Aen.* 1.647; also Prop. 4.7.40; Juv. 6.259–60), again for a women.

ac modo in crepidis vel coturnis, modo in speculatoria caliga, nonnumquam socco muliebri: Footwear: *Crepidae* (κρηπῖδες) were sandals, Greek slippers, not for Roman business (Cic. *Rab. Post.* 27; Gell. 13.22.6–8; *crepidatus,* Sen. *Dial.* 2.18.3). When Tiberius put them on, they symbolized his retirement to Rhodes (*redegitque se seposito patro habitu ad pallium et crepidas,* Suet. *Tib.* 13.1). *Socci* were also Greek slippers worn by comic actors and women (Pliny *HN* 37.17). *Coturni* (κόθορνοι), on the other hand, were the tragic actor's high boots, another reference to Gaius' interest in the stage and as- sociation with actors (11, 33, 54, 55.1). *Caligae* (on 9) were synonymous with military service itself (Sen. *Ben.* 5.16.2). They were worn by the *speculatores,* the praetorians who were special agents and executioners (44.2; see on 30.2 and 32.3 for Gaius as an executioner).[106]

---

[106] A story circulated that separated Gaius from the general's role that he acted so badly (43– 48): He objected to being called Caligula after he had changed his soldier's boots (*caligae*) for "actor's buskins" (*Caligulam convicium et probrum iudicabat coturnatus,* Sen. *Dial.* 2.18.4). The

plerumque vero aurea barba: He alternated between being clean-shaven and bearded (Dio 59.26.7), and he wore wigs (11; Dio 59.26.8; Jos. *AJ* 19.30). For his beard when he mourned his sister, 24.2.

fulmen tenens aut fuscinam aut caduceum deorum insignia: On what occasions did he dress up like this? Probably in private, although Dio puts him on a pedestal dressed as Jupiter giving oracles (59.26.8). He allegedly invented religious rites that included costumes (Jos. *AJ* 19.30). But dressing up had precedent: In addition to triumphant generals who properly dressed as Jupiter, Antony played Dionysius (Dio 48.39.2; Vell. 2.82.4; Plut. *Ant.* 24.3) and accused Augustus of presiding as Apollo over eleven guests at his banquet of "the twelve gods" (Suet. *Aug.* 70.1–2; Scott 1929, 140; Charlesworth 1933a, 172, 175). Gaius, as often, may not have understood the acceptable limits of this sort of thing. He imitated Jupiter with the thunderbolt (*fulmen,* 22.4; Dio 59.26.7), Neptune with the trident (*fuscinam,* Dio 59.26.7; see on 19, 46 and 50.3 for his special relationship with the sea god) and Mercury with the caduceus (*caduceum*). Philo says that he first imitated Dionysus, Hercules and the Dioscuri (*Leg.* 78–92) and then Hermes, Apollo and Ares (*Leg.* 93–110) and digresses at length on how far short he fell in comparison with each. Dio is inclusive, listing Jupiter, Neptune, and Apollo, as well as Hercules and Dionysus and then "all the rest" (τούς τε ἄλλους, 59.26.5–6). Divine props and clothing were appropriate for statues of emperors but not for living persons (Price 183–84).

atque etiam Veneris cultu conspectus est: Female impersonation is noted separately; cf. Jos. *AJ* 19.30. Dio writes that he imitated Juno, Diana and Venus (59.26.6).

triumphalem quidem ornatum etiam ante expeditionem assidue gestavit, interdum et Magni Alexandri thoracem repetitum e conditorio eius: The expedition (*ante expeditionem*) was the one to the northern frontier (43) which began at some point after the bridge affair at Baiae (19.3,

---

joke was that when he wanted to be taken seriously it was as an actor but not the serious sort that he aspired to be; his critics thought the *soccus* more appropriate. Another footwear joke makes the same point about the failed soldier turned soft: Gaius insults a senator by making him kiss his foot (Dio 59.29.5 for foot kissing) so that he can show off an elaborate shoe: *aiunt socculum auratum, immo aureum, margaritis distinctum ostendere eum voluisse...parum enim foede furioseque insolens fuerat qui de capite consularis viri soccatus audiebat, nisi in os senatoris ingessisset imperator epigros suos!* (Sen. *Ben.* 2.12.1–2). Real *caligae* were studded with nails (Pliny *HN* 9.69; Jos *BJ* 6.85), but the hobnails (*epigri*) on Gaius' *caligae* have become pearl studs on his soft shoes (*socculum*). His shoes are again important when they become emblematic of his attitude when he supervises executions during his leisure hours (32–33): *quantulum fuit lucem expectare denique, ne senatores populi Romani soleatus* [wearing sandals] *occideret!* (Sen. *Dial.* 5.18.4).

note 39). Augustus had Alexander's sarcophagus (*conditorium*) brought out from its shrine at Alexandria so that he could revere it but did not remove anything (Suet. *Aug*.18.1; Strab. 17.1.8). Gaius was more arrogant and wore the breastplate when he paraded across the bridge—or so he said (ὥς γε ἔλεγε, Dio 59.17.3; on 19.2). Since he never got to Egypt, doubt is justified. Metaphorically, to view the icon was to think of turning East; to wear it was to take action (on 23.1).

The rubric of Gaius' education, especially in rhetoric. Even from the most strenuous of his detractors there is praise for his speaking ability, and his instability did not interfere with it: *etiam G. Caesaris turbata mens vim dicendi non corrupit* (Tac. *Ann*. 13.3.4). See note 103 for verbal dexterity associated with mania. For his delivering Livia's funeral oration, 10.1; for the rhetorical contests he sponsored at Lugdunum, 20.

53.1 *ex disciplinis liberalibus minimum eruditioni:* Gaius was not well educated in the traditional areas of mathematics, music, literature, law and rhetoric (for the subjects, Cic. *de Or*. 3.127; Levick 1990, 17) in contrast not only with Germanicus (3.1) but also with Tiberius (Suet. *Tib*. 11.3) and Claudius (Suet. *Cl*. 3.1; Tac. *Ann*. 6.46.1; Dio 60.2.1; Jos. *AJ* 19.164). Josephus disagrees, claiming that Gaius competed with Tiberius in erudition although it did him no good (*AJ* 18.207, 19.209–10). The idea was that the *disciplinae liberales* contributed to virtue (Sen. *Ep*. 88.23; Cic. *Ac*. 2.1); consonance between education and character was expected just as with physical appearance and character (50.1).

eloquentiae plurimum attendit: Gaius shared with his father a talent for oratory (and skinny legs). Germanicus was *ingenium in utroque eloquentiae doctrinaeque genere praecellens* (3.1), and Gaius too was proficient in both Latin and Greek (Jos. *AJ* 19.208; Tac. *Ann*. 13.3.4; Dio 59.19.3–8; for his Greek, see 22.1 and 4, 29.1, 47). Augustus (Dio 45.2.7–8), Claudius (Suet. *Cl*. 44.1, 3) and especially Tiberius (*Tib*. 56, 70) also knew both languages well.

quantumvis facundus et promptus, utique si perorandum in aliquem esset: Perorandum = "complete an argument" (cf. *peroraturus,* 53.2), and so for Gaius, have the final word, make the clever retort. He could reply spontaneously to the well-prepared speeches of others (Jos. *AJ* 19.208). The Jewish embassy from Alexandria was stung by his flip responses (Philo *Leg*. 361–62). The quick tongue merits its own rubric (29–31; also Dio 59.8.5, 8.8, 13.6, 28.6, 29.2).

irato et verba et sententiae suppetebant, pronuntiatio quoque et vox, ut neque eodem loci prae ardore consisteret et exaudiretur a procul stantibus: Gaius was an agitated speaker. Many of his *sententiae* are introduced by verbs of exclaiming, threatening and shouting (22.1), and the loud clear voice is attested elsewhere: *maxima voce* (49.1); *voce clarissima* (Sen. *Dial*. 2.18.2).

53.2 *peroraturus stricturum se lucubrationis suae telum minabatur:*
Cf. *perorandum*, 53.1. His sleepless nights (*lucubrationes*, 50.3) were productive
if he used them to prepare speeches. But a double-entendre beneath the nocturnal
exertions and the drawn weapon should be considered (cf. *capulum gladii crebro
verberans*, 49.1; Adams 156–57 for sexual exercise as work).

lenius comptiusque scribendi genus adeo contemnens: When applied to
rhetoric *lenis* means gentle and flowing (Cic. *Off.* 1.134, *de Or.* 183; Sen.
Controv. 7.4.8), and *comptus* means carefully worked, smoothly polished (Quint.
Inst. 10.1.79; Tac. *Hist.* 1.19.1). The contrast is with the sharp attack (*telum*) of
Gaius' own speech.

ut Senecam tum maxime placentem: Since Suetonius is ambiguous in his use
of the simple undesignated "Seneca" (*Tib.* 73.2; Grisart 304–8), it is possible that
this is Seneca the Elder, "the orator" (L. Annaeus Seneca, *PIR*² A. 616), the father of the better known Seneca the Younger, "the philosopher" (L. Annaeus
Seneca, *PIR*² A. 617). In favor of Seneca the Elder is the fact that during Gaius'
reign he was more renowned (*tum maxime placentem*) than his son, who was
only beginning his senatorial and literary careers; Seneca the Younger's first
known writing is plausibly dated to 39 or 40 (*Consolatio ad Marciam = Dial.* 6;
Griffin 396–97). But the rivalry between him and Gaius was an important motif
in the tradition, and so this Seneca is probably he. Gaius was so jealous that he
almost had him executed (Dio 59.19.7–8).[107]

commissiones meras componere...diceret: *Commissiones* = contests, but
here the stuff of the contests, exercises, mere show pieces (Suet. *Aug.* 89.3; Pliny
Pan. 54), a characterization which describes the work of the elder Seneca. But
like *lenis* and *comptus* (above), *commissiones* should be read more in contrast
with Gaius' own wit and ability to speak spontaneously than as a detailed comment on either Seneca.

---

[107] Seneca was saved through the intervention of a woman who said that he would soon die of
consumption in any case (Dio 59.19.7–8). This "near escape" is another of the excuses for how a
member of Gaius' team survived him to become a major player in later court politics (Balsdon
1934a, 56; Griffin 54–55; Barrett 1989, 112). It is an explanation for the hostility between them at
least as plausible as speculations about Seneca's role in the "conspiracy of Gaetulicus and
Lentulus" and his residual loyalties to the "party of Sejanus" (Stewart 70–85; Clarke 1965, 62–
69). Seneca was exiled by Claudius for adultery with Julia Livilla, Gaius' youngest sister (Dio
60.8.5), and recalled to be Nero's tutor through the intervention of the other surviving sister
Agrippina, now Claudius' wife (Tac. *Ann.* 12.8.3; Dio 61.32.3). For other survivors, see on 25.1
and 2, 49.3, 57.2 and 3 and note 117.

et harenam esse sine calce: "Sand without lime," from the construction trade. *Harena et calx* or *calx harenatus* were the usual expressions for mortar, mixed three parts sand to one part lime (Vitr. 2.5.1; Cato *Agr.* 18.7). The formula seems to have been common knowledge and so available as a metaphor (Vell. 2.22.4). Badly compounded mortar might describe the somewhat disjointed nature of the younger Seneca's writing accurately, but once again, the real point is Gaius' preference for his own more vigorous oratory (above).[108]

solebat etiam prosperis oratorum actionibus rescribere et magnorum in senatu reorum accusationes defensionesque meditari ac, prout stilus cessarat, vel onerare sententia sua quemque vel sublevare: Always unpredictable, he wrote (and delivered, *ad audiendum,* below) speeches in favor of whichever side seemed the more convenient at the moment (*prout stilus cessarat*) and wrote rebuttals (*rescripta*) to speeches which favored positions he himself took (*actiones prosperae*). The senatorial court met at the senate's regular meetings (*in senatu*). It came into being with the Empire and dealt largely with cases that concerned its own members and with those that affected the princeps and his family (i.e., *maiestas* cases); it followed the prejudices of the emperor in its decisions (Talbert 460–74). Claudius was one such *magnus reus.* He was charged with being a signatory of a forged will (Suet. *Cl.* 9.2). Less likely is the story that he was accused by his own slave on a capital charge; Gaius was supposedly disappointed by his acquittal (Jos. *AJ* 19.13).

equestri quoque ordine ad audiendum invitato per edicta: He deliberately set the equestrian order against the senate by inviting them to watch him perform in the senatorial court (above). Favor to the *equites: edixit et reverti se...equestri ordini et populo,* 49.1.

Gaius' four unacceptable amusements are first listed and then developed in this well-constructed rubric. The occupations match the persons with whom he supposedly spent his time and took as his advisors—gladiators, chariot drivers and actors (33, 55.1; Dio 59.5.2, 4–5).

---

[108] The construction of this sentence is difficult since the subject of the second half of the compound indirect statement is unclear. It might be read: "Gaius said that Seneca, who enjoyed a fine reputation at that time, composed mere school exercises and that his sand was without lime" with *harenam* as the subject accusative of the second indirect statement; or again, "Gaius said that Seneca...composed mere exercises and that [he/his eloquence, ability, etc.] was sand without lime." A possible confusion of or pun on *commissiones* (above) and *commissurae* (joints, splices between parts as in a structure) would continue the building metaphor across both statements and make the reading somewhat more satisfactory: "Gaius said that Seneca wrote mere exercises / disjointed pieces and that his sand [for the connecting mortar] was without lime" (Stroux 349–55; *contra,* Braun 229–32).

54.1 *sed et aliorum generum artes studiosissime et diversissimas exercuit. Thra<e>x et auriga, idem cantor atque saltator:* Cf. 52 for another careful topic sentence. The four entertainments, gladiatorial combat, chariot driving, singing and dancing, had either very masculine or very effeminate associations (*diversissimas*). He began by observing them (Dio 59.5.2), and ended by participating (Dio 59.5.4–5), but probably in private. See on 18.3, 32.2.

battuebat pugnatoriis armis: This evidently refers to the time when he played the *Thraex* in an exhibition match and killed the opponent who had obligingly fallen before him (32.2). *Battuere* is the verb in both instances.

aurigabat extructo plurifariam circo: Plurifariam, "in many places," suggests that he blocked out more than one track for racing. With great effort Gaius brought from Egypt the obelisk that now stands in front of St. Peter's, not far from its original position at the center of a race course that he established in the Gardens of Agrippina, across the Tiber from the city proper (Suet. *Cl.* 20.3; Pliny *HN* 16.201–2; *CIL* 6.882). The area had apparently begun as one of his private courses (18.3; Dio 59.14.6), but under Claudius and then Nero it became a public site and a monumental stone circus called the Circus Vaticanus (Suet. *Cl.* 21.2; *Ner.* 22.2; Tac. *Ann.* 14.14.2, 15.44.5; J. H. Humphrey 550–51). Suetonius does not mention it among his building projects (21), but Pliny calls it the "Vatican Circus of Gaius and Nero" (*tertius* [obelisk] *est Romae in Vaticano Gai et Neronis principum circo... HN* 36.74). A practice place called the Gaianum (Dio 59.14.6) seems to have been a different site.

canendi ac saltandi voluptate ita efferebatur, ut ne publicis quidem spectaculis temperaret quo minus et tragoedo pronuntianti concineret et gestum histrionis quasi laudans vel corrigens palam effingeret: Gaius' interest in performance had been anticipated in his youth: *scaenicas saltandi canendique artes studiosissime appeteret* (11). Gesturing was an important part of pantomime (Beare 139, 173), and it was a short distance from prompting the performers (*histriones*) to climbing onto the stage (54.2). He watched "with mad enthusiasm" (ἐκμανῶς, Philo *Leg.* 42). *Cantor* and *saltator* are often paired as terms of abuse (Tac. *Dial.* 26.3; Ov. *Ars Am.* 1.595, *Rem. Am.* 333–34; Cic. *Cat.* 2.23).

54.2 *nec alia de causa videtur eo die, quo periit, pervigilium indixisse quam ut initium in scaenam prodeundi licentia temporis auspicaretur:* This stage debut was another of the things that Gaius did not bring off (see 34.2 and 48.1 for "intentions"). But his plan is nonetheless credited with precipitating his assassination; his desire to extend the *ludi Palatini* (56.2) in order to provide himself with the occasion of taking the final step to the stage it-self proved the last straw for his assassins (Dio 59.29.6; Jos. *AJ* 19.77). A ritual of some sort was planned for the night of the day he was killed, quite probably the celebration of Isiac mysteries (57.4; Jos. *AJ* 19.104). *Pervigilium* = an all night religious festival but with overtones of debauchery; other *pervigilia:* Suet. *Vit.* 10.3; *Gal.* 4.3. For the "day on which he died," see 58.1 and note 120.

saltabat autem nonnumquam etiam noctu; et quondam tres consulares secunda vigilia in Palatium accitos multaque et extrema metuentis super pulpitum conlocavit: Despite *nonnumquam* only one example is given. This too was plausibly Isiac ritual (Wiseman 1991, 30 on Jos. *AJ* 19.30; Köberlein 33, n. 9), and the details of the consulars and the second watch (around midnight) lend credibility. For Nero summoning senators disrespectfully in the middle of night, Dio 63.26.4.

deinde repente magno tibiarum et scabellorum crepitu cum palla tunicaque talari prosiluit ac desaltato cantico abiit: Desaltato cantico abiit = "after dancing one number, he departed" (*desaltare,* only here among classical writers). *Scabella* (*scabilla*) were ankle castanets or rhythm instruments attached to the feet with which he beat time (Cic. *Att.* 1.16.3; *Off.* 1.150; Quint. 11.3.58; Fronto *Ep.* Nab. p. 160; *RE* 4A.2061–63). They were associated par-ticularly with the *ludus talarius,* dance accompanied by music but not by singing, suitable for a "low-grade music hall" (Bailey on Cic. *ad Att.* 1.151 = 1.16.3). Both the *palla* and the *tunica talaris,* a garment reaching the ankles were im-proper, non-Roman garb, women's garments (Cic. *Cat.* 2.22; *Verr.* 5.31). Cf. the long garments in 52, all plausibly Isiac.

atque hic tam docilis ad cetera natare nesciit: Docilis = apt, teachable, in other areas at least. Swimming was a standard upper class accomplishment; even Gaius' sister Agrippina knew how (Tac. *Ann.* 14.5.3). It was part of the basic ed-ucation of Gaius and Lucius Caesar, the adopted sons of Augustus: *nepotes et litteras et natare aliaque rudimenta...docuit* (Suet. *Aug.* 64.3; for upper class swimming, see also Hor. *Carm.* 1.8.8, 3.7.28, 3.12.7). Gaius' inability is a wonderfully ironic (anti)climax for this rubric of disreputable skills.[109]

Gaius was as unpredictable in his loves as in his hates; he could pardon unexpectedly (16.4) and be charming when he chose (Jos. *AJ* 19.87). Philo writes, "He answered in such a moderate and kindly fashion that we feared not only for our case but also for our lives" (ὁ δὲ οὕτως ἐπιεικῶς καὶ φιλανθρώπως ἀντιπροσηγόρευσεν, ὡς μὴ μόνον τὴν ὑπόθεσιν ἀλλὰ καὶ τὸ ζῆν

---

[109] For the danger of swimming for epileptic children (Benediktson 1991, 159–60). But there are many reasons for not knowing how to swim.

ἀπογνῶναι, *Leg.* 352). This and chapter 51 are as close as Suetonius comes to generalizing about Gaius' capricious behavior.

55.1 *quorum vero studio teneretur, omnibus ad insaniam favit Mnesterem pantomimum etiam inter spectacula osculabatur:* The social kiss had become a mark of favor (Suet. *Gram.* 23; Sen. *Dial.* 4.24.1; Sen. *Ben.* 4.30.2) and was so common that Tiberius thought it necessary to put forth an edict against the *cotidiana oscula* for hygenic reasons (Suet. *Tib.* 34.2; Pliny *HN* 26.3; *RE* S5.513–15). An emperor's kiss, given or received, was of course especially significant (Tac. *Agr.* 40.3; Sen. *Ep.* 118.3), a sign of his gracious respect: *gratum erat cunctis, quod senatum osculo exciperes, ut dimissus osculo fueras...* (Pliny, *Pan.* 23.1). Gaius flattered few in this way and so his special attention to Mnester (already introduced among Gaius' sexual partners, 36.1) was noteworthy (Dio 59.27.1). Nero did not give kisses either (Suet. *Ner.* 37.3). Gaius usually offered a hand or foot instead (56.2 and note 106).

ac si qui saltante eo vel leviter obstreperet, detrahi iussum manu sua flagellabat: For his insistence on everyone sharing his tastes, see 30.2–3; 35.2–3; also Dio 59.5.4, 14.4.

equiti R. tumultuanti per centurionem denuntiavit: Denuntiare followed by a subjunctive clause (*abieret sine mora,* below) indicates an order, and delivered by one of the praetorian centurions, it was a threat. The knight's misbehavior may (or may not) be related to the incident in which "more than twenty knights were killed" (*per eum tumultum,* 26.4).

abieret sine mora Ostiam perferretque ad Ptolemaeum regem in Mauretaniam codicillos suos; quorum exemplum erat: ei quem istoc misi, neque boni quicquam neque mali feceris: An example of capricious clemency (cf. 16.4). This cryptic anecdote evidently bears on the summons that brought Ptolemy to Rome or Lugdunum; it may have been in another document that the knight carried. The story rests on the old traditions that the bearer of bad tidings was subject to punishment or that a messenger carried the order for his own death. Gaius scared the knight but nothing happened; it was "wit...by anticlimax" (Plass 126). This evidently took place in 39 before Gaius left Rome since Ptolemy of Mauretania was killed during the following winter (35.1).

55.2 *Thr<a>eces quosdam Germanis corporis custodibus praeposuit:* He chose commanders for his German guards from among his favorite Thracians (32.2, 35.2, 54.1). One former gladiator, Sabinus (*PIR¹ S.* 25) commanded a detachment (Bellen 43–46) and led it against Gaius' assassins (58.3; Jos. *AJ* 19.122).[110]

murmillonum armaturas recidit: The very heavily armed *murmillones* (on 30.3, 32.2, on 35.2) were the opponents of his Thracians, and Gaius wanted to reduce their advantage.

Columbo victori, leviter tamen saucio, venenum in plagam addidit, quod ex eo Columbinum appellavit: Columbus (*PIR²* C. 1260), a *murmillo*, won anyway. There seem to be overtones of erotic competition in this story (cf. Colosseros, 35.2). *Columbus*, the male counterpart to the dove of Venus, was a term of endearment (Pers. 3.16. Catull. 29.8; as a gladiator's name, *CIL* 12.3325; another gladiator dove named Palumbus was in the arena under Claudius, Suet. *Cl.* 21.5). The adjective *columbinus* means dovelike but also dove colored (light gray) and was applied to plants and other natural substances (Pliny *HN* e.g., 14.40, 17.43). Its connection with the gladiator Columbus probably worked in the opposite direction from the way described here; i.e., the name of the gladiator provided the explanation for an already existing substance. For Gaius and poison, note 11.[111]

sic certe inter alia venena scriptum ab eo repertum est: This is the box of poisons found on the Palatine along with the two *libelli* of Protogenes (49.3). *Sic certe* shows Suetonius' conviction that *columbinus* was at least on the list, whether or not it had a connection with the gladiator. Suetonius often uses *certe* to affirm his acceptance of a point about which he thought there was some question (12.3; *Jul.* 50.1; *Cl.* 1.1; *Ner.* 33.1; *Oth.* 7.1; *Vit.* 2.2). For the possibility of doubt about the entire incident, see on 49.3 and note 9.

prasinae factioni ita addictus et deditus, ut cenaret in stabulo assidue et maneret: *Prasinus* = "leek green" (πράσον = leek). For Gaius' favorite "Greens," see 18.3. The *vicus stabularius* was in the Campus Martius, not far

---

[110] Sabinus survived into the reign of Claudius when he was supposed to die fighting in the arena, perhaps as a punishment for killing some of the assassins (Levick 1990, 36; see note 126). But Messalina saved him, allegedly because he was her lover (Dio 60.28.2). Nero had a favorite *murmillo* (Spiculus, *PIR¹* S. 579), an officer in his guard, who died because of his loyalty to his master (Suet. *Ner.* 30.2, 47.3; Plut. *Gal.* 8.5; Bellen 45–46).

[111] Gaius also poisoned rival charioteers and horses (τούς τε ἀρίστους καὶ τοὺς ἐνδοξοτάτους σφῶν φαρμάκῳ διέφθειρε, Dio 59.14.5). D'Erce suggests that the poison Gaius used on Columbus was arsenic because it is effective when applied externally (1969, 123–48). He takes his argument from Gaius' interest in turning orpiment (yellow sulphide of arsenic) into gold (Pliny *HN* 33.79), an interest that he thinks was stimulated by Gaius' imagining that Germanicus had been poisoned by arsenic (1.2).

from a practice course called the Trigarium that ran along the bank of the Tiber. Near the stables were the clubhouses for the Green and Blue factions. The Greens headquarters was on the site of the present church of San Lorenzo in Damaso (San Lorenzo in Prasino in the Middle Ages, J. H. Humphrey 558; Coarelli 840–43). One could eat and drink and perhaps sleep at the clubhouse, and this was where Gaius spent large amounts of time.

agitatori Eutycho comisatione quadam in apophoretis vicies sestertium contulit: Eutychus (*PIR²* E. 134), "Lucky," was appropriate for a charioteer. Gaius' attachment to him was obviously notorious. Josephus writes that after the assassination, Chaerea sarcastically told the praetorians that he would satisfy their demand for a new emperor (Claudius) if he got the password from Eutychus (*AJ* 19.256–57). Since it was the emperor whose task it was to give the password of the day to the praetorian tributes (58.2), Gaius and his charioteer were assimilated. Eutychus received two million sesterces, twenty (*vicies*) times 100,000 (*sestertium*), along with other party favors (*apophoretis* = things to take away from a banquet). *Apophoreta* were not normally cash (Suet. *Aug.* 75; *Ves.* 19.1; Petron. *Sat.* 27, 64), although this may have been more usual for athletes and entertainers than for social equals (*Ves.* 19.1).

55.3 *Incitato equo, cuius causa pridie circenses, ne inquietaretur, viciniae silentium per milites indicere solebat:* Incitatus ("Swift"), the best known member of Gaius' entourage. The stories about him have their origin in Gaius' racing obsession (18.3, 19.2). The name is also attested for drivers (*ILS* 9027; Mart. 10.76.9, 11.1.16; Syme 1977b, 87).

praeter equile marmoreum et praesaepe eburneum praeterque purpurea tegumenta ac monilia e gemmis: The stables and clubhouses were probably established during the reign of Augustus, but Gaius built new stables and used the praetorians for the job, a demeaning non-military assignment that angered them (Jos. *AJ* 19.257). See chapter 21 for praetorian involvement with the Corinthian canal.

domum etiam et familiam et supellectilem dedit, quo lautius nomine eius invitati acciperentur: There must have been elaborate meals in the Greens clubhouse (*cenaret in stabulo assidue,* above). Gaius invited his horse to dinner, gave him golden food and toasted him in golden goblets (Dio 59.14.7).

consulatum quoque traditur destinasse: Suetonius does not state it as fact that Gaius intended to make Incitatus a consul (*traditur destinasse*), and Dio writes that he only "promised" (59.14.7). But the preceding information has been in the indicative, and this influences the reader to accept the final outrageous allegation.[112] The joke about Incitatus the consul is related to Chaerea's to sarcastic remark that he would get the watchword from Eutychus (on 55.2; Jos *AJ* 19.256–57). If the charioteer could be princeps, why then was his horse not consul? In a similar inference about Gaius' intimacy with the stable, Incitatus is a priest of his cult along with Caesonia and Claudius (Dio 59.28.6; on 22.3). Another aspect of the Incitatus joke is the parody of the great man's special horse. Alexander had his Bucephalus (Pliny *HN* 8.154; Plut. *Alex.* 6; Gell. 5.2) and Julius Caesar a horse with almost human feet (Suet. *Jul.* 61; Dio 37.54.2; Pliny *HN* 8.154). Germanicus wrote a poem about the tomb of Augustus' horse (Pliny *HN* 8.154–55). It was thoroughly appropriate that this ersatz general's warhorse be a racehorse (note the *biiugi famosorum equorum* at the bridge parade, 19.2).

The narrative is picked up from 49.2. But since Suetonius is interested in telling the story of his emperor and not the story of the conspiracy, he only broadly summarizes the events that led to the assassination. He writes that two conspiracies were intercepted, that others never got off the ground and that the two persons (he names no names at this point) who were responsible for the final succesful one had the help of a freedman and the praetorian prefects who became involved after Gaius accused them falsely. The lines between conspiracies blur and blend into an amorphous threat. For more detail (even in epitome) see Dio 59.29–30.2 and especially Josephus *AJ* 19.17–273. Plots precipitated *maiestas* prosecutions. Suetonius has already gathered the executions of this period into his rubric of cruelty (27.4, 28, 32.1).

56.1 *ita bacchantem atque grassantem non defuit plerisque animus adoriri:* Cf. *periit, ingentia facinora ausus et aliquanto maiora moliens* where Suetonius' left the story at 49.2; similarly at Dio 59.25.5[b].

sed una <atque> altera conspiratione detecta: Both the epitome of Dio and Seneca describe two (*una <atque> altera*) conspiracies together, two of the father-son pairs noted at 27.4, one of which involved Betilienus Capito and his son Betilienus Bassus (also on 26.3, 32.1 and below; see note 68). Others who were punished by Gaius during these last months were Scribonius Proculus (28) and perhaps Julius Graecinus (on 23.3; Sen. *Ben.* 2.21.5; Tac. *Agr.* 4.1; Barrett 1989, 158; Syme 1958, 20).

aliis per inopiam occasionis cunctantibus: Nothing is known about these, but there is a sense of opportunities almost missed by Chaerea (58.1).

---

[112] Allegations gain credibility when they are placed among facts (Gascou 705). Suetonius uses the same trick elsewhere: *creditur etiam…* (*Ner.* 37.2); *suspectus et…* (*Vit.* 14.5); *fertur etiam…* (*Tib.* 44.2).

duo consilium communicaverunt perfeceruntque: The two were Cassius
Chaerea (on 16.4, 32.3, 40, named and identified at 56.2) and Cornelius Sabinus
(*PIR²* C. 1431, named and identified at 58.2), both tribunes of the praetorian
guard.[113] According to Josephus, the final successful conspiracy had three divi-
sions. Aemilius Regulus of Cordova (*PIR²* A. 397) led one group (no more is
heard of him), Chaerea another, and the senator L. Annius Vinicianus (*PIR²* A.
701) the third (*AJ* 19.17–23). Vinicianus was or had been a member of Gaius' inner circle and a friend of the once powerful Aemilius Lepidus (24.1, 3; Jos. *AJ*
19.20, 49); he was made an Arval Brother in the revision of May 24, A.D. 38 (on
23.3, 25.1; *Docs.* no. 3 p. 10; Scheid and Broise 221, 225; still present at a sacrifice in early June of 40, *Docs.* no. 10 p. 14). Vinicianus was the most important
political personality known to be involved in the conspiracy and was perhaps its
real power (Jos. *AJ* 19.52; Timpe 1962, 79–83; Barrett 1989, 161–62). He escaped being killed in the aftermath of the assassination, played a part in the
aborted attempt to reestablish the Republic on the following day (Jos. *AJ* 19.153,
252) and died as a major player in the A.D. 42 conspiracy against Claudius (Dio
60.15.1–2, 5; Swan 155–64). For the idea that Claudius himself was a tacit party
to the assassination, Jung 382–86; Levick 1990, 35–39. Tacitus writes that
Valerius Asiaticus (on 36.2) was one of the ringleaders (*principuum auctorem
Asiaticum interficiendi G. Caesaris, Ann.* 11.1.2) but too cowardly to face the
hostile crowd after the deed was done; Josephus, on the other hand, writes that he
told the same crowd that he wished that he had done it (*AJ* 19.160). There is
much about the conspiracy that is not known; "the assassination and what was intended to follow were planned in secret...and did not go according to plan"
(Levick 1990, 34).

*non sine conscientia potentissimorum libertorum praefectorumque
praetori:* Of all groups, freedmen and praetorian prefects should have been the
most loyal to the princeps since their status was totally dependent on his benefactions. Only extraordinary provocation could make such men disloyal, and so the
story is told so as to emphasize its existence. The freedman in question (the only
one identified) was Callistus (C. Julius Callistus, *PIR²* I. 229), a very wealthy,
powerful and trusted confidant of Gaius (Dio 59.19.6; Jos. *AJ* 19.64–65) who did
indeed remain loyal to Claudius (Tac. *Ann.* 11.29, 12.1.2; Sen. *Ep.* 47.9; Pliny
HN 33.134, 36.60). He may have courted Claudius before Gaius was dead (Jos.

---

[113] Praetorian tribunes commanded the praetorian cohorts and were the officers below the prefect or prefects (Durry 143). Papinius (*PIR¹* P. 73) is a third named as a conspirator (Jos. *AJ*
19.37). The otherwise unidentified Aquila (*PIR²* A. 980) who struck the blow that finally killed
Gaius (Jos. *AJ* 19.110) must also have been a praetorian. Cornelius Sabinus is not the Sabinus
who was a gladiator turned bodyguard (55.2 and note 110).

AJ 19.66–69) and in any case knew when to abandon a sinking ship. Two praetorian prefects seem to have been appointed in Macro's place (on 26.1; ὑπάρχους, Dio 59.25.7, 8; Balsdon 1934a, 39–40), but the name of only one, M. Arrecinus Clemens (*PIR²* A. 1073), is known. He was of senatorial rank (Jos. *AJ* 19.154), and his daughter married the emperor Titus (T. Flavianus Vespasianus [Augustus], *PIR²* F. 399; Suet. *Tit.* 4.2; Tac. *Hist.* 4.68.2; Jos. *AJ* 19.37). Clemens released Vinicianus (above) from custody after the assassination and made a speech about the justice due to tyrants (Jos. *AJ* 19.154–56). The praetorian guard was split between the senate and Claudius, and the other prefect may not have committed himself so quickly if at all (Jos. *AJ* 19.188; Barrett 1989, 160). Claudius appointed a replacement (Rufrius? Pollio, *PIR¹* R. 123; Jos. *AJ* 19.267; Dio 60.23.2; Sen. *Apocol.* 13.5) for one of them within hours.[114] Josephus portrays Clemens as more privy to the conspiracy than an active participant (Jos. *AJ* 19.37–47), a nice compromise for the reputation of someone who would one day be connected with an emperor by marriage.

quod ipsi quoque etsi falso in quadam coniuratione quasi participes nominati, suspectos tamen se et invisos sentiebant: The story was that when Betilienus Capito (above) was in danger of death, he implicated others in conspiracy and included Caesonia, Callistus and the prefects among the guilty. These highly unlikely names (especially Caesonia) threw his entire testimony into doubt (Dio 59.25.7). But his accusations suggested to Gaius the possibility that persons close to him could be disloyal and made Callistus and the prefects realize that they could be the objects of suspicion.

nam et statim seductis magnam fecit invidiam destricto gladio affirmans sponte se periturum, si et illis morte dignus videretur: Dio puts different words into Gaius' mouth: "I am one but you are three; I am defenceless but you are armed. If you hate me and wish to kill me, strike" ("εἷς εἰμί" ἔφη, "τρεῖς δὲ ὑμεῖς, καὶ γυμνὸς μὲν ἐγώ, ὡπλισμένοι δ᾽ ὑμεῖς· εἰ οὖν μισεῖτέ με καὶ ἀποκτείνειν θέλετε, φονεύσατε," 59.25.8). Both versions of the story illustrate Gaius' vulnerability.

nec cessavit ex eo criminari alterum alteri atque inter se omnis committere: Gaius himself is made responsible for their complicity because he played the three of them off against one other until they would have nothing more to do with him and left him to the conspirators (Dio 59.25.8). Their

---

[114] But for which one? For Clemens according to Jung (385); for the nameless one according to Levick (1990, 37–38).

involvement was his fault, not theirs, a neat solution for persons who would serve the next princeps.

56.2 cum placuisset Palatinis ludis spectaculo egressum meridie adgredi: Cf. *hora fere septima cunctatus an ad prandium surgeret* (58.1). The Palatine games that Livia established in honor of the deified Augustus began on January 17 (Tac. *Ann.* 1.73.3; Dio 56.46.5; for their duration, see note 120). There was some urgency because Gaius was soon to depart for the East (49.2, 51.3; Jos. *AJ* 19.81). But not too soon; the sailing season was still about six weeks away (on 15.2).

primas sibi partes Cassius Chaerea tribunus cohortis praetoriae depoposcit: It was convenient to give Chaerea the major share of the responsibility since it was he who was executed in order to discourage similar disloyalty to the next emperor (Suet. *Cl.*11.1; Dio 60.3.4–5; Jos. *AJ* 19.268–71); but see on 59 and note 126 for the real reason why he was chosen. Josephus especially emphasizes his central role (ἀναθείη δ' ἄν τις τὴν πρᾶξιν Χαιρέᾳ, *AJ* 19.111). Sabinus was not condemned but took his own life after Chaerea was executed (Dio 60.3.5; Jos. *AJ* 19.273; note 126). He in fact may have been equally important in carrying out the action (*duo consilium communicaverunt perfeceruntque*, 56.1; also 58.2). *Primas...partes* = leading role; see the *secundae* (*partes*) for the actors at 57.4.

quem Gaius seniorem iam et mollem et effeminatum denotare omni probro consuerat: *Denotare* = insult (Sen. *Ben.* 4.30.2). The defection of the praetorian tribune, like that of the freedman and the prefects (56.1), had to be explained, and so Chaerea is shown sorely provoked. *Senior* = a man past the age of military service, i.e., over forty-five (Gell. 10.28.1). Chaerea was perhaps fifty years old in 41. He had been a centurion in the Army of Lower Germany during the mutiny of 14 when he acted decisively and saved himself when others were being lynched (Tac. *Ann.* 1.32.2). His name was probably preserved in connection with this because of his later role (*mox caede Gai Caesaris memoriam apud posteros adeptus, tum adulescens et animi ferox*, Tac. *Ann.* 1.32.2); it helped refute Gaius' assessment of him as *mollis* and *effeminatus*. Gaius insulted him by calling him soft (Dio 59.29.2; Jos. *AJ* 19.21, 30), but his weak voice belied his courage (Sen. *Dial.* 2.18.3; also Jos. *AJ* 19.113, 270), and the tradition turned his gentle manner into a virtue when he pitied those from whom he collected harsh taxes (40.1) and those whom he was forced to torture (16.4).

et modo signum petenti Priapum aut Venerem dare: Πόθος o r Ἀφροδίτη in Greek (Dio 59.29.2). Each day it was the emperor's task to give the watchword to the praetorian officer in charge (on 55.2). The obscenities that Gaius used with Chaerea were a degrading insult that became thematic in the assassination story (58.2).[115] The entire city knew about them (after the fact at least) and even Chaerea's fellow officers derided him (Jos. *AJ* 19.31, 53). Although Venus means "desire" in this context, it had already been used as a watchword by another Gaius Julius Caesar to refer to Venus Genetrix, the mother of the Julian clan (App. *BCiv* 2.104). When *libertas* became the conspirators' watchword of the day (Jos. *AJ* 19.54, 186; on 58.2), it marked the change from the obscenity of Julian tyranny to constitutional freedom; see 60 for the desire to erase all things Julian.

modo ex aliqua causa agenti gratias osculandam manum offerre formatam commotamque in obscaenum modum: Gaius perverted the kiss of favor (55.1) by substituting his foot (especially the less propitious left one), an act that required a person to bow low before him (Dio 59.29.5; see note 106) or by offering his hand in an obscene gesture, either the "fig," a fist with the thumb protruding between the closed fingers (Ov. *Fast.* 5.433–34), or the *digitus impudicus*, the extended middle finger (Juv.10.52–53; Mart. 2.28.1–2; Pers. 2.33; Adams 6; Courtney on Juv.10.53; Elworthy 414–16). Both hand gestures implied that the person at whom they were aimed was a pathic (*mollis* and *effeminatus*, above).

A rubric of portents inserted at this point postpones the action and increases the suspense (Gugel 50–52; Lounsbury 85). They are ingenious and a number have something to do with Julius Caesar; the analogy between the two was inescapable since both died in public of multiple stab wounds at the hands of a Cassius. Others introduce the idea of substitute sacrifice that is important in the telling of the assassination story. The omens begin at some distance from the time and place and gradually come closer (*pridie quam periret* and *illo ipso die paulo prius*, 57.3).[116] Most of Suetonius' emperors have a rubric of prodigies, especially Julius Caesar (*Jul.* 81; *Aug.* 97.1–2; *Tib.* 74; *Cl.* 46; *Ner.* 46; *Gal.* 18; *Vit.* 9; *Dom.* 15.3–16). Suetonius provides the fullest list for Gaius; a smaller number at Dio 59.29.3–4 and Jos. *AJ* 19.94–95.

57.1 *futurae caedis multa prodigia extiterunt:* About Julius Caesar: *sed Caesari futura caedes evidentibus prodigiis denuntiata est* (Suet. *Jul.* 81.1).

---

[115] They were widely reported. In addition to here: *Huic Gaius signum petenti modo Veneris, modo Priapi dabat* (Sen. *Dial.* 2.18.3); καὶ τὸ σύνθημα αὐτῷ...Πόθεν ἢ Ἀφροδίτην ἢ ἕτερόν τι τοιοῦτον ἐδίδου (Dio 59.29.2); θήλεά τε ἐδίδου τὰ ὀνόματα, καὶ ταῦτα αἰσχύνης ἀνάπλεα (Jos. *AJ* 19.29–30).

[116] Gugel (50–51) sees the structure of chapter 57 as a ring composition of increasing intensity; the first group of three omens (Jupiter, Cassius and the lightning strikes, 57.1–2) matches the second group (Cassius, Jupiter and the bloodly incidents, 57.3–4). They surround the one actual prediction (57.2).

Olympiae simulacrum Iovis, quod dissolui transferrique Romam placuerat: This was one of the works of art that Gaius removed or intended to remove to Rome (22.2; other split episodes are 19 and 32.1, 14.2 and 27.2, perhaps 32.2 and 54.1).

tantum cachinnum repente edidit, ut machinis labefactis opifices diffugerint: The statue of Olympian Zeus contributed to the tradition about Gaius in three ways: It was emblematic of his divine pretensions because he intended to exchange the head on the statue for one of his own (22.2; Dio 59.28.3–4). Secondly since it was referred to the end of his life, it functioned as a fatal omen (here and Jos. *AJ* 19.8–10); the statue laughed whenever anyone approached it, and the ship intended to transport it was appropriately struck by the god's own thunderbolts (Dio 59.28.4). But there was a practical reason for abandoning the project—it was too big to be moved without damage (Jos. *AJ* 19.9). Gaius himself had evidently given up on bringing it to Rome in time to make alternate arrangements for the shrine to his *numen* on the Palatine (22.3; see note 43). The story's third function was the rescue of Memmius Regulus (17.1), legate of Achaea where Olympia was located and in charge of removing the statue (22.2). When he reported his failure, he risked Gaius' anger and his own life, and only the emperor's opportune death saved him (Jos. *AJ* 19.10).[117] See on 25.2 for another way of rescuing him from association with Gaius.

supervenitque ilico quidam Cassius nomine: Ilico, i.e., there at Olympia. Nothing is known about this Cassius (*PIR²* C. 472), not surprising since nothing mattered but his name. Another Cassius at 57.3.

iussum se somnio affirmans immolare taurum Iovi: Gaius will become a sacrificial victim to the god whose statue he was molesting. Cf. Dio: "...and he became a sacrifice at the hands of those by whom he was called and written to as Zeus and god" (καὶ ὑφ' ὧν τε Ζεὺς καὶ θεὸς ὠνομάζετό τε καὶ ἐγράφετο, σφάγιον ἐγίνετο, 59.30.1ᵃ). The conceit of Gaius as surrogate sacrifice continues in details of the bloody garment (57.4) and the assassination itself (58.2).

57.2 Capitolium Capuae Id. Mar<t.> de caelo tactum est: Lightning struck (*de caelo tactum est*) on the anniversary of Julius Caesar's death in 44 B.C.,

---

117 A similar reprieve was granted P. Petronius (*PIR¹* P. 198), legate of Syria, who defied Gaius by delaying the installation of his statue in the temple in Jerusalem. When Petronius reported resistance to the project, Gaius condemned him to death but was himself dead before his order arrived in the East (Jos. *AJ* 18.261–309; *BJ* 2.202–3; Philo *Leg.* 207–60). See note 107 for Seneca and on 57.3 for C. Cassius Longinus. Pertinent also are the lists of those who would have been killed if the emperor had not died (49.3).

not really close to the time of the assassination since Gaius was killed in January (58.1). The ancient city of Capua in Campania near the Bay of Naples had a Capitolium with a temple of Jupiter modeled after Rome's (Suet. *Tib.* 40; Tac. *Ann.* 4.57.1). A bronze tablet found in the same neighborhood had predicted dire events shortly before the death of Caesar (Suet. *Jul.* 81.1). Lightning strikes were often portents of change (*haruspicem...qui consultus de fulgure mutationem rerum praedixerat,* Suet. *Dom.* 16.1). They predicted both Augustus' birth (Suet. *Aug.* 94.2) and death (*Aug.* 97.2) and the death of Claudius (*Cl.* 46). All the Ides belonged to Jupiter and his thunderbolts (Ov. *Fast.*1.56, 587–88, 4.621, 6.650; Macr. 1.15.14; Fowler 129). For the parallel treatments of Gaius and Caesar, Mouchova 53–54.

item Romae cella Palatini atriensis: The thunderbolts came closer. The *cella* belonged to the palace steward, the *atriensis,* the highly trusted slave who supervised the household. *Atrienses* of the imperial house are well attested (*TLL* 2.1100.20–22). To be noted is an undated inscription: *Chaerea Caesaris atriensis* (*CIL* 6.8739).

nec defuerunt qui coniectarent altero ostento periculum a custodibus domino portendi, altero caedem rursus insignem, qualis eodem die facta quondam fuisset: The interpretation of one lightning strike (the second mentioned here) was easy since it was a reference to the noteworthy (*insignem*) public murder of Julius Caesar (*eodem die*). As for the other, the trusted praetorian tribune Chaerea was equated with the trusted household steward. It meant that the threat would originate close to home, from within Gaius' own establishment (*a custodibus domino*), i.e., from the praetorians (56.2, 58.2). Ingenuity in interpreting omens, especially after the fact, was never lacking.

consulenti quoque de genitura sua Sulla mathematicus certissimam necem appropinquare affirmavit: The ancients often recorded the names of their astrologers (19.3; Suet. *Ner.* 36.1; *Dom.* 15.3). This Sulla (*PIR¹* S. 703), who actually predicts Gaius' death, is otherwise unknown. Dio reports that the prediction was made by an Egyptian named Apollonius (*PIR²* A. 926), who was summoned to Rome but luckily did not arrive until the day Gaius died and so was saved—yet another near miss (59.29.4). The information that a horoscope (*genitura*) provided about the date of death was not really welcome, and the *mathematicus* was routinely suspect because he seemed to know too much. Domitian also condemned a soothsayer (Suet. *Dom.* 16.1).

57.3 *monuerunt et Fortunae Antiatinae, ut a Cassio caveret:* The second notice of a hostile Cassius (cf. 57.1). There was an important shrine of two sister goddesses of Fortune (*Fortunae*) at Gaius' favored Antium (8.1 and 5, 49.2; for the shrine, Mart. 5.1.3; Tac. *Ann.* 3.71.1, 15.23.3). His personal deities were protecting him.

qua causa ille Cassium Longinum Asiae tum proconsulem occidendum delegaverat inmemor Chaeream Cassium nominari: C. Cassius Longinus (*PIR*[2] C. 501), consul suffect in A.D. 30, was brother to the first husband of Gaius' sister Drusilla (24.1). According to Dio, he was brought back from Asia to Rome as a prisoner, but his life was saved when Gaius was killed before his punishment could be carried out (59.29.3; see 57.1 and notes 107 and 117). He survived to be governor of Syria under Claudius (Jos. *AJ* 20.1; Tac. *Ann.* 12.11.3) and to be exiled by Nero (Suet. *Ner.* 37.1; Tac. *Ann.* 16.7–9.1). A direct descendant of the C. Cassius Longinus who was chief among the assassins of Julius Caesar (Dio 59.29.3), to Nero's annoyance he kept a portrait of his anti-Caesarian ancestor among his *imagines* (Suet. *Ner.* 37.1; Tac. *Ann.* 16.7.1–2). His very tangential role in the story of Gaius' death (indeed, non-role since he appears only in this prediction that was obviously conceived after the assassination was led by another Cassius) suggests that he was retrojected into Gaius' story as yet another of his subordinates whose reputation had to be cleansed for a continuing role under a later emperor.

pridie quam periret, somniavit consistere se in caelo iuxta solium Iovis impulsumque ab eo dextri pedis pollice et in terras praecipitatum: The omens appear closer to the fatal day. Julius Caesar also dreamed on the eve of his assassination (Suet. *Jul.* 81.3), and Nero and Domitian had predictive dreams as well (Suet. *Ner.* 46.1; *Dom.* 15.3). Caesar dreamed that he saw himself flying above the clouds with his right hand in that of Jupiter (*ea vero nocte, cui inluxit dies cadis, et ipse sibi visus est per quietem interdum supra nubes volitare, alias cum Iove dextram iungere,* Suet. *Jul.* 81.3; also Dio 44.17.1). But instead of being hand in hand with Jupiter like Caesar (or closer yet, *in contubernium ultro invitatus,* 22.4), Gaius was kicked out of heaven by the god's big toe, not even given the dignity of a solid shove with the whole foot. Was his dream a comment on the practice of foot kissing? The message was that Gaius was no *divus,* the same message that was in the witticism that when he was killed, "he learned that he was not a god" (ὡς οὐκ ἦν θεὸς ἔμαθεν, Dio 59.30.1). The banishment of Claudius from heaven in the *Apocolocyntosis* is not totally dissimilar (*Cyllenius illum...trahit ad inferos a caelo,* Sen. *Apocol.* 11.5). Parody of deification (or non-deification) was clearly an available strategy.

prodigiorum loco habita sunt etiam, quae forte illo ipso die paulo prius acciderant: The tension increases with the day itself at hand (*illo ipso die*). As Suetonius himself admits, events were deemed significant in retrospect.

Several bloody things occurred on his last day. These prodigies that show life imitating art are all exceptionally clever.

57.4 *sacrificans respersus est phoenicopteri sanguine:* First, the blood on Gaius' garment made him a surrogate sacrifice (57.1, 58.2). Josephus has a different version of this conceit: When Gaius entered the theater, he sacrificed to Augustus in whose honor the *ludi Palatini* were held; the temporary theater was plausibly set up in the vicinity of the altar to Augustus' *numen* (Wiseman 1987, 171–72). And it was not Gaius but P. Nonius Asprenas, *consul ordinarius* of 38 (17.1), whose robe was sprinkled with the blood of an unspecified victim (πίπτοντος τῶν ἱερείων τινὸς, Jos. *AJ* 19.87). He was the first to lose his life in the confusion that followed the assassination (58.3; Jos. *AJ* 19.123). The garment bloodied during sacrifice was a stock omen of imminent death, and so it is probable that neither Gaius nor Asprenas was bloodied by a flamingo or anything else. Before the battle of Idistaviso in A.D. 15, Germanicus dreamed that he was spattered with a victim's blood and that Livia supplied him with a fresh toga, a reprieve from disaster in the battle to come (*nox eadem laetam Germanico quietem tulit, viditque se operatum et sanguine sacri respersa praetexta pulchriorem aliam manibus aviae Augustae accepisse,* Tac. *Ann.* 2.14.1). For the flamingo as a sacrifice to his *numen* and for Gaius' participation in his own cult, see 22.3.

Events on the stage would soon be acted out in the real world. A conversation in the audience also referred to life imitating art: the program for the day would include "the assassination of a tyrant" (τυραννοκτονίας ἀγὼν πρόκειται, Jos. *AJ* 19.92).[118] The *ludi Palatini* (56.2) were *ludi scaenici* (58.1).

et pantomimus Mnester tragoediam saltavit: Mnester also at 36.1 and 55.1. Pantomimes, more or less serious productions derived from tragedy, were "danced" (on 18.2, 55.1).

quam olim Neoptolemus tragoedus ludis, quibus rex Macedonum Philippus occisus est, egerat: Neoptolemus (Diod. 16.92.3; Dem. 5 [= Περὶ

---

118 So said "Bathybius" to the "consular" Cluvius (Jos. *AJ* 19.91–2), plausibly Cluvius Rufus (*PIR²* C. 1206), courtier of Nero and writer of history. This apparently gratuitous introduction of Cluvius into the story suggested to Mommsen that a history written by Cluvius Rufus was Josephus' Latin source (Mommsen 1870, 320, 322), an idea that has been widely accepted. But *contra,* Feldman 1962, 322–33; Timpe 1960, 500–502; Ritter 1972; Wardle 1992.

τῆς εἰρήνης] 6–7) was a well-known tragic actor of the court of Philip II of Macedon (359–36 B.C.). His performance at the wedding of Philip's daughter included an ode that taught that sudden death was bound to overtake the proud (*TGF adespota* no. 127, vol. 2, p. 53 = Diod. 16.92.3). In order to appear civil, Philip had separated himself from his bodyguard when he entered the theater and, thus exposed, was killed by one of them (Diod. 16.91–94; Paus. 8.7.6). January 24 was not the anniversary of his death as Josephus writes; Philip's daughter's marriage took place in the autumn (Feldman 1965) or summer (Wiseman 1991 at Jos. *AJ* 19.95). But assassination by a member of the guard in the context of a theatrical production had a clear parallel in Gaius' end, and the content of the play was also relevant. It was an otherwise unattested pantomime called *Cinyras*, the incestuous story of Myrrha who fell in love with her father (*TGF adespota* no. 5d, vol. 2, p. 11; Ov. *Met.* 10.298–502). It ended in bloody death (Jos. *AJ* 19.94). Another parallel between Philip and Gaius was an oracle delivered shortly before Philip's death that declared that a bull stood wreathed and ready for the sacrifice (Diod. 16.91.2; Paus. 8.7.6). Both became victims themselves (57.1, on 58.2).

et cum in Laureolo mimo: In addition to the pantomime *Cinyras*, the mime *Laureolus* was presented (Jos. *AJ* 19.94). It was by a Catullus, either the well-known Republican poet (Wiseman 1985, 187–95) or another Catullus (*PIR²* C. 581) who wrote during the first century. It concerned the adventures, capture and crucifixion of a runaway slave become a bandit chief (Juv. 8.187; Mart. *Spect.* 1.7.3; *CRF* 2.392; see Wiseman 1985, 258–59 for testimonia; Fantham 158, n. 27). By implication Gaius was a brigand king who got his painful deserts. For Gaius as a runaway slave, see the *rex Nemorensis* (35.3).

in quo a[u]ctor proripiens se ruina sanguinem vomit: *Ruina,* probably a stage "fall" as he rushed offstage (Schmidt 156–60). Abrupt endings were frequent in mime (Beare 143–44), and Gaius would soon make his own bloody exit.

plures secundarum certatim experimentum artis darent, cruore scaena abundavit: *Secundae* = *secundae partes,* the actors who played secondary roles. A mime was dominated by a single actor to whom all the others were very subordinate (Beare 143). *Secundae* (and *tertiae*) *partes* used figuratively indicated inferior status in general (Sen. *Dial.* 5.8.6; Pliny *HN* 7.54). The vigorous performances of this supporting cast not only added to the quantity of fake blood (αἷμά τε ἦν τεχνητὸν πολύ, Jos. *AJ* 19.94) that was already on the stage from both tragedy and mime but also showed how well those of the second rank (such as praetorian tribunes) could improvise and play starring roles. A subordinate, Chaerea, had the *primae partes* (56.2) in the assassination.

parabatur et in noctem spectaculum: The *pervigilium* at which he would make his stage debut has already been introduced (54.2).

quo argumenta inferorum per Aegyptios et Aethiopas explicarentur: By that night Gaius would be able to supply first hand information about the *argumenta inferorum* = "explanations about the gods of the dead" (54.2; Jos. *AJ* 19.30, 71, 104; *media nocte...deos inferos et deos superos accessi coram,* Apul. *Met.* 9.23; Köberlein 32). Ethiopians were black Africans but more specifically inhabitants of the upper Nile who were guardians of the Isiac tradition along with the Egyptians (Apul. *Met.* 11.4; Thompson 89; Snowden 1956, 112–16).

The moment was at hand but a few more delays continue to increase the suspense (58.1). Chaerea's action was postponed so often that the opportunity was almost lost (Jos. *AJ* 19.70–74, 78–83, 96–99).

58.1 *VIIII. Kal. Febr.:* January 24. Suetonius reckons Gaius' reign as lasting three years, ten months and eight days (59). Counting from March 18, A.D. 37, the date of his *dies imperii* (on 14.1), this is January 25. A correction to seven days from eight in Suetonius' calculation (59, *apparatus*) would bring it to January 24. Dio counts three years, nine months and twenty-eight days (59.30.1). This gives January 22, 23 or 24[119] when counted from March 28, apparently when he thought that Gaius' reign began (14.1 and note 15). Josephus is much less precise with four years less four months, *AJ* 19.201). Suetonius loved dates and calculations (on 59), and it is a fair assumption that he at least thought he knew when Gaius was killed.[120]

---

[119] Wardle notes that Dio's reckoning could have been by inclusive, conpensative or exclusive calculations (1991, 159).

[120] There is no epigraphical corroboration for the date. A problem arises from the fact that January 24 may not tally with indirect dating from the *ludi Palatini*. When the Palatine games were instituted after the death of Augustus, they began on January 17 and lasted for three days (56.2). Dio writes that the conspirators restrained themselves through the five days of the festival and then, when Gaius decided to extend it three more so that he could make his debut (54.2), they acted (Dio 59.29.5–6); this seems to imply that the date was January 22, the first of the three extra days. Josephus writes of three appointed days (*AJ* 19.77) and that the assassination was on the "last" (*AJ* 19.77, 96). Although vague, this makes it January 22 again according to Wiseman (1987, 167–8, 1991, at Jos. *AJ* 85; accepted by Barrett 1989, 169–70), who assumes that the three appointed days were followed by three extra. By the fourth century, the *ludi Palatini* lasted six days; how long they lasted in 41 is unknown, but Wissowa accepted Dio's five days for this period (458 n. 5). Gaius liked *munera* and *ludi* so much (18) that "almost every day something was presented" (ὥστε καθ᾽ ἑκάστην ὀλίγου ἡμέραν πάντως τι τοιοῦτον ἄγεσθαι, Dio 59.5.3). Claudius put a stop to unlimited extensions of the games (60.6.4–5; noted by Wardle 1991, 160). Since

hora fere septima cunctatus an ad prandium surgeret: *Hora fere septima*
= about 1:00. The usual hour for a light meal (*prandium* = lunch) was noon
(Balsdon 1969, 25); cf. *egressum meridie adgredi* (56.2). It was about the ninth
hour (περὶ ἐνάτην ὥραν), 2:30 or so according to Josephus (*AJ* 19.99). Gaius'
custom was to bathe and eat and then return, but on this day he considered not
taking his break (Jos. *AJ* 19.96).

marcente adhuc stomacho pridiani cibi onere: His stomach was "weak"
because "burdened" by too much food of the preceding day, this detail supplied
only by Suetonius who takes one last opportunity to note Gaius' self-indulgence
(37.1; Philo *Leg.* 14). The participle of *marcere* was often used for the general
disfunctioning of body parts but only here for the stomach (*TLL* 8.373.42–57).

tandem suadentibus amicis egressus est: Vinicianus (on 56.1) tried to per-
suade him to go by getting up to go himself. Asprenas (on 17.1, 57.3) urged him
also (Jos. *AJ* 19.96–98).

cum in crypta, per quam transeundum erat: *Crypta* = a covered passageway. The *ludi Palatini* were given on the Palatine itself where a temporary stage
was set up in an open area every year. No terribly large area was available but it
would not have been needed since these were private games attended by the nobility. It was nonetheless very crowded and this benefitted the conspirators (Jos.
AJ 19.75; Beare 166–67; Tamm 1963, 66–67; Wiseman 1987, 169–70, 172, 175).
Gaius left by way of a portico that was connected in some way with the complex
of imperial dwellings, still individual structures at this time (59; Jos. *AJ* 19.89–
90; Bellwald, et al. 18–19) and proceeded through a narrow passageway toward
the baths (Jos. *AJ* 19.103–4). The conspirators wisely chose a confining place for
their attack so that they would be able to isolate Gaius and protect themselves.

***pueri nobiles ex Asia ad edendas in scaena operas evocati
praepararentur:*** One of Gaius' motives for leaving the theater, or at least for
turning into the narrow corridor, was to inspect these youths who were being
rehearsed. The group was to perform Pyrrhic dances at the games (*ad edendas in
scaena operas*). These were a common entertainment performed by upper class
youths from the East;[121] another group would sing a hymn to him in the

---

Josephus and the epitome of Dio are rather vague about the length of the games, it is best to accept
the reckoning of reign and life that Suetonius and Dio make, both of whom thought that they were
calculating correctly. Since they reckoned from different dates for Gaius' *dies imperii* a number of
independent interrelated errors would have to be postulated if they are wrong. See note 15.

[121] *Pyrricham saltaverunt Asiae Bithyniaeque principum liberi* (Suet. *Jul.* 39.1); *pyrrichas
quasdam e numero epheborum* (Suet. *Ner.* 12.1). Pyrrhic dances had originally been war dances
that mocked combat and trained youth for war (Xen. *An.* 6.1.5–13; Strab. 10.3.8, 4.16).

mysteries he would celebrate that night (*in noctem spectaculum*, 57.4; Jos. *AJ* 19.104; Dio 59.29.6).

ut eos inspiceret hortareturque restitit ac nisi princeps gregis algere se diceret, redire ac repraesentare spectaculum voluit: It was cold in Rome's January chill. The affair is given a chance aspect. Gaius almost skipped lunch; he happened to turn aside into this narrow passageway; the dancing master was cold. But luck finally favored the conspirators.

Multiple accounts of chaotic events should be expected even without the addition of imaginative interpretation. The assassination took on narrative and rhetorical shape as it was told and retold. Gaius fell as though at the hand of an executioner and not unlike the sacrificial victim that has been anticipated (57.1, 4); the emphasis is as much on the words that were spoken as on the blows themselves. The obscene watchword that Gaius gave Chaerea (56.2) came back to haunt him.

58.2 *duplex dehinc fama est:* There are other indications that Suetonius used more than one source (8.1, 12.3, 23.3, 25.1; for Dio's multiple sources, notes 42 and 94). It should be assumed that when he calls attention to differing versions that the references are his own (Gascou 335–39; Wallace-Hadrill 1983, 62–66). Neither of Suetonius' two accounts really coincides with Josephus' detailed one (*AJ* 19.99–113) although they are not contradictory in spirit. The epitome of Dio is too sparse to add much (59.29.5–7).

alii tradunt: Suetonius may be accurate when he says that there were two basic versions (*famae*, above), each of which was transmitted more than once (*alii...alii*, below), but the plurals are more likely his usual generalizations.

adloquenti pueros: Gaius was set upon while indulging his persistent interest in performance artists.[122]

a tergo Chaeream cervicem gladio caesim graviter percussisse praemissa voce: hoc age!: The description of Gaius' assassination actualizes the metaphor of sacrifice (57.1, 4) and includes elements of execution (30.2) as well. When a sacrifice began, the *victimarius* (*popa*, 32.3) struck the unsuspecting victim from its blind side and knocked it senseless, just as Chaerea's first blow from the rear disabled Gaius. According to Josephus, the first non-fatal blow

---

122 Although it is dramatically satisfying that Gaius was waylaid at the very moment when he was talking with the dancing boys, it creates a problem. It was generally agreed that Gaius was killed when he was isolated (*summota per conscios centuriones turba*, below) and in a tight place (τρέπεται δὲ κατὰ στενωπὸν ἠρεμηκότα, Jos. *AJ* 19.104; ἄλλως τε στενῶν οὐσῶν τῶν ὁδῶν, καθ᾽ ἃς ἔπραξαν τὸ ἔργον, Jos. *AJ* 19.116; ἀπέκτειναν ἐν στενωπῷ τινι ἀπολαβόντες, Dio 59.29.6). But the boys must have been grouped in a somewhat more spacious area, and Dio and Josephus write that he was on his way to see them when it happened.

landed between shoulder and neck and was stopped by the collarbone, and then Sabinus pushed Gaius to the ground where he was vulnerable (*AJ* 19.105–6, 109–10) like the animal forced to the ground before it was stabbed (Latte 388–89; cf. 32.3 where the metaphor is reversed, and Gaius is an inept *victimarius* who accidentally kills his fellow attendant). Some said, continues Josephus, that this first blow was intentionally not fatal so that the tyrant could die slowly and painfully as he had enjoyed watching others suffer (*ita feri ut se mori sentiat*, 30.1; Jos. *AJ* 19.106–8).[123] *Hoc age* was the affirmative answer to the formulaic question with which a sacrifice began: *agone?* = "Do I proceed?" = "Do I strike now?" *Hoc age* = "Strike" (Ov. *Fast.* 1.321–22; Sen. *Controv.* 2.3.19; noted by Rolfe 1913–1914). By another interpretation it was the command of the presiding official that all present "mark this," "pay attention," be silent for the sacred business (Plut. *Num.* 14.2, *Cariol.* 25.2; Latte 383–88). In either case, it was the cue for the sacrifice to begin. The expression *hoc age* was also used in connection with execution because it shared with sacrifice the extended neck (Suet. *Gal.* 20.1; Tac. *Hist.* 1.41.2; Sen. *Controv.* 2.3.19; Sen. *Clem.* 1.12.2). And it is as an execution that Seneca describes Gaius' death: *Gaius Caesar iussit Lepidum Dextro tribuno praebere cervicem; ipse [cervicem] Chaereae praestetit* (Sen. *Ep.* 4.7); Chaerea's slashing blow (*caesim*) also fits.[124] The executioner who wished that the Roman people had a single neck was himself executed (*utinam p. R. unam cervicem haberet!* 30.2; see note 123).

dehinc Cornelium Sabinum, alterum e coniuratis, tribunum ex adverso traiecisse pectus: Sabinus, the second leader among the tribunes (56.1), is named and his rank is given. *Ex adverso* = "from the opposite side" and so in the chest from the front if Chaerea struck him *a tergo* (above). Cf. Josephus *AJ* 19.104–6, 110.

alii Sabinum summota per conscios centuriones turba signum more militiae petisse: Everyone, including Claudius, was thrust out of the passageway (*summota...turba*, Suet. *Cl.* 10.1; Jos. *AJ* 19.101–2). This is the only version

---

[123] Josephus is properly skeptical of such a risky plan. Gaius' wish that the Roman people had a single neck (30.2) was also turned against him in the end when it was he who had the single neck and they the many hands (Dio 59.30.1ᶜ). Both reversals are noted by Charlesworth (1933b, 112).

[124] *Caesim* was the adverb appropriate for execution by decapitation; *punctim* was for something less official, a stabbing thrust. Cf. the *gladius* and *pugio* at 49.3. The two sorts of attack were often contrasted; *"Sed decollaberis." quid interest caesim moriar an punctim?* (Sen. *Rem. Fort.* 3.1; also *Pan.* 2(12).36.1; Liv. 22.46.5). A brave man stuck his neck out firmly and thus perished by a single clean stroke of the executioner's sword: *ille* [Chaerea] *cervicem mediam uno ictu decidit* (Sen. *Dial.* 2.18.3). A slow death was a coward's portion; see on 59 for the execution of the assassins. Gaius died slowly.

of the story in which the watchword motif is associated with Sabinus. According to Josephus, it had been Chaerea's day to ask for the watchword. When Gaius gave him one of the usual insulting kind (56.2), Chaerea returned the verbal abuse and then struck him with his sword (Jos. *AJ* 19.85, 105). Or as Seneca writes, [Gaius] *coegit itaque illum* [Chaerea] *uti ferro, ne saepius signum peteret* (*Dial.* 2.18.3).

et Gaio Iovem dante Chaeream exclamasse: accipe ratum! respicientique maxillam ictu discidisse: Chaerea strikes the first blow to the jaw (not the neck, above) after Gaius looks around in response to his shout. The watchword "Jupiter" connected Gaius with the god whom he had challenged (22.4) but for whom he was no match (57.3). Chaerea's answer, *accipe ratum* = "Receive [the watchword] as fulfilled," i.e., "take back what you gave" = "may Jupiter [with his thunderbolts] turn against you." The lightning (57.2) finally strikes home. Both this and the obscene watchword (above, 56.2) make the same point: Gaius got back what he had given—with interest. See also the conspirators' watchword *libertas* (on 56.2, 60).

58.3 *iacentem contractisque membris clamitantem se vivere:* The manner of death revealed character. The ugly picture of Gaius writhing in pain on the ground suited his ugly life. He was cowardly and wanting in dignity because he refused to acknowledge what was happening to him (Steidle 91; Gugel 97–98). For the cry that he was still alive as it related to the confusion in the theater he had just left, see 60. Josephus writes that he was too stunned to call for help (Jos. *AJ* 19.109).

ceteri vulneribus triginta confecerunt: After the first brave blows, others joined in and could not exercise their fury enough; they spat upon him (Dio 59.30.1) and continued to strike him after he was dead (Dio 59.29.7), surrounding him and cheering one another on (Jos. *AJ* 19.110) as they avenged personal injuries (Sen. *Dial.* 2.18.3). Dio's statement that some even tasted his flesh (59.29.7) confirms the analogy with sacrifice (58.2); it was appropriate to eat a victim after the sacred business was finished. The tally of his wounds is another parallel with Caesar, who suffered twenty-three (Suet. *Jul.* 82.2; App. *BCiv.* 2.117). The greater number for Gaius seems to make him "worse" (i.e., more hated) than Julius.

nam signum erat omnium: repete!: Signum is yet another play on the watchword theme. *Repete!* ("again!") is perhaps the word of encouragement (ἀφ' ἑνὸς ἐγκελεύσματος) that Josephus reports (*AJ* 19.110).

quidam etiam per obscaena ferrum adegerunt: Julius Caesar modestly covered his lower body as he fell (*sinistra manu sinum ad ima crura deduxit, quo honestius caderet etiam inferiore corporis parte velata,* Suet. *Jul.* 82.2). Gaius again comes up short in comparison. A stab wound in the groin was probably thought appropriate for bad emperors; also Domitian (Suet. *Dom.* 17.1).

ad primum tumultum lecticari cum asseribus in auxilium accucurrerunt: His litter bearers came to his aid, their only weapons the detachable poles (*asseres*) that fitted through the sides of the couch that they carried (Mart. 9.22.9; Juv. 3.245, 7.132). But *asseres,* poles fitted with points (not litter poles), were also actual weapons (Tac. *Hist.* 4.30.1; Caes. *BCiv.* 2.2). A pun seems intended, and the *lecticari* themselves are probably a joke. Litters were a mark of luxury (Juv. 1.32, 3.242; Brown 269–82), properly reserved for women (Dio 60.2.3) and invalids (27.4; Suet. *Aug.* 33.1, 43.5). Gaius was ridiculed for using the especially elaborate *octophorus* for his progress to Gaul (43). The idea is once again that few remained loyal at the end—only his horse (55.3), his wife (on 59) and now his porters.

mox Germani corporis custodes: Josephus writes that it was the loyal German bodyguards (the *Batavi,* 43) who arrived first, rushing out of their station on the Palatine (Jos. *AJ* 19.119–22). This makes more sense. For their leader Sabinus, notes 110 and 126.

ac nonnullos ex percussoribus, quosdam etiam senatores innoxios interemerunt: Chaos followed and the German guard killed guilty and innocent alike (Jos. *AJ* 19.114–200). The first to fall was the consular Nonius Asprenas (17.1) upon whose toga the sacrificial victim's blood had fallen (on 57.4); his severed head was brought into the theater. He was evidently involved in the conspiracy (Jos. *AJ* 19.98, 123, 143). Another was Norbanus (*PIR²* N. 161), "one of the noblest Romans" and descended from generals (Jos. *AJ* 19.123–24; perhaps = L. Norbanus Balbus, *PIR²* N. 165, consul A.D. 19; Dio 57.18.3); it is not known whether he was involved in the plot. Anteius (*PIR²* A. 729), also a senator, encountered the German guard when he went to view Gaius' body with his own eyes; his father had been one of those whom Gaius first exiled and then killed in his place of exile (28; Jos. *AJ* 19.125). Chaerea and Sabinus escaped through the labyrinth of passages that led the conspirators to the "house of Germanicus" contiguous with other buildings (Jos. *AJ* 19.115–18).

59 *vixit annis viginti novem, imperavit triennio et decem mensibus diebusque octo:* He would have been twenty-nine later in the year. For the date of his death, see 58.1 and note 120. Suetonius makes similar calculations about either the age of most of the emperors or the length of their reigns or both, and he breaks the shorter reigns down as far as months and days (Suet. *Oth*. 11.2; *Tit.* 11) and for Augustus even the hour (Suet. *Aug*. 100.1; see also *Tib*. 73.1; *Ner.* 57.1; *Gal.* 23; *Vit.* 18; *Ves.* 24; *Dom.* 17.3).

cadaver eius clam in hortos Lamianos asportatum: Herod Agrippa, the friend of Gaius' youth (on 16.4), dressed his body and placed it on a bier (Jos. *AJ* 19.237). It should be imagined that Claudius approved minimal decency; with Gaius' sisters in exile, he was the only family. The *horti Lamiani* were just outside the city limits on the Esquiline. Probably laid out by L. Aelius Lamia (*PIR*² A. 200, consul A.D. 3), they came into the possession of the imperial family when they were left to Tiberius (*PA* 267–68). It was a logical burial site since it was both family property and outside the *pomerium*. Gaius had at least one house there (Phil. *Leg*. 351).

et tumultuario rogo semiambustum levi caespite obrutum est: The hastily constructed pyre, the body not fully burned and the shallow grave are tokens of haste and disrespect; each insult was separately remedied (*erutum et crematum sepultumque*, below).

postea per sorores ab exilio reversas: For the exile of Agrippina and Julia Livilla, 24.3 and 29.1. Claudius soon recalled them and restored their property (Dio 60.4.1).

erutum et crematum sepultumque: The disrespectful treatment of the corpse (above) was reversed. The family tomb was the Mausoleum of Augustus (on 15.1), and without further explanation a quiet placement of his urn there is probably implied (Smallwood 1961 at Philo *Leg*. 351). But a site on family property such as the same *horti Lamiani* is also possible. Nero was buried in the family tomb of the Domitii (Suet. *Ner.* 50), and the ashes of Domitian, who like Gaius had a pauper's grave at first, were later removed to the temple of the Flavii (Suet. *Dom.* 17.3). Agrippina and Livilla could have done nothing without Claudius' approval.

satis constat: "It was common knowledge..." For *satis constat* used for a somewhat problematical assertion that was nonetheless generally accepted, Suet. *Jul.* 1.3; *Tib.* 49.1; *Vit.* 72; *Dom.* 1.1.

prius quam id fieret, hortorum custodes umbris inquietatos: Both those deprived of proper burial and those who were murdered might become ghosts (Porph. on Hor. *Ep.* 2.2.209; Pliny *Ep.* 7.27.11; Ov. *Fast.* 2.555–56). Augustus haunted his birthplace but without malice (Suet. *Aug.* 6). For procurators as caretakers of the *horti Lamiani,* Philo *Leg.* 351; *CIL* 6.8668.

in ea quoque domo, in qua occubuerit, nullam noctem sine aliquo terrore transactam, donec ipsa domus incendio consumpta sit: Note that the passageway in which he was killed lay within a particular *domus* (*in ea...domo*) within the accretion of Julio-Claudian structures on the northwest part of the Palatine, the so-called *domus Tiberiana* (Tac. *Hist.* 1.27.2). It burned in 80 (Suet. *Tit.* 8.3) and was replaced with a new structure built by Domitian (Tamm 1963, 75–77). It seems appropriate that this Julian ghost was finally laid to rest in Flavian times. Suetonius makes the assumption that his readers know the topography of the Palatine and of Rome in general (cf. on *Gelotiana,* 18.3; also Lugdunum? 27.1, 41.2).

perit una et uxor Caesonia gladio a centurione confossa et filia parieti inlisa: Cf. Dio; 59.29.7. Vengeance was a motive, but Chaerea took the position that Caesonia and little Drusilla could not be left alive to cause difficulty in the future. The story of the love potion that made Gaius mad instead of passionate helped rationalize Caesonia's murder (50.2). But not all parties to the conspiracy agreed that it was neccesary to kill her. A second story betrays the ambivalence: She was found at her husband's body, reproaching him for not believing her predictions. Had she told him that he would meet this end if he continued his reign of terror? Or had she warned him about the assassination? Her complicity depended on the interpretation of her words (Jos. *AJ* 19.190–97). The centurion who killed her was Julius Lupus (Ti. Julius Lupus, *PIR²* I. 388; Josephus calls him a tribune), who was related by marriage to the praetorian prefect Clemens (*AJ* 19.190–91; on 56.1).[125] He was executed along with Cassius Chaerea. The specific charge against them must have been the murder of Caesonia and Drusilla. Killing Gaius was justifiable tyrannicide (Jos. *AJ* 19.150–53), but going after the rest of the family (which included Claudius of course) was not (ἔπραξε δὲ τοῦτο οὐχ ὡς καὶ τῷ Γαΐῳ τιμωρῶν, ἀλλ' ὡς ἑαυτῷ ἐπιβουλεύσαντα αὐτὸν λαβών, Dio 60.3.4; Timpe 1968, 91; Jung 383).[126]

---

[125] According to Josephus, Lupus was chosen for the dirty job precisely for this reason—to implicate Clemens in the conspiracy (*AJ* 19.191). This may mean that Clemens was active within Chaerea's faction (Jung 384–85), or again, that this was an attempt to make him appear to be (Levick 1990, 37–38).

[126] The fact that Cornelius Sabinus, the other leader of the conspiracy, was not executed (on 56.2) seems to reveal the crime that was actually being punished (Levick 1990, 36). Claudius also intended to punish the Sabinus who led out the German guard against the assassins (on 55.2, 58.3 and note 110). This Julius Lupus may have been the father of Ti. Julius Lupus (*PIR²* I. 390), prefect of Egypt under Vespasian in 70–71, who oversaw the closing of the temple of the Jews in

Julius Lupus died only after repeated blows (Jos. *AJ* 19.269–71; see note 124). The violent manner of baby Drusilla's death only here.

Suetonius briefly summarizes the fluid situation in the hours that followed Gaius' death when the praetorian guard transferred *imperium* to Claudius (Dio 60.1; Jos. *AJ* 19.127–271). More detail did not suit the biographer's priorities (similarly with the conspiracy itself, 56.1). It was Claudius' story in any case (Suet. *Cl.* 10.2–11.1).

60 condicionem temporum illorum etiam per haec aestimare quivis possit. nam neque caede vulgata statim creditum est, fuitque suspicio ab ipso Gaio famam caedis simulatam et emissam, ut eo pacto hominum erga se mentes deprehenderet: Rumors flew about the theater that Gaius had just left, and the German guards who brought in the heads of persons whom they had killed did nothing to calm fears (on 58.3). It was reported that a wounded and bloody Gaius, still playing the demagogue in opposition to the senate, had gone to the Forum to address the people. If he had only been wounded, anyone who accepted the report of his death too eagerly or too quickly would have been in danger (Jos. *AJ* 19.127–44). His last words (*clamitantem se vivere*, 58.3) were possibly derived from the rumors of his survival.

neque coniurati cuiquam imperium destinaverunt: Did some of the conspirators truly hope to "restore the Republic," share power among themselves? If the assassination of Gaius was indeed a last Republican gasp, it represented a failure to understand the extent to which power had shifted to the military in the course of seventy years.[127]

et senatus in asserenda libertate adeo consensit, ut consules primo non in curiam, quia Iulia vocabatur, sed in Capitolium convocarent: *In asserenda libertate* = "in declaring their independence," legal language for manumission (Suet. *Vit.* 10.2l; *Gram.* 21). According to Suetonius elsewhere (*Cl.* 10.3) and to Josephus (*AJ* 19.158, 248), the senate met twice. Later in the day on January 24, after Gaius' death had been confirmed, it gathered, apparently in the Curia Julia (*accitusque* [Claudius] *et ipse per tr. pl. in curiam*, Suet. *Cl.* 10.3).

Alexandria (Jos. *BJ* 7.420, 433), an action that would not have endeared the family to a Jewish writer. Josephus' portrayal of Lupus is particularly unflattering.

127 Reconstructions of events: Timpe 1962, 77–93; Swan 149–64; Jung 368–86; Wiseman 1982, 59–63; Levick 1990, 29–39. Josephus and presumably his source(s) took a pro-senatorial position and saw the assassination as an atttempt to restore the Republic. This is especially true in the idealistic speech that he puts into the mouth of the consul Saturninus (17.1; *AJ* 10.167–84). His regret for the loss of the senate's past dignity is similar to that expressed by Tacitus, and this has prompted Timpe (1960, 500–502) to think that Josephus' source was the Fabrius Rusticus (*PIR*[2] F. 62) whom Tacitus much admired (Tac. *Agr.* 10.3). The strong anti-Julian line suggests a Flavian date for the source in any case (Ritter 1972, 88; Wiseman 1991, xii–xiv).

This first meeting ended with some hope of restoring the Republic with the senate deciding (*consensit*) to declare its independence (*in asserenda libertate; asserturi communem libertatem,* Suet. *Cl.* 10.3; also Jos. *AJ* 19.186–87). It met again very early the next morning for that purpose, probably on the Capitoline (*verum postero die,* Suet. *Cl.* 10.3; Jos. *AJ* 19.248).[128] But by the time of this second meeting Claudius' position was firm, and the senate had no choice but to accept the situation as it existed (Dio 60.1.4; Jos. *AJ* 19.212–53). Suetonius' *primo* apparently means that the consuls called a meeting for the Capitol "for the first time" since the Curia Julia had been dedicated in 29 B.C. The change of location was significant because it recalled government from its imperial center on the Palatine to its Republican location; cf. Palatine vs. Capitoline in Gaius' challenge to Jupiter (22.4). The consuls transferred the state treasuries there for safe keeping (Dio 59.30.3). Josephus records the symbolism of the change when he writes that Gaius' death came a neat hundred years after "liberty" was first lost, i.e., in 59 B.C., the first consulship of Caesar (*AJ* 19.186–87, also 173, 184; see 56.2 for the watchword *libertas*). The senatorial (Republican) viewpoint found it fitting that this "last" emperor would meet his end at the Palatine games established in honor of the "first" (Jos. *AJ* 19.75).

quidam vero sententiae loco abolendam Caesarum memoriam ac diruenda templa censuerint: Sententiae loco = "when it was their turn to express an opinion" (Tac. *Ann.* 2.33.1; Pliny *Ep.* 6.19.3, 9.13.8–9). This gives the impression of an orderly meeting of the senate in contrast with the actual power game that was taking place in the praetorian camp. The city was replete with temples that had been built according to the imperatives of a Julian public relations agenda. Obvious were the temples of Venus Genetrix, Clementia Caesaris, Divus Julius, Mars Ultor and the one that Gaius himself had recently dedicated, the new temple of Augustus (21). Their demolition would have changed the Roman landscape radically.

Suetonius makes the comparison between the two Gaius Julius Caesars his final emphatic point. The biography that began with Germanicus (*Germanicus, C. Caesaris pater*... 1.1) ends fittingly with Julius Caesar. The early promise had been reduced to a second rate dictatorship.

---

[128] Josephus writes that the second meeting was in the temple of Jupiter Victor (*AJ* 19.248). But other accounts (including Josephus' elsewhere, *BJ* 2.205) say that this early morning meeting was on the Capitoline, i.e., in the temple of Jupiter Capitolinus. The epitome of Dio has only one meeting and that on the Capitoline (60.1.1). Although there was probably a small temple of Jupiter Victor on the Palatine, perhaps close to the site of the Palatine games (Wiseman 1981), this must be an error.

observatum autem notatumque est in primis: In primis = imprimis, here "above all" (cf. 26.1).

Caesares omnes, quibus Gai praenomen fuerit, ferro perisse, iam inde ab eo, qui Cinnanis temporibus sit occisus: Not strictly true. Julius Caesar's father, a Gaius Julius Caesar, died a natural death (Suet. *Jul.* 1.1; Pliny *HN* 7.181) as did Augustus and the Gaius who was Gaius Caligula's brother (7, 8.2). Suetonius (and the tradition) had in mind Julius Caesar himself and Gaius, the grandson of Augustus, who died of a wound acquired in Asia (Dio 55.10ᵃ.8– 9; Vell. 2.102.2–3; Sen. *Dial.* 11.15.4; Tac. *Ann.* 1.3.3) as well as the first in the series, Gaius Julius Caesar Strabo (d. 87 B.C.) referred to here. The great uncle of the dictator, he became involved in political conflict when he stood for the consulship without serving as praetor first (Cic. *Phil.* 11.11). He was killed during the bloody years when the dictator L. Cornelius Cinna (consul 87–84 B.C.) was in power. The phrase *Cinnana tempora* stood for total chaos (Cic. *Brut.* 307; *de Or.* 3.9.10; *Fam.* 1.9.11; *Red. Sen.* 9). The point is nonetheless made that Gaius followed Caesar's lead—even in death.

Bibliography

Classical texts included in this list are those whose commentaries have been used as sources of information. They are listed by editor. Abbreviations are those used in *L'Année Philologique*.

Adams, J. N. *The Latin Sexual Vocabulary*. London, 1982.

Adler, A., ed. *Suidae Lexicon*. 5 vols. Leipzig, 1928.

Aiardi, A. "Optimus Maximus Caesar: Considerazioni sull'interesse di Caligola per il culto di Giove." *AIV* 136 (1977–78): 99–108.

Alföldy, G. "Zur Beurteilung der Militärdiplome der Auxiliarsoldaten." *Historia* 17 (1968): 215–27.

Audin, A. *Lyon, miroir de Rome*. Paris, 1979.

Audin, A, and J. Guey. "Une belle découverte epigraphique à l'amphithéâtre des Trois-Gaule." *CH* 3 (1958): 99–101.

Auguet, R. *Caligula ou le pouvoir à vingt ans*. Paris, 1975.

Bagnall, R. "A Trick a Day to Keep the Tax Man at Bay? The Prostitute Tax in Roman Egypt." *BASP* 28 (1991): 5–12.

Bailey, D. R. S., ed. *Cicero's Letters to Atticus*. 6 vols. Cambridge, 1965–1970.

Baldwin, B. *Suetonius*. Amsterdam, 1983.

Balsdon, J. P. V. D. *The Emperor Gaius (Caligula)*. Oxford, 1934a. Reprint. Westport, Conn., 1977.

———. "Gaius and the Grand Cameo of Paris." *JRS* 26 (1936): 152–60.

———. *Life and Leisure in Ancient Rome*. New York, 1969.

———. "Notes Concerning the Principate of Gaius." *JRS* 24 (1934b): 13–24.

Barrett, A. A. *Caligula: The Corruption of Power*. New Haven, 1989.

———. "Claudius, Gaius and the Client Kings." *CQ*, n.s., 40 (1990): 284–86.

———. "Gaius' Policy in the Bosporus." *TAPhA* 107 (1977): 1–9.

Barron, J. P. "The Sixth-Century Tyranny at Samos." *CQ*, n.s., 14 (1964): 210–29.

Bauman, R. *Impietas in Principem*. Munich, 1974.

Baumgarten-Crusius, L. F. O. *C. Suetonii Tanquilli Opera*. 2 vols. Turin, 1823.

Beare, W. *The Roman Stage*. 2nd ed. London, 1955.

Bell, H. I. "The Acts of the Alexandrians." *JJP* 4 (1950): 19–42.

Bellen, H. *Die germanische Leibwache der römischen Kaiser des julisch-claudischen Hauses*. Mainz, 1981.

Bellwald, U., Cassatella A. and others. *Domus Tiberiana: neue Forschungen: Studien zur Restaurierung*. Translated by R. Sartorio and D. Ugolini. Zurich, 1985.

Benediktson, D. T. "Caligula's Madness: Madness or Interictal Temporal Lobe Epilepsy?" *CW* 82 (1989): 370–75.

———. "Caligula's Phobias and Philias: Fear of Seizure." *CJ* 87 (1992): 159–63.

Berger, A. *Encyclopedic Dictionary of Roman Law*. *TAPhS* 3, part 2. Philadelphia, 1953.

Bernardi, A. "L'Interesse di Caligola per la successione del *Rex Nemorenisis* e l'arcaica regalità nel Lazio." *Athenaeum* 31 (1953): 273–87.

Berthet, J.-F. "La culture Homérique des Césars d'après Suétone." *REL* 56 (1978): 314–34.

Bicknell, P. T. "The Emperor Gaius' Military Activities in A.D. 40." *Historia* 17 (1968): 496–505.

———. "Gaius and the Sea-shells." *AClass* 5 (1962): 72–74.

Bieber, M. *The History of the Greek and Roman Theater*. Princeton, 1961.

Birch, R. A. "The Settlement of 26 June A.D. 4 and its aftermath." *CQ*, n.s., 31 (1981): 443–56.

Birt, T. "Woher stammen die Amoretten?" In *Aus dem Leben der Antike*, 134–64. 2nd ed. Leipzig, 1919.

Blanck, H. *Wiederverwendung alter Statuen als Ehrendenkmäler bei Griechen und Römern*. Cologne, 1963.

Boissevain, U. P. *Cassii Dionis Cocceiani Historiarum Romanarum quae supersunt*. 5 vols. Berlin, 1895–1931.

Bollinger, T. *Theatricalis Licentia*. Winterthur, 1969.

Bömer, F. "Der Eid beim Genius des Kaisers." *Athenaeum* 44 (1966): 77–133.

Borzsák S. "Das Germanicusbild des Tacitus." *Latomus* 28 (1969): 588–600.

———. "Zum Verständnis der Darstellungskunst des Tacitus." *AAntHung* 18 (1970): 279–92.

Boswith, A. B. *Conquest and Empire: The Reign of Alexander the Great*. Cambridge, 1988.

Bourne, E. *A Study of Tibur, Historical, Literary and Epigraphical, from the Earliest Times to the Close of the Roman Empire*. Menasha, Wis., 1916.

Bowersock, G. "Suetonius and Trajan." In *Hommages à Marcel Renard*, 119–25. Edited by J. Bibauw. 3 vols. Brussels, 1969.

Bradley, K. R. "The Composition of Suetonius' *Caesares* Again." *JIES* 1 (1973): 257–63.

———. "Ideals of Marriage in Suetonius' *Caesares*." *RSA* 15 (1985): 77–85.

———. "Imperial Virtues in Suetonius' *Caesares*." *JIES* 4 (1976): 245–53.

———. "The Significance of the *Spectacula* in Suetonius' *Caesares*." *RSA* 11 (1981): 129–37.

———. *Suetonius' Life of Nero: An Historical Commentary*. Brussels, 1978.

Braun, E. "Harena sine calce (zu Sueton. Calig. 53,2)." *JŒAI* 38 (1950): 229–32.

Braund, D. C. *Rome and the Friendly King*. London, 1984.

Brilliant, R. "An Early Imperial Portrait of Caligula." *AAAH* 4 (1969): 13–17.

Bringmann, K. "Zur Tiberiusbiographie Suetons." *RhM* 114 (1971): 268–85.

Brown, R. D. "The Litter, a Satirical Symbol in Juvenal and Others." In *Studies in Latin Literature and Roman History*, edited by C. Deroux, 266–82. Brussels, 1983.

Brunt, P. A. "The Fiscus and its Development." *JRS* 56 (1966): 75–91.

———. "Principes and Equites." *JRS* 73 (1983): 42–75.

———. "Publicans in the Principate." In *Roman Imperial Themes*, 354–432. Oxford, 1990.

———. "The Revenues of Rome." Review of *Untersuchungen zu den Direkten Staatsabgaben der Römischen Kaiserzeit*, by L. Neesen. *JRS* 71 (1981): 161–72.

Buckland, W. W. *A Textbook of Roman Law from Augustus to Justinian*. 3rd ed. Revised by P. Stein. Cambridge, 1963.

Burian, J. "Caligula und die Militärrevolte am Rhein." In *Mnema: Vladimír Groh*, 25–29. Prague, 1964.

Buttrey, T. V. "The Spintriae as a Historical Source." *NC* 13 (1973): 52–63.

Cameron, A. *Circus Factions*. Oxford, 1976.

———. *The Greek Anthology from Meleager to Planudes*. Oxford, 1993.

Campbell, J. B. *The Emperor and the Roman Army*. Oxford, 1984.

Carney, T. F. "How Suetonius' Lives Reflect on Hadrian." *PACA* 11 (1968): 7–24.

Cary, E., trans. *Dio's Roman History*. 9 vols. Cambridge, Mass., 1914–1927. Reprint. 1968–1970.

Casson, L. *Ships and Seamanship in the Ancient World*. Princeton, 1971.

————. *Travel in the Ancient World.* London, 1974.

Castagnoli, F. "Sulla topografia del Palatino e del Foro Romano." *ArchClass* 16 (1964): 173–99.

Ceausescu, P. "Caligula et le legs d'Auguste." *Historia* 22 (1973): 269–83.

Cerutti, S. M., and L. Richardson, Jr. "The *Retiarius Tunicatus* of Suetonius, Juvenal, and Petronius." *AJP* 110 (1989): 589–94.

Charlesworth, M. P. "Deus Noster Caesar." *CR* 39 (1925): 113–15.

————. "Gaius and Claudius." In *The Augustan Empire,* edited by S. A. Cook, F. E. Adcock, and M. P. Charlesworth, 653–701. Vol. 10 of *The Cambridge Ancient History.* 12 vols. Cambridge, 1934.

————. "Some Fragments of the Propaganda of Mark Antony." *CQ* 27 (1933a): 172–77.

————. "The Tradition about Caligula." *CHJ* 4 (1933b): 105–119.

————. "The Virtues of the Roman Emperor: Propaganda and the Creation of Belief." *PBA* 23 (1937): 105–33.

Chilver, G. E. F. *A Historical Commentary on Tacitus' Histories I and II.* Oxford, 1979.

Christ, K. "Antike Siegesprägungen." *Gymnasium* 64 (1957): 504–33.

Cichorius, C. *Römische Studien.* Leipzig, 1922. Reprint. Stuttgart, 1961.

Cizek, E. *Structures et idéologie dans "Les vie des douze Césars" de Suétone.* Bucharest, 1977.

Clarke, G. W. "The Burning of Books and Catullus 36." *Latomus* 27 (1968): 575–80.

————. "Seneca the Younger under Caligula." *Latomus* 24 (1965): 62–69.

Coarelli, F. "Il Campo Marzio occidentale: storia e topografia." *MEFR* 89 (1977): 807–46.

Colin, J. "Les consuls du césar-pharaon Caligula et l'heritage de Germanicus." *Latomus* 13 (1954): 394–416.

Conington, J. *The Satires of A. Persius Flaccus.* Edited by H. Nettleship. Oxford, 1893.

Couissin, J. "Suétone physiognomoniste dans les *Vies des XII Césars.*" *REL* 31 (1953): 234–56.

Courtney, E. *A Commentary on the Satires of Juvenal.* London, 1980.

Crook, J. *Law and Life of Rome.* Ithaca, N. Y., 1967. Reprint. 1984.

Cumont, F. "La salle Isiaque de Caligula au Palatine." *RHR* 114 (1936): 127–29.

D'Anna, G. *Le Idee Letterarie di Suetonio.* Florence, 1954.

D'Arms, J. *Romans on the Bay of Naples: a Social and Cultural Study of the Villas and their Owners from 150 B.C. to A.D. 400.* Cambridge, Mass., 1970.

Davies, R. W. "The 'Abortive Invasion' of Britain by Gaius." *Historia* 15 (1966): 124–28.

Davis, R. *Service in the Roman Army.* Edited by R. Bagnall and W. V. Harris. New York, 1989.

Debevoise, N. C. *A Political History of Parthia.* Chicago, 1938.

Déchelette, J. "Les Gladiateurs Pegniares." *RA* (1904): 308–16.

Degl'Innocenti Pierini, R. "Caligola come Fetone [Sen. *ad Pol.* 17.3]." *GIF* 37 (1985): 73–89.

Della Corte, F. *Suetonio, Eques Romanus.* Milan, 1958.

D'Erce, F. "La Mort de Germanicus et les Poisons de Caligula." *Janus* 56 (1969): 123–48.

————. "La Tour de Caligula à Boulogne-sur-Mer." *RA,* n.s., 1 (1966): 89–96.

Dessau, H. *Geschichte der römischen Kaiserzeit.* 2 vols. Berlin, 1924–1926.

Dihle, A. Review of *Sueton und die antike Biographie,* by W. Steidle. *Göttingischen gelehrte Anzeige* 208 (1954): 45–55.

Dobrowski, A. M. "Problems in the Tradition about the Principate of Gaius." Ph.D. diss., University of Toronto, 1972.

Dobson, B. "The Significance of the Centurion and 'Primipilaris'." *ANRW II* 1 (1974): 392–434.

Doer, B. *Die römische Namengebung.* Stuttgart, 1937.

Dorey, T. A. "Adultery and Propaganda in the Early Roman Empire." *University of Birmingham Historical Journal* 8 (1961): 1–6.

Downey, G. *A History of Antioch in Syria from Seleucus to the Arab Conquest.* Princeton, 1961.

Drinkwater, J. F. *Roman Gaul: The Three Provinces, 58 B.C.–A.D. 260.* London, 1983.

Duff, A. M. *Freedmen in the Early Roman Empire.* Cambridge, 1958.

Duncan-Jones, R. *The Economy of the Roman Empire.* Cambridge, 1974.

Dupont, F. *L'Acteur roi, ou le theatre dans la Rome antique.* Paris, 1985.

Durry, M. *Les cohortes prétoriennes.* Paris, 1938.

Eden, P. T., ed. *Seneca: Apocolocyntosis.* Cambridge, 1984.

Eitrem, S. "Zur Apotheose." Parts 1–3. *SO* 10 (1932a): 31–56; 11 (1932b): 11–34; 15 (1936): 111–37.

Elworthy, F. T. *The Evil Eye.* London 1895. Reprint. New Jersey, 1982.

Enking, R. "Minerva Mater." *JDAI* 59–60 (1944–1945): 111–24.

Esser, A. *Cäsar und die julisch-claudischen Kaiser im bioliogisch-ärzlichen Blickfeld.* Leiden, 1958.

Evans, E. C. *Physiognomics in the Ancient World. TAPhS* 59, part 5. Philadelphia, 1969.

———. "Roman Descriptions of Personal Appearance in History and Biography." *HSPh* 46 (1935): 43–84.

———. "The Study of Physiognomy in the Second Century A.D." *TAPhA* 72 (1941): 96–108.

Fairweather, J. *Seneca the Elder.* Cambridge, 1981.

Fantham, R. E. "Mime, the Missing Link in Roman Literary History." *CW* 82 (1989): 153–63.

Faur, J.-C. "Caligula et la Maurétanie: La fin de Ptolémée." *Klio* 55 (1973a): 249–71.

———. "Un discours de l'empereur Caligula au Sénat (Dion, Hist. rom. LIX, 16)." *Klio* 60 (1978): 439–47.

———. "La première conspiration contre Caligula." *RBPh* 51 (1973b): 13–50.

Fears, J. R. "Jupiter and Roman Imperial Ideology." *ANRW II* 17.1 (1981): 3–141.

Feldman, L. H., ed. and trans. *Josephus: Jewish Antiquities.* Vol. 9, *Books XVIII–XIX.* 10 vols. Cambridge, Mass., 1965. Reprint. 1981.

———. "The Sources of Josephus' 'Antiquities,' Book 19." *Latomus* 21 (1962): 320–33.

Ferrill, A. *Caligula, Emperor of Rome.* London, 1991.

Filtzinger, P. "Kastell Koblenz." *BJ* 160 (1960): 168–203.

Finley, M. I. *Ancient Sicily.* London, 1979.

Fishwick, D. "The Annexation of Mauretania." *Historia* 20 (1971): 467–87.

———. "Claudius *Submersus.*" *AJAH* 3 (1978): 76–77.

———. *The Imperial Cult in the Latin West: Studies in the Ruler Cult of the Western Provinces of the Roman Empire.* 2 vols. Leiden, 1987–1992.

Fishwick D., and B. D. Shaw. "Ptolemy of Mauretania and the Conspiracy of Gaetulicus." *Historia* 25 (1976): 491–94.

Flach, D. "Zum Quellenwert der Kaiserbiographien Suetons." *Gymnasium* 79 (1972): 273–89.

Flory, M. B. "Pearls for Venus." *Historia* 37 (1988): 498–504.

Förster, R. *Scriptores Physiognomonici Graeci et Latin.* 2 vols. Leipzig, 1893.

Fowler, W. W. *The Religious Experience of the Roman People.* London, 1911.

Fraschetti, A. "La *Tabula Hebana,* La *Tabula Siarensis* e il *iustitium* per la Morte di Germanico." *MEFR* 100 (1988): 867–89.

Frazer, J. G. *The Golden Bough.* 3rd ed. 12 vols. London, 1923–1935.

Frei-Stolba, R. "Inoffizielle Kaisertitulaturen im 1. und 2. Jahrhundert." *MH* 26 (1969): 18–39.

Friedländer, L. *Roman Life and Manners under the Early Empire.* 4 vols. Translated by J. H. Freese, L. A. Magnus, and A. B. Gough. London, 1913. Originally published as *Darstellungen aus der Sittengeschichte Roms.* 7th ed. Leipzig, 1907–1913.

Fronzheim, J. "Das Geburtsjahr der jüngeren Agrippina." *Philologus* 31 (1872): 185–88.

———. "Ein Widerspruch bei Tacitus (ann. I 44 – XII 27) und seine Lösung." *RhM* 32 (1877): 340–52.

Funaioli, G. "Suetonius." *RE* 4A (1931): 594–642.

Funke, H. "Sueton, Cal. 26.4." *Hermes* 105 (1977): 252.

Furneaux, H., ed. *The Annals of Tacitus.* 2nd ed. 2 vols. Oxford, 1896.

Gain, D. B., ed. *The Aratus Ascribed to Germanicus Caesar.* London, 1976.

Gallivan, P. A. "The *Fasti* for the Reign of Claudius." *CQ,* n.s., 28 (1978): 407–26.

————. "The *Fasti* for the Reign of Gaius." *Antichthon* 13 (1979): 66–69.

————. "Some Comments on the *Fasti* for the Reign of Nero." *CQ*, n.s., 24 (1974): 290–311.

Garnsey, P. *Social Status and Legal Privilege in the Roman Empire*. Oxford, 1970.

Garnsey, P,. and R. Saller. *The Early Principate: Augustus to Trajan. Greece and Rome: New Surveys in the Classics* 15. Oxford, 1982.

————. *The Roman Empire, Economy, Society and Culture*. Berkeley and Los Angeles, 1987.

Garzetti, A. "La data dell'incontro all'Eufrate di Artabano III e L. Vitellio legato di Siria." In *Studi in onore di Aristide Calderini e Roberto Paribeni*, 211–29. 3 vols. Milan, 1956–1957.

————. *From Tiberius to the Antonines: A History of the Roman Empire, AD 14–192*. London, 1974. Revised edition. Translated by J. R. Foster. Originally published as *L'Impero da Tiberio agli Antonin*. Bologna, 1960.

Gascou, J. *Suétone historien*. Rome, 1984.

Gatti, C. "Un compromesso politico dell'imperatore Gaio all' inizio del suo regno (nota in margine a Dione Cassio LIX 3.1–2)." In *Miscellaneo di studi classici in onore di Eugenio Manni*, 1055–64. 6 vols. Rome, 1980.

Gelzer, M. "Iulius (Caligula)." *RE* 10 (1918): 381–423.

Gelzer, M., and H. Kroll. "Iulius (Germanicus)." *RE* 10 (1918): 435–64.

Gergel, R. A. "A Julio-Claudian Torso in the Walters Art Gallery." *JWAG* 45 (1987): 19–31.

Gill, C. "The Question of Character-Development: Plutarch and Tacitus." *CQ*, n.s., 33 (1983): 469–87.

Ginsburg, J. *Tradition and Theme in the Annals of Tacitus*. Salem, N. H., 1981.

González, J. "Tabula Siarensis, Fortunales Siarenses et Municipia Civium Romanorum." *ZPE* 55 (1984): 55–100.

Goodyear, F. R. D., ed. *The Annals of Tacitus, Books 1–6*. 2 vols. Cambridge, 1972–1981.

————. "Tiberius and Gaius: Their Influence and Views on Literature." *ANRW II* 32.1 (1984): 603–10.

Grant, M. *Aspects of the Principate of Tiberius*. New York, 1950.

Griffin, M. *Seneca: a Philosopher in Politics*. Oxford, 1976.

Grisart, A. "Suétone et les deux Sénèque." *Helikon* 1 (1961): 302–8.

Guastella, G., ed. and trans. *La Vita di Caligola*. Rome, 1992.

Guey, J. "Les 'bains d'or' de Caligula *immensi aureorum acervi* (Suétone, *Cal.*, 42.3)." *MEFR* 89 (1977): 443–46.

Gugel, H. *Studien zur biographischen Technik Suetons*. Vienna, 1977.

Harris, W. V. "The Theoretical Possibility of Extensive Infanticide in the Greco-Roman World." *CQ*, n.s., 32 (1982): 114–16.

Hayne, L. "The Last of the Aemilii Lepidi." *AC* 42 (1973): 497–506.

Henzen, W., ed. *Acta Fratrum Arvalium quae supersunt*. Berlin, 1874.

Herz, P. "Die Arvalakten des Jahres 38 n. Chr.: Eine Quelle zur Geschichte Kaiser Caligulas." *BJ* 181 (1981a): 89–110.

————. "Diva Drusilla." *Historia* 30 (1981b): 324–36.

————. "Kaiserfeste des Prinzipatszeit." *ANRW II* 16.2 (1978): 1135–1200.

Heubner, H. *P. Cornelius Tacitus: Die Historien; Kommentar*. 5 vols. Heidlelberg, 1963–1982.

Hirschfeld, O. "Zur annalistischen Anlage des taciteischen Geschichtswerkes." *Hermes* 25 (1890): 363–73.

Hohl, E. "Der Cupido der Augustusstatue von Primaporta und der große pariser Cameo." *Klio* 31 (1938): 269–84.

————. "Der große pariser Cameo als geschichtliches Zeugnis." *AA* 63–64 (1948–1949): 255–60.

Hopkins, K. "Brother-Sister Marriage in Roman Egypt." *CSSH* 22 (1980): 303–54.

————. "Murderous Games." In *Death and Renewal*, 1–30. Cambridge, 1983.

Humphrey, J. "The Three Daughters of Agrippina Maior." *AJAH* 4 (1979): 125–143.

Humphrey, J. H. *Roman Circuses: Arenas for Chariot Racing.* Berkeley and Los Angeles, 1986.

Humphrey, J. W. *An Historical Commentary on Cassius Dio's Roman History, Book 59 (Gaius Caligula).* Ph.D. diss., University of British Columbia, 1976.

Humphrey, J. W., and P. M. Swan. "Cassius Dio on the Suffect Consuls of A.D. 39." *Phoenix* 37 (1983): 324–27.

Hurley, D. W. "Gaius Caligula in the Germanicus Tradition." *AJPh* 110 (1989): 316–38.

Ihm, M. "Beitrage zur Textgeschichte des Sueton." *Hermes* 37 (1902): 507–97.

Jakobson, A., and H. M. Cotton. "Caligula's Recusatio Imperii." *Historia* 34 (1985): 497–503.

Jerome, T. S. "The Historical Tradition about Gaius, 37–41 A.D." In *Aspects of the Study of Roman History,* 381–421. New York, 1923.

Jolowicz, H. F., and Nicholas, B. *Historical Introduction to the Study of Roman Law.* 3rd ed. Cambridge, 1972.

Jones, A. H. M. *Cities of the Eastern Roman Provinces.* 2nd ed. Oxford, 1971.

———. "The Elections Under Augustus." *JRS* 45 (1955): 9–21.

———. "'I Appeal unto Caesar'." In *Studies Presented to David Moore Robinson,* 918–30. 2 vols. Edited by G. E. Mylonas and D. Raymond. St. Louis, 1953.

———. "Imperial and Senatorial Jurisdiction in the Early Principate." *Historia* 3 (1954): 464–88.

———. "The Imperium of Augustus." *JRS* 41 (1951): 112–19.

———. *The Roman Economy: Studies in Ancient Economic and Administrative History.* Edited by P. A. Brunt. Totowa, N. J., 1974.

———. *Studies in Roman Government and Law.* Oxford, 1960. Reprint. 1968.

Jucker, H. "Iulisch-claudische Kaiser- und Prinzenporträts als 'Palimpseste'." *JDAI* 96 (1981): 236–316.

———. "Die Prinzen auf dem Augustus-Relief in Ravenna." In *Mélanges d'histoire ancienne et d'archéologie offerts à Paul Collart,* 237–67. Edited by P. Ducrey and others. Lausanne, 1976.

Jullian, C. *Histoire de la Gaule.* 2nd ed. 8 vols. Paris, 1908–1926. Reprint. Brussels, 1964.

Jung, H. "Die Thronerhebung des Claudius." *Chiron* 2 (1972): 368–86.

Katz, R. S. "Caligula's Illness Again." *CW* 70 (1977): 451.

———. "The Illness of Caligula." *CW* 65 (1972): 223–25.

Kessler, G. *Die Tradition über Germanicus.* Berlin, 1905.

Keil, H. *Grammatici Latini.* 8 vols. Leipzig, 1857–1880. Reprint. Hildesheim, 1981.

Köberlein, E. *Caligula und die ägyptischen Kulte.* Meisenheim am Glan, 1962.

Koestermann, E., ed. *Cornelius Tacitus Annalen.* 4 vols. Heidelberg, 1963–1968.

———. "Die Feldzüge des Germanicus 14–16 n. Chr." *Historia* 7 (1958): 429–79.

———. "Die Mission des Germanicus im Orient." *Historia* 6 (1957): 331–75.

Kolb, F. "Römische Mäntel: *paenula, lacerna,* μανδύη." *MDAI(R)* 80 (1973): 69–167.

Krauss, F. B. *An Interpretation of the Omens, Portents, and Prodigies Recorded by Livy, Tacitus, and Suetonius.* Philadelphia, 1930.

Lambrechts, P. "Caligula dictateur littéraire." *BIBR* 28 (1953): 219–32.

Lana, I. *"Civilis, Civiliter, Civilitas,* in Tacito e in Suetonio." *AAT* 106 (1972): 465–87.

Lasfargues, M. J., and M. Le Glay. "Découverte d'un sanctuaire municipal du culte impérial à Lyon." *CRAI* (1980): 394–414.

Latte, K. *Römische Religionsgeschichte.* 2nd ed. Vol. 5.4 of *Handbücher klassischen Altertumswissenschaft.* 1967. Reprint. Munich, 1976.

Le Glay, M. Review of *Caligula und die ägyptischen Kulte,* by E. Köberlein. *Latomus* 22 (1963): 346–48.

Leo, F. *Die griechisch-römische Biographie nach ihrer literarischen Form.* Leipzig, 1901.

Levick, B. *Claudius.* New Haven. 1990.

———. "Drusus Caesar and the Adoptions of A.D. 4." *Latomus* 25 (1966): 227–44.

———. "Imperial Control of the Elections Under the Early Principate: Commendatio, Suffragatio, and 'Nominatio'." *Historia* 16 (1967): 207–30.

————. "The *Senatus Consultum* from Larinum." *JRS* 73 (1983): 97–115.

————. *Tiberius the Politician.* London, 1976.

Liebenan, W. "Bemerkungen zur Tradition über Germanicus." *Fleckeissens Jahrbuch = Neue Jahrbücher für Philologie* 143 (1891): 717–36.

Liechtenhan, E. "Das Ziel des Aufstandes der Rheinarmee." *MH* 4 (1947): 52–67.

Linderski, J. "The Mother of Livia Augusta and the Aufidii Lurcones of the Republic." *Historia* 23 (1974): 463–80.

Lippold, A., ed. *Orosio. Le Storie contro i Pagani.* Translated by A. Bartolucci. Milan, 1976.

L'Orange, H. P. "Das Geburtsritual der Pharaonen am römischen Kaiserhof." *SO* 21 (1941): 105–16.

Lounsbury, R. C. *The Arts of Suetonius: an Introduction.* New York, 1987.

Lucas, J., "Un empereur psychopathe: contribution à la psychologie du Caligula de Suétone." *AC* 36 (1967): 159–89.

Lugend, R. "Suétone et Caligula." *REA* 32 (1930): 9–13.

Luttwak, E. N. *The Grand Strategy of the Roman Empire.* Baltimore, 1976.

Lyketsos, C. G., Stoline, A. M., and others. "Mania in Temporal Lobe Epilepsy." *Neuropsychiatry, Neuropsychology, and Behavioral Neurology* 6 (1993): 19–25.

Macé, A. *Essai sur Suétone.* Paris, 1900.

Magie, D. *Roman Rule in Asia Minor to the End of the Third Century after Christ.* 2 vols. Princeton, 1950.

Maiuri, A. "Note di Topografia Campana." *RAI,* 7th ser., 2 (1941): 249–60.

Malcovati, H. "De Gaetulico, Graecorum Epigrammatum Scriptore." *Aethenaeum,* n.s., 1 (1923): 32–38.

Manning, C. "'Actio Ingrati'." *SDHI* 52 (1986): 61–72.

Marrone, G. C. "Germanico tra mito d'Alessandro ed *exemplum* d'Augusto." *Sileno* 4 (1978): 209–26.

Marsh, F. B. *The Reign of Tiberius.* Oxford, 1931.

Marx, F. A. "Aufidius Bassus." *Klio,* n.s., 11 (1936a): 94–101.

————. "Die Quellen der Germanenkriege bei Tacitus und Dio." *Klio,* n.s., 8 (1933): 323–29.

————. "Die Überlieferung der Germanenkriege besonders der Augusteischen Zeit (Velleius und Dio)." *Klio,* n.s., 11 (1936b): 202–18.

Massaro, V., and I. Montgomery. "Gaius (Caligula) doth murder Sleep." *Latomus* 38 (1979): 699–700.

————. "Gaius—Mad, Bad, Ill or all Three?" *Latomus* 37 (1978): 894–909.

Maurer, J. A. *A Commentary on C. Suetonii Tranquilli Vita C. Caligulae Caesaris (chapters I–XXI).* Philadelphia, 1949.

Maxfield, V. A. *The Military Decorations of the Roman Army.* London, 1981.

Mayor, J. E. B. *Thirteen Satires of Juvenal.* 3rd ed. London, 1881.

McDermott, W. C. "Suetonius, *Caligula,* 50.3." *Latomus* 31 (1972): 527.

McGinn, T. A. J. "The Taxation of Roman Prostitutes." *Helios* 16 (1989): 79–111.

Meise, E. *Untersuchungen zur Geschichte der julisch-claudischen Dynastie.* Munich, 1969.

Mensching, E. "Zu den namentlichen Zitaten in Tacitus' Historien und Annalen." *Hermes* 95 (1967): 457–69.

Merkelbach, R. *Isisfeste in griechisch-römischer Zeit: Daten und Riten.* Meisenheim am Glan, 1963.

Millar, F. *The Emperor in the Roman World (31 B.C., A.D. 337).* Ithaca, N. Y., 1977.

————. *A Study of Cassius Dio.* Oxford, 1964.

Misener, G. "Iconistic Portraits." *CPh* 19 (1924): 97–123.

Möbius, H. "Zweck und Typen der römischen Kaiserkameen." *ANRW II* 12.3 (1985): 32–88.

Momigliano, A. "Osservazioni sulle Fonti per la Storia di Caligola, Claudio, Nerone." *RAL* 7 (1932a): 293–336.

————. "La Personalità di Caligola." *ASNP* 1 (1932b): 200–28.

Mommsen, T. "Bruchstücke der saliarischen Priesterliste." *Hermes* 38 (1903): 125–29.

———. "Cornelius Tacitus und Cluvius Rufus." *Hermes* 4 (1870): 295–325.

———. "Die Familie des Germanicus." *Hermes* 13 (1878): 245–65.

———. "Iusiurandum in C. Caesarem Augustum." *Ephemeris Epigraphica* 5 (1884): 154–58.

———. "Relief aus Kula." *MDAI(A)* 13 (1888): 18–21.

———. *Römische Staatsrecht*. 3 vols. Leipzig, 1871–1888. Reprint. Munich, 1979.

———. *Römische Strafrecht*. Leipzig, 1899.

Morgan, M. G. "Caligula's Illness Again." *CW* 66 (1973): 327–29.

———. "Once Again Caligula's Illness." *CW* 70 (1977): 452–53.

Moss, G. C. "The Mentality and Personality of the Julio-Claudian Emperors." *Medical History* 7 (1963): 165–75.

Mouchova, B. *Studie zu Kaiserbiographien Suetons*. Prague, 1968.

Musurillo, H. A., ed. *Acts of the Pagan Martyrs: Acta Alexandrinorum*. New York, 1954.

Münzer, F. "Die Quelle des Tacitus für die Germanenkriege." *BJ* 104 (1899): 67–103.

Neraudau, J. P. *La jeunesse dans la littérature et les institutions de la Rome républicaine*. Paris, 1979.

Nesselhauf, H. "Das Bürgerrecht der Soldatenkinder." *Historia* 8 (1959): 434–42.

Newbold, R. F. "Social Tensions at Rome in the Early Years of Tiberius' Reign." *Athenaeum*, n.s., 52 (1974): 110–43.

———. "Suetonius' Boundaries." *Latomus* 43 (1984): 118–32.

Nicholas, B. *An Introduction to Roman Law*. Oxford, 1962.

Nicols, J. "The Chronology and Significance of the M. Agrippa Asses." *ANSMusN* 19 (1974): 65–86.

Nock, A. D. "Severi and Augustales" In *Essays on Religion and the Ancient World*, 348–56. Edited by Z. Stewart. 2 vols. Cambridge, Mass., 1972

Nony, D. *Caligula*. Paris, 1986.

Ogilvie, R. M., and I. Richmond, eds. *Cornelii Taciti de Vita Agricolae*. Oxford, 1967.

Oliver, J. H. "Lollia Paulina, Memmius Regulus and Caligula." *Hesperia* 35 (1966): 150–53.

Oliver, J. H., and R. E. A. Palmer, eds. "Text of the Tabula Hebana." *AJPh* 75 (1954): 225–49.

Parker, E. R. "The Education of Heirs of the Julio-Claudian Family." *AJPh* 67 (1946): 29–50.

Parker, H. M. D. *The Roman Legions*. Oxford, 1928.

Pareti, L. *Storia di Roma e del mundo*. 6 vols. Turin, 1955.

Pasoli, E., ed. *Acta Fratrum Arvalium, quae post annum MDCCCLXXIV reperta sunt*. Bologna, 1950.

Pease, A. S. ed. *M. Tulli Ciceronis de divinatione liber I, II*. 2 vols. Urbana, Ill., 1920–1923.

Pelling, C. "Tacitus and Germanicus." In *Tacitus and the Tacitean Tradition*, 59–85. Edited by T. J. Luce and A. J. Woodman. Princeton, 1993.

Phillips, E. J. "The Emperor Gaius' Abortive Invasion of Britian." *Historia* 19 (1970): 369–74.

Pike, J. B., ed. *Gai Suetoni Tranquilli De Vita Caesarum Libri III–VI*. Boston, 1903.

Plass, P. *Wit and the Writing of History: the Rhetoric of Historiography in Imperial Rome*. Madison, Wis., 1988.

Pollini, J. "Gnaeus Domitius Ahenobarbus and the Ravenna Relief." *MDAI(R)* 88 (1981): 117–40.

Prevost, M.-H. *Les adoptions politiques à Rome sous la république et le principat*. Paris, 1949.

Price, S. R. F. *Rituals and Power: The Roman Imperial Cult in Asia Minor*. Cambridge, 1984.

Questa, C. *Studi sulle Fonti degli Annales di Tacito*. 2nd. ed. Rome, 1963.

———. "Tecnica biographica e tecnica annalistica nei ll. LIII–LXIII di Cassio Dione." *StudUrb (ser. B)* 31 (1957a): 37–53.

———. "Il viaggio di Germanico in Oriente e Tacito." *Maia* 9 (1957b): 291–321.

Quidde, L. *Caligula; eine Studie über römischen Cäsarenwahnsinn*. Leipzig, 1894.

Radin, M. "The Lex Pompeia and the Poena Cullei." *JRS* 10 (1920): 119–30.

Ramage, E. S. "Denigration of Predecessor under Claudius, Galba, and Vespasian." *Historia* 32 (1983): 201–14.

Ransom, C. L. *Couches and Beds of the Greeks, Etruscans and Romans.* Chicago, 1905.

Reynolds, L. D. *Texts and Transmission: A Survey of the Latin Classics.* Oxford, 1983.

Richlin, A. *The Garden of Priapus: Sexuality and Aggression in Roman Humor.* Revised edition. New Haven, 1992.

Ritter, H.-W. "Adlocutio und corona civica unter Caligula und Tiberius." *JNG* 21 (1971): 81–96.

————. "Cluvius Rufus bei Josephus? Bemerkungen zu Ios. ant. 19, 91f." *RhM* 115 (1972): 85–91.

Ritterling, E. "Legio (Caligula)." *RE* 12 (1924): 1244–49.

Robert, L. "Le culte de Caligula à Milet et la province d'Asie." *Hellenica* 7 (1949): 206–38.

————. *Les gladiateurs dans l'orient Grec.* Paris, 1940.

Rogers, R. S. "The Roman Emperors as Heirs and Legatees." *TAPhA* 78 (1947): 140–58.

Rolfe, J. C. "Some Temporal Expressions in Suetonius." *CPh* 8 (1913): 1–13.

————, trans. *Suetonius.* 2 vols. Cambridge, Mass., 1913–1914. Reprint. 1979.

Rosborough, R. R. *An Epigraphic Commentary on Suetonius's Life of Gaius Caligula.* Philadelphia, 1920.

Ross, D. O., Jr. "The Tacitean Germanicus." *YCIS* 23 (1973): 209–27.

Rostovtzeff, M., *Social and Economic History of Rome.* 2nd ed. Revised by P. M. Fraser. Oxford, 1957.

Roxan, M. M. *Roman Military Diplomas 1978 to 1984.* London, 1985.

Rutland, L. W. The Tacitean Germanicus: Suggestions for a Re-Evaluation." *RhM* 130 (1987): 153–64.

Ryberg, I. S. *Rites of the Roman State Religion.* Rome, 1955.

Sachs, H. *Caligula.* Translated by H. Singer. London, 1931. Originally published as *Bubi, die Lebensgeschichte des Caligula.* Berlin, 1930.

Sallmann, K. "Der Traum des Historikers: zu den 'Bella Germaniae' des Plinius und zur julisch-claudischen Geschichtsschreibung." *ANRW II* 32.1 (1984): 578–601.

Salmon, P. *Population et dépopulation dans l'empire Romain.* Brussels, 1974.

Salway, P. *Roman Britain.* Oxford, 1981.

Sandison, A. T. "The Madness of the Emperor Caligula." *Medical History* 2 (1958): 202–9.

Scarborough, J. *Roman Medicine.* Ithaca, N. Y., 1969.

Scheid, J., and H. Broise. "Deux nouveaux fragments des Actes des Frères Arvales de l'année 38 ap. J.-C." *MEFR* 92 (1980): 215–48.

Schilling, R. *La religion Romaine de Vénus depuis les origines jusqu'au temps d'August.* Paris, 1954.

Schmidt, V. "La *ruina* du mime Mnester. A propos de Suétone, *Cal.,* 57,4." *Latomus* 42 (1983): 156–60.

Schönberger, H. "The Roman Frontier in Germany: An Archaeological Survey." *JRS* 59 (1969): 144–97.

Schwartz, E. "Cassius Dio." *RE* 3 (1899): 1684–1722.

Scott, K. "Ein Ausspruch des Tiberius an Galba." *Hermes* 67 (1932): 471–73.

————. "Greek and Roman Honorific Months." *YCS* 2 (1931a): 201–79.

————. "Octavian and Antony's 'de sua ebrietate'." *CP* 24 (1929): 133–41.

————. "The Significance of Statues in Precious Metals in Emperor Worship." *TAPhA* 62 (1931b): 101–23.

Seager, R. *Tiberius.* Berkeley and Los Angeles, 1972.

Seston, W. "Les chevaliers Romains et le "iustitium" de Germanicus." *Revue historique de droit Français et étranger* 30 (1952): 159–77.

Sharbrough, F. W. "Complex Partial Seizures." In *Epilepsy: Electroclinical Symptoms,* 279–302. Edited by H. Lüders and R. P. Lesser. London, 1987.

Sherk, R. K., ed. *The Roman Empire: Augustus to Hadrian.* Cambridge, 1988.
Sherwin, I., Peron-Magnan, P. and others. "Prevalence of Psychosis in Epilepsy as a Function of Laterality of the Epileptogenic Lesion." *Archives of Neurology* 39 (1982): 621–25.
Sherwin-White, A. N. *The Letters of Pliny: A Historical and Social Commentary.* 2nd ed. Oxford, 1985.
———. "Procurator Augusti." *PBSR* 15 (1939): 11–26.
———. *The Roman Citizenship.* 2nd ed. Oxford, 1973.
Shotter, D. C. A. "Tacitus, Germanicus and Tiberius." *Historia* 17 (1968): 194–214.
Simon, E. "Zur Augustusstatue von Prima Porta." *MDAI(R)* 64 (1957): 46–68.
Simpson, C. J. "The 'Conspiracy' of A.D. 39." In *Studies in Latin Literature and Roman History II,* 347–66. 6 vols. Edited by C. Deroux. Brussels, 1979–1984.
———. "The Cult of the Emperor Gaius." *Latomus* 40 (1981): 489–511.
Slater, W. J. "Pueri, Turba Minuta." *BICS* 21 (1974): 133–40.
Smallwood, E. M. *The Jews under Roman Rule: From Pompey to Diocletian, a Study in Political Relations.* Leiden, 1981.
———, ed. *Philonis Alexandrini Legatio ad Gaium.* Leiden, 1961.
Snowden, F. M., Jr. *Blacks in Antiquity.* Cambridge, Mass., 1970.
———. "Ethiopians and the Isiac Worship." *AC* 25 (1956): 112–16.
Snyder, W. F. "On the Chronology in the Imperial Books of Cassius Dio's Roman History." *Klio* 33 (1940): 39–56.
Stambaugh, J. *The Ancient Roman City.* Baltimore, 1988.
Steidle, W. *Sueton und die antike Biographie.* Munich, 1951.
Sternkopf, W. "Cäsars gallischen Feldzug in Ciceros Briefen." *NJA* 23 (1909): 638–66.
Stevenson, G. H. "Ancient Historians and their Sources." *JPh* 35 (1920): 204–24.
Stewart, Z. "Sejanus, Gaetulicus and Seneca." *AJPh* 74 (1953): 70–85.
Studniczka, F. "Zur Augustusstatue der Livia." *MDAI(R)* 25 (1910): 27–55.
Stroux, J. "Vier Zeugnisse zur römischen Literatur-geschichte der Kaiserzeit, II." *Philologus* 40 (1931): 349–55.
Stylow, A. U. "Die Quadratanten des Caligula als Propagandamünzen." *Chiron* 1 (1971): 285–90.
Summer, G. V. "Germanicus and Drusus." *Latomus* 26 (1967): 421–33.
Sutherland, C. H. V. *Coinage in Roman Imperial Policy, 31 B.C.–A.D. 68.* London, 1951.
———. "The Intelligibility of Roman Imperial Coin Types." *JRS* 49 (1959): 47–55.
Swan, M. "Josephus, *A. J.* XIX, 251–252: Opposition to Gaius and Claudius." *AJP* 91 (1970): 155–64.
Syme, R. "Biographers of the Caesars." *MH* 37 (1980): 104–28.
———. "The Consuls of A.D. 13." *JRS* 56 (1966): 55–60.
———. "Domitius Corbulo." *JRS* 60 (1970a): 27–39.
———. "'Donatus and the Like.'" *Historia* 7 (1978): 588–603.
———. "The Early Tiberian Consuls." *Historia* 30 (1981): 189–202.
———. "The Enigmatic *Sospes.*" *JRS* 67 (1977): 38–49.
———. "Livy and Augustus." *HSCP* 64 (1959): 27–87.
———. "Marcus Lepidus Capax Imperii." *JRS* 45 (1955): 22–33.
———. "Personal Names in Annals, I–VI." *JRS* 39 (1949): 6–18.
———. *The Roman Revolution.* Oxford, 1939. Reprint. Oxford Paperbacks, 1960.
———. "Seianus on the Aventine." *Hermes* 84 (1956a): 257–66.
———. "Some Pisones in Tacitus." *JRS* 46 (1956b): 17–21.
———. *Tacitus.* 2 vols. Oxford, 1958.
———. *Ten Studies in Tacitus.* Oxford, 1970b.
Taillardat, J., ed. *Suétone: Περι βλασφημιων. περι παιδιων.* Paris, 1967.
Talbert, R. J. A. *The Senate of Imperial Rome.* Princeton, 1984.
Tamm, B. *Auditorium and Palatium.* Stockholm, 1963.

————. "Ist der Castortempel das *vestibulum* zu dem Palast des Caligula gewesen?" *Eranos* 62 (1964): 146–69.

Tandoi, V. "Albivino Pedone e la retorica Giulio-Claudio." Parts 1, 2. *SIFC* 36 (1964): 129–68; 39 (1967): 5–66.

Taylor, L. R. *The Divinity of the Roman Emperor*. Middletown, Conn., 1931. Reprint. Philadelphia, 1975.

Temkin, O. *The Falling Sickness: A History of Epilepsy from the Greeks to the Beginnings of Modern Neurology*. 2nd. ed. Baltimore, 1971.

Thompson, L. A. *Blacks and Romans*. Norman, Okla., 1989.

Timpe, D. "Römische Geschichte bei Flavius Josephus." *Historia* 9 (1960): 474–502.

————. *Der Triumph des Germanicus: Untersuchungen zu den Feldzügen der Jahre 14–16 n. Chr. in Germanien*. Bonn, 1968.

————. *Untersuchungen zur Kontinuität des frühen Prinzipats*. Wiesbaden, 1962.

Townend, G. B. "The Circus of Nero and the Vatican Excavations." *AJA* 62 (1958): 216–18.

————. "Cluvius Rufus in the *Histories* of Tacitus." *AJPh* 85 (1964): 337–77.

————. "The Date of Composition of Suetonius' *Caesares*." *CQ*, n.s., 9 (1959): 284–93.

————. "The Earliest Scholiast on Juvenal." *CQ*, n.s., 22 (1972): 376–87.

————. "The Hippo Inscription and the Career of Suetonius." *Historia* 10 (1961): 99–109.

————. "The Sources of the Greek in Suetonius." *Hermes* 88 (1960): 98–120.

————. "Suetonius and his Influence." In *Latin Biography*, 79–111. Edited by T. A. Dorey. London, 1967.

————. "Traces in Dio Cassius of Cluvius, Aufidius and Pliny." *Hermes* 89 (1961): 227–48.

Toynbee, J. M. C. *Animals in Roman Life and Art*. London, 1973.

————. *Death and Burial in the Roman World*. Ithaca, N. Y., 1971.

Treggiari, S. *Roman Freedmen During the Late Republic*. Oxford, 1969.

Treves, P. *Il mito di Alessandro e la Roma d'Augusto*. Milan, 1953.

Trillmich, W. *Familienpropaganda der Kaisers Caligula und Claudius*. Berlin, 1978.

Ucelli, G. H. *Le nave di Nemi*. 2nd ed. Rome, 1950. Reprint. 1983.

Ullman, B. L. "Cleopatra's Pearls." *CJ* 52 (1957): 193–201.

Van Deman, E. B. "The House of Caligula." *AJA* 28 (1924): 368–98.

Veyne, P. *Bread and Circuses: Historical Sociology and Political Pluralism*. Abridged and with an introduction by O. Murray. Translated by B. Pearce. London, 1990. Penguin Books 1992. Originally published as *Le pain et le cirque*. Paris, 1976.

————. *"Titulus Praelatus:* offrande, solennisation et publicité dans les ex-voto Gréco-Romains." *RA* (1983): 281–300.

Vidman, L. "Inferiae und iustitium." *Klio* 53 (1971): 209–12.

Ville, G. *La gladiature en occident des origines à la mort de Domitien*. Rome, 1981.

Von Petrikovits, H. "Mogontiacum—das Römischen Mainz." *MZ* 58 (1963): 27–36.

Walker, B. *The Annals of Tacitus*. Manchester, 1952.

Wallace-Hadrill, A. "Civilis Princeps: Between Citizen and King." *JRS* 72 (1982): 32–48.

————. "The Emperor and His Virtues." *Historia* 30 (1981): 298–323.

————. Review of *Suétone historien*, by J. Gascou. *CR* 36 (1986): 243–45.

————. *Suetonius: the Scholar and his Caesars*. London, 1983.

Walser, G. *Rom, das Reich und die fremden Völker in der Geschichtsschreibung der frühen Kaiserzeit: Studien zur Glaubwürigkeit des Tacitus*. Baden-Baden, 1951.

Wardle, D. "Cluvius Rufus and Suetonius." *Hermes* 120 (1992): 466–82.

————. "When did Gaius Caligula Die?" *AClass* 34 (1991): 158–65.

Wardman, A. E. "Description of Personal Appearance in Plutarch and Suetonius: the Use of Statues as Evidence." *CQ*, n.s., 17 (1967): 414–20.

Warren, L. B. "Roman Triumphs and Etruscan Kings: the Changing Face of Triumph." *JRS* 60 (1970): 49–60.

Watson, A. *The Law of Succession in the Later Roman Republic.* Oxford, 1971.

Webster, G. *The Roman Imperial Army.* 3rd ed. London, 1985.

Weinstock, S. *Divus Julius.* Oxford, 1971.

————. "The Image and Chair of Germanicus." *JRS* 47 (1957): 144–54.

————. "The Posthumous Honors of Germanicus." In *Mélanges d'archéologie et d'histoire offerts à André Piganiol,* 891–99. 3 vols. Edited by R. Chavallie. Paris, 1966.

Wellesley, K., ed. *Cornelius Tacitus: The Histories Book III.* Sydney, 1972.

Wells, C. M. *The German Policy of Augustus: An Examination of the Archaeological Evidence.* Oxford, 1972.

Wightman, E. M. *Roman Trier and the Treveri.* London, 1970.

Wilkes, J. "Julio-Claudian Historians." *CW* 65 (1972): 177–203.

Willrich, H. "Caligula." Parts 1–3. *Klio* 3 (1903): 85–118, 288–317, 397–470.

Wilson, L. M. *The Clothing of the Ancient Romans.* Baltimore, 1938.

Wiseman, T. P. "Calpurnius Siculus and the Claudian Civil War." *JRS* 72 (1982): 57–67.

————. *Catullus and his World: A Reappraisal.* Cambridge, 1985.

————. *Cinna the Poet and other Roman Essays.* Leicester, 1974.

————, ed. and trans. *Death of an Emperor: Flavius Josephus.* Exeter 1991.

————. "The Definition of 'Eques Romanus' in the Late Republic and Early Empire." *Historia* 19 (1970): 67–83.

————. "Josephus on the Palatine." In *Roman Studies Literary and Historical,* 167–75. Liverpool and Wolfeboro, N. H., 1987.

————. "The Mother of Livia Augusta." *Historia* 14 (1965): 334–35.

————. "The Temple of Victory on the Palatine." *Antiquaries Journal* 61 (1981): 35–52.

Wissowa, G. *Religion und Kultus der Römer.* 2nd ed. Vol. 4.5 of *Handbücher klassischen Altertumswissenschaft.* 1912. Reprint. Munich, 1971.

Witt, R. E. *Isis in the Graeco-Roman World.* Ithaca, N. Y., 1971.

Woodman, A. J. [T.] "Questions of Date, Genre and Style in Velleius: Some Literary Answers." *CQ,* n.s., 25 (1975): 272–306.

————. "Self-Imitation and the Substance of History: Tacitus *Annals* 1.61–5 and *Histories* 2.70, 5.14–15." In *Creative Imitation and Latin Literature,* 143–55. Edited by T. Woodman and D. West. Cambridge, 1979.

————. "Tacitus' Obituary of Tiberius." *CQ,* n.s., 39 (1989): 197–205.

————, ed. *C. Velleius Paterculus Historiae Romanae II.* 2 vols. Cambridge, 1977–1983.

Yavetz, Z. "Levitas popularis." *A & R* 10 (1965): 97–110.

————. *Plebs and Princeps.* Oxford, 1969.